Reflexivity in Criminological Research

Reflexivity in Criminological Research

Experiences with the Powerful and the Powerless

Edited by

Karen Lumsden
Senior Lecturer in Sociology, Loughborough University, UK

Aaron Winter
Senior Lecturer in Criminology and Criminal Justice, University of East London, UK

First published 2014 by
PALGRAVE MACMILLAN

Palgrave Macmillan in the UK is an imprint of Macmillan Publishers Limited, registered in England, company number 785998, of Houndmills, Basingstoke, Hampshire RG21 6XS.

Palgrave Macmillan in the US is a division of St Martin's Press LLC, 175 Fifth Avenue, New York, NY 10010.

Palgrave Macmillan is the global academic imprint of the above companies and has companies and representatives throughout the world.

Palgrave® and Macmillan® are registered trademarks in the United States, the United Kingdom, Europe and other countries.

ISBN 978–1–137–37939–9

This book is printed on paper suitable for recycling and made from fully managed and sustained forest sources. Logging, pulping and manufacturing processes are expected to conform to the environmental regulations of the country of origin.

A catalogue record for this book is available from the British Library.

Library of Congress Cataloging-in-Publication Data
Reflexivity in criminological research : experiences with the powerful and the powerless / edited by Karen Lumsden, Aaron Winter.
    pages   cm
    Summary: "Doing research with criminals or deviants has inspired much academic reflection, particularly in respect of the risks and dangers which researchers may face in these contexts, as well as the ethical, legal and moral dilemmas they provoke. This collection contributes to, advances and consolidates discussions of the range of methods and approaches in criminology through the presentation of diverse international case studies in which the authors reflect upon their experiences with both powerless and/or powerful individuals/groups. Reflexivity, and the need to be reflexive, permeates all criminological research and the chapters in this collection cover various aspects of this, including gaining access to the field, building relationships with the researched, the impact of the researcher's identity on the research (including gender, class and race), ethics, risk, bias and partisanship, policy implications, and how to disseminate findings and 'give voice' to the researched. A range of research settings are drawn from including those typically involving the powerful, such as state institutions, courts and prisons, to those typically conceived of as powerless, such as deviant and dangerous individuals as well as subcultures including boy racers and hooligans. Research participants defined as vulnerable, for example victims of crime, are also considered. This comprehensive collection explores a variety of methods including interviews, participant observation, virtual ethnography and feminist research. Acknowledging the fluid nature of power relations and dynamics, this volume will be a valuable resource to scholars of criminology and sociology." — Provided by publisher.
    ISBN 978–1–137–37939–9 (hardback)
    1. Criminology—Research.   2. Criminology—Research—Methodology.
    I. Lumsden, Karen.   II. Winter, Aaron.
    HV6024.5.R44 2014
    364.072—dc23   2014024794

Contents

Acknowledgements

Karen would like to thank colleagues at Loughborough University and Dr Heather M. Morgan at the University of Aberdeen for her assistance with the initial call for papers. Aaron would like to thank former colleagues in the Sociology Division at Abertay University and Professor Jeffery Ian Ross (University of Baltimore) for their support. He would also like to thank his family, Alexandra, Matthew and Shane, for their love and support. We would also like to thank those academics who voiced their support for an edited collection of this nature, to expand and enhance discussions of reflexivity in criminological research. Finally, we would like to thank all of the contributors, who through their rich and honest reflections demonstrate the lively and diverse criminological research carried out internationally.

Contributors

Ruth Armstrong is a Research Associate in the Prisons Research Centre at the Institute of Criminology, University of Cambridge, UK. She is currently working on an ESRC-funded project under the new 'Transforming Social Science' initiative, entitled 'Locating and Building Trust in a Climate of Fear: Religion, Moral Status, Prisoner Leadership and Risk in Maximum Security Prisons'. In her spare time she is busy publishing her PhD thesis 'An Ethnography of Life After Prison in Bible Belt USA'. She is interested in the intersections and interactions between prisons, faith communities, post-prison criminal justice supervision processes and people convicted of criminal offences.

James Banks is Senior Lecturer in Criminology at Sheffield Hallam University, UK. He has published in a number of journals including *Crime, Media, Culture, Critical Criminology, The Howard Journal of Criminal Justice* and the *European Journal of Crime and Criminal Law*. He is currently engaged in research examining the regulation of the online gambling market.

Monish Bhatia is Lecturer in Criminology at the University of Abertay Dundee. His research focuses on prison and detention experiences of asylum seekers and 'illegal' migrants, administration of justice in immigration and criminal courts, drug use, self-harm and mental health of asylum seekers. Monish also works as a volunteer for a refugee charity organisation called REVIVE (Greater Manchester), and he is in the process of evaluating the refugees' well-being and suicide prevention services.

Gemma Birkett completed her PhD at the Centre for Law, Justice and Journalism, City University London. Her current research spans the areas of media criminology, public policy and penology. Prior to her career in academia she worked as a researcher in Parliament and has extensive experience of working on criminal justice consultations and legislation, speechwriting and political briefings. Gemma has also worked in the third sector as a researcher and lobbyist for various charities such as the Centre for Social Justice and the Magistrates' Association. Gemma currently lectures on various subjects related to criminology, penology and media at City University London.

Jarrett Blaustein is Lecturer in Criminology at Aberystwyth University, UK. He earned his PhD in Law (Criminology) from the University of Edinburgh in 2013 and has published articles in the *European Journal of Criminology* and *Policing & Society*. His research focuses on sociological analyses of international criminal justice policy transfers and the politics of police development assistance to the Global South. He is currently working on a monograph based on his doctoral research in Bosnia-Herzegovina.

Oona Brooks is Lecturer in Criminology at the Scottish Centre for Crime and Justice Research (SCCJR), University of Glasgow, UK. She has worked as a researcher and practitioner in the field of gender-based violence for over 15 years. Oona's main research interests include rape and sexual assault, domestic abuse, criminal justice responses to sexual offences, the prevention of gender-based violence, gender and alcohol. She has published her work in journals including the *British Journal of Criminology* and *Sociology*.

Stephen Case is Associate Professor in the Centre for Criminal Justice and Criminology at Swansea University, UK. He is the author of *Understanding Youth Offending: Risk Factor Research, Policy and Practice* (with Professor Kevin Haines, 2009) and has published in a range of journals including *Youth Justice, Children and Society* and the *Journal of Substance Use*. His research interests include youth crime prevention and social inclusion.

Ben Crewe is Deputy Director of the Prisons Research Centre and Director of the Penology Programme at the Institute of Criminology, University of Cambridge, UK. He has written widely on prisons and imprisonment and is the author of *The Prisoner Society: Power, Adaptation and Social Life in an English Prison* (2009). He is currently undertaking a study (with Susannah Hulley and Serena Wright) of long-term imprisonment from young adulthood.

Julie T. Davies is Senior Lecturer in Criminology at Edge Hill University and has a Master's degree in Criminology, Rights and Justice from the University of Lancaster. Her research interests include marginalised populations and she has published in a range of journals such as *Criminal Justice Matters* and *Journal of Criminal Justice Education*.

Vanina Ferreccio is Lecturer in Sociology at the University of Litoral, Argentina. She is a PhD candidate in Social Sciences at the University of Padua, Italy. She has participated in several studies on the conditions of detention in the prisons of Argentina and has coordinated the 'Prisons and Human Rights Observatory' in the province of Santa Fe. She is the author of *El código modelo y los procesos penales de los países iberoamericanos* (2005) and has published in several journals. Her research interests include institutional violence, effects of imprisonment on families of prisoners and the sociology of deviance.

Kate Fitz-Gibbon is Lecturer in Criminology at Deakin University, Victoria, Australia. Her research focuses on legal responses to lethal violence and the effects of homicide law reform in Australian and international jurisdictions. This research has been undertaken with a focus on issues relating to gender and justice and is informed by over 100 interviews conducted with members of the Australian and English criminal justice systems. The findings have been published in leading criminology and law journals. Kate is the author of *Homicide Law Reform, Gender and the Provocation Defence: A Comparative Perspective* (Palgrave Macmillan, 2014).

Loraine Gelsthorpe is Professor of Criminology and Criminal Justice and Director of the Centre for Community, Gender and Social Justice at the Institute of Criminology, University of Cambridge, UK. Her publications include contributions to the *Oxford Handbook of Criminology* (edited by Maguire, Morgan and Reiner), the *Handbook of Probation* (edited with R. Morgan, 2007) and over 170 articles on criminological and criminal justice related topics, book chapters and reports. Recent interests revolve around criminal and social justice in sentencing, youth justice issues, women and criminal justice (including the criminalisation of migrant women), community penalties and social exclusion, crime and justice. Loraine maintains a strong interest in methodological issues (particularly psychoanalytical dimensions of the research process). She is the current President of the British Society of Criminology.

David Glisch-Sánchez is a doctoral candidate in Sociology at the University of Texas at Austin. He is completing his dissertation tentatively titled '"Listen to what your *jotería* is saying": Queer Latin@s Confronting Social Harm, Seeking Justice'. His research interests include Latina/o studies, queer studies, violence and deviance, feminist theory and methods and queer of colour critique.

Hannah Graham is Associate Lecturer in Criminology in the School of Social Sciences at the University of Tasmania, Australia. Hannah's research interests include innovative justice, desistance scholarship, penal cultures and practices, vulnerability and people with complex needs, alcohol and other drugs rehabilitation, euthanasia and ethics. Together with Rob White, she is the co-author of two books: *Working with Offenders: A Guide to Concepts and Practices* (2010) and *Innovative Justice* (2014).

Elias le Grand is a researcher at the Department of Sociology, Stockholm University. He has previously held post-doctoral fellowships at Kyoto University and the Swedish School of Textiles, and visiting fellowships at Birkbeck and Goldsmiths, University of London. A cultural sociologist, his research has focused on class identity, consumer culture, spatiality and youths, particularly the formation of white working-class identities in Britain. He is currently working on an historical research project on territorial stigmatisation and council housing in South London.

Clare E. Griffiths is Lecturer in Criminology at Keele University, UK, where she also studied for her PhD in Criminology entitled *Civilised Communities: Immigration and Social Order in Changing Neighbourhoods*. Clare's research is particularly interested in dispelling some of the myths surrounding immigration and its impacts on crime and security in communities. It shows how 'civilised relationships' between newcomers and the established residents can exist in these changing neighbourhoods. Other areas of research interest include fear of crime, quantitative research methods, community, social control and trust in the police.

Kevin Haines is Head of the Centre for Criminal Justice and Criminology at Swansea University, UK. He is the author of *Young People and Youth Justice* (with Professor Mark Drakeford, Palgrave, 1998) and has published in a range of journals including *Youth Justice*, the *Howard Journal of Criminal Justice* and the *British Journal of Social Work*. His research interests include youth justice, children's rights and complexity theory.

Emily Luise Hart is Lecturer in Criminology at Liverpool Hope University, UK. She gained her PhD from the University of Leeds in 2013. She also has an MA in Research Methods (University of Leeds) and an MSc in Sociology (London School of Economics). Her research interests include women and crime, critical and feminist criminology and feminist research methods but more specifically women prisoners, their resettlement and desistance. She has a particular interest in how the possession of capital and the process of responsibilisation can impact on women prisoners' ability to desist from crime and plan for their future.

Meghan E. Hollis is Assistant Professor with the School of Criminal Justice at Michigan State University (MSU), USA. Her current research focuses on police organisations, situational crime prevention and environmental criminology. She has published in academic journals including *Crime, Law, and Social Change*, *Journal of Experimental Criminology*, *Security Journal* and *Crime Prevention and Community Safety*. She has also co-authored systematic reviews for the *Cochrane* and *Campbell Collaborations* and has authored and co-authored several book chapters. Before joining MSU, she was Research Associate with Northeastern University and the Netherlands Institute for the Study of Crime and Law Enforcement.

Stephanie C. Kane is a Professor in the School of Global and International Studies and Adjunct Professor in the Department of Criminal Justice of Indiana University. She is the author of three reflexive, experimental ethnographies: *Where the Rivers Meet the Sea: The Political Ecology of Water* (2013); *AIDS Alibis: Sex, Crime and Drugs in the Americas* (1998); and *The Phantom Gringo Boat: Shamanic Discourse and Development in Panama* (1994, 1st edition; 2004, 2nd edition). She co-edited *Crime's Power: Anthropologists and the Ethnography of Crime* (Palgrave Macmillan, 2003). Her current research focuses on environmental and social justice.

Karen Lumsden is Senior Lecturer in Sociology at Loughborough University, UK. She has a PhD in Sociology from the University of Aberdeen. She is the author of *Boy Racer Culture: Youth, Masculinity and Deviance* (2013) and has published in a range of journals including *Sociology, Qualitative Research, Sociological Research Online, Policing & Society, Policing: A Journal of Policy and Practice, YOUNG: Nordic Journal of Youth Research* and *Mobilities*. She is also on the Associate Board of the BSA *Sociology* journal. Her research interests include the sociology of crime and deviance, policing, car culture and youth culture.

Rimple Mehta is Assistant Professor at the School of Women's Studies, Jadavpur University, India, and is also a doctoral candidate there. She was a recipient of the Ryoichi Sasakawa Young Leaders Fellowship Fund (Sylff) from 2010 to 2013 for her doctoral studies. She was also awarded the SYLFF Research Abroad (SRA) award to visit Central European University, Budapest, as a visiting scholar for six months. Her research interests include border criminologies, 'honour', gender-based violence and feminist methodology. She has worked and volunteered with various non-governmental organisations working largely on issues of gender and justice.

Nicola O'Leary is Lecturer in Criminology at the University of Hull, UK, where she previously studied, gaining her PhD in 2012. She teaches in the areas of criminological theory, punishment and media and crime. Her principal research interests are based around the intersections between crime, media and culture, with a particular emphasis on the issues of media representation and collective victimisation as well as around the notions of stigma and identity.

Eleanor Peters is Senior Lecturer in Criminology at Edge Hill University and has a PhD from the University of Bristol, UK. She has published in a range of journals such as *International Journal of Social Research Methodology, Gender and Education, Journal of Social Welfare* and *Family Law*. Her research interests include youth justice, parenting and motherhood.

Emma Poulton is Lecturer in Sociology of Sport within the School of Applied Social Sciences at Durham University, having obtained her PhD from Loughborough University. She is co-author (with Laura Kelly and Peter Millward) of a forthcoming book *Sport and Crime: A Critical Perspective* and has published in a range of peer-reviewed journals including *Sociological Research Online*, *International Review for the Sociology of Sport*, *Sociology of Sport Journal*, *Sport in Society*, *Media, Culture, Society*, *Continuum: Journal of Media and Cultural Studies* and *Internet Journal of Criminology*. Her research interests centre upon media representations of sport, in particular football-related violence; anti-Semitism in football; and forms of crime and deviance in the context of sport.

Francesca Vianello is Lecturer in Sociology of Law at the University of Padua, Italy. She is the Scientific Coordinator of the 'European Prison Observatory. Detention Conditions in the European Union', teaching 'Sociology of Deviance' and 'Prison Life and Convict's Rights' for the Sociology Degree, University of Padua. She is the author of *Il carcere. Sociologia del penitenziario* (2012), *Sociologia della devianza e della criminalità* (2010) and *Diritto e mediazione* (2004) and has published in several journals. Her research interests include crime and deviance, prison rights and prison life, social safety and policing.

Michael Wearing is Senior Lecturer in the School of Social Sciences, University of New South Wales (UNSW) Sydney, Australia. He completed a PhD in Sociology at the Social Policy Research Centre UNSW in 1989 and has gone on to teach full time and publish in social policy and political sociology while an academic at Sydney University and then UNSW. He is the author of several books and over 50 refereed publications. His current research interests are young people, edge living and crime, the environment and eco-tourism, the politics of crime and welfare rhetoric and comparative youth justice and social policy.

Rob White is Professor of Criminology and Director of the Criminology Research Unit in the School of Social Sciences at the University of Tasmania, Australia. Rob has made extensive contributions in research, teaching and publishing across the areas of green criminology and transnational environmental justice, juvenile justice and youth studies, critical criminology, restorative justice and mainstream criminal justice. His recent books include *Youth Gangs, Violence and Social Respect* (Palgrave Macmillan, 2013), *Environmental Harm: An Eco-Justice Perspective* (2013) and *Climate Change from a Criminological Perspective* (2012).

Breea C. Willingham is a scholar, journalist, researcher and writer. She is a PhD candidate in American Studies at SUNY Buffalo and Visiting Assistant

Professor in Sociology at SUNY Oneonta. Her dissertation, 'Incarcerated Education: The Paradox and Politics of Teaching Higher Education in Women's Prisons', examines how instructors navigate the politics of teaching in prison to create safe learning spaces for women. Her research interests include women and prison and race, crime and justice. Her article 'Black Women's Prison Narratives and the Intersection of Race, Gender and Sexuality in US Prisons' appeared in the *Critical Survey* (23:3) journal.

Aaron Winter is Senior Lecturer in Criminology and Criminal Justice at the University of East London. He holds a DPhil in Social and Political Thought from the University of Sussex. His research interests include right-wing extremism, terrorism, hate crime and institutional racism in the criminal justice system. He is co-editor of *Discourses and Practices of Terrorism: Interrogating Terror* (2010) and *New Challenges for the EU Internal Security Strategy* (2013) and a contributor to the *Encyclopedia of Street Crime in America* (2012) and *Extremism in America* (2013). He is co-convener of the British Sociological Association Race and Ethnicity Study Group and on the editorial board of *Sociological Research Online*.

1
Reflexivity in Criminological Research

Karen Lumsden and Aaron Winter

The discipline of criminology can and often does involve doing research *for* the powerful, those social control agents and organisations responsible for the creation and maintenance of definitions, labels and boundaries of crime and markers of criminality. According to Barbara Hudson (2000, 177),

> [o]f all the applied social sciences, criminology has the most dangerous relationship to power: the categories and classifications, the labels and diagnoses and the images of the criminal produced by criminologists are stigmatizing and pejorative. The strategies of control and punishment which utilize those conceptions have implications for the life-chances, for the opportunities freely to move around our cities, and for the rights and liberties, of those to whom they are applied.

Hence, a reliance on 'state and legally defined conceptions of crime' is 'per-haps the biggest hurdle to be faced in the search for a series of self-reflexive replacement discourses in which transgression might be understood with-out reference to crime, harm reduced without recourse to criminalisation and social justice achieved without recourse to criminal law' (Muncie 2000, 7). Jock Young (2011, 180–81), a pioneer in the development of critical criminology founded in the 1970s–1980s as a challenge to the dominance of positivist and normative criminology, also conveys this sentiment in his call for a 'criminological imagination', claiming that

> [t]here are two criminologies: one grants meaning to crime and deviance, one that takes it away; one which uses an optic which envisages the wide spectrum of human experience: the crime and law-abiding, the deviant and the supposedly normal – the whole round of human life, the other a lens that can only focus on the negative, the predatory, the supposedly pathological.

For Young (2004, 13), we are confronted with an 'orthodox criminology which is denatured and desiccated. Its actors inhabit an arid planet where they are either driven into crime by social and psychological deficits or make opportunistic choices in the criminal marketplace'. Loïc Wacquant is also critical of the 'science-politics nexus in criminology', which he claims is forged through the

> hierarchical articulation of the academic field, of which the criminological domain is a sector, the bureaucratic field, the political field and the journalistic field – in short, by the changing location and uses of justice scholarship in the patterned space of struggles over instruments of rule that Bourdieu calls the *field of power*.
>
> (2011a, 441–42 original emphasis, see also Bourdieu 1990)

The current criminological context involves a renewed and growing dominance of and push for positivist and normative criminology and crime science, and the related push for applied and evidence-based research, which further includes increased professionalisation, use of metrics[1] and the impact agenda in the United Kingdom, the pursuit of knowledge transfer opportunities, enterprise activities and funding. This is within the wider societal context of a return of conservative law and order politics in several countries during the recession, as well as growth areas such as security and terrorism studies post-9/11 and 7/7, which have provided state/system supportive research and consultancy opportunities and funding for criminologists. It is within this context that the contributors to this collection reflect on their experiences of 'doing' criminological research with powerful and/or powerless groups. We argue that evidence-based research and engagement with the criminal justice system or other powerful institutions must be done in a tempered, critical and reflexive manner, as the chapters in this collection shall demonstrate. Reflexivity in social research draws our attention to the ways in which knowledge is produced not just by the academic, but in collaboration (and often conflict) with the researched and those in positions of power who grant us access to, or seek research on, various 'criminal' or 'deviant' groups and also often fund criminological research thus having a vested interest in our results and in their application. Reflexivity not only provides an extra layer of critical distance and engagement – one that ironically promotes subjectivity as a way of interrogating the un-interrogated hidden biases, conflicts of interest and assumptions of so-called objective scientific research – but is a process, permeating all aspects of the research from selection of the research topic, search for funding, access to and engagement with participants and settings, data collection, analysis, interpretation, dissemination, application of findings and our theoretical and methodological location in the disciplinary field of criminology itself. As Alvesson and Sköldberg (2000, 6) argue

> The research process constitutes a (re)construction of the social reality in which researchers both interact with the agents researched and, actively interpreting, continually create images for themselves and for others: images which selectively highlight certain claims as to how conditions and processes – experiences, situations, relations – can be understood, thus suppressing alternative interpretations.

Hence, this book provides examples of the multiple ways in which knowledge is created with the researched and the influence of the researcher's social background and location, including gender, race, ethnicity, social class, sexuality, embodiment and other sites and positions of power and privilege or lack thereof, on the research process, relationships with respondents and thus the interpretation and representation of the social worlds in question. We argue that criminologists must openly acknowledge, reflect upon and share their experiences of research in various settings, crucially highlighting instances where internal or external power dynamics are at play and problematising such relations and knowledge production. It is crucial that as criminologists we reflect upon the research we do, whom we do it for and to what purpose it will be used. Chan (2000, 131–32) claims that the task for criminologists is to

> relentlessly contest inappropriate performance indicators or evaluative criteria. The proliferation of contract research and the rise of criminologists in the private sector must be subject to close scrutiny, because, more than anything else, there is a distinct danger that the acceleration of these trends will spell the end of critical – reflexive – criminology.

Doing criminological research with the powerful and the powerless

Foundational studies of crime and deviance such as William Whyte's (1943) *Street Corner Society*, Ned Polsky's (1967) *Hustlers, Beats and Others*, Laud Humphrey's (1970) *Tearoom Trade*, Ken Pryce's (1979) *Endless Pressure*, Patricia Adler's (1985) *Wheeling and Dealing*, Howard Becker's (1963) *Outsiders*, Dick Hobbs' (1988) *Doing the Business*, Jock Young's (1971) *The Drugtakers* and Elijah Anderson's *Code of the Street* (1999) and *A Place on the Corner* (2003) (to name just a few) provide valuable insights into the challenges the authors faced in the course of their research. Doing research with criminals or deviants has inspired much academic reflection among sociologists of crime and deviance, particularly those using ethnographic methods. These accounts highlight the risks and dangers which researchers may face in these contexts, as well as the host of ethical, legal and moral dilemmas they provoke. This is also reflected in the work of sociologist Stephen Lyng (2005) and cultural criminologists such as Mike Presdee (2001), Keith Hayward, Jeff Ferrell and Stephen Hamm (see Ferrell and Hamm 1998; Parnell and Kane 2003; Vaaranen 2004; Ferrell and Hayward 2011), who suggest that ethnographers engage in 'edgework', which involves experientially immersing themselves in the risky activities and behaviours of the culture in question. Weber's notion of *Verstehen* is adopted within the context of criminological research to denote 'a process of subjective interpretation on the part of the social researcher, a degree of sympathetic understanding between social researcher and subjects of study' (Ferrell 1998, 27).

These works mainly focus on research with those perceived or labelled as 'deviant', who are often already marginalised subjects based on their lack of power (socially, economically, politically or in terms of youth, class, race, ethnicity, gender or sexuality), or, to put it more bluntly, those groups who are *powerless* – the 'underdogs' (Gouldner 1973), in the face of the criminal justice system and state authorities. Thus, it is imperative that criminologists and sociologists working in the area of crime reflect on the relationship between 'deviance' not only as a label, but also as it relates to wider issues of social power, particularly when such research requires – as it often does – engagement with and the involvement of institutions and participants identified as *powerful*: institutional mechanisms of control, regulation and surveillance (including prisons, courts, police, security services and social work settings). This can present three main issues or challenges, particularly if that research is being done for or on behalf of the *powerful*.

The first of these is the issue of becoming (or not becoming) complicit in the mechanism of power and the construction and application of such labels and, by effect, the further stigmatisation and marginalisation of powerless subjects. The second issue is that of trust and access to the *powerless*. In that, if such subjects belong to a group or subculture that has historically been labelled as 'deviant' and/or criminalised (such as black youths or the Muslim community), are involved in criminal activity or stigmatised social, cultural or sexual practices, have negative experience with the law enforcement and the wider criminal justice system or have fears about contact with it, they may not trust the researcher who is doing work for or with agencies within that system and may withhold participation or be less than candid. It is worth noting that the relationship between 'deviant' or criminalised research participants and the criminal justice system may not only affect the research in terms of a lack of trust and participation by the researched, but if the researcher is conducting research on a politically charged topic such as extremism and terrorism, he/she may find themselves coming under scrutiny from the police or security services for meeting with members of a 'suspect community' or group or under scrutiny by that community or group if conducting research for the state. The level of scrutiny, access and trust from either party may also be contingent on the race, ethnicity or religion of the researcher in relation to the community or group in question. The third issue is that of access to the *powerful* and autonomy. Researchers investigating topics under the remit of criminology which engage with or involve the *powerful* have tended to remain quiet regarding their experiences (see Ashworth 1995; Richards 2011). In many cases this is because such research is on the 'deviant' or criminal/crime and not the system or agency, merely using the latter as a source of expertise and data, thus leaving it unexamined or even hidden behind a normative blind spot. It could also be posited that explicitly reflecting on experiences when conducting research in these politically controlled and sensitive contexts is more problematic, as access to certain settings and participants could be restricted, denied or curtailed, and the research might be funded by governments or official bodies with a vested interest in how findings are publicly disseminated. This may particularly be the case when the agency or body involved is – although in a position of power – under great political and public scrutiny like the police or deals with issues of national security.

Hence, as criminologists, how can we openly and honestly reflect on research which is being done *for and on behalf of the powerful* without compromising valuable relationship and resources? And what do we do when our research questions and agendas involve the voices of *both powerful* and *powerless* groups and potential conflicts arise? How do we navigate, negotiate and reflexively approach the ways in which these scenarios affect the research, access to research participants and data, funding, credibility, integrity, ethics, dissemination and impact?

The chapters herein contribute to this gap in social methods' reflections on criminologists' experiences with the powerful, while highlighting the benefit of adopting a reflexive approach overall in criminological research. In the social sciences, the question is no longer whether we should 'be' reflexive, but how do we go about 'doing' or practising reflexivity (Finlay 2002), while crucially avoiding reducing this to mere navel-gazing whereby our reflections centre solely or primarily on us as the researcher? We must remember that knowledge is co-produced with the researched, who can have an influence on it not only through who they are and the information they provide, but also through how they affect funding and allow or limit access, and thus the role of the researched must be included in our accounts and reflections. Moreover, as noted above, often those in powerful positions have their own agendas and ideas about how this knowledge should be constructed, disseminated and applied in the 'real world'. This highlights the problematic nature of positivist criminological research and the growing impetus in criminology towards crime science and the evidence base. Crucially, in addition, power relations and dynamics between the researcher and the researched (whether powerful or powerless) are fluid, contextual and often unpredictable, challenging and shaping our identities and resulting in the co-production of knowledge and findings. As a result, reflexivity is an essential tool for aiding how we 'do' criminological research and furthering awareness of how we situate ourselves, and our methods practices, within the disciplinary field of criminology.

Reflexivity in criminological research

Reflection can be viewed as 'interpretation of interpretation' (Alvesson and Sköldberg 2000, 6). Bourdieu and Wacquant (1992; see also Wacquant 1989; Bourdieu 1990) highlight different varieties of reflexivity including ethnomethodological ethnography as text, social scientific studies of the sciences, post-modern sociology, critical phenomenology and double hermeneutics. These

> different uses of reflexivity or reflection … typically draw attention to the complex relationship between processes of knowledge production and the various contexts of such processes as well as the involvement of the knowledge producer.
>
> (Alvesson and Sköldberg 2000, 5)

'Reflective research' has two basic characteristics which include consideration of the importance of interpretation and reflection, turning attention 'inwards' 'towards the person of the researcher, the relevant research community, society as a whole, intellectual and cultural traditions, and the central importance, as well as problematic nature, of language and narrative (the form of presentation) in the research context' (Alvesson and Sköldberg 2000, 5–6). The reflexive turn in the social sciences draws attention to the researcher as part of the world being studied and to the ways in which the research process constitutes what it investigates (Taylor 2001, 3). It reminds us that those individuals involved in our research are 'subjects', not 'objects', and hence 'they should not be treated as would a chemist treat a chemical substance or a geologist would treat a rock. The objects of criminological inquiry are not inanimate' (Jupp 1989, 130). For Michel Foucault (1976), the products of social research reflect its social character, rather than representing some world that is independent of it. Therefore, different 'regimes of truth' are established in different contexts, reflecting the play of diverse sources of power (Hammersley and Atkinson 1995).

Feminist researchers have made a number of convincing arguments as to the importance of reflexive research. As Gelsthorpe and Morris (1990, 88) point out, the feminist principle involves 'viewing one's involvement as both problematic and valid and of recording the subjective experiences of doing research, for these experiences underpin the creation of knowledge'. Theoretical developments in feminist criminology have begun to permeate mainstream criminology, and the benefits of research methodologies favoured by feminist criminologists are gradually being recognised by other streams of criminology (Mason and Stubbs 2010; and see for instance work by Smart 1976, 1989; Carlen 2002; Cain 1990; Britton 2000; Chesney-Lind 1989; Daly and Chesney-Lind 1988; Daly and Maher 1998; Gelsthorpe 1990, 2010; Gelsthorpe and Morris 1988, 1990; Mason and Stubbs 2010; Heidensohn 1996, 2012). For Gelsthorpe and Morris (1988, 97 original emphasis) it is important to recognise that a singular 'feminist criminology' cannot exist, for feminist criminologists 'reflect the tensions and differences which exist within [criminological] perspectives'.

Moreover, (feminist) criminology faces the challenge of formulating theory and carrying out empirical studies which prioritise 'race, class, and sexual inequality', 'rather than relegating one or more of them to the background for the sake of methodological convenience' (Britton 2000, 72–73). However, it is still the case that more generally, despite the proliferation of publications on reflexivity in disciplines such as sociology, gender studies and anthropology, the discipline of criminology has thus far largely glossed over reflexivity in discussions of research methods (for exceptions see Jupp 1989; Jupp et al. 2000; Nelken 1994; Gadd et al. 2000; Hudson 2000; King and Wincup 2007; Davies and Francis 2011).

The significance of the feminist intervention and promotion of reflexivity is often also cited in relation and comparison to race and ethnicity. They are related in a list of 'subgroups' or sites of otherness, inequality and identity (and identity-politics) that require critical intervention and representation and would benefit from reflexive approaches in research. Feminism has dominated such work, but, as a result, is often brought in to cover or frame the reflexive intervention or work for all the 'others' as illustrated earlier. Alvesson and Sköldberg (2012, 227–28, original emphasis) refer to the 'study of subgroups' and argue that

> [e]thnicity is an emerging topic, but we cannot *yet* call it a strong theme in social science research. On the other hand, gender now indisputably occupies a leading position in our research area ... the dominating thrust in contemporary research can be accused not only of male domination and inadequate reflection in terms of gender, but also of a predominance of white (Western) middle-class contributors and the overly powerful influence of their (our) culture.

While the authors are correct that there has been a relative lack of work in the area, it would be wrong to merely subsume or subordinate race and ethnicity under another framework, particularly one that is not designed around, addresses or reflects on the racial order or the politics and complexity of race and ethnicity (including in relation to gender) as subject positions and subject matter. In 'Race and Reflexivity', Mustafa Emirbayer and Matthew Desmond (2012, 589) do acknowledge a problem, arguing that '[e]ver since its inception, race scholarship has paid too little heed to the cardinal principle of reflexivity'. Although they recognise some strides in the last 40 years, they claim that 'far too much work today fails to incorporate a rigorous stance of reflexivity into its analyses of the American racial order' (Emirbayer and Desmond 2012, 589). While they highlight the American case, general claims about the state of the discipline are made without discussing examples from elsewhere. What concerns Emirbayer and Desmond particularly is where reflexivity has

> been conceived in too narrow and underdeveloped a fashion: what the vast majority of thinkers typically have understood as reflexivity has been the exercise of recognizing how aspects of one's identity or social location can affect one's vision of the social world.
>
> (Emirbayer and Desmond 2012, 577)

They argue that 'our understanding of the racial order will remain forever unsatisfactory so long as we fail to turn our analytic gaze back upon ourselves, the analysts of racial domination, and inquire critically into the hidden presuppositions that shape our thought' (Emirbayer and Desmond 2012, 574). What Emirbayer and Desmond propose is that reflexivity goes beyond the identification and analysis of the researcher's location in the racial order and is 'directed at three levels of hidden presuppositions: the social, the disciplinary, and the scholastic' (Emirbayer and Desmond 2012, 574). Such an approach would, they argue, enable a better understanding of racial structures and practices, the elaboration of ways to think about and address racial injustice and more thoughtful ways of understanding and appreciating racial differences (Emirbayer and Desmond 2012, 590).

The authors call for a collective undertaking, 'one which requires not merely the subjective conversion of the race scholar, but an objective transformation of the social organization of race scholarship, a restructuring of the enterprise' (Emirbayer and Desmond 2012, 591). In order to achieve this, they call for sanctions, such as the loss of scientific prestige, difficulty getting work published and public critiques 'when one fails to take into account advances in reflexivity already accomplished by others' (Emirbayer and Desmond 2012, 591).

In response to Emirbayer and Desmond, in 'A Race to Reflexivity', Sudhir Venkatesh (2012, 635) asks 'how one would institutionalize this sort of policing', an apt metaphor for a book on reflexivity and criminological research. Venkatesh is critical not only of this strict regulation, but also of their lack of acknowledgement of reflexive race scholarship by the authors.

In response to their statement that reflexivity is a matter of 'engaging in rigorous institutional analyses of the social and historical structures that condition one's thinking and inner experience' (Emirbayer and Desmond 2012, 591), he cites several omitted examples, including those in the area of criminological research, most notably Stuart Hall's and Paul Gilroy's work on the role of the state in racialising the discourse on crime in Britain and Aaron Cicourel's and John Kitsuse's studies of school tracking and juvenile justice (Venkatesh 2012, 635). There is also more recent reflexive work by researchers who engage reflexively with not only the issue of race and ethnicity and the criminal justice system and wider social structure, but also the methods, discipline, research enterprise and scholarship itself. Moreover, this work addresses race and ethnicity in the American context as well (which Emirbayer and Desmond claimed is in need of reflexive analysis) and in relation to other sites and positions of identity, subjectivity and power(lessness) such as class, as opposed to merely subsuming race and ethnicity within one of them, for instance, Loïc Wacquant's *Urban Outcasts* (2008) on the ghetto and *Deadly Symbiosis* (2011b) on prison and 'race'. This body of work is interlinked with Bourdieu and Wacquant's (1992) call for a 'reflexive sociology' (highlighted earlier), which extends to criminology (Wacquant 2011a).

Returning to the wider need for, and challenges of, reflexivity in criminological research specifically, Nelken (1994, 9) points out that 'claims that criminology need [*sic*] to be more reflexive do not always refer to the same thing and rarely spell out all the implications of this requirement'. The overshadowing of reflexivity is in part a reflection of the disciplinary factions, state-driven criminology (Barton et al. 2007) and related shift towards positivism that was discussed at the beginning of this introduction (for criticisms of this shift see Wacquant 2011a; Young 2000, 2011; Cohen 1988; Hudson 2000; Garland 2001; Chan 2000; Maguire 2000). Hence, focusing primarily on qualitative studies (Brookman et al. 1990) (and specifically on ethnographies of crime and deviance), reflexivity has thus far largely been the terrain of feminist criminologists, critical criminologists (Schwartz and Hatty 2003; Nelken 1994), sociologists of crime and deviance (Hobbs 1988; Young 1971, 2011; Cohen 1988), cultural criminologists (Presdee 2001; Ferrell and Hamm 1998; Ferrell and Hayward 2011) and sociologists of race and ethnicity (for instance see Anderson 1999, 2003), ironically further forging interdisciplinary walls within criminology itself. Thus, this edited collection is a call for a more nuanced and open dialogue, with critical reflections on how criminologists engage with, and do research on, or on behalf of, the powerful and the powerless, particularly in the current academic climate of universities in countries such as the United Kingdom, which as mentioned pushes for measurable and immediate research impact, visible enterprise activities, knowledge transfer and thus engagement with police, criminal justice agencies and the state for access to resources and funding.

In this wider context it is even more urgent that we communicate the need for, and benefits of, a reflexive approach to our students.

Reflexivity in this sense is conceived of as an active process, not a personal quality of the researcher, and it covers all aspects of the research process. Reflexivity is not about navel-gazing, merely placing the researcher at the centre of the work, but is instead a means of acknowledging and further emphasising the co-construction of knowledge and understanding that occurs between researchers and their participants. As Adkins (2002) and Skeggs (1997, 2004) point out, reflexivity tends to inscribe a 'hierarchy of speaking positions' in social research and the 'narration of the self' is given authority in the research practice rather than reflexivity. Thus, how we 'give voice' to those involved in our studies and how we interpret and represent their social worlds are crucial issues for criminological researchers who wish to adopt a critical, open and honest interpretation of their research and the challenges they faced along the way. Hence, '[r]eflexivity is not a self-indulgent exercise akin to showing photographs to others to illustrate the "highs" and "lows" of a recent holiday, rather it is a vital part of demonstrating the factors which have contributed to the social production of knowledge' (Davies and Francis 2011, 284).

Book structure

Reflexivity in Criminological Research contributes to, advances and consolidates discussions of the range of methods and approaches in criminology through the presentation of diverse international case studies from the United Kingdom and wider Europe, Australia, America, India and South America, in which the authors reflect upon their experiences with both powerful and/or powerless individuals/groups. Chapters are interdisciplinary, written by criminologists and other social scientists working on crime, deviance and/or criminal justice. As noted, reflexivity enhances our understandings of a diverse range of research experiences and relationships. Hence, the chapters in this collection cover aspects such as gaining access to the field or setting, building rapport and relationships with the researched, the impact of the researcher's identity on the research (including gendered interactions, race and ethnicity, bodily presentation, social class and emotions), how space in the research context structures our interactions with the researched, risk and danger in the field (and their relationship to wider ethical debates), bias and partisanship, policy implications, how we disseminate our findings and 'give voice' to the researched and, finally, reflections on attempts to shape the discipline of criminology itself via various forms of research innovation. The chapters cover a range of criminological research settings from the powerful, such as courts, prisons, legal professionals, criminal justice agencies, the police and the media, to the powerless such as individuals and subcultures labelled as 'criminal' or 'deviant', including criminals and criminalised subjects, prison inmates, online gambling sub-cultures, youths and subcultures such as boy racers, football hooligans, those belonging to the lesbian, gay, bisexual, transgender and queer (LGBTQ) community, racial/ethnic minorities, immigrant communities and research participants defined as vulnerable, such as victims of sexual assault and other crimes. The fluid nature of power relations and dynamics is acknowledged in, and through, the authors' experiences with the researched and encoun-ters of barriers to research projects and/or the dissemination of research findings. We also explore ethics, risk and danger in criminological research and finish with consideration of the future of criminological research itself, drawing on examples such as international innovative justice research and participation in policy nodes.

The chapters cover a range of qualitative research methods including interviews, participant observation, ethnography, feminist research, virtual ethnography and also one instance of quantitative research. Each section contains a short Editors' Introduction, to tease out the central themes cov-ered in the chapters, highlighting how the author's reflections add to our understandings of criminological research and power relations, and address and contribute to the collection's themes and thesis.

Part I: Research relationships

Part I begins with a discussion of *Research Relationships*. In Chapter 2, Nicola O'Leary examines the role of researcher reflexivity when exploring a com-munity which has experienced collective victimisation in the wake of a serious and high-profile crime. Much of this reflexive account deals with how the researcher gained access to the field and negotiated (and renegoti-ated) relations in an unfamiliar and at times unreceptive environment. Julie T. Davies and Eleanor Peters in Chapter 3 also highlight the problematic process of gaining and sustaining access to individuals or groups, but in this case via powerful institutions such as prisons. They consider issues of power, ethics and hierarchy in conducting research with vulnerable popu-lations who are incarcerated or subject to criminal justice sanctions in the community. In Chapter 4, Rimple Mehta focuses on the role of the mango tree in the female ward of a prison for both men and women, in shaping the relationship between the researcher and Bangladeshi female prisoners in a correctional home in Kolkata, India. Through the example of a mango tree, she highlights the role that space plays in shaping relationships in the field. In Chapter 5, Stephen Case and Kevin Haines present 'Reflective Friend Research', a paradigm founded in a long-standing research partner-ship between researchers, practitioners and young people. They argue that researchers functioning as critical friends offer evidence-based recommen-dations for radical, systemic changes to traditional practices of knowledge generation, engagement and integrating research findings into practice. Nur-turing long-term reflective relationships with researched parties can facilitate levels of access to research participants, data sets, internal documentation and knowledge generation processes seldom enjoyed by positivists conducting research on research subjects rather than with research participants/contributors.

Parts II and III: Researcher identities, subjectivities and intersectionalities

The second and third parts of the book focus on *Researcher Identities, Subjectivities and Intersectionalities*. Here, we focus on the role of *Gender and Class* and *Race and Ethnicity* in research and, particularly, shaping relationships with research participants. In Part II, the authors focus on the role of *Gender and Class* in their research. In Chapter 6, Emma Poulton identifies the methodological challenges and concerns which she had to (re)negotiate and manage as a female academic researching the hyper-masculine subculture of 'football hooliganism'. According to Poulton doing gendered research (especially with deviant subcultures) can sometimes require the researcher (male or indeed female) to demonstrate that they have the metaphorical 'balls' in terms of handling particular situations and power relations – including sometimes feeling powerless. In Chapter 7, Oona Brooks draws on feminist literature to offer an account of her research with young women about safety in bars and clubs in Scottish cities. She discusses how consideration was given to addressing potential imbalances of power between the researcher and the researched. The feminist identity of the researcher directly influenced the focus of the study and the interpretation of findings. In Chapter 8, Emily Luise Hart explores how her pregnancy impacted on a series of qualitative semi-structured interviews with female prisoners. The researcher's visible pregnancy gave access to particular insights that may not have otherwise been possible, for instance aiding access to sensitive data, helping to establish a positive rapport and supporting the development of a trusting relationship in the interview setting. In Chapter 9, Elias le Grand provides us with an account of his fieldwork experiences with working-class youths in a deprived South London suburb. He explores how writing the ethnographic self can inform our understanding of the performance of class and masculinity in the field. In this case, reflexive analysis of the interactions between the middle-class researcher and the young working-class respondents elucidated the classed dynamics of masculine performances and how these are tied to the embodied knowledge of cultural codes.

In Part III, the authors focus on the role of *Race and Ethnicity* in their research and the need for reflexivity in this area. Although the focus is on race and ethnicity, several highlight the ways in which other sites of identity, subjectivity and powerlessness overlap and intersect with race and ethnicity in their research, most notably sexuality and gender. In Chapter 10, David Glisch-Sánchez discusses his research on hate crimes against LGBTQ Latinas and Latinos and examines the power relationship between researcher and research participant. He also looks at wider issues and challenges for researchers working in this area, most notably the social and institutional mechanisms that create criminological scholars as institutional agents of the state and academic discipline and institutions. He discusses how reflexive practices are commonly reduced to the indexing of differences across various categories of identity, such as race, ethnicity, sexuality and national origin. He argues that collective reflexive practice must incorporate a deep understanding of how the intersections of socially significant identities intersect with our roles as institutional agents. In Chapter 11, Breea C. Willingham provides a reflexive account of how being an African American woman with male relatives incarcerated in the American penal system presented unique challenges when conducting research on incarcerated African American fathers. She argues that a reflexive approach creates not only challenges but also opportunities for researchers like her to tell powerful stories of powerless and marginalised groups and individuals, as well as highlight the ways in which the researcher often may not only serve either the powerful or powerless, but also share overlapping social positions and experiences with either. In Chapter 12, Meghan E. Hollis outlines her experiences of researching minority police officers during a three-year ethnographic study of a police department in a north-eastern coastal metropolitan city in the United States. She highlights difficulties accessing the experiences of the non-white and/or female police officers, examining the position of the researcher as a white female. In Chapter 13, Monish Bhatia discusses his research on the United Kingdom's immigration policies and procedures on asylum seekers and 'illegal' migrants. He examines the role of emotional reflexivity in research and the ways in which it can offer an effective navigation tool for researchers, driving critical criminological knowledge and exposing state and structural violence and injustice against asylum seekers and 'illegal' migrants. Bhatia highlights the ethical and methodological dilemmas faced while conducting sensitive qualitative research with oppressed and marginalised populations. He argues that emotions are epistemologically relevant and should not be hidden or left undisclosed from the text, but rather addressed appropriately to enhance the value and credibility of the data collected. In Chapter 14, Clare E. Griffiths discusses a quantitative research project that sought to capture the perspectives of an established local community and a transient immigrant community on crime and disorder in their local neighbourhood in an English city, after a period of increased migration and debates about it. She reflects on incidents that raised questions for the random and objective principles of a quantitative research project and shows how special considerations are needed when researching such 'hidden' populations. In Chapter 15, Michael Wearing discusses how qualitative criminology helps to frame 'law and order' agendas of state surveillance. Focusing on research on child sexual assault in remote Aboriginal communities in Northern Australia and in the crime biographies of life course, he interrogates the positivist creation of subjectivities in qualitative research as legitimating false constructions of the 'other'.

Part IV: Risk, ethics and researcher safety

Part IV moves to discussions of *Risk, Ethics and Researcher Safety* in criminological studies in the United Kingdom and South America. In Chapter 16, Ruth Armstrong, Loraine Gelsthorpe and Ben Crewe candidly describe the ethical compromises of a UK postgraduate conducting ethnographic work with prisoners and ex-prisoners in the United States. They question whether being ethical is synonymous with following ethical protocols to the letter or whether taking risks might respect the values that underpin ethical regulations more than trying to rule out these risks entirely. They also reflect on the discomfort of undertaking and supervising these risks and describe the importance of trust, honesty and 'ethical sensibility' in the process of fieldwork and research reporting. Then, in Chapter 17, Stephanie C. Kane provides an account of the gendered cultural process through which crime affectively circulates in the community, beyond victims, perpetrators and agents of social control through widening spheres of social relations. She shows how reflexive methods clarify the contingent process of knowledge production and amplify criminology's cultural imagination. A knife assault witnessed on a globally popular beach in Salvador da Bahia, Brazil, illuminates the 'political unconscious' of crime and its dynamic relationship to place. Serendipitously in the scene of a crime, a distressingly mundane act of violence enhances communicative trust between co-witnesses, the ethnographer and her interlocutor.

Part V: Power, partisanship and bias

Part V highlights the role of *Power, Partisanship and Bias* in research involving those in *powerful* positions, such as legal professionals, courts, criminal justice agencies, politicians, the police and the media. As Hughes (2000, 235) observes, '[a]ll social science has a political dimension, in the non-party-political sense. All aspects of research necessarily involve the researcher in both the analysis and practice of power and, in turn, have the potential to generate conflicts of interest between a whole host of interested parties'. In Chapter 18, Gemma Birkett describes her research with criminal justice professionals in the British government. She addresses the distinct issues involved in interviewing female policy elites and considers the difficulties encountered in the dissemination of political research findings. In Chapter 19, Kate Fitz-Gibbon also focuses on her research experiences with powerful groups. She argues that at the time when academia is increasingly recognising the importance of policy application and the transfer of research into practice, interviews with legal practitioners provide an opportunity for criminologists to validate and support research findings with the experiences of those working within the field. In Chapter 20, Vanina

Ferreccio and Francesca Vianello observe how their research in prisons in Italy and Argentina involved a balancing exercise between the strategies developed and implemented by the institutional actors of the prison with the aim of influencing and directing research and the existing possibilities for the researcher to resist and construct a space of partial autonomy within the research field. In Chapter 21, Karen Lumsden then reflects on her experience of conducting research with both the powerless – boy racers – and powerful groups including the police, local council, politicians and media. She focuses on the role of bias and partisanship in her study of boy racers and the tendency for sociologists of deviance to side with the powerless. She also draws attention to how we 'give voice' to our research participants, focusing on her interactions with the media.

Part VI: Reflexivity and innovation: New contexts, challenges and possibilities

In the final part of the book, *Reflexivity and Innovation*, we turn to discussions of the future of criminological research and examples of innovation in policy, practice and research methods in particular cases and contexts – from the virtual to the international. In Chapter 22, James Banks describes his research on online gambling, examining a context and social subculture made possible through technological innovation and presenting new challenges to the ethnographer. He considers the responsibility of criminologists as virtual ethnographers to reflexively interrogate their roles, methods and interpretations when examining online cultures, as well as how the researcher's biography, presuppositions and cultural position impacted upon the study of an online gambling subculture. In Chapter 23, Jarrett Blaustein then describes how a researcher's direct immersion in an active policy node can create unique opportunities to exercise reflexivity and achieve a transnational criminology of harm production. This involves moving beyond ex post facto critiques of ethnocentrism and the structural inequalities associated with transnational criminology and actively mitigating the potential consequences of one's participation in the field. Blaustein reflects on the ethical dilemmas he encountered while completing ethnographic fieldwork with UNDP's Safer Communities project in Bosnia-Herzegovina. Finally, in Chapter 24, Hannah Graham and Rob White discuss the challenges, paradoxes and opportunities encountered in conducting international criminological research about innovative justice initiatives and creative ways of working with offenders. They argue that claims of 'innovation' and 'success' are inevitably relative and contextualised, subject to diverse interpretation and frequently contested. Yet, innovation inspires and resonates beyond itself; 'quiet revolutions' are being achieved in unorthodox ways and unlikely places around the world.

By sharing and critically examining our research experiences and challenges in the course of doing criminological research, we illustrate the 'messy' nature of social research and the complex and myriad power contests and relationships which must be negotiated, and implications that must be attended to in the course of our research – from design to dissemination and impact. This edited collection is a reminder of the need for criminologists to retain a critical and reflexive stance in their research as they work with a host of powerless and powerful groups in contemporary society, challenging always how notions and labels of 'crime' and 'deviance' are socially constructed and interrogating the role of criminologists in the construction or legitimisation of these concepts, particularly as they are applied by those with power and authority to those with little or no power, with serious consequences for the lives of those individuals whose identities and life chances are intertwined with such categorisations and employment of them by state and criminal justice agencies.

Note

1. For instance, in the United Kingdom this includes the Research Excellence Framework (REF), a system for assessing the quality of research in UK higher education institutions.

References

Adkins, L. (2002) 'Reflexivity and the Politics of Qualitative Research'. In T. May (ed.) *Qualitative Research in Action*, London: Sage, pp.332–348.

Adler, P. (1993[1985]) *Wheeling and Dealing: An Ethnography of an Upper-Level Drug Dealing and Smuggling Community*, 2nd edn, New York: Columbia University Press.

Alvesson, M. and Sköldberg, K. (2000) *Reflexive Methodology: New Vistas for Qualitative Research*, 1st edn, London: Sage.

Alvesson, M. and Sköldberg, K. (2012) *Reflexive Methodology: New Vistas for Qualitative Research*, 2nd edn, London: Sage.

Anderson, E. (1999) *Code of the Street: Decency, Violence and the Moral Life of the Inner City*, New York: W.W. Norton.

Anderson, E. (2003) *A Place on the Corner: A Study of Black Street Corner Men*, 2nd edn, Chicago: University of Chicago Press.

Ashworth, A. (1995) 'Reflections on the Role of the Sentencing Scholar'. In C.M.V. Clarkson and R. Morgan (eds) *The Politics of Sentencing Reform*, Oxford: Clarendon Press, pp.251–265.

Barton, A., Corteen, K., Scott, D. and Whyte, D. (eds) (2007) *Expanding the Criminological Imagination*, Devon: Willan Publishing.

Becker, H.S. (1963) *Outsiders: Studies in the Sociology of Deviance*, New York: Free Press of Glencoe.

Bourdieu, P. (1990) *In Other Words: Essays Towards a Reflexive Sociology*, trans. M. Adamson, Oxford: Polity Press.

Bourdieu, P. and Wacquant, L.J.D. (1992) *An Invitation to Reflexive Sociology*, Chicago: University of Chicago Press.

Britton, D.M. (2000) 'Feminism in Criminology: Engendering the Outlaw' *ANNALS of the American Academy of Political and Social Science* 571: 57–76.

Brookman, F., Noaks, L. and Wincup, E. (1990) *Qualitative Research in Criminology*, Aldershot: Ashgate.

Cain, M. (1990) 'Towards Transgression: New Direction in Feminist Criminology' *International Journal of the Sociology of Law* 18: 1–18.

Carlen, P. (2002) *Women and Punishment*, Cullompton: Willan Publishing.

Chan, J. (2000) 'Globalization, Reflexivity and the Practice of Criminology' *Australian & New Zealand Journal of Criminology* 33(2): 118–35.

Chesney-Lind, M. (1989) 'Girls' Crime and Women's Place: Toward a Feminist Model of Female Delinquency' *Crime and Delinquency* 35(1): 5–29.

Cohen, S. (1988) *Against Criminology*, New Brunswick: Transaction Publishers.

Daly, K. and Chesney-Lind, M. (1988) 'Feminism and Criminology' *Justice Quarterly* 5: 497–538.

Daly, K. and Maher, L. (1998) 'Crossroads and Intersections: Building from Feminist Critique'. In K. Daly and L. Maher (eds) *Criminology at the Crossroads*, New York: Oxford University Press, pp.1–17.

Davies, P. and Francis, P. (2011) 'Reflecting on Criminological Research'. In P. Davies, P. Francis, and V. Jupp (eds) *Doing Criminological Research*, 2nd edn, London: Sage, pp.281–85.

Emirbayer, M. and Desmond, M. (2012) 'Race and Reflexivity' *Ethnic and Racial Studies* 35(4): 574–99.

Ferrell, J. (1998) 'Criminological *Verstehen*: Inside the Immediacy of Crime'. In J. Ferrell and M.S. Hamm (eds) *Ethnography at the Edge: Crime, Deviance and Field Research*, Boston: Northeastern University Press, pp.20–42.

Ferrell, J. and Hamm, M.S. (eds) (1998) *Ethnography at the Edge: Crime, Deviance and Field Research*, Boston: Northeastern University Press.

Ferrell, J. and Hayward, K. (eds) (2011) *Cultural Criminology: Theories of Crime*, Aldershot: Ashgate.

Finlay, L. (2002) 'Negotiating the Swamp: the Opportunity and Challenge of Reflexivity in Research Practice' *Qualitative Research* 2(2): 209–30.

Foucault, M. (1976) 'Truth and Power'. In P. Rabinow (ed.) *Essential Works of Foucault, Volume 3*, New York: the Free Press, pp.111–33.

Gadd, D., Karstedt, S. and Messner, S. (eds) (2000) *The SAGE Handbook of Criminological Research Methods*, London: Sage.

Garland, D. (2001) *The Culture of Control: Crime and Social Order in Contemporary Society*, Chicago: University of Chicago Press.

Gelsthorpe, L. (1990) 'Feminist Methodologies in Criminology: A New Approach or Old Wine in New Bottles?' In L. Gelsthorpe and A. Morris (eds) (1998) *Feminist Perspectives in Criminology*, Milton Keynes: Open University Press, pp.89–106.

Gelsthorpe, L. (2010) 'Women, Crime and Control' *Criminology & Criminal Justice* 10: 375–86.

Gelsthorpe, L. and Morris, A. (1988) 'Feminism and Criminology in Britain' *British Journal of Criminology* 28(2): 93–110.

Gelsthorpe, L. and Morris, A. (eds) (1990) *Feminist Perspectives in Criminology*, Milton Keynes: Open University Press.

Gouldner, A. (1973) *For Sociology*, London: Allen Lane.

Hammersley, M. and Atkinson, P. (1995) *Ethnography: Principles in Practice*, 2nd edn, London: Tavistock.

Heidensohn, F. (1996) *Women and Crime*, 2nd edn, Basingstoke: Macmillan.

Heidensohn, F. (2012) 'The Future of Feminist Criminology' *Crime, Media, Culture* 8(2): 123–34.

Hobbs, D. (1988) *Doing the Business: Entrepreneurship, the Working Class, and Detectives in the East End of London*, New York: Oxford University Press.

Hudson, B. (2000) 'Critical Reflection as Research Methodology'. In V. Jupp, P. Davies and P. Francis (eds) *Doing Criminological Research*, London: Sage, pp.175–92.

Hughes, G. (2000) 'Understanding the Politics of Criminological Research'. In V. Jupp, P. Davies and P. Francis (eds) *Doing Criminological Research*, London: Sage, pp.234–48.

Humphreys, L. (1970) *Tearoom Trade: Impersonal Sex in Public Places*, London: Duckworth.

Jupp, V. (1989) *Methods of Criminological Research*, London: Unwin Hyman.

Jupp, K., Davies, P. and Francis, P. (eds) (2000) *Doing Criminological Research*, London: Sage.

King, R. and Wincup, E. (2007) *Doing Research on Crime and Justice*, 2nd edition, Buckingham: Open University Press.

Lyng, S. (2005) *Edgework: The Sociology of Risk Taking*, New York: Routledge.

Maguire, M. (2000) 'Researching Street Criminals in the Field: A Neglected Art?'. In R. King and E. Wincup (eds) *Doing Criminological Research*, Oxford: Oxford University Press, pp. 121–152.

Mason, G. and Stubbs, J. (2010) 'Feminist Approaches to Criminological Research'. In D. Gadd, S. Karstedt and S. Messner (eds) *The SAGE Handbook of Criminological Research Methods*, London: Sage, pp.486–499.

Muncie, J. (2000) 'Decriminalising Criminology'. *British Criminology Conference: Selected Proceedings*. Volume 3. Papers from the British Society of Criminology Annual Conference 1999. URL (accessed 8 January 2014): http://britsoccrim.org/volume3/010.pdf

Nelken, D. (ed.) (1994) *The Futures of Criminology*, London: Sage.

Parnell, P. and Kane, S.C. (eds) (2003) *Crime's Power: Anthropologists and the Ethnography of Crime*, Basingstoke: Palgrave Macmillan.

Polsky, N. (1967) *Hustlers, Beats and Others*, Chicago: Aldine Publishing Co.

Presdee, M. (2001) *Cultural Criminology and the Carnival of Crime*, London: Taylor & Francis.

Pryce, K. (1979) *Endless Pressure*, London: Penguin Books.

Richards, K. (2011) 'Interviewing Elites in Criminological Research: Negotiating Power and Access and Being Called "Kid"'. In L. Bartels and K. Richards (eds) *Qualitative Criminology: Stories from the Field*, Victoria: The Federation Press, pp.68–79.

Schwartz, M. and Hatty, S. (eds) (2003) *Controversies in Critical Criminology*, Cincinnati: Anderson Publishing.

Skeggs, B. (1997) *Formations of Class and Gender*, London: Sage.

Skeggs, B. (2004) *Class, Self, Culture*, London: Routledge.

Smart, C. (1976) *Women, Crime and Criminology: A Feminist Critique*, London: Routledge & Kegan Paul.

Smart, C. (1989) *Feminism and the Power of Law*, London: Taylor & Francis.

Taylor, S. (ed.) (2001) *Ethnographic Research: A Reader*, London: Sage.

Vaaranen, H. (2004) 'Stories from the Street: Some Fieldwork Notes on the Seduction of Speed'. In J. Ferrell, K. Hayward, W. Morrison and M. Presdee (eds) *Cultural Criminology Unleashed*, London: the Glasshouse Press, pp.245–48.

Venkatesh, S. (2012) 'A Race to Reflexivity' *Ethnic and Racial Studies* 35(4): 633–36.

Wacquant, L.J.D. (1989) 'Towards a Reflexive Sociology: A Workshop with Pierre Bourdieu' *Sociological Theory* 7(1): 26–63.

Wacquant, L.J.D. (2008) *Urban Outcasts: A Comparative Sociology of Advanced Marginality*, Cambridge: Polity Press.

Wacquant, L.J.D. (2011a) 'From "Public Criminology" to the Reflexive Sociology of Criminological Production and Consumption' *British Journal of Criminology* 51(2): 438–48.

Wacquant, L.J.D. (2011b) *Deadly Symbiosis: Race and the Rise of the Penal State*, Cambridge: Polity Press.

Whyte, W.F. (1943) *Street Corner Society*, Chicago: University of Chicago Press.

Young, J. (1971) *The Drugtakers: The Social Meaning of Drug Use*, London: Paladin.

Young, J. (2004) 'Voodoo Criminology and the Numbers Game'. In J. Ferrell, K. Hayward, W. Morrison and M. Presdee (eds) *Cultural Criminology Unleashed*, London: Glasshouse Press, pp.13–28.

Young, J. (2011) *The Criminological Imagination*, Cambridge: Polity Press.

Part I
Research Relationships
Editors' Introduction
Karen Lumsden and Aaron Winter

This section focuses on *research relationships*. Here, we look at the challenges faced when attempting to successfully negotiate access to a variety of groups and settings. Deviant cultures have little to gain by allowing researchers access to their daily lives and various illegal activities (Winlow et al. 2001). Moreover, even if initial access is granted, deviant activities can be obscured from view by what Best and Luckenbill (cited in Lee 1993, 133) refer to as 'command of place' where by means of physical separation and the use of shielding mechanisms, participants free themselves from surveillance by social control agencies. Relationships with gatekeepers and participants in official settings such as prisons must also be continually renegotiated throughout the course of the research, highlighting the imbalance of power relations within the field that leads directly to bargaining in the access situation. Despite gaining access in an official sense, in certain settings and circumstances the researcher can be denied access to certain 'backstage regions' (Goffman 1959). Negotiating access in institutional settings such as prisons also draws attention to the ways in which the researched are involved in shaping the study, and thus the construction of knowledge on life in that setting. However, as Mehta's chapter herein demonstrates, these instances in the prison setting can conversely open up new avenues for dialogue with the researched, highlighting the role that space plays in shaping social relations and the willingness of the researched to share their life stories.

In Chapter 2, Nicola O'Leary begins by examining the role of researcher reflexivity when exploring a community which has experienced collective victimisation in the wake of a serious and high-profile crime. Much of this reflexive account deals with how the researcher gained access to the field and negotiated (and renegotiated) relations in an unfamiliar, and at times unreceptive, environment. Julie T. Davies and Eleanor Peters in Chapter 3 also highlight the problematic process of gaining and sustaining access to individuals or groups, but in this case via powerful institutions such as prisons. They consider issues of power, ethics and hierarchy in conducting research with vulnerable populations who are incarcerated or subject to criminal justice sanctions in the community. In Chapter 4, Rimple Mehta focuses on the role of the mango tree in the female ward of a prison for both men and women, in shaping the relationship between the researcher and Bangladeshi female prisoners in a correctional home in Kolkata, India. Through the example of a mango tree she highlights the role that space plays in shaping relationships in the field. In Chapter 5, Stephen Case and Kevin Haines present 'Reflective Friend Research', a paradigm founded in a long-standing research partnership between researcher, practitioners and young people. They argue that researchers functioning as critical friends offer evidence-based recommendations for radical, systemic changes to traditional practices of knowledge generation, engagement and integrating research findings into practice. Nurturing long-term reflective relationships with researched parties can facilitate levels of access to research participants, data sets, internal documentation and knowledge generation processes seldom enjoyed by positivists conducting research on research subjects rather than with research participants/contributors.

References

Goffman, E. (1959) *The Presentation of Self in Everyday Life*, New York: Doubleday Company Inc.

Lee, R.M. (1993) *Doing Research on Sensitive Topics*, London: Sage.

Winlow, S., Hobbs, D., Lister, S. and Hadfield, P. (2001) 'Get Ready to Duck: Bouncers and the Reality of Ethnographic Research on Violent Groups' *British Journal of Criminology* 41: 536–48.

2

Negotiating 'Victim Communities': Reflexivity and Method in Researching High-Profile Crimes

Nicola O'Leary

Introduction

Certain crimes seem to embody the mood of the times, entering the public consciousness in such an enduring way that they almost become public property. Crimes such as the killing of James Bulger in 1993 and the disappearance of Madeleine McCann in 2007 have reached such prominence, attracting large amounts of sustained media coverage and popular attention. However, many such serious crimes typically involve a range of harms to multiple victims, not only to individuals or immediate groups, but also often on a broader level to others that live and are connected to the location where the crime took place.

This chapter aims to contribute to the discussions of reflexivity in criminological research by detailing some of my own reflective experiences as a qualitative researcher attempting to explore such 'victim communities'. The research reflections below are based on a combination of semi-structured interviews and observations at two research sites as part of my doctoral research. These communities were witness to two of the most high-profile and highly mediatised crimes in recent decades in the United Kingdom: the school shootings in Dunblane in 1996 and killings of school girls Holly Wells and Jessica Chapman in Soham in 2002. As a previously un-researched and powerless group who have experienced victimisation, this research attempts to explore how a serious crime event may affect the wider community involved and how they collectively come to terms with the trauma, stigma and aftermath of a highly mediatised 'signal crime' (Innes 2003). Innes defines signal crimes as events that, in addition to affecting immediate participants, impact in some way upon a wider audience (2003, 52). In addition, the notion bears some similarity to 'moral panics' and the 'broken windows' thesis, where an offence or incident, when experienced or seen, may trigger a change in public behaviour or beliefs.

Reflexivity in method

All social actors are *reflexive agents*, in the sense that they are able to continually alter their behaviour in response to the situations they are experiencing (Giddens 1990). What is different about the reflexivity of social researchers is that they attempt to moderate their own responses while observing the responses of other social agents; as such 'subsequent activity can be altered by virtue of reflection-based knowledge' (Ransome 2013, 83). However, a reflexive approach to social science research is not for everyone. Some criminological researchers are not prepared, nor do they see the value in interrogating the notion of self in their research, not least because they see self-reflection as a distraction from what the research is 'really about' (Crewe 2009). However, although by no means universal, in many other social science fields and indeed in some criminological research discussions, the importance of being reflexive is increasingly acknowledged with the attention focused on recognising the social location of the researcher, as well as the ways in which the researcher's emotional responses to participants shape the emotional account (Piacentini 2013). Significantly, reflexivity in such cases emphasises the importance of self-awareness, political and cultural consciousness and ownership of one's perspective, all of which are vital in academic research seeking to maximise the significance of emotional experience. Relationships and our reflexive awareness of them have an impact at every level of the research process.

With the above in mind, this chapter details a reflexive approach to some of the theoretical and practical issues involved in conducting empirical fieldwork of a sensitive nature with members of a 'victim community' and addresses how I as the researcher negotiated an unfamiliar and sometimes unreceptive environment. Although the fieldwork entailed both practical and methodological challenges, the focus here particularly concerns research relationships, more specifically the building of those relationships, access to the field and the constant renegotiation of both. By adopting a reflexive approach, this chapter seeks to explore how reflexivity can feed into method and practice and hopes to advance discussions on reflexive methodologies in criminological research, while also offering some concrete accounts of how to 'be' reflexive.

Research approach and choices

As with almost all methodological choices, there is a tension between getting rich and valid material on the one hand, and scale and representativeness of data on the other. Following a broadly qualitative strategy, this research engaged in several methods of analysis, including observation and informal interviews which when used in conjunction can serve to provide a holistic and inclusive description of cultural membership (Lindlof 1995). Such methods (primarily semi-structured interviews) were chosen, as the experience of these potential 'communities of victims' had not been researched previously (and rarely acknowledged in the existing literature). The aim was therefore to concentrate on the private discourse of individuals involved through an exploration of 'victims' as a collective identity. This choice of method would further our knowledge and understanding of 'victims' rather than an appreciation through the extrapolation of theories, arguments and politics based on taken for granted assumptions about a transient concept. As Stanley and Wise (1983, 167) have suggested, 'the best way to find out about people's lives is for people to give their own analytical accounts of their own experiences'.

With reference to the context of the research approach and methods chosen, I am drawn to the view that such qualitative research is partly autobiographical (Liebling 1999; Jewkes 2012), reflecting the researcher's personality and psyche as well as those of the respondents participating in the interpretative dialogue. As Jennifer Hunt (1989, 42) insightfully notes, 'fieldwork is in part, the discovery of the self through the detour of the other'. There is no doubt that the research process is a complex enterprise; in attempts to understand the role of the researcher within feminist perspectives, for example, Ann Oakley (1981) has emphasised that drawing on and theorising about one's personal experience can be valuable to the research process. In some areas of criminology, too, there has been a growing recognition that the research process must be an inherently personal, political and partial endeavour (Ferrell 1998). Thus, it is suggested that the self is always present and affects every aspect of the research process from the choice of project to the presentation of 'findings' whether acknowledged or not (Stanley and Wise 1983). Issues of reflexivity and reflection are an extremely important part of research, and researcher identities need to be made explicit throughout the research process.

For this doctoral research I settled on two primary research sites in the United Kingdom, Dunblane in Scotland and Soham in Cambridgeshire. The reasons for these particular sites were twofold. First, both had experience of what has been termed a 'signal crime' (Innes 2003) and the proposal was to explore whether these highly mediatised crime events had left a tainted legacy for the wider community, which had permeated the collective memory. Second, I was keen to give a comparative edge to the research. The inclusion of a more recent 'victim community' such as Soham, in contrast to Dunblane, where the serious crime in question is not quite so 'new' in the collective memory (although this can be a temporal state), would give an element of longevity and temporal analysis to the understanding of the subject, adding value and depth to the findings.

With any academic research it is vitally important to have practical access to the sample population, yet in some situations this can be difficult. The process of starting to build relationships begins before a researcher enters the field, but how does one go about obtaining that initial access? This of course takes some form of planning but spontaneity, evolution and organic growth also play their part.

Approaching the field, building relationships

In what can be described as the pre-research phase, I set about gathering as much relevant secondary data as I could on the proposed research sites and the serious crime events, including national and local newspaper articles and images covering the crime (for a separate media analysis of the crime events see O'Leary 2012). My primary approach was to use this material to identify and locate potential contacts from within each community. At this point I did not have a firm idea of the size of the intended sample but hoped that via these 'primary definers' (Hall et al. 1978), a networking system of recommendations would emerge, where the number of participants to the research would 'snowball'. As others have illustrated, from these first contacts, information about the research disseminates and such projects can often develop their own momentum (Sharpe 2000). My own research path was not quite as smooth, although I did manage to engage an initial contact at one location that effectively acted as my champion and sponsor. This individual did much to ensure that I was introduced and at least accepted in the first instance, by some others in the community and their recommendations no doubt helped to encourage more to participate in the research. However, this was not always the case and there were several instances when those who were recommended to me declined to take part in the study.

Gaining access is unpredictable, particularly where the research is seen as sensitive in nature, because as John Johnson (1975) argues the one thing needed to ensure successful access is a detailed theoretical understanding of the social organisation of the setting one is attempting to enter. In other words, 'that which is most likely to secure access can only be gained once the researcher is actually inside the setting' and has carried out the fieldwork (cited in Lee 1993, 121). In addition I was careful not to address the issue of access as one that only takes place at the initial phase of entry to the research setting. Instead it is an ongoing and implicit process, which needs to be continually renegotiated, often on a personal and one-to-one basis. Access had to be revisited not only each time I made a new contact, but also when revisiting those who had not previously responded or when returning to participants at a later date. Although physical access is a likely precondition of the social (Lee 1993) the latter should not be taken for granted and can remain problematic. The concept of access can be helpfully thought of as a journey where social access is the 'process of "getting along" through establishing a research role, building a rapport with participants and securing their trust' (Noaks and Wincup 2004, 63). Past experiences of research for participants (or in this case, previous experience of media attention, which they judged as one in the same) can often make group members cynical and they may assume the worst about an outsider (Lee 1993). This was particularly resonant given the nature of this research subject and the intense media coverage of the serious crimes both at the time and subsequently. As a prospective outsider attempting to enter these communities I was acutely aware that I may be considered as part of that interest and assigned a negative role on that basis.

Entering the field: Accessing a sensitive community

During the pre-research phase of information gathering, I initially travelled several times to the research sites to get a 'feel' for the place and the communities and to gather any background and local community information that I felt would be instructive. This also gave me the opportunity to familiarise myself with the geography and the physical space of the places where I would be spending so much time. I spoke to people in the local shops and in the pubs and chatted to residents on the street about everyday issues, passing the time of day, but not talking about my research. At the time I did not consider these actions as research in the formal sense, yet on reflection in addition to informal information gathering I was clearly 'getting my face known' and attempting to move some way from my assumed identified position as a complete 'outsider' or someone whose interest came with dubious intentions. From some of that information and together with the newspaper articles collated for the media analysis I was able to identify names of some in the community to approach to partake in this study. Initial contact was by letter, explaining the aims and process of the research, as well as details and assurances of anonymity and confidentiality (issues which had become highly visible in both sites during this pre-research process). From these preliminary contacts and after further communications, a handful of interviews were arranged with participants at the two sites. At the end of each of these interviews and where appropriate, each participant was asked if they felt they could recommend anyone else in the community to take part in the research. The overall response rate to these requests for participation was not high and while the numbers of community members who participated did reach the target set (39 in total), there were several within the community who declined to take part in the research study before having a fully informed understanding of the details of the research aims and process. This in itself gives an interesting indication of the level of emotion and stigma attached to the locality and members of the community at a collective level.

Keeping the gate open: Negotiating relationships

Researching in and around serious and high-profile crimes can be an extremely sensitive and emotional activity. Such research requires consideration of the sociopolitical and cultural context within which the project is undertaken and received. Ethical practices should permeate all stages of the research process, and by reflecting on potential problems that may occur, methods of how to minimise the effect on research participants can be devised.

Informed consent and confidentiality

Informed consent can be viewed as the linchpin of the relationship between the researcher and the participants and the point in the research process at which ethical considerations are brought definitively to the foreground. The principle of informed consent is deeply embedded in professional codes of practice and achieving it is generally promoted as a fundamental guiding principle for an ethically informed approach to social science research. Informed consent can be described as research conducted in such a way that participants have 'a complete understanding, at all times, of what the research is about and the implications for themselves in being involved' (Noaks and Wincup 2004, 45). Such transparency of approach is commendable but often difficult to achieve in some practical situations, as it may discourage certain potential participants' willingness to reveal sensitive information. At times the researcher has to balance the competing questions of consent and validity (Jupp et al. 2000). However, part of the rapport and trust that a qualitative researcher aims to build with participants involves privacy and confidentiality, something which participants need to be aware of and understand from the outset of the fieldwork. In addition it was apparent during this research that, as with the issue of access, ongoing consent should not automatically be assumed. Informed consent also implies the right to discontinue participation, to withdraw consent, even once the research is underway, and where relevant has to be renegotiated throughout the various stages of the fieldwork.

The ethical approach adopted with my own research participants in this case was to offer them assurances regarding confidentiality and although this was less important for some than others, the default position of anonymity. This of course was not possible when considering the community more generally and the notion of place. Research, which is grounded in a sense of place, cannot credibly anonymise place names (Loader et al. 1998). Some community members and research participants had understandable concerns about how the image of their community may be negatively affected by the research attention. However, they also clearly understood that by their very nature, these were locations where extremely high-profile crimes had taken place and, as such, are already likely to have negative connotations for wider audiences. Therefore, the inability to disguise the location of the research sites was explained fully to the participants in terms meaningful to them and an understanding of this issue and its implications was agreed before any data collection took place.

The process of research can be an emotionally intense experience for any researcher and participant. When researching in a community, the collective element can be equally significant. Researchers will often need to be aware of and navigate community biases and partisanships. Resonance is felt here with Lynn Hancock's (2000, 378) writings on conducting research in high-crime communities where she calls for researchers to be 'mindful of the sensibilities that exist in a community and consider their implications'. Not only then does research conducted within a community need to be conscious of the attitudes to the research, but also it needs to be aware of neighbourhood collectives and sensitive to how they may cut across the willingness of some to be involved in the research or not. This was certainly an important dimension of my own research, as I often had requests from participants and potential participants enquiring as to who else had contributed and what their thoughts had been. There was a distinct concern from some to know whether they were 'on' or 'off' message with others who had participated in the research and almost all were at pains to insist they were not speaking on behalf of the community as a whole. I found the situation difficult when respondents enquired in this way but strict notions of anonymity and confidentiality had been promised and were adhered to at all times. I dealt with this by talking in general terms of the 'many people from different sections of the community who had kindly agreed to participate'. Given the nature of community relations at one of the research sites in particular, confidentiality and anonymity from other members of their wider community was a particularly important issue. While it was reiterated throughout the research process and to all participants that I was simply interested in their thoughts and experiences as individuals as part of a community, it transpired that others had fallen foul of this before with interviews given to the media and it had become almost a local 'taboo' to be talking about community issues, as a spokesperson for, or on behalf of the community.

Collective sensibilities, emotions and neutrality

Defining what constitutes 'sensitive' research is not as straightforward as it sounds. A relatively broad and safe definition may be to say that a research topic is sensitive if it involves potential cost or harm to those who are or who have been involved, harm or cost that goes beyond the incidental or merely onerous (Lee 1993). Of course, it should be recognised that there are different ideas of harm for different people and at different stages of the process. With regard to this research, I was reminded of what can be described as the 'messy realities' of social research. This research project explores a subject matter that is complex and emotional in nature for many in the community, whether participating in the research directly or not. As such, as the researcher I had to be constantly aware of the sensitivity of the situation with specific regard to issues of intrusion and vulnerability; it is particularly important to be aware that research about emotional and sensitive issues may bring forward vulnerable people as others have suggested (Stanley and Wise 1983; Finch 1984). Paying attention to the sensitivity of the research and the issue of intrusion in particular, I aimed to reduce the extent that this may have been a significant factor for my participants by careful consideration throughout the research process of methods, the nature, breadth and depth of the questions and the impingement on the time of those involved and by warning participants of the potential sensitive nature of the content.

Staying neutral when conducting research of an emotional nature is also difficult. In 'Whose Side Are We On?' Howard Becker (1967) firmly believes that qualitative research can never be totally value free. While ethics is undoubtedly a vital component of robust research, Becker suggests that in order to produce authentic and quality data one must take sides, particularly if researching a 'powerless' or subordinate group. Due to the individual and 'hands-on' nature of much qualitative research there is little chance that the researcher will not have some sympathy and possible attachments to the group being researched. This may put in jeopardy the 'value-free' stance attempted by the researcher to the extent that Becker (1967) firmly believes that all research is unavoidably contaminated by the researcher's beliefs. Although individual biases and values can be minimised, they cannot be completely eradicated. Being sympathetic and maybe even taking sides could certainly distort the data to a degree but it does not make it unusable. Historically the qualitative researcher or ethnographer invariably leaves one's individual mark on the data collection process. This has certainly been my own experience.

Reflections on research relations

Qualitative research takes place in a vast variety of situations and there is much variation within each type of setting that is relevant and has bearing on the nature of relationships that are possible with the participants in these settings. As such, generalisations when discussing relations in the field are necessarily subject to multiple exceptions. Therefore this account can only be a discussion of the methodological and practical considerations as they relate directly to this doctoral research study.

My research experience leads me to believe that researcher identity and status are important and complex issues and encountering suspicion about a researcher's presence in the field is not uncommon. I am aware that my initial attempts to enter the field at both sites were sometimes thwarted or certainly made more difficult because of the doubt of some community members as to my true intentions. Due to the nature of the research subject and my interest in the role of the media in the representations of community, many potential respondents were suspicious that I was in fact part of the media myself. My greatest (and ongoing) hurdle in this respect was to convince participants of my interests in their own views and day-to-day experiences rather than the more media-driven, voyeuristic elements of the crime itself. In this regard I worked extremely hard throughout the research process, and through the fieldwork stage in particular, to encourage the view that my interest in their community and these issues was intellectual in nature and more importantly, genuine.

These discussions have highlighted many elements to consider of a practical and emotional nature when approaching, accessing and negotiating the field. Emotional involvement and experience can certainly play a part in the formulation of knowledge. Although not technically essential to the research process, the ability to draw on one's own experience and resources can allow connections to be made and rapport to be developed between researchers and researched at a crucial early stage of the fieldwork. In this way the role of the researcher in the research process as a whole, including generating the data collected must be recognised (Hammersley 1992). There is a vast amount of literature on the role of the researcher and one of the most pertinent themes to emanate is that establishing a research role takes time and one needs to adopt different roles throughout the research process (Hammersley and Atkinson 1995). For these reasons and in order to be accepted, researchers need to be adaptable in how they manage their role (Goffman 1963) within the fieldwork setting. In my own experience this role adjustment was not an overt or conscious decision, rather a critical awareness of the level of sensitivity that was needed to manage what were often acute relations in the field.

Reflexivity in method and practice

There is always the risk of the researcher altering what is said or done in a specific situation by his/her very presence (Jewkes 2002). Why is it important for some researchers to be reflexive, to discuss and to analyse research methods and reasons for their use, when for others it is simply not an issue? Many significant and influential studies, even those employing ethnographic methods, have been written and published with very little discussion in this area. Often elements of context have not informed a substantial part of the text in accounts of research. Where they have been provided, they are sometimes tucked away in a short appendix or are often highly generalised accounts. Although as Davies (2000) notes, within more recent mainstream criminological publications, descriptive accounts of research processes have become more prominent and transparent, still many empirical accounts only pay lip service to issues of reflexivity. While factually describing methods employed, there is often little description or discussion of the more personal reasons for, or elements of, the research. This does not allow the audiences to consider the research process or project in its entirety. With no reflexive account there is nothing of the author's personality or identity within, no recognition of self. This leaves the audience in a weakened position as it becomes more difficult to analyse and consider the representativeness and validity of the research process and findings without this information. Whether these are key issues for all is a decision for the individual researcher, but a reflexive awareness of the many influences on data collection, presentation and the research process as a whole is crucial to my mind. Using reflexivity in this way, we can claim to be more aware of the factors affecting and underpinning the investigation of social phenomena. This is all part of the learning process of social research (Ransome 2013).

Conclusion

This discussion has presented a reflexive insight into the practical process of conducting research on a sensitive issue at a community level. Its contribution to the discussion of reflexivity in criminological research foregrounds the primacy of emotion and sensitivity within the research process, particularly at a community level. Such discussions must do more than fulfil the requirements of a 'methods' section or chapter of a research project; self-awareness and emotion are the conduits to understanding the process of 'doing' research. This chapter has also detailed the reflexive experiences of exploring a previously un-researched and relatively powerless group. These groups have experienced victimisation in the wake of a serious and high-profile crime but as a collective have not had their voices heard. As such this work is able to challenge the more public, stereotypical and simplistic discourses of those who are 'recognised' as victims. The doctoral research on which this chapter is based owes a clear debt to the work of Erving Goffman (1961, 1963) concerning stigma and spoiled identity and the classic works of Howard Becker (1963, 1967) regarding labelling and neutrality in social research. These formative studies of crime and deviance are refracted in another direction by examining the impact of issues of identity, stigma and social reaction through a collective or community lens.

The power of qualitative research is in showing how there are alternative explanations for any outcome, and also that there can be many different outcomes. This diversity and variation is not a shortcoming, but rather a strength. With that in mind I do not suggest that this work is representative of all who are part of a physical community in the aftermath of a serious and high-profile crime, nor is it necessarily indicative of others' experiences of qualitative research with emotional communities. I do hope, however, that it does have value in explanatory terms and that it may be relevant to other researchers who find themselves in similar situations.

References

Becker, H. (1963) *Outsiders: Studies in the Sociology of Deviance*, New York: Free Press.
Becker, H. (1967) 'Whose Side Are We On?' *Social Problems* 14: 239–47.
Crewe, B. (2009) *The Prisoner Society: Power, Adaptation and Social Life in an English Prison*, Oxford: Oxford University Press.
Davies, P. (2000) 'Doing Interviews with Female Offenders'. In V. Jupp, P. Davies, and P. Francis (eds) *Doing Criminological Research*, London: Sage, pp.82–96.
Ferrell, J. (1998) 'Criminological *Verstehen*: Inside the Immediacy of Crime'. In J. Ferrell and M.S. Hamm (eds) *Ethnography at the Edge: Crime, Deviance and Field Research*, Boston, MA: Northeastern University Press, pp.20–42.
Finch, J. (1984) 'It's Great to Have Someone to Talk To: The Ethics and Politics of Interviewing Women'. In C. Bell and H. Roberts (eds) *Social Researching: Politics Problems, Practice*, London: Routledge and Kegan Paul, pp.70–87.
Giddens, A. (1990) *The Consequences of Modernity*, Cambridge: Polity Press.
Goffman, E. (1961) *Asylums: Essays on the Social Situation of Mental Patients and Other Inmates*, Harmondsworth: Penguin.
Goffman, E. (1963) *Stigma: Notes on the Management of Spoiled Identity*, Harmondsworth: Penguin.
Hall, S., Critcher, C., Jefferson, T., Clarke, J. and Roberts, B. (1978) *Policing the Crisis: Mugging, the State and Law and Order*, London: Macmillan.
Hammersley, M. (1992) *What's Wrong with Ethnography?* London: Routledge.
Hammersley, M. and Atkinson, P. (1995) *Ethnography: Principles in Practice*, London: Routledge.
Hancock, L. (2000) 'Going Around the Houses: Researching in High Crime Areas'. In R. King and E. Wincup (eds) *Doing Research on Crime and Justice*, Oxford: Oxford University Press, pp.373–83.
Hunt, J. (1989) *Psychoanalytic Aspects of Fieldwork*, London: Sage.
Innes, M. (2003) '"Signal Crimes": Detective Work, Mass Media and Constructing Collective Memory'. In P. Mason (ed.) *Criminal Visions: Media Representations of Crime and Justice*, Cullompton, Devon: Willan, pp.51–69.
Jewkes, Y. (2002) *Captive Audience: Media, Masculinity and Power in Prisons*, Cullompton, Devon: Willan.
Jewkes, Y. (2012) 'Autoethnography and Emotion as Intellectual Resources: Doing Prison Research Differently' *Qualitative Inquiry* 18(1): 63–75.
Jupp, V., Davies, P. and Francis, P. (eds) (2000) *Doing Criminological Research*, London: Sage.
Lee, R. (1993) *Doing Research on Sensitive Topics*, London: Sage.
Liebling, A. (1999) 'Doing Research in Prison: Breaking the Silence?' *Theoretical Criminology* 3(2): 147–84.
Lindlof, T. (1995) *Qualitative Communication Research Methods*, Thousand Oaks, CA: Sage.
Loader, I., Girling, E. and Sparks, R. (1998) 'Narratives of Decline: Youth, Dis/order and Community in an English "Middletown"' *British Journal of Criminology* 38: 388–403.
Noaks, L. and Wincup, E. (2004) *Criminological Research: Understanding Qualitative Methods*, London: Sage.
Oakley, A. (1981) 'Interviewing Women: A Contradiction in Terms'. In H. Roberts (ed.) *Doing Feminist Research*, London: Routledge, pp.30–61.
O'Leary, N. (2012) 'Negotiating Collective Identity: Crime, the Media and the Growth of Victim Communities', Unpublished PhD thesis, University of Hull, UK.

Piacentini, L. (2013) *Handle with Care: New and Established Methodologies in Prison Research*. URL (accessed 26 August 2013): http://ssrn.com/abstract=2240953.

Ransome, P. (2013) *Ethics and Values in Social Research*, Basingstoke: Palgrave Macmillan.

Sharpe, K. (2000) 'Mad, Bad and (Sometimes) Dangerous to Know: Street Corner Research with Prostitutes, Punters and the Police'. In R. King and E. Wincup (eds) *Doing Research on Crime and Justice*, Oxford: Oxford University Press, pp.363–72.

Stanley, L. and Wise, S. (1983) *Breaking Out*, London: Routledge & Kegan Paul.

3

Relationships Between Gatekeepers and Researchers: The Experience of Conducting Evaluations into Parenting Programmes in Community and Penal Settings

Julie T. Davies and Eleanor Peters

Introduction

The idea of reflexivity in research and how biographies intersect with the field is one which has been discussed by various authors in a number of settings (Finlay 2002; O'Reilly 2012). Although we address some of these issues as critical criminologists[1] (Carrington and Hogg 2008), the chapter will focus on 'social critique' (Finlay 2002) in terms of the power imbalance between researcher and respondents, and the dynamics involved between the researcher and the professionals, such as social workers and criminal justice professionals, who act as gatekeepers. In a critical research approach, issues of power and powerlessness are paramount if we are to be reflexive in our research – critically analysing power, personalities, politics and marginalisation.

This chapter draws on two research projects into parenting programmes provided by a voluntary organisation in a city in the North of England. The organisation is a charity which delivers a number of interventions within the social care setting and the work with families in conflict with the law is just one part of their remit. The community parenting classes were provided to parents who were experiencing severe problems with their child's behaviour, either involvement in crime and antisocial behaviour and/or truancy. The objective was to improve parents' relationships with their children, boost confidence in their parenting skills and provide specific guidance in dealing with issues associated with problematic behaviours. The organisation's work with incarcerated fathers grew from work in the community providing parenting classes and with some adaptions this work was introduced in a local prison. The objective of the work in the prison was to not only provide fathers with parenting skills, but also provide a link for these fathers while incarcerated with their children by holding family visit days. These included specific activities that permitted more freedom of association, allowing parents to fully engage with their children. The research was conducted in order to evaluate the success of the projects, and this involved 52 semi-structured interviews with parents, approximately 80 hours of observation during parenting classes in the prison and community, in court, during family visit days in the prison and over an activity weekend for parents and their children.

This chapter is specifically concerned with the gatekeeper–researcher relationship arising from our research into parenting programmes in the community and a penal setting. Gatekeepers are an integral part of the process of gaining access to conduct research and the researcher needs to develop a relationship with the gatekeeper in order to gain access. Gatekeepers are individuals who can introduce the researcher to the field, either an organisation or a group of people, or both. The process of gaining and sustaining entry to institutions and to groups or individuals is often a problematic area for researchers, and these difficulties are exacerbated if the research population is deemed to be vulnerable. Although vulnerability is a fluid and poorly defined category, it usually includes children, people who have been abused, people with communication impairments and those who are incarcerated, many of whom are likely to be of interest to criminologists. For example, access to the prison estate in particular is notoriously problematic, 'secret places' that are shut-off to all but those who reside at Her Majesty's pleasure or those who 'hold the keys' (King and Liebling 2008, 431). However, access to so-called vulnerable populations can be difficult in a number of settings (Scourfield 2012). The vulnerability of the research participants in this study stemmed from their involvement in the criminal justice system. The fathers in prison were obviously vulnerable due to their incarceration; the mothers in the community parenting classes were also vulnerable through issues such as alcohol and drug addiction, mental health issues, domestic violence and poverty.

Vulnerable, 'hard-to-reach' populations and research ethics

There is a tradition in social science research of using gatekeepers in ethnographic work, for example, the archetypal 'Doc' in *Street Corner Society* (Whyte 1955), and although this role has been analysed to some extent in ethnographies of gangs (e.g. Armstrong and Harris 1991), the role of gatekeepers in social research conducted within organisations has received less attention. There has been some recent consideration of issues of access and gatekeeping in social research and this is particularly the case when researchers want to access people who are deemed to be vulnerable, which is where formal research ethics has its part.

Research ethics can have a significant impact on how research is conducted, controlled and facilitated and there is a suggestion that researchers in the field of criminology have been particularly slow to consider the ethics of research in their discipline (Dupont 2008). This criticism can be explained by the fact that much criminological research takes the form of applied research aimed at assisting criminal justice agencies with crime detection, prevention and control. There has been a long-standing issue about how government-funded research focuses on a narrow definition of crime, usually to meet the specific and immediate policy needs of governments targeting particular marginalised populations (Hillyard et al. 2004; Walters 2007).

What this chapter intends to do is, by focusing on the reflections of the authors' experiences in conducting their research, develop an analysis about the relationship between gatekeepers and researchers and how these can affect every stage of the research, focusing particularly on issues of power. We begin by exploring who and what gatekeepers are, then we highlight some of the critical stages of research and how the relationships between individuals affect these stages. We conclude by reflexively considering power dynamics and how these affected relationships between us as researchers and the gatekeepers we encountered.

What is gatekeeping?

Accounts of research fieldwork tend to underplay the role and potential impact of gatekeepers often focusing on the instrumental role that gatekeepers play in facilitating researchers' access, rather than issues of trust and power (Emmel et al. 2007). Little has changed since Broadhead and Rist (1976, 331) remarked how few 'researchers have discussed the control that gatekeepers exercised in forcing them either to revise or depoliticize their analysis'. In social research terms the gatekeeper is the person who provides access to the research field, although it is quite likely that there will be more than one gatekeeper and there may also be formal (official) and informal (unofficial) gatekeepers. The distinction between different gatekeepers is important at various stages of research as input gatekeepers can make the initial stages difficult, and the output gatekeeper can suppress findings from being produced and disseminated, or politically motivated pressure can be applied regarding the interpretation of findings. There is also a difference between being granted access by gatekeepers at the top of the organisation and gaining the cooperation of gatekeepers further down the organisational structure (Wanat 2008; Scourfield 2012). By looking at gatekeepers in this way makes it clear that negotiating access via these actors is an ongoing process.

Gatekeepers within organisations can be very helpful to the research process by encouraging potential respondents with whom they already have a relationship to participate. They can also introduce the researcher to new sources of information and consideration of new ways of looking at the issues being researched. Gatekeepers also play a valuable role in scrutinising researchers' intentions and motivation, as it would be naïve to assume that all requests to conduct research can be accommodated as some will be unsuitable, not feasible or even harmful. However, gatekeepers can ultimately choose to prevent research from being conducted, and often this is done through the gatekeeper making a decision of non-participation on behalf of his/her 'clients' without consultation (Scourfield 2012). This decision may be made because the gatekeeper feels the people in question are particularly vulnerable.

There are a number of reasons why a gatekeeper might decide not to cooperate, but occasionally gatekeepers may display an overprotectiveness which amounts to denying the rights of would-be participants to take part in research in the first place. Their actions may result in a failure to provide them with genuine opportunities to exercise their agency (Scourfield 2012). The decision of the gatekeeper is therefore a proxy for the assent or refusal of potential research participants, although they may not have actually been consulted at all. Researchers who have analysed the gatekeeper relationship have frequently found that gatekeepers are not always the most appropriate person to make the decision whether someone is capable of taking part in research, or indeed capable of being asked whether they want to participate (Wanat 2008).

Getting in: Access and negotiations

The aforementioned research projects under consideration in this chapter began through personal contacts with senior managers of a voluntary organisation project supporting families and children in the North of England. The initial contact was made with a manager at director level, and then meetings were held with the managers of the two parenting projects, one located in the community and the other in a local prison. Managers of both projects felt that the work would benefit from independent research. Both evaluations were conducted in tandem with one of us (JTD) taking the lead on the prison project, and the other (EP) the community project. Our two connected projects had a common gestation but were experienced very differently by us; both researchers had some of the same personnel to deal with (higher and slightly lower management) but 'on the ground' the personalities were different. In addition, one of us (JTD) had to negotiate additional access via Her Majesty's Prison Service.

One aspect of research which occurs to almost every researcher is that of delays. These can occur at all stages of research, but are particularly apparent at the access stage. One of us (JTD) had to negotiate many different layers of gatekeepers including those in the voluntary organisation with whom the research was being conducted, and the prison itself. For example, there was a lengthy delay while enhanced security checks were processed by the prison. There were also negotiations to be had with the person who acted as 'overseer' of the varied voluntary groups located within the prison, all of these factors leading to inevitable delays and interruptions to the research.

Initial meetings at the prison had to be arranged via the voluntary organisation prison project manager and the researcher was allowed 'in' on a visitor's pass while awaiting security clearance which would allow direct access to the prison. The researcher was well aware of and acknowledged the strict guidelines, procedures and practices existent within the prison estate and fully anticipated varying levels of impediments that could be encountered. The nature of prisons themselves, self-contained environments in which activity is tightly regulated and monitored, can make access difficult (Patenaude 2004). There is a long history of prison research in Britain, but as King (2008, 288) states, a crucial issue of concern is that 'the Home Office is both gatekeeper as far as access is concerned and [in some cases] principle funder of research'. This shows how issues of control, power and knowledge are closely interlinked. The issue as highlighted by a number of researchers (Fox et al. 2010; Ramluggun et al. 2010) is the difficulty of gaining access to the prison estate. Control is wielded by governors and the Ministry of Justice and access can be easily denied. Even if access is granted there can be restrictions on the kind of work done and the tendency is to allow 'safe' projects through, meaning that knowledge gained is partial.

One of the biggest hurdles experienced in starting our research was receiving information from the voluntary organisation itself. For example, conducting an outcomes-based evaluative research project meant that the framework of the research was based on the organisation's key aims, objectives and outcomes for the parenting programmes. This actually took several months to acquire, with the voluntary organisation placing the blame for the hold up on the external funders of the project. Promises were made, and not kept, in respect of appointments or meetings arranged with associated partners, and this highlights the need for good forward planning and for gatekeepers to be aware of what research can be realistically conducted given time and financial constraints. This was all highly problematic for us because it impeded the commencement of the research, and then once the projects' outcomes were received, a number were unachievable given the allotted time frame.

The research process can be hindered when gatekeepers delay or refuse to give or withhold information. Gatekeepers can refuse to provide information in a manner that does not involve directly withholding information by classifying it as 'official only' or by limiting access to information so that it is managed, partial and distorted. In the community setting, one example we encountered was obtaining a list of who was involved in the programme, the length of time they had been in contact with the organisation, the status of their involvement (voluntary, court ordered, referred by other agency) which was not forthcoming until a number of requests had been placed by the researcher.

If the gatekeeper sees the research as straying into areas they have an interest in protecting and managing, this may preclude cooperation. Clark (2011) suggests that the researcher's world view needs to be congruent with that of the gatekeepers regarding 'political representation'; therefore, if the gatekeeper suspects that the researcher will represent their work with an alternative viewpoint, they may feel threatened. We suggest that a new manager (as the community project manager was) may not feel comfortable with the research project particularly because new working practices were being introduced to the organisation. There are risks for the gatekeeper in research being conducted on their work, particularly 'if it threatens to reveal an area of practice that the gatekeeper does not want to be represented with the public domain' (Clark 2011, 11). We felt that there were differences in acceptance of our epistemological position between the prison personnel and the parenting workers in the community. The prison personnel led the National Offenders Management Services (NOMS) Children and Families pathway. Therefore, their role was primarily one of maintaining family ties between the incarcerated father and his family, rather than issues of prison security. Consequently, they were able to adopt the position of 'comprehensive gatekeeper' (Emmel et al. 2007) who have a special remit for the care of their 'clients' having a comprehensive role which included referral to other agencies. In the community, the workers were more what Emmel et al. (2007) describe as 'formal gatekeepers' in that their work with socially excluded people is to achieve a certain end through control and supervision, often via disciplinary enforcement such as court-ordered parenting interventions (Peters 2012).

There is a perception that the researcher will cause harm (Hugman et al. 2011) to the participants, to the workers, to the managers, to the service and institution and its reputation. So while there is formal ethical clearance (e.g. via university committees), there is also an allusion to ethics as a tactic some gatekeepers use for blocking access. Here is obviously a means by which the gatekeeper can wield power.

Power is a complex concept but it is worth stressing that what we may encounter as researchers is most probably a combination of what Wolf (1999, 5) calls 'tactical or organizational power' which refers to how actions of others can be constrained or directed within an organisational setting and a more relational power which 'is manifested in interactions and transactions among people' (Wolf 1999, 5). The research studies analysed here are examples not only of power in the institutional sense (the voluntary organisation, the prison), but also of the social (the relationship between the researchers and others). Although as discussed above, there seems to be a contention that researchers are powerful and that ethical considerations and gatekeepers are necessary to keep them in check, it is important not to underestimate the fragmentary nature of power.

Staying in: Rapport

In the prison setting, both the prison chaplain[2] and voluntary organisation manager were readily available for interview and talked quite freely and candidly regarding the parenting programme that they had initiated. Immersion in the research process encourages a greater rapport with respondents and the researcher achieved this by attending and participating in family days, conversing with fathers, families and staff in order to break down any perceived power/trust relations before discussing their participation in the research process. The level and amount of 'good will' afforded to the researcher must be acknowledged as an extremely positive development.

Previous researchers have highlighted how identifiable commonalities between researcher and respondents can engender rapport and hence encourage trust, both of which can add to the richness of the findings, although this is not without its problems (Glesne 1989). It was felt that such commonalities, such as gender, marital and single-parent status, as well as a keen interest in penal policy and practice, enhanced rapport, an affinity which did indeed encourage trust and shared understanding which encouraged a free flow of information and cooperation. A problem, if indeed it can be called such, was that such rapport did lead to the prison project manager calling for a few 'off the record' meetings away from the prison. It was certainly felt by the researcher that such occasions were utilised in order for the key worker to put her 'side of things' forward first, before meetings took place with others involved in the programme; this included discussions regarding her perceived perceptions of individual personalities and the power dynamics that existed between individuals. She was very 'open' in that many aspects of her private life were divulged and although 'researchers [can] involve themselves in activities through which reciprocal relationships are developed' (Emmel et al. 2007, 3) the researcher (JTD) only shared what she considered both relevant and professional – invitations to 'nights out' were respectfully declined.

The impact of personalities is an important consideration in thinking reflexively about research. In their paper, Roesch-Marsh et al. (2011) discuss how their identities, particularly the aspect of being a social work practitioner or non-practitioner, affected their relationships with gatekeepers. The researchers who were social workers had ambivalent feelings about whether this shared professional status benefited them during the research, for example, it could help with the social worker gatekeepers, but impede their relationship with social work 'clients'. Therefore, research relationships are not unidirectional but rather rely on complex interactions between a number of people. Ideally, the gatekeeper asks respondents if they want to take part; they agree and contact details are given to the researcher to contact the individual; slightly less ideally, the gatekeeper approaches respondents and gives them the researcher's contact details for them to follow up (although this puts the onus on the respondent). Preferably the gatekeeper provides access to the 'field' and then remains hands off.

In our research studies it was made very clear to staff and potential participants, via consent forms, information sheets and discussions that all those involved in the research would receive information about the research and it would be ensured that full voluntary consent was obtained, and that no person felt coerced into participating. We wanted to make sure that potential participants were fully informed about what the research entailed and could make a free decision whether to take part and ensure that participants knew they did not have to take part and the service they received from the voluntary organisation would be unaffected by their decision.

However, the manager of the parenting programme in the community setting would often suggest that the parents were too chaotic, their lives were in crisis and asking them to participate in research was not advisable. By not asking parents whether they wanted to participate in the research meant that the researcher could not look at their files as the organisation stated the researcher could not analyse parents' files without their explicit consent. However, by deeming the parent incapable of being asked about the research, the parent could not consent to the researcher looking at the files and therefore the researcher is stuck in a 'Catch-22' situation, whereby the researcher is deprived of all opportunity to contact parents. The difficulty for the researcher was that parents were not making an informed decision about whether to engage with the research or not; parenting workers were declining on their behalf. However, once the researcher did manage to engage the respondents they were happy to speak to her and did not seem especially chaotic nor unable to consent to what was being asked of them (Wanat 2008; Scourfield 2012).

This was less of an issue in the prison research as there was no direct obstruction from staff regarding who was deemed capable of being involved. The dilemma here for the researcher was when and where to see the respondents as she was conscious that it was unfair if the men were taken from their work or leisure pursuits in order to be interviewed. It was especially important not to encroach on the restricted time available to the men to see their families during prison visits and family visit days.

However, another of the manoeuvres that gatekeepers can use to exert their power is by only introducing researchers to 'safe' informants, cherry picking who the researcher has access to (Davies 2011). It may be that those 'clients' who are the keenest to talk to researchers may not necessarily be the most typical; the people that parenting workers offer to you as participants may be ones that can be relied upon to 'say the right things'; however, this may be inadvertent, as the following example shows.

Although in the prison project, the prison chaplain and the voluntary organisation manager were extremely keen to help the researcher achieve a favourable evaluation, this was not without its problems. During initial meetings with fathers, consent was arranged in respect of conducting one-to-one interviews with them inside the prison and confirmation sought that they were happy for the researcher to approach their families outside of the prison, although obviously consent was gathered from the family members as well. The researcher had been promised that the fathers would be brought to her to interview within the chaplaincy offices; however, this did not happen and the researcher was taken to various settings within the prison, namely workshops, the gym and recreation area, where individuals were brought to her and the interview took place with a key worker in close proximity. While we acknowledge that an appropriate escort would and indeed should enable the researcher to access the fathers, the researcher felt that this could have impeded on the level and frankness of the information given when being asked about the standard and effect of the parenting programme. This is not an uncommon experience in prison research (see Patenaude 2004). Quraishi (2008), whose movements inside prison were also dependent upon being accompanied by chaplains, felt that senior officers might be filtering participants and presenting those likely to give favourable responses.

Conclusion: Reflections on the research process

This chapter analysed issues of access, power and research relationships in the context of parenting programmes in a penal and community setting. By focusing on the relationship between gatekeepers and researchers, it has contributed to discussions of reflexivity by highlighting the pluralistic nature of the gatekeeper – the access-giver, the facilitator, but also the controller, the obstructer. As this chapter has highlighted, there is not just one gatekeeper (or even just one level of gatekeeping), and gatekeepers can often be in conflict with each other about what they desire from the research process (Walker and Read 2011).

We believe that the assumption that power is held (mostly) by the researchers is overestimated. As a result of this power imbalance, gatekeepers may also fear being judged by researchers and therefore become suspicious of their motives. However, in our experience gatekeepers can wield a huge amount of power and influence. One aspect we have discussed is how the gatekeeper can control the research process by various means, one of which is denying the agency of the respondent; the gatekeeper who precludes the respondent's participation has removed from that individual his/her right to be heard. This leads to questions, well versed in feminist research in particular, about who has knowledge, who governs it and who are those who control which individuals are allowed to generate it (Harding 1991)?

The chapter has utilised a critical criminological framework, particularly around issues of denying the voices of those usually excluded from research (Faulkner 2004; Walker and Read 2011). A desire to highlight the 'view from below' was an important factor in our research because the respondents are often not consulted about anything in their lives, incarcerated young men and mothers living in extreme poverty. Whereas in the prison setting the gatekeepers were keen to have the voices of the fathers heard, there was a disjuncture between the ethos of the community manager and that of the researcher because the manager was keen to focus almost solely on parenting while the researcher was interested in looking at how parents could do this given their socio-economic disadvantages, and as discussed there are risks for the gatekeeper if the research is perceived as being critical towards their practice (Clark 2011).

There are lessons that as researchers we can take forward which may be of use to others. One is that doing a wide range of preparatory work cannot be understated. Ensuring that all members of staff are involved and 'on board' is a difficult matter and many may feel obliged to 'play along' if senior managers are present at meetings. As Wanat (2008) clearly set out in her research, access from 'the top' does not always mean cooperation from others, and therefore perhaps a 'bottom-up' approach is more advantageous because this may minimise the feeling that researchers are trying to catch people out and the feeling that the research has been forced on them by their managers.

We all experience doing research in a personal way; it is impossible not to consider how you as a person affect the relationships in the field, and the dynamics of personalities can sometimes make or break a research project (Spradley 1979). But it is perhaps worth keeping in mind what Scourfield (2012, 3) says: 'there can ... be factors about certain fields where the difficulties in gaining effective access go beyond solving relational problems'. With careful planning, mutual trust and forethought, research can be a rewarding exercise for the researcher in highlighting important issues that may normally remain hidden, and as a form of empowerment for those not normally given the opportunity to be heard.

Notes

1. Critical criminology questions the power of the state to define crime and deviance and therefore the criminalisation and social control of marginalised groups in society.
2. The chaplain was the prison lead for the NOMS Children and Family pathway and initial instigator of the project.

References

Armstrong, G. and Harris, R. (1991) 'Football Hooligans: Theory and Evidence' *Sociological Review* 39(3): 427–58.

Boden, R., Epstein, D. and Latimer, J. (2009) 'Accounting for Ethos or Programmes for Conduct? The Brave New World of Research Ethics Committees' *Sociological Review* 57(4): 728–49.

Broadhead, R.S. and Rist, R.C. (1976) 'Gatekeepers and the Social Control of Social Research' *Social Problems* 23(3): 325–36.

Carrington, K. and Hogg, R. (2008) 'Critical Criminologies: An Introduction'. In K. Carrington and R. Hogg (eds) *Critical Criminologies: Issues, Debates, Challenges*, Cullompton; Willan, pp.1–14.

Clark, T. (2011) 'Gaining and Maintaining Access: Exploring the Mechanisms That Support and Challenge the Relationship Between Gatekeepers and Researchers' *Qualitative Social Work* 10(4): 485–502.

Davies, P. (2011) 'Doing Interviews in Prison'. In P. Davies, P. Francis and V. Jupp (eds) *Doing Criminological Research*, London: Sage, pp.161–78.

Dupont, I. (2008) 'Beyond Doing No Harm: A Call for Participatory Action Research with Marginalized Populations in Criminological Research' *Critical Criminology* 16: 197–207.

Emmel, N.D., Hughes, K., Greenhalgh, J. and Sales, A. (2007) 'Accessing Socially Excluded People – Trust and the Gatekeeper in the Researcher-Participant Relationship' *Sociological Research Online* 12(2): http://www.socresonline.org.uk/12/2/emmel.html

Faulkner, A. (2004) *The Ethics of Survivor Research: Guidelines for the Ethical Conduct of Research Carried Out by Mental Health Service Users and Survivors*, Bristol: Polity Press.

Finlay, L. (2002) 'Negotiating the Swamp: The Opportunity and Challenge of Reflexivity in Research Practice' *Qualitative Research* 2(2): 209–30.

Fox, K., Zambrana, K and Lane, J. (2010) 'Getting In (and Staying In) When Everyone Else Wants To Get Out: 10 Lessons Learned from Conducting Research with Inmates' *Journal of Criminal Justice Education* 22(2): 304–27.

Harding, S. (1991) *Whose Science? Whose Knowledge?* Ithaca, NY: Cornell University Press.

Hillyard, P., Sim, J., Tombs, S. and Whyte, D. (2004) 'Leaving a "Stain upon the Silence" Contemporary Criminology and the Politics of Dissent' *British Journal of Criminology* 44(3): 369–90.

Hugman, R., Pittaway, E. and Bartolomei, L. (2011) 'When "Do No Harm" Is Not Enough: The Ethics of Research with Refugees and Other Vulnerable Groups' *British Journal of Social Work* 41 (7): 1271–87.

King, R.D. and Liebling, A. (2008) 'Doing Research in Prisons'. In R.D. King and E. Wincup (eds) *Doing Research on Crime and Justice*, Oxford: Oxford University Press, pp.431–54.

O'Reilly, K. (2012) 'Ethnographic Returning, Qualitative Longitudinal Research and the Reflexive Analysis of Social Practice' *Sociological Review* 60(3): 518–36.

Patenaude, A.L. (2004) 'No Promises, But I'm Willing to Listen and Tell What I Hear: Conducting Qualitative Research Among Prison Inmates and Staff' *The Prison Journal* 84: 69S.

Peters, E. (2012) 'Social Work and Social Control in the Third Sector: Re-Educating Parents in the Voluntary Sector' *Practice: Social Work in Action* 1(13): 41–93.

Quraishi, M. (2007) 'Researching Muslim Prisoners' *International Journal of Social Research Methodology* 11(5): 453–67.

Ramluggun, P., Lindsay, B. and Pfeil, M. (2010) 'Research in Prison: a Researcher Practitioner's View' *Nurse Researcher* 17(3): 60–71.

Roesch-Marsh, A., Gadda, A. and Smith, D. (2011) '"It's A Tricky Business!" The Impact of Identity Work in Negotiating Research Access' *Qualitative Social Work* 11(3): 249–65.

Scourfield. P. (2012) 'Defenders Against Threats or Enablers of Opportunities: The Screening Role Played by Gatekeepers in Researching Older People in Care Homes' *The Qualitative Report* 17(28): 1–17.

Spradley, J.P. (1979) *The Ethnographic Interview*, New York: Rinehart & Winston.

Walker, S. and Read, S. (2011) 'Accessing Vulnerable Research Populations: An Experience with Gatekeepers of Ethical Approval' *International Journal of Palliative Nursing* 17: 14–18.

Walters, R. (2007) 'Critical Criminology and the Intensification of the Authoritarian State'. In A. Barton, K. Corteen, D. Scott and D. Whyte (eds) *Expanding the Criminological Imagination: Critical Readings in Criminology*, Cullompton: Willan, pp. 15–37.

Wanat, C. L. (2008) 'Getting Past the Gatekeepers' *Field Methods* 20(2): 191–208.

Whyte, W.F. (1955) *Street Corner Society: The Social Structure of an Italian Slum*, Chicago: University of Chicago Press.

Wolf, E. (1999) *Envisioning Power: Ideologies of Dominance and Crisis*, Berkeley: University of California Press.

4

The Mango Tree: Exploring the Prison Space for Research

Rimple Mehta

Introduction

Relationships are negotiated in and across space, whether it is within a court-room, a hospital, a public street, a home or the prison. 'Space' plays a crucial role in shaping the direction that research takes, but is often left out of discussions on the relationship between a researcher and research partici-pants in the field. Gupta and Ferguson (1997, 34–36) point out that in the social sciences 'space itself becomes a kind of neutral grid on which cul-tural difference, historical memory, and societal organisation is inscribed'. Space does feature as a central organising principle in the social sciences, but at the same time it disappears from analytical purview. There are dis-cussions of techniques, representation and power relations in the context of ethnographic work (see Stanley and Wise 1983; Visweswaran 1996; Bosworth 1999; Bandyopadhyay 2010), but there is little dialogue about the role space plays in formulating these. Space is an active participant in the research process. This active participant becomes even more prominent when it is a closed institution, for example, a prison, a hospital, or a government-run shelter home. Mills (2003, 693) proposes to see space as a 'set of super-imposed spatial frameworks, as many social spaces negotiated within one geographical place and time'. One needs to engage in a discussion of spa-tiality to determine which of the many spaces in the prison, a common site for criminological research, are less oppressive and how they facilitate an interaction between the researcher and the research participants. This dis-cussion needs to be situated in the context of the larger social frameworks that interact in the given prison space.

The fieldwork for my doctoral thesis, on which this paper is based, began as an endeavour to gather the narratives of Bangladeshi women imprisoned in two correctional homes in Kolkata, India, under section 14[1] of the For-eigners Act 1946, who had entered India without valid documents and visa.[2] The research objective was to explore how the agency and experiences of these women were shaped in the context of 'honour' and violence in the process of 'illegal' migration and their interaction with the criminal justice system in India. The fieldwork involved participant observation, formal interview sessions as well as informal conversations and group discussions[3] with around 40 Bangladeshi women prisoners in two correctional homes in Kolkata for nine months between December 2011 and December 2012. The research participants selected the point in their lives they wanted to begin talking from. It is important to note that although I made every effort to have a reciprocal relationship in the process of research, the communication setting was a pre-designed one. The questions that the research participants asked me about my life were often more spontaneous and reactive in comparison to the questions I asked them. Though I did share some intimate details of my life when faced with questions, it would be incorrect to say that there was complete parity between the position of the research participants and myself in the research process. There was a difference in our locations in the research process.

The Bangladeshi women, largely in the age group of 18–22 years, were from extremely impoverished backgrounds, and most of them did not have a permanent residence in Bangladesh. A number of them worked as domestic help from a very young age, earning a meal or two in return along with a meagre salary. The average years spent in formal education was five. Some of them had been to *Madrasas*[4] but the majority of them could neither read or write. Of the women I interacted with, five were Hindu and the others were Muslim. Only one of the 15 married women had migrated with her child and husband. The others came with distant relatives and people from the neighbourhood but a large number of them came to India alone but with the help of touts.[5]

Of the two prisons in which I carried out ethnographic field work, the first one housed both men and women. The female ward comprised approximately 35–40 Bangladeshis and two Indian women at any given time. The second prison, with a capacity of 400 women inmates, was an all-women's prison with approximately 12 per cent Bangladeshis. The prison space that the research participants inhabited needs to be broken down into multiple spaces such as the various corners of the female ward, registration desk, interview room, hospital/out patient department, school room, trees, warders' duty room and toilets in order to understand how inmates experienced different spaces, where they felt comfortable and where they felt threatened with the power which constantly subjected them to a discursive surveillance. It is important for a prison researcher to be reflexive of the various 'sub-spaces' within the 'given' anthropological space of the prison because they impact on the performance of narratives and gestures of the research participants differently. The comfort level of the women prisoners within a certain space was analysed based on the change in their behaviour (as observed by me) and the changing nature of the narratives as we moved our conversations from one place to another within the prison.

By focusing on a mango tree in the female ward of the prison for both men and women, this paper seeks to show that the relationship between the researcher and the research participants, which is an important component of reflexivity, is intersected by space and has an impact on critical inquiry. It will further show how the mango tree is used and understood by Bangladeshi women prisoners and how it influences their narratives and experience of what Goffman (1961) calls a 'total institution'. Hence, this chapter emphasises that in order to incorporate reflexivity in criminological research it is important to highlight its linkages with space.

Reflexivity and space

According to Flavin (2001) mainstream criminology is androcentric. It relies on masculine ideals and works within the positivist framework for carrying out research. It emphasises neutrality and therefore values objectivity and a detached knower. Such an approach does not allow for or acknowledge the lived experience of both the researcher and research participants. Reflexivity, therefore, is not the core of a positivist androcentric framework. According to Burns and Chantler (2011, 72) 'reflexivity is primarily about challenging the notion of objective, neutral and value-free research, focusing instead on accounting for subjectivity'. They further emphasise that reflexivity focuses on the researcher as embedded in relationships and understanding the power relations that are inherent to and reproduced through research, in order to move towards more egalitarian research practices. Flavin (2001, 278) points out that reflexivity refers to 'identifying the assumptions underlying the research endeavour and often includes the investigator's reaction to doing the research'. Therefore, in order to incorporate reflexivity in criminological research it is important to consider how the subjectivity of the researcher plays a role in the research process. This chapter will show how the space where research is being carried out plays a role in shaping the subjectivity of the researcher.

This discussion draws on feminist criminological theories and research. There is no one theory of criminology or feminism, but broadly speaking, feminist interventions at the methodological level have been welcomed largely by critical, Marxist and interactionist approaches in criminology (Britton 2000). One of the key features of feminist methodology is the use of reflexivity in research. The researcher is considered on the same plane as the research participants and not as a neutral or absolute figure of authority, but as a real historical individual with concrete, specific desires and interests. This relationship and awareness of the subjectivities of both the researcher and the research participants form an important component of reflexivity in feminist research. Feminist scholarship offers rich conceptual frameworks to understand how relations of power are produced in and through sexuality, gender, race, ethnicity, class, caste and citizenship, among other position-alities (see Collins 1986, 1998, 2000; Crenshaw 1991); however, there is little discussion of the way that space intersects in creating different relations of power. It is important to take note of the way in which the space in which research is conducted choreographs research relationships as well as individual subjectivities.

In the following section, a description of the research activities around the mango tree will be illustrative to draw linkages between research relationships, reflexivity and space.

From the school room to the mango tree

From passing through a metal detector, depositing the mobile phone to the duty officer, waiting on a chair opposite the men's toilet in a chaotic office to be escorted to the female ward by a male guard, watching the large red iron gate being unlocked with a voluminous bunch of keys, walking through the prison spaces with loitering male prisoners staring at me, to finally reaching the small unassuming gate of the female ward, the rituals of entry into the prison set the rules for conducting myself in these spaces. The aura of the prison space warned me against any untoward utterance or gesture and compelled me to reflect on my own safety and the safety of the research participants while navigating the apparently secure spaces within it. This aside, I had to be careful of every move I made as there was always a threat of denial of access to the prison. The prison and its spaces also played a major role in mediating the interactions between the research participants and me. There was both an invisible and a visible barrier which controlled our conversations. The invisible barrier was in the form of a discursive surveillance and the visible barrier was present in the architectural form as well as the stationed warders and guards.

The prison space needs to be seen in terms of its temporality as well. Activities in the prison like various institutions are organised around time. Distribution of food, labour, *Gunti*,[6] court dates and arrival of non-governmental organisation workers were all organised around time. Prison time in some senses was separate from other parallel times 'outside' and within prison time there are various other conceptions of time. Prison time comprised not only the everyday life in prison but also the time they had suspended and the time in which they visualised their return. Time spent with me to contribute to the research process also became a part of prison time. Time for the staff members/warders was organised in terms of their duty hours, shift timings, holidays and so on. Their time was also organised on the basis of the temporal space that they shared with the prisoners. It was within this temporal space that they jostled over moments of power and certain specific subjectivities were produced. There can be a separate discussion to highlight the lived experience of women prisoners in terms of temporality but here it is important to understand the link between time and space to highlight how they worked together to shape the interactions between the research participants and myself.

During the first few months of fieldwork in the first prison, the staff instructed me to sit in the school room where they would ask the inmates to come and talk to me one after another. The very first day there were two female police constables, a welfare officer, an executive officer of the chief controller, a female warder and a school teacher who sat around me and the research participants. They heard our conversation which went on for about an hour. I felt awkward and Hasina,[7] a 21-year-old, married, Muslim Bangladeshi prisoner, who was the first research participant, hardly opened her mouth to speak. She had been in the prison for more than a year when I first met her that day and had recently received her sentence and date of release. She answered in a monosyllabic manner. I tried to prolong the interview so that the people who were sent by the administration to keep an eye on us would be dissuaded from doing so the next time. As I had predicted, the boredom of sitting and listening to the same questions caught on and the large contingent was not sent to keep an eye on me and the research participants from the second day. Probably, their curiosity around my visits had also been settled by being witness to a prolonged discussion, which made them think that this was *just something to do with women* and therefore harmless. Also, they claimed to empathise with my position as a researcher and said they realised that the inmates would not talk if they were around. From the next day the research participant and I were left to speak with each other without much interference by the prison staff. The teacher of the school insisted that I sit on a chair and the research participants would sit on the floor. It was a proposal I rejected without much ado and asked for a mat on which both the research participants and I would sit.

The school room was a dark damp place with dim lights, a sewing machine in one corner and a teacher who spent most of her time reading magazines in another corner of the room. The walls had some dusty, worn-out paintings and artwork which were made by the prisoners. This room once served as a space where non-governmental organisations would come and carry out educational programmes with the prisoners and their children. This was evident from some teaching material which hung on the walls coated with cobwebs and dust. Ever since the Indian women were transferred to an all-women's prison and the number of women in the female ward decreased, the non-governmental organisations gradually stopped coming to this prison. This had created some amount of unrest among the Bangladeshi women who felt that they were being denied their right to study in the prison in the way the Indian women used to do. Though a government-employed teacher came to the school room every day, no classes were held. The room would remain open only while she was there and was locked by the warders as soon as she left. Some exceptions were made for me if my interview continued a little after the teacher had to leave.

Initially the women found the process of coming and talking to me in the school room an intimidating one and sometimes even humiliating. They would often wonder why they were being hauled up to the school room by the warder, especially because it was not a space commonly used by them. They felt a certain sense of isolation from the rest of the inmates and felt like they were being subjected to a 'secret' investigation. This gave rise to a lot of suspicion and angst. This continued for a couple of months. The women were selected by either the warder on duty or the Indian life convict (who was one of the inmates in charge of the cells) and sent to the school room. Though I insisted that none of the women be forced to come and speak with me, it was obvious that some of them had been coerced or threatened. The women would speak so softly that I could often not hear them clearly despite sitting next to them on a mat spread out on the floor. Often I had to go back and listen to the recordings to make sense of what they said. Needless to say, the volume of their narratives was soft so that the teacher and some of her chatting warder friends could not hear them. Gradually I started making use of my walk from the school room to the main gate of the female ward to exchange a few informal conversations with groups of women who would be lurking around the school room out of curiosity to see me and speak with me.[8] The narratives that emerged as a result of this fear, angst, awkwardness and surveillance were a replica of each other. With minor variations, the women narrated stories with similar life trajectories. It seemed to be a mechanism through which they ensured that they were not singled out because of some misleading information that may emerge from their narrative. There was immense amount of curiosity and discussions around my visit. These details were disclosed to me by the research participants themselves as they gradually began to trust me and speak with me in an uninhibited manner.

On a particular day, approximately four months after my first visit, I was told that the school room was locked for various administrative reasons. One of them was the superannuation of the school teacher. The warders were unable to take a decision with regard to where I would sit and in a moment of confusion I was asked to sit with the women under a mango tree. In the peak of Kolkata summer, I was not sure if the women would want to come and sit under the mango tree instead of being comfortable under a fan in their damp but cool cells. But surprisingly, the mango tree seemed like a more acceptable place to the women. Moreover, the warders did not come to check on us under the mango tree in the sweltering heat. The space was less significant in the eyes of the authorities, less formal more casual. It was available to public gaze but paradoxically it gave the research participants more privacy.

I realised that under the mango tree the women did not feel like they were being pulled up and asked to talk about their lives to a stranger. The mango tree was in an open space; it was a part of nature and duplicated a space in their own village so it gave them a sense of familiarity. I gradually discovered that a number of activities revolved around the mango tree. The mango tree was a space they looked for shade in the scorching heat, had informal conversations with the warders, meetings with the Superintendent as well as their hunger strikes.[9] Now this became a place where they could come out and sit at a time when they were supposed to be locked up in their cells. Apart from all these, there was the greed for mangoes. Each one hoped that a mango would fall while they were talking to me so that they could take it without having to share it with other women who were in the cell at that time. The contour of the space around the mango tree was unpredictable and it changed throughout the day and in different seasons, as opposed to the overall monotonous and predictable environment and routine of the prison. Since they could be out of the cell at their lock-up time, a number of them started to compete for my attention so that I would request the warder to take them out of the cell so that I could speak with them. A group of women prepared and performed two plays around their lives and insisted to perform it under the mango tree while the audience (the warders on duty and I) sat on the concrete platform built around the tree. The tree was one of the ways in which they made meaning of their everyday lives. Their narratives and interactions with me became uninhibited with time and the change in space. The women did not look at the mango tree as an unnatural setting that the school room appeared to be. They would keep moving around and doing their daily chores in between interviews, go and drink water and stroll back. It seemed like very comfortable surroundings to them and even I got a better view of their activities. The tree was visible from one of the cells and the girls would signal each other when one of them was sitting outside with me. Some of them would talk to me and continue to stitch or embroider a piece of cloth for the warders. The mango tree and their interactions with me became a part of their everyday life in the prison. There was a specific way in which the physical and emotional space interacted to create their subjectivity as research participants and mine as a researcher. The skyline, air, walls, trees, cells, the female ward within a male-dominated prison, each individual unit signified an emotional as well as physical space which influenced the research process in varying ways.

The content of the narratives of the research participants changed to a great extent with a shift from the school room to the mango tree. From tailor-made narratives with predictable story lines, the narratives shifted to issues which pertained to their day-to-day life in the prison, its relations with their life before they entered prison and their imagination of their life thereafter. An important shift in the research process was a shift in their narratives from 'violence' to 'love'. Soon after the change in space from the school room to the mango tree the women started talking about their love stories, with both men and women, in prison, which later became an important part of my research. As a feminist researcher I went to the prison to understand their experiences of violence through their narratives, but they preferred to talk about their experiences of love in the prison. They challenged my intentions to hear their stories of violence and established through their narratives that it was a certain idea of love and being in love in prison which helped them go through their everyday life. They had silenced their memories of violence and did not want to think about it anymore. This shift in their narratives necessitated efforts on my part to understand the nuances of their experiences and I realised that it was a shift in space from the dark damp empty school room to the mango tree which gave them a sense of thrill and was already a part of a number of their daily activities.

Discussions of space become important in the context of incarcerated foreigners. The prison space in the case of the Bangladeshi research participants was an institutional space in a different country, where they were not only foreigners, but their status was that of an 'illegal' one. This 'foreign' space was marked by an absence of their family members and acquaintances who could have otherwise visited them had they been in a prison in their own country. Hence, the Bangladeshi women's narratives were mediated by not only time and memory but also the external environment in which they were generated.

Conclusion

Qualitative criminological researchers undertaking regular visits to detention and imprisonment facilities assume and take note of the constraints in the field that a researcher needs to confront and address in the process of field work. However, most of these considerations tend to overlook the spaces within this enclosed field which are a source of survival for the inmates. There are spaces which allow the inmates to make meaning of their everyday monotonous predictable life of incarceration, in this instance; one of these spaces was the mango tree. It seemed that the research participants found meaning in the unpredictability of the mango falling from the tree which was in sharp contrast to their predictable prison routine. It seemed to provide them with a sense of continuity of life, a life which progressed each day in contrast to their lives which seemed to be in inertia of rest.

The chapter owes a debt to Gupta and Fergusson's (1997) conceptualisation of space and feminist literature on methodology and reflexivity. It develops these and weaves them together by foregrounding prison space as playing an important mediating role in understanding the relations of power and powerlessness between the researcher and research participants. The emphasis given to 'space' in the social sciences by Gupta and Fergusson (1997) has been extended by drawing its connections with reflexivity and its importance in the research process.

Through a process of reflexivity one can become aware of the power relations and exploitative research relationships but it is important to bear in mind that it cannot always be eliminated. In this chapter I have focused on just the mango tree within the premises of the female ward of a prison. There can be further comparative investigations in terms of change in narratives and behavioural patterns of research participants in different spaces in the prison.

There have been several discussions between feminists on the intersections of gender, caste, class and colour which influence the relationship between the researcher and the research participant. This chapter has contributed to discussions of reflexivity by highlighting the importance of space as an intersection while discussing the factors which contribute towards creating a hierarchy between the researcher and the research participants. It points to the need to be reflexive not only about how the researcher conducts herself but also where she conducts herself within the specified field. It has contributed to discussions of reflexivity in criminological research by breaking down the criminological research space into sub-spaces and has showcased the need to go beyond the institutional constraints confronting the researcher in order to strive towards building stronger research relationships.

Notes

1. Provisions of section 14 of the Foreigners Act 1946 state that a person arrested under this act could be sentenced for imprisonment up to five years and is also liable to pay a fine.
2. Bangladeshi women come to India for varied reasons, most of which revolve around the aspiration for a better life. Some of them come with the hope of making a living, to escape violent marriages; others come to meet relatives on the other side of the border, which they viewed as an extension of Bangladesh and not necessarily a separate country. Sometimes the migration was 'voluntary' at other times it was not. The women I spoke with were either arrested from the railway or bus stations upon their arrival, in their attempt to go back to Bangladesh, or from a brothel.
3. The discussions revolved around broad themes of an interview guide. The themes were *Migration Decision, Understanding and Process of Crossing Borders, Experiences of Arrest, Imprisonment and Legal Proceedings, Change in Gender Roles and Responsibilities, Deportation.*
4. *Madrasa* is the Arabic word for any type of educational institution whether secular or religious. However, when the research participants referred to a *Madrasa*, they implied the religious education that they received there.

5. Touts or agents, commonly known as *Dalals* in Bengali, facilitate the movement of people across the Indo-Bangladesh border, often at a hefty price. Agents who smuggle persons across the border may also double up as traffickers, making money by selling girls and women to brothel owners. There is a well-knit network of agents. The people crossing the border are often referred to different people at different points in their journey from Bangladesh to India. The already perilous journey becomes even more daunting when the people do not know who they are following.
6. The inmates were counted about five times in the day, both before and after lock-up. All the inmates were required to be present at that time as the heads were counted and noted down. The numbers were then sent to the administrative office in the prison.
7. The names of the research participants have been changed in order to keep their identities confidential. The interviews were recorded with oral consent from the participants. Few signed the consent letter but most feared to do so, lest it proved to be detrimental to their legal case. There were many who did not know how to sign their names.
8. One of the time slots between which the women were kept in the lock-up was from 12 noon to 3 pm. The Superintendent of the prison suggested that I visit the prison during that time so that I could request the warder to release one or two women from the lock-up so that I could speak with them. He said this was to ensure my safety. I tried to prolong my stay a little after 3 pm so that I could meet groups of women who were released from the lock-up. Gradually I could prolong my stay for much longer especially after I started sitting under the mango tree.
9. The Bangladeshi women often went on hunger strikes to protest against the delay in the process of being sent back to Bangladesh.

References

Bandyopadhyay, M. (2010) *Everyday Life in a Prison: Confinement, Surveillance, Resistance*, New Delhi: Orient Blackswan Private Limited.

Bosworth, M. (1999) *Engendering Resistance: Agency and Power in Women's Prisons*, Aldershot: Ashgate.

Britton, D.M. (2000) 'Feminism in Criminology: Engendering the Outlaw' *Annals of the American Academy of Political and Social Science* 571: 57–76.

Burns, D. and Chantler, K. (2011) 'Feminist Methodologies'. In B. Somekh and C. Lewin (eds) *Theory and Methods in Social Research*, 2nd edn, New Delhi: Sage Publications India Pvt. Ltd., pp.70–77.

Collins, P.H. (1986) 'Learning from the Outsider Within: The Sociological Significance of Black Feminist Thought' *Social Problems* 33(6): 14–32.

Collins, P.H. (1998) 'The Tie That Binds: Race, Gender, and US Violence' *Ethnic and Racial Studies* 21(5): 917–38.

Collins, P.H. (2000) 'Gender, Black Feminism, and Black Political Economy' *Annals of the American Academy of Political and Social Science* 568(1): 41–53.

Crenshaw, K.W. (1991) 'Mapping the Margins: Intersectionality, Identity Politics, and Violence Against Women of Color' *Stanford Law Review* 43(6): 1241–99.

Flavin, J. (2001) 'Feminism for the Mainstream Criminologist: An Invitation' *Journal of Criminal Justice* 29: 271–85.

Goffman, E. (1961) *Asylums*, New York: Anchor Books.

Gupta, A. and Ferguson, J. (1997) 'Beyond "Culture": Space, Identity, and the Politics of Difference'. In A. Gupta and J. Ferguson (eds) *Culture, Power, Place: Explorations in Critical Anthropology*, Durham, NC: Duke University Press, pp.33–51.

Mills, S. (2003) 'Gender and Colonial Space'. In R. Lewis and S. Mills (eds) *Feminist Postcolonial Theory: A Reader*, New York: Routledge, pp.692–719.

Stanley, L. and Wise, S. (1983) *Breaking Out: Feminist Consciousness and Feminist Research*, London: Routledge.

Visweswaran, K. (1996) *Fictions of Feminist Ethnography*, New Delhi: OUP.

5

Reflective Friend Research: The Relational Aspects of Social Scientific Research

Stephen Case and Kevin Haines

Introduction

The starting point for this chapter is that the historically dominant research paradigm in the social sciences, *Positivism*, is based on a misunderstanding and an oversimplification of methodological principles and that social scientific research, if it is to be fully 'social', requires a more reflective and reflexive paradigm. Positivist research methodology has privileged experimental, quasi-experimental and quasi-clinical methods, structured, quantified measurement and assessment instruments (e.g. questionnaires, interviews, observation schedules), randomised controlled trials and 'what works' evaluation criteria (Farrington 2003 for a critique see Haines and Case 2014; Hope 2009; Sherman 2009) as the gold standard of methodological excellence. Moreover, these various methods are deployed – in fullest expression of the gold standard – in a cloak of quasi-clinical rationality and *independence* of the researcher from the individuals and organisations being researched. This quality of 'independence' (free from researcher bias) is at the core of the argument for the validity of Positivist research. The result, it is claimed, is the production of ostensibly 'generalisable', 'reliable' and (experimentally) 'valid' conclusions regarding the causes and predictors of human behaviour and 'effective' and 'evidence-based' responses to it – free from human 'interference'. Our position is that the requirement for researchers to be independent – and the methods utilised in the service of this objective – has, in reality, offered at best restricted and partial explanations and, at worst, invalid knowledge and understandings of people's lives and experiences. Purportedly dispassionate, objective and value-free Positivist social science research has negated a more reflective consideration of how research methods are necessarily social constructions between participating actors (see Cunliffe 2008) in favour of a 'white-coated' researcher (conducting research on inanimate subjects) model. In this way, Positivist social science research excludes the 'social', it excludes and renders power-less important researched parties in the research process (the eponymous research 'subjects'), neglecting their potential to function as 'research part-ners' who can influence and augment research processes, relationships, outcomes and impacts. The highest quality social science research is, we believe, *not* conducted by independent 'white-coated' researchers on inan-imate subjects, but rather is a reflective and reflexive activity, the product of embedded, situated research and relationships, that facilitates the emer-gence of more nuanced understandings of the realities of everyday lives and practice contexts and permits these to be exposed to detailed scrutiny.

This chapter presents and discusses *Reflective Friend Research* (RFR), a 'real-world' model of social enquiry wherein academic researchers work in close reflective collaboration with the 'researched'. RFR has certain defining and interactive characteristics that enhance its utility and recommend it above Positivist social science research that is 'done to' passive subjects. These char-acteristics emphasise the context and conduct of social science research in order to shape (not dictate) the choice of research methods.

Reflective friend research: Situated, reflective and critical engagement

> We don't see research as something tagged on and in a sort of remote orbit to a project. It is something inherent and fundamental and a part of the project itself.
>
> (Swansea YOS Manager)

The positivist method, and its notion of clinical independence, has eschewed the *relational* aspects of social science research – the importance and value of the researcher–researched relationship for research quality and validity – thus paradigmatically excluding one of the most important ingre-dients of high-quality research. Conversely, our position is that what is required for methodologically sound, high-quality social science research is a deep *engagement* with the field and the participants in research (hereafter 'the researched'). Moreover, we posit that the type of engagement with the researched advocated here can be achieved not only through maintaining the independence of the researcher, but by enhancing it and the conse-quent impact of the research findings – as judged by the quality of the research product – thus achieving and even enhancing a key objective of social scientific research.[1] The key elements and advantages of RFR are

- Situated learning: In RFR, the researcher actively participates in the work-ing/practice contexts of the researched. Consequently, researchers and the researched co-construct their learning, understandings and practical realities within research-informed partnerships akin to 'communities of practice' (see Lave and Wenger 2002, 1991; Bredo 2005), with researchers embedded within and part of the practical contexts of the researched, simultaneously functioning as situated learners and 'knowledgeable' experts (see Vygotsky 1978). The situated nature of the research relationship, therefore, enables research partners to co-construct and co-develop research agendas, with description, explanatory frameworks and conclusions that are underpinned and informed by the active participation of the researched in the research venture, as opposed to conceiving of the researched as inanimate objects of the research exercise.

- Enhanced access: Situating researchers within the practice and decision-making contexts of the researched facilitates *access* (granted by research partners) to research participants (individuals, organisations, institutions), key data sets (e.g. practice monitoring databases; crime statistics), internal documentation (minutes, policies, drafts of governmental papers) and knowledge generation processes (meetings, steering groups, committees, advisory panels). The knowledge and understandings that emerge from this access are thus more context sensitive and ecologically and practically valid than possible through more didactic researcher–subject approaches preferred in Positivist social science research.

- Research partnerships: RFR promotes *research partnerships* between the researcher and the researched, who collaborate in the co-construction of knowledge/understandings through, what others have termed, 'legitimate peripheral participation' in the research process (see Lave and Wenger 1991), contributing their own expert knowledge, experience, perspectives and meanings to the foci of research projects, the design of research methods, the implementation of research tools and the interpretation and application of research results. Knowledge and understandings (research outcomes) are not imposed on research 'subjects' through a prescriptive 'master–apprentice' working dynamic. In this context, independence is maintained and enhanced via a joint journey to the truth in which researcher and researched collaborate to expose the focus of the research and subject it to scrutiny.

- Reflective engagement: RFR prioritises the relational aspects of research, employing situated learning to enhance engagement between the researcher and the researched. *Reflective engagement* is an inherent quality of the situated research/learning context, achieved through regular dialogue, exchange of views and researcher feedback. Practitioners' expectations for constructive and regular feedback and specific support from researchers are common to (social science) research processes (e.g. Iedema et al. 2004) and thus handling these expectations is a practical, undervalued, yet important challenge for researchers (see Alvesson and Sköldberg 2000) and a priority within RFR. Therefore, reflective engagement is a means of producing better quality (in the sense of a closer and more accurate depiction of social reality) research than can be achieved in the absence of a 'relationship'. The 'dense relations of mutual engage-ment' (Wenger 1998, 74) that drive RFR are founded in reciprocal respect, trust, confidence, interactivity and competence (see also Cousin and Deepwell 2005). The importance of the relationship between researchers and researched that characterises RFR has been largely overlooked (or viewed critically) within empirical social science research papers (Bar-ley 1990; Iedema et al. 2004), in favour of deconstructing the practice of others (e.g. Alvesson and Sköldberg 2000).

• Critical friendship: Researchers involved in RFR engage critically with partner organisations and their staff over a sustained period of time, such that the research relationship evolves as both partners interact with and observe each other (see also Tuckermann and Ruegg-Sturm 2010). Researchers operate as a *critical friend*, working in close collaboration with research partners, including regular dissemination of research pro-cesses and findings. In this way, regular feedback loops to operate within research relationships, which encourage individual practitioners and the organisation more broadly to assess their own knowledge and practice critically. Consequently, critical friendship is a key relational aspect of RFR that maintains independence for the researcher (and researched), thus insulating them from the invalidating influences of bias, subjectivity and proselytising on behalf of the research partner. The critical friend role illustrates the importance of the relational foundations of social science research for reflective engagement between research partners as a tool to improve research validity, breadth/depth of knowledge produced and potential research impact, for example, the willingness of the researched to listen, reflect on and accept constructive critique of their philoso-phies, understandings and practices, and to apply research findings to their practice. Consequently, the effective relational practices promoted by RFR enhance the quality of connections between the parties involved in social science research and as such are pivotal for enabling healthy, enriching and generative research projects (see also Dutton and Dukerich 2006).

We acknowledge that we are not the first researchers to identify the range of issues discussed above as pivotal to effective social science research. Indeed, we have been influenced by a cogent body of work critiquing traditional Positivist approaches and advocating more focus on the relational aspects of research (cf. Alvesson and Sköldberg 2000; Dutton and Dukerich 2006; Tuckermann and Ruegg-Sturm 2010). While the contribution of others' work influences and complements our central thesis, the current chapter brings these arguments together in one place and augments them with empiri-cal illustrations from our own work in order to present a coherent and evidenced paradigm for conducting reflective social science research. Accord-ingly, we proceed to develop the concept of RFR and detail the benefits and advantages of this approach. In doing so, we will illustrate our arguments with reference to research we have conducted since 1996 in partnership with Swansea Youth Offending Service (YOS).

The origin and development of RFR

The genesis of the RFR model and the illustrations employed in this chapter can be traced back to 1996, when a research partnership between Swansea University's Centre for Criminal Justice and Criminology (CCJC) and Swansea Youth Justice Team (now Youth Offending Service/YOS[2]) was established following a meeting to discuss the research and evaluation of local youth justice policies, practices and programmes aiming to prevent youth offending. Thus began what was characterised as

> a partnership with the University that would give us [YOS and Community Safety Department] that resource to take a more objective look – first of all at the evidence from what we were doing and then secondly the evaluation of what we were doing.
>
> (Community Safety Manager)

Over a near 20-year period, Swansea YOS has opened its doors to researchers, offering unrivalled access to its Management Board, senior management team, frontline practitioners, operational meetings, policy and practice documentation, statistical databases and, perhaps most importantly, to the young people who have come into contact with the Youth Justice System. A series of long-term reflective research and evaluation projects have resulted, with YOS staff and researchers working collaboratively to identify issues, strengthen relationships, improve practice and enhance outcomes for young people in the Youth Justice System. Researchers leading independent, funded evaluations of YOS prevention programmes and completing related postgraduate degrees have been allocated office space at Swansea YOS, while open access 'hot desk' space has been granted to researchers and undergraduate students on work placement since 2008. In addition, a CCJC researcher has been based full time at the YOS since 2010, collaborating with staff on range of programmes and evaluations.

The evolution of the Swansea University–Swansea YOS research partnership has been situated in nature. Researchers have been immersed (situated) physically and contextually in the working environments, cultures and practices of the YOS on a daily basis, having regular discussions with staff, both formally (e.g. research interviews) and informally (e.g. liaising and relationship building in team offices and staff rooms), attending policy and practice monitoring and development meetings (e.g. YOS Management Board, sub-team meetings, team days, multi-agency panels to which the YOS is affiliated), accompanying staff on their daily practice functions (e.g. visits to families, schools, secure institutions, partner agencies, affiliated projects). Researchers acting as critical friends have also disseminated and presented their research progress, outcomes and conclusions/recommendations for policy and practice improvements to internal YOS bodies (e.g. YOS Management Board, YOS sub-team and project team meetings, YOS team days) and externally to affiliated organisations such as the Youth Justice Board for England and Wales, the Youth Justice Board Wales (YJB Cymru), the Welsh Government Youth Justice Division, the Welsh Youth Justice Advisory Panel,[3] Swansea Substance Misuse Action Team, South Wales Police and local magistrates.

Reflective friend research: Enhancing the relational foundations of research for higher-quality outcomes

The RFR model articulates how research can function as a situated, social, communicative practice, just like the practice it explores (cf. Morgan 1983). An effective research–researched relationship is developed through reciprocity, with data collected in situ over a prolonged time period within a research relationship that evolves through social interaction involving systematic challenges regarding roles, expectations and differing interests (see Tuckermann and Rüegg-Stürm 2010). Those who are, or have their work, subject to the prying eyes of researchers are frequently distrustful of the researchers and nervous about the outcome – often resulting in a guarded approach towards the research. This was certainly the situation we have encountered many times and hesitancy about engaging with researchers and research certainly characterised our initial experiences locally. This distrust, nervousness, guardedness and hesitancy must be overcome if research is to be effective. However, employing the RFR model has enabled researchers to establish and nurture long-term reflective relationships with the researched as a means of conducting better quality research. Ongoing reflective discussion between the researcher and the researched permits refinement and improvement of data collection and research findings. This reflective relationship also has the benefit of increasing the degree of trust, respect, confidence and honesty between research partners and enhancing the breadth, depth and ultimately the user-friendly nature of research findings, conclusions and recommendations. Close, constant attention to developing the relational foundations of our research, we suggest, has enabled better quality research to be produced and utilised. Situating researchers within practice and decision-making contexts engenders research partnerships wherein researchers and researched engage with and learn from one another, co-constructing understandings by sharing their particular expertise and skills. Researchers benefit from legitimate peripheral participation in the daily working practices of research partners, while research partners are enabled to pursue legitimate peripheral participation in the development, interpretation and dissemination of research methods and findings relating to their practice.

In Focus: Improving Participatory Practice in Swansea YOS

Research and the co-presence of researchers has become a normal and accepted part of daily (working) life for staff in Swansea YOS. This normalcy was evidenced in a recent discussion between two senior practitioners from adjoining Welsh YOSs. In a discussion about a knotty professional matter, the Swansea Senior Practitioner remarked: 'What does your researcher think?' The extent to which the context of an ongoing research relationship can facilitate short-term projects is illustrated by our experience of introducing research-based placements for undergraduate students.

In 2012, a third-year undergraduate student was situated in Swansea YOS for two months as part of a research internship, under the daily supervision of a CCJC staff member (also situated within the YOS). This student conducted a qualitative research study examining the extent to which Swansea YOS was promoting participatory practice for young people within its review system (Lelliot 2013) – the focus of the research emanating from interaction between YOS and CCJC staff. A focus group and interview method accessed the views of YOS practitioners and young people referred to the YOS regarding their experiences of the review system. YOS staff actively facilitated the student's access to research participants and data, and this engagement in the research process facilitated informal feedback from the student researcher at key stages of the research. Consequently, it is clear that *access* was seen as a reciprocal process by the research partners – access to the critical researcher for the researched was as important as researcher access to the information and systems of the researched. This embedded,[4] situated research process fostered trust between research partners, deepened researcher appreciation of the meaningfulness of the project and engendered a view of the researcher as 'being genuinely interested' (see Dutton and Dukerich 2006).

The research highlighted areas of strong participatory practice, primarily the positive relationships between young people and YOS staff that enhanced the young people's confidence to participate in review meetings. However, several barriers were identified that inhibited or deterred participation, such as the power imbalance between practitioners and young people, neglect of young people's individual needs and failures in information sharing with the young person. The student researcher presented these findings to the YOS Management Board and the YOS staff group, recommending that future review meetings revolve around the capabilities of young people, rather than implementing a single generic system that only focuses on reaching the highest level of participation available to the young person while under the statutory obligation to finish their sentence. Further recommendations were made that practitioners utilise their positive relationship with young people to ensure that individual needs are the primary focus of review meetings (Lelliot 2013). As a result of this research, in fact during the presentation, YOS staff embraced the findings and actively engaged in a discussion about how their practice could be improved – to the extent that some changes were immediately agreed and implemented. A 'Participation Think Tank' was established, comprising representatives from all YOS operational teams and independently chaired by the CCJC researcher based at the YOS. The Think Tank has facilitated the development of a new, rights-based 'Participation Policy' for Swansea YOS, 'Participation Action Plans' (linked to the implementation of research findings) and an internal overview system to ensure that participation is positively being promoted and mainstreamed. Hence, research has fuelled process, systems and practice change.

The example above illustrates how *situated learning* and *enhanced acc*ess have been facilitated through the RFR model. Research has become an accepted daily working practice within Swansea YOS, constantly focused on maximising utility of *research partnerships* as a means of enhancing practice outcomes for the researched and the recipients of the research (e.g. young people). By being situated in the practice community and physical contexts of the researched, reflective and critical researchers were made available for contact inside and outside formal research processes (e.g. informal discussions with partners, participating in training sessions, team days and policy and practice development meetings, formal dissemination reports and presentations), in order to meet practitioner expectations for consistent, accessible and constructive feedback and guidance on their practice. The constructive processes and outcomes of this research internship illustrate how attention to the much-neglected relational aspects of social science research have increased investment and commitment to research projects among research and have promoted engagement (often through joint interpretation) with the findings of research, thereby enhancing their impact.

Promoting reflective research partnerships as a driver for change

The sustained, intensive and proximal *research partnership* between the CCJC and Swansea YOS has produced outcomes and recommendations that have been critically reflective on policy, practice and programme development. Prolonged *reflective engagement* with staff and privileged access to the operation of Swansea YOS have enabled researchers to conduct in-depth evaluations of policy making and practice at key decision-making points in the youth justice process. Indeed, our research has, at times, reached conclusions that are highly critical of existing YOS policy and practice. Crucially, these research findings and their dissemination locally have, however critical, been received, reflected on and acted upon constructively by YOS staff. As the YOS Manager has commented '... because agencies have been part of the research, things have begun to change'.

In an era when the impact of research is attracting much attention and has significant implications for research reputations and funding, the importance of achieving the sorts of outcomes described above is heightened. Achieving such outcomes is, as we have illustrated, enhanced by the application of RFR. The sustained engagement (relationship building) and enhanced access to practice networks, staff, data and decision-making processes derived from the RFR model have enabled researchers to develop a situated, nuanced appreciation of practice/policy contexts and to foster mutual trust and respect with research partners in order to increase levels of cooperation and to maximise the impact of dissemination processes and action on recommendations.

In Focus: Innovative and Reflective Risk Assessment in Swansea as a Stimulus for Radical Practice and Policy Change

Ongoing access to local and national youth justice databases has been facilitated through the YOS–University partnership. This has enabled two researchers to evaluate the efficacy of the established risk assessment process in the Youth Justice System (known as the 'Scaled Approach' – Youth Justice Board 2009) through a secondary analysis of key statistical outcomes for young people, notably reoffending rates (Haines and Case 2012). Detailed secondary data analysis was conducted over a three-year period (2010–2012) in partnership with the YOS Information Manager, who facilitated data access and advised on data cleaning and interpretation. Comparative analyses of statistical outcomes established that the rights-based, discretionary approach to risk assessment adopted by Swansea YOS, which included a built-in practitioner override of designated 'scaled' outcomes where appropriate (a substantial departure from the prescriptive, technical YJB Scaled Approach model), had produced reductions in reoffending that rated within the top 5 per cent of all YOSs in England and Wales. In direct contrast, analysis identified an increase in reoffending rates within a neighbouring YOS that had piloted and applied the Scaled Approach in an assiduous manner, placing it within the bottom 5 per cent of YOSs (see Haines and Case 2012).

The Scaled Approach example illustrates how RFR has enabled research to have impact and to serve as a driver for change. Privileged access to key data sets facilitated statistical analyses that indicated the advantages of a rights-based model of youth justice when compared to the standard Scaled Approach. These research findings provided Swansea YOS with the evidence and confidence to deepen its implementation of a rights-based model, which had also benefitted from the evidence produced as part of the CCJC evaluation of YOS participatory practice. Subsequently, the impact of this research extended further to contribute to the YJB's abandonment of the risk-focused Scaled Approach (see Haines and Case 2012) and its replacement with the 'AssetPlus' model, for which Swansea YOS will serve as a pilot area.

The RFR approach has evolved by embedding and building in recursive (reoccurring, reciprocal) and reflective feedback loops between researchers and the researched. Researchers have been built into the very decision-making processes under scrutiny as an embedded way of improving practice through evidence generation, research partnership and critical friendship. This partnership approach was explicated by the Swansea YOS Manager when questioned about the YOS–University research relationship:

An action research model was developed at an early stage...very much looking at using input from the University at a number of levels...establishing what was happening and why it was happening, and contributing to that process of development to make sure we did the right thing...For example, researchers had an interpretive input within the YOS Operational Management Group...and formed part of project management groups.

The action research and partnership model has facilitated interaction between the researcher and the researched such that these interactions have become a normal aspect of the working practices of both partners. As such, RFR processes of situated reflective engagement grounded in reciprocal feedback mechanisms have promoted a 'mutual learning dynamic' (Dutton and Dukerich 2006) that enriches the quality and volume of learning derived from social science research, facilitating more meaningful interpretation and dissemination of research findings. This virtuous circle of mutual learning stands in contrast to a white-coated approach to research and is more suited to take advantage of the iterative and dynamic nature of reflective and recursive research processes. The RFR model enables practitioners and organisations to address this complexity through its emphasis on developing and implementing a variety of participatory and inclusionary research [partnership] methodologies with a range of appropriate stakeholder participants (including young people and their families as priority stakeholders) in order to co-construct a practical and valid knowledge base to inform practice. For example, researcher feedback in team and project meetings related to prevention programmes (Haines and Case 2005), children's rights compliant practice (Charles 2011) and the YOS review system (Lelliott 2013) has been critical of the relative lack of engagement and participation of young people in determining, implementing and interpreting assessment and intervention processes across the YOS. This formal critique has motivated YOS staff to expand the level of participation by young people in subsequent research and evaluation methodologies and in the development of rights-focused and participatory practice.

In Focus: Evolving Rights-Based, 'Positive Prevention' Through Recursive and Reflective Feedback

Feedback from CCJC research and evaluation has underpinned an iterative series of multi-agency (YOS-led) prevention programmes that coalesce to form a coherent, reflective evolution of prevention policy and practice locally. The independent evaluation of the Promoting Positive Behaviour (PPB) programme to prevent secondary school exclusion ran from 1996 to 1999 and identified indicators/correlates with problem behaviour that were located in key domains of young people's lives (school, family, neighbourhood, peer group, thinking and attitudes). Researchers disseminated these results to the PPB steering group, the YOS Management Board and the local authority Education Department in meetings, consolidated by an official report (Haines et al. 1999) and a peer-reviewed journal article (Haines and Case 2003). The CCJC and the key 'researched' partner (Swansea YOS) made recommendations to the local authority and its affiliated partner agencies (e.g. police, health, probation) that the identified indicators/correlates were likely to be common influences on a variety of problem behaviours for local young people (e.g. offending, antisocial behaviour, substance use, social exclusion). As such, recommendations were made that local preventative intervention programmes should be broadened out to address a wider range of potentially negative outcomes for young people and to incorporate a wider range of local agencies in their delivery. These conclusions and recommendations led the CCJC and Swansea YOS into further collaboration on a successful bid for Youth Justice Board funding for a multi-agency programme and associated research/evaluation entitled 'Promoting

Prevention' (2000–2004), which was to be focused on preventing youth offending, substance use and antisocial behaviour through interventions located within the YOS and outside of school hours. Findings mirrored those of PPB in terms of identified correlates with problem behaviours (Case and Haines 2004; Haines and Case 2005) and prompted researcher recommendations to roll-out local prevention approaches further still (in terms of their foci and contributing partners) into the wider community beyond the YOS and the school (e.g. in the family, neighbourhood, community). Consequently, the CCJC and YOS collaborated on a successful bid for funding from the National Institute for Social Care and Health Research and thus giving rise to the 'Pentrehafod Prevention Project' (PPP) to address social inclusion through universal family, school and community intervention, which is subject to ongoing evaluation (see Case, Haines and Charles 2012).

CCJC reflections and recommendations from evaluative research have generated and catalysed an iterative local approach to the prevention of problem behaviours, moving from first-generation-targeted preventative provision within schools (e.g. PPB – see Haines and Case 2003) to second-generation YOS- and community-based out-of-school preventative targeted services (Promotion Prevention – see Case and Haines 2004; Haines and Case 2005) to universal service delivery penetrating the everyday lives of young people through systemic changes to how agencies and young people engage with one another to achieve positive life-changing outcomes (PPP – Case et al. 2012). Local programmes and interventions have evolved from simply targeting the underlying influences upon problem behaviours and the barriers to young people achieving positive outcomes to explicitly addressing how best to promote and sustain pro-social and positive outcomes for young people such as social inclusion, community engagement, academic success and accessing their universal rights as children.

The research connections that have resulted from embedding the RFR approach in Swansea benefit from a tensility and flexibility that allow them to withstand stress and a strong connectivity that renders partners more open to new ideas and influence (Losada and Heaphy 2004), as the above example shows. It is the quality of these research connections that drive the relational and reflective nature of RFR, enabling research projects and research-informed practice to adapt to the new information and new understandings as they progress and develop over time (see also Gittell 2003).

Critical friendship as the foundation for independent research and policy development

Situated reflective engagement is built into and catalyses the RFR relationship between the CCJC and Swansea YOS. However, from an external perspective, this working relationship/partnership could be open to accusations of *researcher bias* and a *lack of researcher independence*. Potential criticisms of this approach include excessive researcher subjectivity and immersion in the local practice context (e.g. 'going native'), the pursuit of mutually beneficial, but self-fulfilling research and practice agendas (e.g. the generation of 'policy-based evidence'), the privileging of appreciative inquiry over independent research/evaluation and mutual respect/confidence/trust translating into preferential loyalty and protectiveness[5] (Fuller cited in Lewis-Beck et al. 2004). It is, therefore, essential to emphasise that the foundation and central driver of RFR is *critical friendship*, researchers conducting independent research that produces reflective yet critical findings, conclusions and recommendations relating to existing working principles, practices, programs and policies. The extent and nature of situated learning, enhanced access, recursive feedback, research partnership and reflective engagement, central to the operationalisation of the RFR model, are ingredients that foster a research context grounded in reciprocity, trust, confidence and mutual respect. This creates a virtuous circle whereby closer research relationships enhance the quality of situated learning, the degree of access and feedback, the extent of reflective engagement and so on. Within this context, practitioners become less cynical, defensive, guarded and protective of their principles and daily practices. The power and utility of the critical friendship, therefore, is the ability it confers on researchers and researched to raise 'difficult' issues, expose them to scrutiny and to respond to research findings – whatever they may be:

> Research has been part of a process of enabling practitioners and senior practitioners to be more self-critical about what they do.
>
> (YOS Manager)

In Focus: The Evolution of a Local Approach to Diversion Underpinned by Critical Friendship from Researchers

Since 2010, CCJC researchers located in Swansea YOS have been conducting an independent evaluation of the 'Swansea Bureau', a YOS–police partnership aimed at diverting young people from the formal Youth Justice System by providing mechanisms that normalise offending, while promoting positive behaviour, children's rights, participation and engagement in the family, school and community and tackling the underlying causes of offending. A multi-method evaluation of the first year of the Bureau using secondary data analysis and interviews with key stakeholders (YOS and police staff) identified a 44 per cent decrease in 'first-time entrants' into the Youth Justice System (the target population for the Bureau) and a reoffending rate of 7 per cent among Bureau recipients after 12 months of the programme, alongside positive qualitative feedback from key stakeholders regarding the promotion of children's rights and young people's engagement (Haines et al. 2013).

Researchers fed back the evaluation findings to the researched in an official report, an academic article and targeted presentations to the Bureau steering group. A key critical conclusion was that the programme has remained restricted and exclusionary in its focus on first-time entrants and thus had impacted on a limited extent of diversionary outcomes (e.g. for young people subject to pre-court sentences and Referral Orders), rather than also tackling re-entrants into the YJS. As a direct result of the research, Bureau processes have been extended to encompass all young people coming to the attention of the YJS and the YOS, not only first-time offenders/entrants.

The enhancement of the Bureau approach in terms of practice and evaluation methodology is illustrative of the centrality and utility of critical friendship to the refinement and evolution of practice. Critical feedback from researchers has been responded to constructively by practitioners and has motivated (research) evidence-based, reflective changes to working philosophies and practices that seek to benefit all key stakeholders and to feed into further research/evaluation that offers a more holistic and valid examination and development of local approaches.

Conclusion

We believe that reflective practice is what puts the 'social' in social science research. Research that treats its 'subjects' as inanimate objects is not social science research. The research participants addressed in this chapter are YOS staff and the young people they work with. For us, to think about conducting research on YOS practice and its impact on young people without directly and meaningfully engaging these participants in the research is anathema.

In this chapter, we have set out a reflective paradigm for conducting research, which we believe has wider applicability to social science research. Utilising RFR engages the researched in the research process in a variety of ways: it encourages (and gives confidence to) the researched to engage with researchers in defining the nature of research questions; it facilitates their engagement in designing research methodologies and

methods, alongside researchers, and it engages the researched in the reflective process of evaluating the conclusions/consequences of the research for
their practice or, in the case of young people, their lives. RFR also brings benefits to the researchers: it facilitates the depth, breadth and speed of access
to the researched, their data and their decision-making processes, while
increasing the willingness of the researched to engage in reflective, meaningful consideration of research and conclusions, which in turn enhances
the impact of the research findings and recommendations.

To us, RFR seems natural. It is a way of conducting social science research
that is fit for purpose, which gives due recognition and expression to the
'social' in the search for answers to questions. In the introduction, we stated
that Positivism as it has been implemented in much social science research
is based on a misunderstanding of methodological principles. Perhaps paradoxically, we find the strongest endorsement for the RFR model in the work
of the scientist who did more than any other to give expression to Positivist
methodology, R. A. Fisher. In the early 20th century, Fisher published pro-
lifically on statistics – pioneering many of the statistical methods still in use
today – and was a hugely influential figure in his time (Box 1978). Fisher's
(1925, 1935) influence, however, extended beyond statistics to embrace
research methodology. While he remained committed to scientific excellence and Positivist method, Fisher was equally committed to a high level
of engagement between the researcher and the researched, in a manner
lost to modern-day Positivists, as the means of conducting high-quality,
attuned research (see also Box 1978). Fisher believed that the independence
of the researcher was not compromised by a reflective relationship between
researcher and researched. Indeed, he argued that such a relationship was
critically related to the quality of the research process. Our experience over
nearly two decades of developing and conducting what we have presented
here as RFR echoes, evidences and reinforces this view.

Notes

1. In this way, it is not the objective of independence, seen as central to the justification of Positivist method, that we question, but the way in which this
independence is achieved.
2. Swansea Youth Justice Team was reformed under the Crime and Disorder Act 1998
and renamed Swansea Youth Offending Team (now Service). YOSs are statutory
multi-agency organisations in each local authority area in England and Wales
with the primary objective to prevent youth offending. YOSs are constituted by
representatives of the four statutory agencies (police, probation, health and local
authority – typically social services, education and youth services), along with representatives from voluntary and charitable agencies where appropriate in the local
area.
3. The *Youth Justice Board for England and Wales (YJB)* is a government quango that
monitors and evaluates the performance and outcomes of the Youth Justice System (particularly YOSs) and identifies, disseminates and funds 'effective' practice

in preventing and reducing youth offending. Wales has its own regional arm of the YJB, known as *YJB Cymru* (Wales), which is one of five divisions of the larger YJB for England and Wales (the others being Corporate Services Division, Community Division, Secure Division and Effective Practice Division). The Welsh Government's *Youth Justice Division* advises colleagues with policy-making responsibilities on how to address (non-devolved) youth justice issues in the Welsh context. The *Welsh Youth Justice Advisory Panel* is a multi-agency body that advises the Welsh Government and the YJB on the implementation of policy and practice to prevent offending/reoffending by children and young people in Wales.
4. It is not a requirement of RFR that researchers maintain an embedded presence with the researched – just that this represents a maximum version of the implementation of this model. Researchers able to spend much shorter durations engaged in particular projects can evince and exhibit the characteristics of RFR.
5. We have certainly been exposed to such criticism from various quarters over time.

References

Alvesson, M. and Sköldberg, K. (2000) *Reflexive Methodology: New Vistas for Qualitative Research*, London: Sage.
Barley, S. (1990) 'Images of Imaging: Notes on Doing Longitudinal Field Work' *Organization Science* 1(3): 220–47.
Box, J. (1978) *R. A. Fisher: The Life of a Scientist*, New York: Wiley.
Bredo, E. (2005) 'Reconstructing Educational Psychology'. In: P. Murphy (ed.) *Learners, Learning and Assessment*, London: Paul Chapman Publishing, pp.23–45.
Case, S.P. and Haines, K.R. (2004) 'Promoting Prevention: Evaluating a Multi-agency Initiative of Youth Consultation and Crime Prevention in Swansea' *Children and Society* 18(5): 355–70.
Case, S.P., Charles, A.D. and Haines, K.R. (2012) *Pentrehafod Prevention Project*. Report for the National Institute for Social Care and Health Research, Swansea: NISCH.
Case, S.P., Haines, K.R. and Charles, A.D. (2012) *Evaluation of Pentrehafod Prevention Project*, Cardiff: NISCHR.
Charles, A.D. (2011) *Young People's Participation in Everyday Decision Making*, PhD thesis, Swansea: Swansea University.
Cousin, G. and Deepwell, F. (2005) 'Designs for Network Learning: A Communities of Practice Perspective' *Studies in Higher Education* 30(1): 57–66.
Cunliffe, A.L. (2008) 'Orientations to Social Constructionism: Relationally-Responsive Social Constructionism and its Implications for Knowledge and Learning' *Management Learning* 39: 123–39.
Dutton, J.E. and Dukerich, J.M. (2006) 'The Relational Foundation of Research: An Underappreciated Dimension of Interesting Research' *Academy of Management Journal* 49(1): 21–26.
Farrington, D. (2003) 'Methodological Quality Standards for Evaluation Research' *Annals of the American Academy* 585: 49–68.
Fisher, R.A. (1925) *Statistical Methods for Research Workers*, Edinburgh: Oliver and Boyd.
Fisher, R.A. (1935) *The Design of Experiments*, New York: Hafner.
Fuller, D. (2004) 'Going Native'. In M.S. Lewis-Beck, A. Bryman and T. Futing Liao (eds) *The Sage Encyclopedia of Social Science Research Methods*, London: Sage, pp.435–36.
Gittell, J.H. (2003) 'A Theory of Relational Coordination'. In K.S. Cameron, J.E. Dutton and R.E. Quinn (eds) *Positive Organizational Scholarship: Foundations of a New Discipline*, San Francisco: Berrett-Koehler Publishing, pp.279–95.

Haines, K.R. and Case, S.P. (2003) 'Promoting Positive Behaviour in Schools: The Youth Social Audit' *Youth Justice* 3(2): 86–103.

Haines, K.R. and Case, S.P. (2005) 'Promoting Prevention: Targeting Family-based Risk and Protective Factors for Drug Use and Youth Offending in Swansea' *British Journal of Social Work* 35(2): 1–18.

Haines, K.R. and Case, S.P. (2012) 'The Failed Approach?' *Youth Justice* 12(3): 212–28.

Haines, K.R. and Case, S.P. (2014) 'Youth Justice: From Linear Risk Paradigm to Complexity'. In A. Pycroft and C. Bartollas (eds) *Applying Complexity Theory: Whole Systems Approaches in Criminal Justice and Social Work*, Bristol: Policy Press, pp.113–39.

Haines, K.R., Isles, E. and Jones, R. (1999) *Evaluation of Promoting Positive Behaviour*, Cardiff: WORD.

Haines, K.R., Case, S.P., Charles, A.D. and Davies, K. (2013) 'The Swansea Bureau: A Model of Diversion from the Youth Justice System' *International Journal of Law, Crime and Justice* 41(2): 167–87.

Hope, T. (2009) 'The Illusion of Control: A Response to Professor Sherman' *Criminology and Criminal Justice* 9(2): 125–34.

Iedema, R., Degeling, P. White, L. and Braithwaite, J. (2004) 'Analysing Discourse Practices in Organisations' *Qualitative Research Journal* 4(1): 5–25.

Lave, J. and Wenger, E. (1991). *Situated Learning: Legitimate Peripheral Participation*, Cambridge: Cambridge University Press.

Lave, J. and Wenger, E. (2002) 'Legitimate Peripheral Participation in Community of Practice'. In R. Harrison, F. Reeve, A. Hanson and J. Clarke (eds) *Supporting Lifelong Learning: Perspectives on Learning*, London and New York: Routledge Falmer, pp.111–26.

Lelliott, K. (2013) *To What Extent is Swansea YOS's Review System Promoting Participatory Practice for Young People?* Unpublished undergraduate dissertation, Swansea University, UK.

Lewis, M.W. and Kelemen, M.L. (2002) 'Multiparadigm Inquiry: Exploring Organisational Pluralism and Paradox' *Human Relations* 55(2): 251–75.

Losada, M. and Heaphy, E. (2004) 'The Role of Positivity and Connectivity in the Performance of Business Teams: A Nonlinear Dynamics Model' *American Behavioral Scientist* 47(6): 740–65.

Morgan, G. (1983). 'Toward a More Reflective Social Science'. In G. Morgan (ed.) *Beyond Method: Strategies for Social Research*, London: Sage, pp.368–76.

Sherman, L. (2009) 'Evidence and Liberty: The Promise of Experimental Criminology' *Criminology and Criminal Justice* 9(1): 5–28.

Tuckermann, H. and Rüegg-Stürm, J. (2010) 'Researching Practice and Practicing Research Reflexively: Conceptualizing the Relationship Between Research Partners and Researchers in Longitudinal Studies' *Qualitative Social Research* 11(3): http://www.qualitative-research.net/index.php/fqs/article/view/1540 (accessed February 2014).

Vygotsky, L. (1978) 'Interaction Between Learning and Development'. In M. Cole (ed.) *Mind in Society*, Cambridge, MA: Harvard University Press, pp.79–91.

Wenger, E. (1998) *Communities of Practice: Learning, Meaning and Identity*, Cambridge: Cambridge University Press.

Youth Justice Board (2009) *Youth Justice: The Scaled Approach. A Framework for Assessment and Interventions. Post-Consultation Version Two*, London: Youth Justice Board.

Part II
Researcher Identities, Subjectivities and Intersectionalities: Gender and Class

Editors' Introduction

Karen Lumsden and Aaron Winter

This section of the book focuses on *researcher identities, subjectivities and intersectionalities*. In the first of two parts, the authors focus on the role of *social class* and *gender* in their research. Although these chapters focus more explicitly on certain aspects of identity, such as gender and class in this section, we highlight the intersections between these, which influence how we relate to research participants and vice versa. Gender, class, race, ethnicity, sexuality, age, religion, our biography and our personal likes and dislikes shape our research interests, access to the field, relationships with the researched and interpretation and representation of the social group in question. Hence, the chapters herein deal with a host of issues and subject matter, highlighting the often unpredictable ways in which our social background and location can shape criminological research.

In Chapter 6, Emma Poulton identifies the methodological challenges and concerns which she had to (re)negotiate and manage as a female academic researching the hyper-masculine subculture of 'football hooliganism'. According to Poulton doing gendered research (especially with deviant subcultures) can sometimes require the researcher (male or indeed female) to demonstrate that he/she has the metaphorical 'balls' in terms of handling particular situations and power relations – including sometimes feeling powerless. In Chapter 7, Oona Brooks draws on feminist literature to offer an account of her research with young women about safety in bars and clubs in Scottish cities. She discusses how consideration was given to addressing potential imbalances of power between the researcher and the researched. The feminist identity of the researcher directly influenced the focus of the study and the interpretation of findings. In Chapter 8, Emily Luise Hart explores how her pregnancy impacted on a series of qualitative semi-structured interviews with female prisoners. The researcher's visible pregnancy gave access to particular insights that may not have otherwise been possible, for instance aiding access to sensitive data, helping to establish a positive rapport and supporting the development of a trusting relationship in the interview setting. In Chapter 9, Elias le Grand provides us with an account of his fieldwork experiences with working-class youths in a deprived South London suburb. He explores how writing the ethnographic self can inform our understanding of the performance of class and masculinity in the field. In this case, reflexive analysis of the interactions between the middle-class researcher and the young working-class respondents elucidated the classed dynamics of masculine performances, and how these are tied to the embodied knowledge of cultural codes.

6
Having the Balls: Reflections on Doing Gendered Research with Football Hooligans[1]

Emma Poulton

Introduction

This chapter provides my own reflexive account of the methodological issues and concerns that arose for me as a female researcher within the hyper-masculine subculture of 'football hooliganism'. Despite polemic academic stances, most scholars at least agree that the phenomenon is underscored by the psycho-social pleasures of violence that are experienced by the (pre-dominantly) male perpetrators, territorial identification, a sense of solidarity and belonging and especially 'hard' or 'aggressive' masculinity (Spaaij 2008). As such, the subculture of football hooliganism is a fertile site for the sym-bolic expression and validation of 'hyper-masculinity', an extreme form of masculine gender ideology, characterised by one or more of the following characteristics: insensitive attitudes towards women; violence as manly; dan-ger as exciting; and toughness as emotional self-control (see Messerschmidt 1993; Connell 1995/2005). Consequently, it may not be a comfortable site for a female researcher.

The principal aim of this chapter is to identify and explain the method-ological challenges and concerns specifically (re)negotiated as a female academic researching this hyper-masculine subculture in order to provide some methodological strategies and field tips that fellow researchers may find useful to manage the performative presentation of self and navigate some of the complicated gender issues and related power issues that can arise during the research process. This is important for criminology and the social sciences more broadly because the sharing of good (and bad) prac-tices and 'warts and all' admissions are all too often absent from the usual research methods textbooks and 'impact-driven' research papers, which usu-ally present 'sanitised' accounts of methodological processes and practice. Notable exceptions include the feminist scholars Bell and Newby (1977)

and Roberts (1981). There is a real need to candidly reflect (both professionally and personally) upon the 'impact' on the actual researcher and the
experiences and emotions confronted with while 'doing research' – which
strategies 'worked', which did not and, equally important, how it *felt* when
it went well or went wrong – and to share and exchange accounts with
colleagues through other academic forums to help facilitate future studies.
We are doing the next generation of researchers a disservice if we are not
more frank and honest in admitting that doing research is not always a neat
and tidy process of data collection, interpretation and analysis. In practice,
it can sometimes be 'messy', requiring the researcher to dig themselves out
of a hole, negotiate power relations and engage in emotional labour. You
may not always feel in command of a (challenging) situation; in fact you
can actually sometimes feel rather powerless.

This chapter explains my reflections on the methodological issues that
have arisen during an ongoing trajectory of qualitative research with 'retired'
football hooligans involving a suite of data collection techniques to explore
their autobiographical narratives and 'post-hooligan careers'.[2] The key challenges and concerns for me were those that emerged from being a female
academic: first, gaining access to the hyper-masculine subculture; second,
entering and developing rapport within the subculture; and third, 'doing
gendered research' in the hyper-masculine field (Poulton 2012). Drawing
conceptually upon Butler (1990) and Goffman (1959) – and acknowledging previous studies by other female researchers working in male-dominated
fields (Sampson and Thomas 2003; Woodward 2008; Lumsden 2009, 2010;
Palmer 2010) and with deviant social groups (Wiseman 1970; Vaaranen
2004; Jewkes 2005, 2012; Ward 2008) – I offer my own contribution to
this body of work by reflecting upon my experiences of doing gendered
research within the hyper-masculine and deviant subculture of football
hooliganism. Central to these experiences was a very conscious performative
presentation of my gendered self for my self-preservation, both physically
and emotionally, in the gender-incongruent field. It is my contention that
doing gendered research (especially with deviant subcultures) can sometimes
require the researcher (male or indeed female) to demonstrate that they have
the metaphorical 'balls' to negotiate certain situations, power relations and
emotions.

Doing gendered research

Many social scientists conducting fieldwork experience dilemmas and difficulties in relating their own identity and personal culture to the field culture
in which they are operating. The issue of gender arises because researchers
undertake fieldwork by establishing relationships. This is done as a person
with a repertoire of status markers – in terms of age, educational background,
class, ethnicity and sexual orientation – together with his/her own beliefs,

preferences and leisure interests. In particular, fieldwork is undertaken as men and women and so is a 'gendered project' (Lumsden 2009, 2010). That said, we must be careful to avoid the simplistic binary model of gender and appreciate the complexities of gender expression and identities. Gender should be recognised as a fluid variable, not the core aspect of our identity, but rather a performance: what we 'do', the way we act and present ourselves in different contexts and at different times (Butler 1990).

Reflexivity has become recognised as an important research skill in the social sciences because it actively takes into account the effect of the social identity and social presentation of the researcher on whom and what is being investigated (Gertsi-Pepin 2009). Moreover, reflexivity acknowledges and appreciates that the researcher and the researched are embedded within the research process. Thus, our personal biographies shape our research interests, access to the field, relationships with the researched and our interpretation and representation of the culture under examination. This is arguably more pronounced when there is gender incongruence between the researcher and the informants. Feminist scholars have been particularly prominent and insightful regarding ways in which status group membership impedes *or* assists with access and rapport (Hunt 1984; Horn 1997; Lumsden 2009; Mazzei and O'Brien 2009). Female researchers generally appear to be more acutely aware of being situated within gendered spaces and of the gendered interactions within them (Gill and Maclean 2002; Woodward 2008), with male researchers more prone to gender blindness.

Gaining access to the (gendered) field

Particular problems of entrée into the subculture of football hooligans have been well documented. Armstrong (1998) and Giulianotti (1995) both advocate the use of snowballing to establish gatekeepers and engender further subjects. Both acknowledge they were at a distinct advantage in that they were natives of the cities where they conducted their ethnographies and knew some of the hooligan firm members as schoolmates, prior to their formal research, through their lifelong support of Aberdeen and Sheffield United football clubs, respectively. What they did not explicitly acknowledge was that they were male. This gave them a distinct advantage. Despite this omission, Giulianotti (1995, 13) registers his scepticism 'on the viability of female sociologists undertaking participant observation with football hooligan groups'.

I fully respect the thoughts of an experienced researcher in the field and for many years was resigned to the fact that, as a female researcher, the door to the subculture of football hooliganism would always remain closed to me. Yet, having studied media representations of football hooliganism (Poulton 2007, 2008), I had often felt a bit of a 'fraud'. How could I offer an informed analysis and interpretation of media representations of football supporter behaviour or the subculture of 'football hooliganism', without experiencing it, or at the very least meeting some of the participants? However, like journalist and hooligan biographer, Caroline Gall (2005, 4), I found myself asking: 'But then where does a young, middle-class, female reporter [or, in my case, sociologist] from the Shires start when trying to gain entry into such an alien world?' (Gall 2005, 4). My gender and other status markers (such as my age, class and profession) were misaligned with their status group membership(s). Given the general dislike of academic 'boffins' (see Pennant and King 2005, 4) together with prevailing misogynist ideas about women within the subculture of football hooliganism (Spaaij 2008), being a woman *and* an academic hardly boded well for pursuing my ambitions to progress my research interests. This confirmed my resignation that the hooligan subculture was a world that would always remain closed to me as a female researcher.

That was until I received what could be seen as a slice of 'plain luck', which Giulianotti (1995, 8) suggests 'can have the greatest influence on who is prioritized for entrée'. This good fortune arrived via an email from a promoter of some 'retired' hooligans who were organising a series of 'events under the banner of "The Real Football Factories LIVE", featuring some of the lads who appeared on the Bravo TV series' (personal correspondence, 7 February 2008). The email outlined some basic details, suggesting the events may be 'a really useful experience for students studying Sociology and football-related violence'. I was invited to contact them if I was interested. My initial reaction upon receipt of the email was scepticism: I suspected it was a 'wind-up'. Experienced colleagues warned me to be wary and not to respond. Nevertheless, my curiosity and the whiff of an opportunity got the better of me and I replied a week later expressing muted interest and requesting more details.

An email exchange ensued over the next few weeks, with the promoter seemingly very keen to sell themselves and attract my interest and/or 'business'. This culminated in a telephone conversation, first with the promoter and then with Chris, one of the retired hooligans, who had conceived the idea. My conversation with him lasted about 45 minutes, which I took as testimony to how well it went. While I was trying to learn more about their project and ensure it was bona fide and would meet any ethics committee approval, it was evident that I was also being 'sounded out', both as a woman and an academic, and that I was being subtly tested, so I needed to 'impress' them. This was a complex strategic situation. Part of our discussion centred upon 'relations' between hooligans and academics. Chris claimed that the latter were 'up themselves' and that there was 'no relationship between the two' (i.e. academics and hooligans). This put me in a disadvantageous position, but I reminded myself that *they* had contacted *me* after all.

Throughout the conversation, I was acutely conscious of my image management and keen to make a good impression, while striking a balance between being professional and personable: I did not want to come across as being a 'naïve woman' nor 'stuck in my ivory tower'. Fortunately, my knowledge of hooliganism and football more broadly meant I was in my 'comfort zone' to some extent. This seemed to help me and we had an interesting, open and relaxed conversation. I was comfortable using some of the vocabulary of the hooligan subculture and able to demonstrate my awareness of recent incidents of football-related disorder. I was also familiar with Chris' autobiography, which I told him I had enjoyed for its candour and humility: a rare feature in hooligan memoirs often characterised by formulaic bragging and exaggeration. This was well received: Chris struck me as someone who sought approval and thrived off praise. Shortly after the phone call, I received an email from the promoter saying that I had 'made a good impression on Chris' and 'It has been a pleasure to talk to you today for both myself and Chris' (personal correspondence, 27 March 2008). From these early exchanges, it seemed that some subtle 'ego-massaging' was going to be the way forward in developing some form of rapport and maybe gaining further access. Consequently, while not always entirely at ease with this personally, I admit that I adopted 'ego-massaging' as a professional strategy (or what some call 'power tactic') to this end. This mainly involved praise, reassurance and endorsement and sometimes taking what was said with 'a pinch of salt'. I saw this as a necessary part of 'research bargaining'.

Research bargaining (either explicit or tacit quid pro quo) is crucial to gaining access to the field and requires skilful negotiation and re-negotiation (Giulianotti 1995; Lumsden 2009). It soon became apparent in my interactions with the hooligans that our 'relationship' (and balance of power) was underpinned by an implicit 'bargaining' that could be mutually beneficial. First and foremost, they seemed to want endorsement from an academic institution to give their event series a form of integrity; they wanted to visit a university and present to undergraduate students, who they said frequently wrote to them for help with dissertations. In return, it appeared that the 'closed door' to the subculture of football hooliganism might be ajar. As with other research where gaining and maintaining access depends on good relations with gatekeepers and respondents (Sampson and Thomas 2003; Palmer 2010), I openly presented my interest in them and stated my purpose as wanting to find out more about their subculture to develop my research. They were happy with this and over the next few months I corresponded frequently with Chris via email, SMS and phone.

During this time, their project took a significant change of direction. Chris explained that one of his partners involved in the 'The Real Football Factories LIVE' was more involved with the active hooligan subculture and that his plans for a national tour 'glorifying their past exploits' conflicted with Chris' 'reformed' principles. Chris decided to break from the project and instead sought to develop an anti-youth crime project. During this 're-think' and the development of his new project, Chris would regularly contact me and I began to operate as a kind of unofficial consultant who they would bounce ideas off about website and presentation content, sources of funding, the barriers they faced given their criminal records, as well as seeking assurance and endorsement. Upon reflection, I believe that my status group membership as a *female* academic actually *helped* facilitate these interactions and the development of rapport, in ways that male academics may not have been able to do. I also think our age gap may have helped because I was not considered a 'threat', either as a sexual predator or 'groupie'. In this way, my gendered self was a useful tool, not a challenge to the research process.

In return – as part of our unspoken research bargain – I gained an exclusive insight into Chris and his firm through the regular conversations we were now having, which came to serve as informal interviews. Five months after their first speculative email, I was invited to attend the official launch of their anti-youth crime project, which coincided with a pre-screening of a hooligan film. Finally I had my ticket, not just to the launch press conference and the cinema, but into the hooligan subculture. At last I was going to meet some hooligans. Chris was acting in the role of 'gatekeeper' and the door had been opened.

Entering and developing rapport in the hyper-masculine subculture

While my research with 'retired' hooligans is ongoing, to date my fieldwork experiences are perhaps limited compared with the time spent by Lumsden (2009), Palmer (2010) or Woodward (2008) in their respective male subcultures. I am certainly *not* claiming to have gained full entrée as a covert observer (Pearson 2009, 2012) or the status of the 'marginal native' (Armstrong 1998) or 'relative insider' (Giulianotti 1995), which reflects the former's immersed ethnography vis-à-vis the latter's more episodic ethnography. Nevertheless, I was still confronted by a need to 'get on' (McKenzie 2009), without standing out, arousing suspicion or antagonising those within the group in any way, while ensuring my personal safety.[3] There are no explicit guidelines for achieving this, but it is of course imperative to try to establish a level of trust and rapport with those being investigated.

This can pose a real challenge for a woman in 'man land' (Palmer 2010, 433): how do you look inconspicuous when so many physical and social status markers (gender, class, generation and biography, signified by comportment, appearance, accent and dress) are incongruent? My field diary records my anxieties about 'what to wear' when meeting the hooligan firm for the first time at the film pre-screening, demonstrates my acute consciousness of and concern about my presentation of self (Goffman 1959):

> What shall I wear? What do you wear to go and meet a firm of hooligans?! If I was a man, it would be so much easier: I could pick from any number of 'casual' designer labels and look to impress, or at least look

inconspicuous! But what to wear as a woman? We're meeting at a pub and going to the cinema. Do I conform to 'emphasised femininity'? Do I power-dress? Neither suggestion comes naturally to me at the best of times and neither seemed appropriate today of all days with the prospect of my imminent company. I'm not a 'girly-girl'. Rarely had I laboured over what to wear – this was like going on a first date! – yet it seemed to really matter. I didn't want to attract any unwanted advances by dressing provocatively, but I was also aware of a need to look 'feminine', as I would be in the presence of men for whom that was important. 'Comfortable shoes' would almost certainly be associated with stereotypical ideas of being a feminist (lesbian) academic, which wouldn't go down well in these circles. I didn't want to dress too formally, but I wanted to look smart and at the same time feel comfortable and also assertive. So what's a girl to wear? I was annoyed with myself for dwelling over the issue, but I knew that how I presented myself was important. They'd be checking me out, in every sense. Finally, I opted for my fitted, short-sleeved, navy and white, gingham-check Ted Baker blouse, a pair of smart boot-cut jeans and a pair of mules, which revealed my painted toe-nails.

(Fieldnotes, 16 July 2008)

For Mazzei and O'Brien (2009), the female researcher is an active participant in how she is perceived and received by informants. They pose the question: 'You got it, when do you flaunt it?' and expound the concept of 'deploying gender' to build an intersectional thesis on the role of the researcher's status group membership for gaining access and rapport. They 'carefully select our attire, are conscious of our body language, and attune our behaviour so as to present ourselves as acceptable to the field' (Mazzei and O'Brien 2009, 379). While I deliberately opted to avoid 'flaunting it', my wardrobe choice inadvertently helped as an 'icebreaker' from which I worked on developing a rapport with Dave at our first meeting, as my fieldnotes capture:

'I like your shirt', he said. Thinking his comment was a bit of an odd thing to say (was it a flirtatious remark?), I thanked him. At least my worrying about what to wear seemed to have worked. 'It's like mine', he added, 'You've got good taste'. It was then I realised that we were both wearing navy and white gingham-checked shirts. We both laughed. My labouring over what to wear had worked: it had at least broken the ice. 'Actually we've got something else in common', I ventured, 'We've got a mutual friend: Barry "Chicken Run", landlord of The Fox in Hertfordshire'. 'Barry "Chicken Run?" You know "Chicken Run?" Yeah, he's a good bloke him, gets up Upton Park, proper West Ham. So how come you know him?' 'My dad lives opposite The Fox; it's where I come from. That used to be my local. My brothers still drink there', I explained. Dave seemed really interested and animated. 'What that cottage with the thatched roof?' he enquired. We were starting to establish something of a rapport. As we sat talking, I noticed we, or rather I, was getting a few funny looks from some of the hooligans who had come to see the guest of honour: as if to say, who's *SHE* commanding Dave's attention?

(Fieldnotes, 16 July 2008)

My labouring over what to wear is an example of active image management in the presentation of my [ethnographic] self (Goffman 1959; Coffey 1999). Further, while keen to establish a good impression and develop a good rapport with Dave, Chris and the other hooligan firm members, I was keenly aware of maintaining a balance in terms of the image I was wanting to project: knowledgeable and well informed, but not a 'prim and proper' University 'boffin'; willing and able to have a laugh, but also an academic researcher who was there to do a job. I believe I achieved this image management, though this was a constant challenge that I had to (re)negotiate and I always felt that I had to be 'on my toes' and 'keep my guard up'. In this way, my image management was also underscored by an implicit power struggle.

For example, after the pre-screening of *Cass*, we returned to the pub, where Chris introduced to me to some of the 'faces' [reputed hooligans] from the firm: men I had read about and seen photos of in his autobiography. It was apparent Chris had briefed them on who I was; they referred to me variously as 'the researcher', 'the university woman' or (a name that stuck) 'the Doc'. One of them put me on the spot when he said: 'We've heard if you had balls, you'd be one of us!' I wasn't quite sure how to take this gendered remark. I still reflect on what this really meant/means about my character and how this sits with me, both personally and professionally. Something I must have said to Chris during our conversations must have given him the idea that, had I been a man, I would have the propensity to be a football hooligan like them. Such a comment certainly seemed at the time to be a kind of seal of 'approval' and 'acceptance'.

As Sampson and Thomas (2003, 174) note, 'being in a fieldwork setting and gaining initial access to a site is no guarantee of acceptance, much less trust or even popularity. Hard won trust and rapport can be quickly lost in the face of a perceived rejection or "social snub"'. This is something I experienced several months later when a misunderstanding arose over Chris' scheduled trip to my institution to give an evening presentation to our students. There had been much discussion over payment for this, with Chris' promoter seeking an all-expenses-paid trip (including travel costs and an 'appearance fee', rather than the standard visiting lecturer rate), which my institution refused to pay. A compromise was finally reached, but then a week before the visit, I received an email cancelling the trip due to 'work commitments'. In my return email I expressed my disappointment given that I thought we had a 'gentleman's agreement'. This evidently caused great offence given the SMS text I then received from Chris, accusing me of 'selfish' motivations because I had 'not got [my] own way'. He signed off: 'It's been very interesting and at times hilarious whilst studying you studying us'.

It is here that I sympathise with the 'emotional labour' experienced by Coffey (1999), Hunt (2009) and Lumsden (2009, 2010). This was the most challenging experience, mentally and emotionally, I had during the research process. The SMS cut me to the quick. I felt vulnerable and powerless. It made me question the 'rapport' that I *thought* we had developed. I felt naïve for thinking that as an academic, indeed as a female researcher, I could have believed that I had developed a 'rapport' with a hooligan. But wanting to set the record straight, I boldly decided to call Chris. My performative presentation of self was vital here for my self-preservation. Not only did I need to keep my key gatekeeper 'onside' for the future of my research, but I had genuinely begun to value his 'friendship' and wanted to resolve relations. This proved to be a very difficult conversation during which I was subjected to more insults and ridicule as Chris vented his mind. He was particularly agitated by the suggestion he had broken a 'gentleman's agreement'. I had used this gendered term blithely, but he had taken it as a personal affront, as if I was challenging his masculine values of valour and honesty. This put me in an acutely disadvantaged position. Finally, after taking a rap and perhaps helped by some further 'ego-massaging' through my consumption of 'humble pie' and apologetic manner, we resolved the situation. The conversation was emotionally exhausting and I had to compromise some of my personal principles to preserve what I now knew was a very precarious professional relationship and power balance. Despite this, I took some solace and indeed pride from the fact Chris thanked me for 'having the balls' to call, an incongruous gendered phrase in the circumstances! I later received an email from the promoter:

> I think that you may have misunderstood some of what was said. We have never laughed or disrespected you either as a woman or an academic... We have always thought highly of you and will continue to do so... You have always given us the impression that you are an independent, intelligent, outgoing, happy and strong lady... We remain friends.
>
> (Personal correspondence, 28 November 2008)

This email came as a great relief and was reassuring. It was also revealing about how my presentation of self was interpreted and a gauge of how I had been received, as a female academic, in 'doing gendered research', negotiating 'outsider' issues and in forging some form of 'rapport'. Reflecting upon gendered interactions also illuminates some of the internal dynamics of the subculture under examination.

Concluding reflections: 'Doing gender' in the hyper-masculine field

This chapter reflects upon the experiences of being a female academic researcher in a hyper-masculine subculture, specifically football hooliganism. Applying existing ideas and experiences, together with my own, the chapter contributes to discussions of reflexivity in criminological research by addressing some of the omissions in the current body of work and advancing debates on the gendered nature of research and the performativity of gender, along with other status markers, in the presentation of (ethnographic) self (Coffey 1999). Consequently, this chapter is conceptually underpinned by the contrasting, yet I believe complimentary, work of Goffman (1959) and Butler (1990).

The chapter highlights some of the methodological challenges and concerns specifically (re)negotiated and managed as a female academic throughout the research process. For me, these were: first, those that emerged from first gaining access to a hyper-masculine subculture; second, entering and developing rapport in the subculture; and third, 'doing gender' in the hyper-masculine field. Central to negotiating these challenges was a very conscious performative presentation of self, sometimes for self-preservation, during the research process. In practice, this sometimes required demonstrating that I had the (metaphorical) 'balls' in terms of handling particular situations and negotiating power relations, the emotional labour this demands and my overall (gendered) image management. However, being a female academic was not entirely problematic, as I had previously feared. Once I had gained access, these status markers were sometimes actually useful research tools that helped me develop a form of rapport with some of my hooligan subjects and encouraged more candid discussions, which male academics may not have been party to. In this sense, I was actually empowered.

This chapter calls for a lifting of the blinkers in social research, not just regarding gender blindness, but also in terms of acknowledging the complexities and disclosing the 'untidiness' of qualitative research practices and the emotional labour it can require. This involves greater consideration of the *real* nature of the research process and more frank admissions about the challenging and awkward situations that can arise, often presenting the researcher with an emotional rollercoaster of 'highs' and 'lows'. Lessons can be learnt from sharing 'what works' (and 'what doesn't') via 'warts and all' scholarship. This is vitally important for future researchers since this kind of advice and candid reflexivity tends to go unrecognised in the sanitised accounts outlined in traditional methodology teaching and textbooks, and likewise in the vast majority of published research articles, which all too often present qualitative research as a clinical process with polished practices.

My intention is that reflecting upon and sharing my experiences and the emotional nature of my research will contribute to the existing body of methodological work by providing useful advice and guidance on the performative presentation of self – as well as support and encouragement – to other researchers, especially those doing gendered research, to help their self-preservation in the field. While the chapter is primarily concerned with (a) being a female academic researcher and (b) football hooliganism, the methodological issues it addresses readily transfer and can contribute to other criminological field settings. These issues are of relevance to anyone faced with gender incongruence between them and their informers, as well as anyone engaged in qualitative research with deviant, (quasi-)criminal or male-dominated subcultures more broadly. In other words, any field where the researcher may be required to reconsider and negotiate their positioning, practices and performativity in their presentation of self.

Notes

1. This chapter is adapted from Poulton, E. (2012) '"If You Had Balls, You'd Be One of Us!" Doing Gendered Research: Methodological Reflections on Being a Female Academic Researcher in the Hyper-Masculine Subculture of "Football Hooliganism"' *Sociological Research Online* 17(4): http://www.socresonline.org.uk/17/4/4.html
2. My fieldwork involved in-depth interviews; informal interviews; social networking; and observation-as-participant in field settings with a group of 'retired' hooligans, who were 'active' during the late 1970s to early 1990s. I had two main subjects, who acted as gatekeepers. For the purpose of anonymity, they will be given the pseudonyms of Chris and Dave, as will all other subjects mentioned. Both were in their late forties/early fifties and were recognised 'top boys' (leading figures) in their respective hooligan 'firms' (organised gangs).
3. My own personal safety strategy when meeting with football hooligans is generally informed by common sense precautions and practices usually employed when meeting strangers (especially men) including meeting in busy, popular places such as pubs and bars; ensuring that several 'appointment monitors' know where I am going, who I am meeting, the due meet time and expected time of completion; and keeping in regular contact with those monitors via SMS messages.

References

Armstrong, G. (1998) *Football Hooligans: Knowing the Score*, Oxford: Berg.
Bell, C. and Newby, H. (eds) (1977) *Doing Sociological Research*, London: Allen and Unwin.
Butler, J. (1990) *Gender Trouble: Feminism and the Subversion of Identity*, New York: Routledge.
Coffey, A. (1999) *The Ethnographic Self: Fieldwork and the Representation of Identity*, London: Sage.
Connell, R.W. (1995/2005) *Masculinities*, Cambridge: Polity.
Gall, C. (2005) *Zulus. Black, White and Blue: The Story of the Zulu Warriors Firm*, Wrea Green: Milo Books Ltd.

Gertsi-Pepin, C. (2009) 'Learning from Dumbledore's Pensieve: Metaphor as an Aid in Teaching Reflexivity in Qualitative Research' *Qualitative Research* 9(3): 299–308.

Gill, F. and Maclean, C. (2002) 'Knowing your Place: Gender and Reflexivity in Two Ethnographies' *Sociological Research Online* 7(2): http://wwwsocreonline.org.uk/7/2/gill.html

Giulianotti, R. (1995) 'Participant Ethnography and Research into Football Hooliganism: Reflections on the Problems of *Entrée* and Everyday Risks' *Sociology of Sport Journal* 12: 1–20.

Goffman, E. (1959) *The Presentation of Self in Everyday Life*, London: Penguin.

Horn, R. (1997) 'Not "One of the Boys": Women Researching the Police' *Journal of Gender Studies* 6(3): 297–308.

Hunt, J. (1984) 'The Development of Rapport Through the Negotiation of Gender in Fieldwork Among Police' *Human Organizations* 43(4): 283–96.

Jewkes, Y. (2005) 'Men Behind Bars: "Doing" Masculinity as an Adaptation to Imprisonment' *Men and Masculinities* 8(1): 44–63.

Jewkes, Y. (2012) 'Autoethnography and Emotion as Intellectual Resources: Doing Prison Research Differently' *Qualitative Inquiry* 18(1): 63–75.

Lumsden, K. (2009) '"Don't Ask a Woman to Do Another Woman's Job": Gendered Interactions and the Emotional Ethnographer' *Sociology* 43(3): 497–513.

Lumsden, K. (2010) 'Gendered Performances in a Male-Dominated Subculture: "Girl Racers", Car Modification and the Quest for Masculinity' *Sociological Research Online* 15(3): http://www.socresonline.org.uk/15/3/6.html

Mazzei, J. and O'Brien, E. (2009) 'You Got It, So When Do You Flaunt It? Building Rapport, Intersectionality, and Strategic Deployment of Gender in the Field' *Journal of Contemporary Ethnography* 38(3): 358–83.

McKenzie, J.S. (2009) '"You Don't Know How Lucky Your Are to Be Here!": Reflections on Covert Practices in an Overt Participation Study' *Sociological Research Online* 14(2): http://www.socresonline.org.uk/14/2/8.html

Messerschmidt, J.W. (1993) *Masculinities and Crime*, Lanham, MD: Rowman and Littlefield.

Palmer, C. (2010) 'Everyday Risks and Professional Dilemmas: Fieldwork with Alcohol-Based (Sporting) Subcultures' *Qualitative Research* 10(4): 421–40.

Pearson, G. (2009) 'The Researcher as Hooligan: Where "Participant" Observation Means Breaking the Law' *International Journal of Social Research Methodology* 12(3): 243–55.

Pearson, G. (2012) *An Ethnography of English Football Fans*, Manchester: Manchester University Press.

Pennant, C. and King, M. (2005) *Terrace Legends*, London: John Black Publishing Ltd.

Poulton, E. (2007) '"Fantasy Football Hooliganism" in Popular Media' *Media, Culture and Society* 29(1): 151–64.

Poulton, E. (2008) 'Towards a Cultural Sociology of the Consumption of "Fantasy Football Hooliganism"' *Sociology of Sport Journal* 25(3): 331–49.

Poulton, E. (2012) '"If You Had Balls, You'd Be One of Us!" Doing Gendered Research: Methodological Reflections on Being a Female Academic Researcher in the Hyper-Masculine Subculture of "Football Hooliganism"' *Sociological Research Online* 17(4): http://www.socresonline.org.uk/17/4/4.html

Ramsay, J. (1996) 'The Development of Rapport Through the Negotiation of Gender in Fieldwork Among Police'. In J. Busfield and E. Stina Lyon (eds) *Methodological Imaginations*. London: Palgrave Macmillan. pp.130–53.

Roberts, H. (ed.) (1981) *Doing Feminist Research*, London: Routledge.

Sampson, H. and Thomas, M. (2003) 'Lone Researchers at Sea: Gender, Risk and Responsibility' *Qualitative Research* 3(2): 165–89.

Spaaij, R. (2008) 'Men Like Us, Boys Like Them: Violence, Masculinity, and Collective Identity in Football Hooliganism' *Journal of Sport and Social Issues* 32(4): 369–92.

Vaaranen, H. (with Presdee, M.) (2004) 'Stories from the Streets: Some Fieldwork Notes on the Seduction of Speed'. In J. Ferrell, W. Morrison and M. Presdee (eds) *Cultural Criminology Unleashed*, London: The Glass House, pp.245–50.

Ward, J. (2008) 'Researching Drug Sellers: An "Experiential" Account from "the Field"' *Sociological Research Online* 13(1): http://www.socresonline.org.uk/13/1/14.html

Wiseman, J.P. (1970) *Stations of the Lost: The Treatment of Skid Row Alcoholics*, Chicago: University of Chicago Press.

Woodward, K. (2008) 'Hanging Out and Hanging About: Insider/Outsider Research in the Sport of Boxing' *Ethnography* 9(4): 536–61.

7

The Interplay Between Power and Reflexivity in Feminist Research on Young Women's Safety

Oona Brooks

Introduction

Contemporary criminological research offers rich insights into the experiences of those positioned as powerful – such as criminal justice agencies and policy makers – and those who are positioned as powerless through the processes of criminal victimisation and marginalisation. Within criminological research, growing attention has been given to the merits of adopting a reflexive approach that situates the researcher both in relation to the groups that they are studying (e.g. the police, the judiciary, prisoners or victims) and within the social world they are studying. This chapter offers a reflexive account of a feminist research study that examined young women's safety in bars and clubs. The underpinning research was conducted using in-depth qualitative interviews and focus groups with young women between the ages of 18–25 years across Scotland.

Adopting a reflexive approach within research entails rejecting an ontological positioning of the social world as independent of the researcher and the research process; rather the researcher is acknowledged as a subjective resource within the research. Contrary to the notion that researchers are a 'neutral' or 'blank' canvass, the way in which researcher knowledge, experience, values and identity colour the research process is articulated within reflexive accounts. Pivotal to the reflexive turn within social and criminological research is a concern with acknowledging and addressing relations between the researcher and the researched, including the power dynamics underpinning these relations. These concerns have been central to feminist methodological debates, hence the considerable contribution that feminist scholarship has made to discussions of power and reflexivity within criminological research and beyond.

This chapter draws upon earlier feminist studies that have made important contributions to critiquing and enhancing methodological approaches, including reflexive approaches within the criminological enterprise (Stanley 1990; Stanley and Wise 1993; Millen 1997; Oakley 1998; Letherby 2002; Skinner et al. 2005; Mason and Stubbs 2010). The insights contributed by earlier feminist work are developed through particular consideration of the identity of the researcher as a feminist and by challenging the assumptions embedded within some of this work about the operation and direction of power within the research process. This chapter begins by contextualising feminist methodological approaches within criminology and elucidating their relationship with the concept of reflexivity. In the account that follows, the identity of the researcher, as a feminist, is then considered in terms of how this influenced the focus of the study, the power dynamics between the researcher and the researched and the interpretation of the data gathered.

Reflexivity and feminist criminological research

Feminist criminology of the 1970s and 1980s critiqued the neglect of women's criminal victimisation and offending as a legitimate focus of study within conventional criminology (Smart 1976; Carlen 1983; Heidensohn 1985). However, feminist scholars have questioned not just the focus of knowledge, but also conventional assumptions about the means in which research is conceived, produced and justified as knowledge in the public domain (Millen 1997, 2). Since the 1970s feminist researchers have, therefore, also extended the anti-positivist methodological positions developed within perspectives such as ethnomethodology, poststructuralism and hermeneutics (Oakley 1998, 724). In other words, feminist scholars have contributed to the dismantling of the notion that social research is conducted in an objective and value-free way. Ann Oakley (1998, 717) offers a telling description of 'popular conceptions' of science, typically associated with positivism:

> Popular conceptions of science portray scientists as 'reasonable men' searching for causal laws with the goal of predicting and controlling nature, and doing so themselves almost like machines, without reference to values or to their own experience. The scientist 'himself' is context free, and science itself has a linear and evolutionary shape, according to which its knowledge gets better and better all the time.

In contrast to research that makes claims of value neutrality, feminist research and other forms of reflexive research acknowledge the researcher as a 'subjective subject' and a resource within the research, while research participants are no longer simply objects of research. Hence, reflexivity is described by Mason and Stubbs (2010, 12) as one of the means used by feminist criminologists to avoid the myth of objective and value-free research.

The merits of adopting a reflexive approach are widely acknowledged within feminist social and criminological research (see Stanley 1990; Stanley and Wise 1993; Millen 1997; Oakley 1998; Letherby 2002; Skinner et al. 2005; Mason and Stubbs 2010). However, the concept of reflexivity is subject to varying interpretations within the broader research literature. Reflexive research has been described, for example, as 'research that looks back at itself' (Alexander 2001, 355). However, this description is somewhat lacking; it appears to constitute reflexivity as mere reflection. Arguably, reflexivity has a greater depth of purpose; the researcher is consciously inserted into the research process with the intention of providing a more honest, ethical and balanced form of knowledge (Mason and Stubbs 2010, 11–12). Crucially, the subjective position of the researcher is acknowledged and documented so that the way in which the social position of the researcher and the research process affects the research results is apparent. Such an approach is also conscious of the potential power of the researcher over the researched (Stanley and Wise 1993). In practice, adopting a reflexive approach entails consideration of how the researcher's personal biography influences the research process, including fundamental choices that are made by the researcher in relation to the topic of research, study design and interpretation of data.

In the account that follows I will attempt to outline how my position as a feminist and the adoption of a feminist methodological approach influenced my study of young women's safety in bars and clubs. Considerable debate exists in relation to what constitutes feminist methodology in the first instance, and indeed whether a distinctive feminist methodology actually exists (Delamont 2003; Wise and Stanley 2003; Ramazanoglu and Holland 2006). It is argued here, and elsewhere, that there is no single or agreed feminist methodology. The discussion that follows, therefore, articulates what the adoption of a feminist approach entailed within the context of the current study.

The identity of the feminist researcher

The research study that provides the basis for this chapter focuses on young women's safety in bars and clubs. This focus was largely determined by my own biography as a feminist researcher who had previously worked in the field of violence against women and my desire to conduct research that was meaningful to the participants engaging in the research. In keeping with feminist research, which strives to address issues that affect the day-to-day lives of women, I was keen to pursue research that would be pertinent to the lives of those engaging in the research rather than simply indulging my own interests.

At the time of developing the study proposal, contemporary young women appeared to have more opportunities to engage in the traditionally male activity of socialising and consuming alcohol in bars and clubs (Plant

1997; Lyons and Willot 2008), and there appeared to be more social acceptance of them doing so (Day et al. 2004). The United Kingdom has witnessed
an expansion of the night-time economy (Winlow and Hall 2006), and bars,
pubs and clubs have become more 'women friendly' through a process of
feminisation (Chatterton and Hollands 2003). This presents a stark contrast
with observations from earlier studies which position drinking in pubs as
a male privilege and an expression of patriarchal society (Whitehead 1976;
Hey 1986).

However, these apparent new freedoms were accompanied by a renewed
emphasis on women's safety in bars and clubs; this was in part due to
the emergence of 'new' concerns about drink spiking, drug-assisted sexual assault and the relationship between women's alcohol consumption
and sexual assault. These concerns were coupled by scrutiny of young
women's alcohol consumption, particularly where this was seen to be excessive or associated with displays of 'unfeminine' behaviour in public spaces.
An intended benefit of the research for participants was, therefore, the
opportunity to express their views on a subject matter where their behaviour
is often scrutinised, but their voices overlooked. Feedback received from participants via an anonymised feedback form used to gather information about
their experience of participating in the research suggests that they welcomed
this opportunity:

> Interesting to hear other peoples point of view on topics which affect
> us all each week on a night out and be part of research which asks
> women their views on safety as opposed to telling them what they
> should/shouldn't do!

> I liked talking about things that happen every weekend to myself, or my
> friends and expressing my views on it.

It appeared that participants welcomed the opportunity to engage in
research on this topic and were able to identify its relevance within the context of their own lives. Mason (1998) describes this as 'ecological validity'
within qualitative research.

With regard to my own biography, prior to conducting this study I had
worked for eight years at a Rape Crisis Centre in Glasgow. During this time
I provided emotional and practical support to women and girls who had
experienced sexual violence and I also trained workers from other agencies on responding to disclosures of sexual violence. This, coupled with
my personal experience of sexual harassment and violence, meant that
I was acutely aware of the nature and extent of sexual violence within society. My own biography, therefore, significantly influenced the focus of the
research. The questions asked by this study were also informed by feminist theory about violence against women, which locates violence against

women as a result of, and contributor to, women's subordination. Feminist literature on the relationship between gender, power and social control was particularly influential, and I was keen to explore the relevance of these concepts to understanding the experiences of contemporary young women within a context of apparent empowerment and new-found freedoms to socialise in bars and clubs. In essence, the study was conducted within a feminist framework which acknowledges women's oppression with a view to challenging this oppression by attempting to understand women's beliefs from their own point of view, and within the context of their own lived experiences.

Conducting my research from a feminist perspective provided a valuable conceptual framework for the study and it also provided congruence with my own identity as a feminist. Indeed, it is difficult to envisage how I could have conducted the study in a way that did not acknowledge my feminist identity. However, one aspect of conducting research which is given relatively little attention within feminist methodological literature is whether the feminist theory and principles guiding the research should be shared overtly with research participants. Millen (1997) acknowledges that some 'methodological difficulties' emerge when doing feminist research on non-feminist populations, and Ramazanoglu and Holland (2006) note that unfavourable perceptions of feminism can mean that such research will be met with suspicion by gatekeepers, resulting in access being denied. However, this observation is not extended to research participants. So, should the researcher openly identify themselves as a feminist? In this particular study, I chose not to disclose this information to participants. This decision was partly borne out of concern that doing so might inhibit or unduly influence participants' responses by suggesting that particular types of response were sought or favoured.

Furthermore, identifying the research project as a feminist study may have alienated participants. For many women, especially young women, feminism has negative connotations and feminists are constructed particularly negatively (Riley 2001). Indeed, Angela McRobbie (2004, 512) even suggests that feminism has been expelled to a state which can be likened to 'a retirement home in an unfashionable rundown holiday resort', which repels young women. Priority was given, therefore, to conducting fieldwork in a way which reflects the ethos of feminist methodology, while identification of the study as grounded in feminist theory remained implicit. Adopting this approach, however, left me with some uncomfortable questions about the extent to which my study was complicit in the distancing of feminism as an accepted and positive identity for young women.

Power dynamics in the feminist research process

Minimising power imbalances within the research process is a fundamental concern of feminist methodology (Skinner et al. 2005); doing so requires a reflexive awareness of the power held by researchers in relation to research participants. Within the current study, specific attention was given to redressing power differentials between the researcher and the researched and to adopting a reflexive approach throughout the study. Mindful of potential power imbalances between the researcher and the researched, care was taken to minimise this dynamic by working to ensure that research participants were able to exercise their own discretion, choice and control in the research process.

Particular care was taken, for example, to ensure that informed consent was secured from all participants. In effect, this meant that all participants were informed, verbally and in writing, of the nature and purpose of the study and given the opportunity to request further information about the study prior to, during or after participation. Consent to participate in the study was viewed as an ongoing agreement, which was actively negotiated throughout the research process. Choice was also exercised by participants in terms of whether they participated in an interview and/or a focus group and where and when this should take place. Moreover, the semi-structured nature of focus groups and interviews allowed these encounters to be guided by a combination of what I, as the researcher, and the research participants considered important to discuss.

However, power is a complex and dynamic concept (Millen 1997), and the measures undertaken within this study did not automatically generate an equal and reciprocal relationship between the researcher and the researched, nor was the power of the researcher and the researched a dichotomous relationship. The issue of power in the research process, particularly in the relationship between researchers and the researched, has been given attention in methodological research literature by feminist writers (Oakley 1981; Finch 1984), suggesting that the qualitative interview process has the potential to overcome the asymmetrical balance of power typical within survey-based interviews, which limit women's self-expression (Lee 1999) and hinder the formation of a reciprocal relationship between the interviewer and the interviewee. It has also been argued that focus groups, a method also used in the current study, are a relatively non-hierarchical method (Wilkinson 1999).

From one feminist perspective, it is argued that women, as interviewers and interviewees, 'share a subordinate structural position by virtue of their gender', which can facilitate shared identification and rapport (Finch 1984, 76). Being female was the most obvious similarity between me and each of the research participants. Echoing the experiences of other feminist researchers interviewing women (Oakley 1981; Finch 1984), responses and feedback from participants would suggest that participants were able to identify with me on this basis and were comfortable in disclosing particular information that they may not have done with a male researcher (e.g. male behaviour which makes them feel uncomfortable but tends to be trivialised by men).

However, Wise (1987) critiques the assumption that power imbalances are dissipated by shared gender alone. Furthermore, while women may occupy a subordinate structural position as a result of their gender, it does not necessarily follow that they share the same experiences of oppression, discrimination, and powerlessness as Finch (1984) would suggest. Essentially, the power dynamic within the research process is likely to be influenced by a range of both structural factors such as sexuality, ethnicity or economic position (Millen 1997, 3), and situational factors (e.g. interviewer skill, time and location of interview).

In addition to structural or situational factors that may impact upon the dynamic of the research process, the researcher and research participants may agree or disagree on a range of factors that impact upon the possibilities of interaction (Ramazanoglu and Holland 2006). Indeed, it was apparent within the current study that shared gender between me and research participants did not necessarily equate to a shared view of the world. During focus groups and interviews, for example, some participants expressed views about appropriate behaviour for women, which were not in keeping with my own personal values; women who wear 'revealing' clothing were described as 'slappers', and it was suggested that women commonly make up stories of rape or may be to blame for sexual assault, particularly if they have been drinking alcohol:

> Suzanne (interview): I think it's really harsh, but if you've had that much to drink, I just think it's a bit kind of tough luck, but that sounds really horrible, but I just think that if you've had that much to drink you should have people around you that are, you know, are looking out for you. I think you shouldn't put yourself in that situation to start with ... but if it does happen I really don't think that it is rape or sexual assault ... I think that it's a mistake, I think that it's a bad decision, you know, you shouldn't have drank that much in the first place.

Prior to engaging in fieldwork, I had considered how best to respond in situations of this nature. I considered it appropriate to explore why participants held particular views, but not to criticise participants' perspectives or silence them in any way. This aspect of the fieldwork was particularly challenging and it raised questions about the feminist principle of 'allowing women's voices to be heard' when women's 'voices' may serve to intentionally or unintentionally discriminate against other women. Further, Ramazanoglu and Holland argue that 'feminists have had to come to terms with the discomforts of producing knowledge of how women exercise power, promote injustice collude in their own subordination, or benefit from the subordination of "others"' (Ramazanoglu and Holland 2006, 148). Nonetheless, I found it difficult to listen to these views in the knowledge that discriminatory views of this nature compound the blame attributed to women following a rape. Based on my experience of working in a Rape Crisis Centre I was aware that, in addition to the emotional distress caused to women, the unjust attribution of blame following an assault can deter women from reporting their experiences to the police and other agencies. In contrast with methodological research literature which highlights the powerlessness of the researched, such situations highlighted the relative powerlessness of the researcher, enforced by the etiquette of the interview (Lee 1999).

The 'privilege' of interpreting and representing participants' experiences

While my experience of conducting fieldwork challenges the conventional dichotomy of power relations between the researcher and the researched, arguably, interpretation and presentation of data is where the power of the researcher is most acute (Smith 1987). On the basis that researchers have the time, skills and resources to make sense of individual experiences within a historic and social context, Kelly et al. (1994, 37) contend that researchers occupy a position which makes the notion of an equal relationship with participants an illusion. While much early feminist research focused on giving women a voice by conducting research from the standpoint of women, this leaves the question of whose 'standpoint' is most valid when conflicting perspectives emerge – particularly, in this instance, between researchers and the researched. Sylvia Walby (1990, 18) problematises the uncritical acceptance of standpoint approaches:

> The limits of this approach to feminist methodology are the limits of the views of the women interviewed. Concepts and notions about structures outside their experience are ruled out. I think this is very problematic, since it is not clear why women's everyday experiences should be any less contaminated by patriarchal notions than are theories.

Walby's critique resonates with my own experience of collecting and gathering data from the young women in my study. That said, while it can be argued that individuals do not always have the knowledge and resources to be the best interpreters of their experiences (Maynard and Purvis 1994, 6), it could equally be argued that on the basis of an interview, neither do I as the researcher. Further questions existed on my part in relation to whether my own feminist interpretation of the data adequately represents the perspectives of the participants within this study. In this regard, I considered the task of interpreting the data and presenting findings based on my own understandings to be both a daunting responsibility and a privilege. In doing so,

I was mindful that my interpretation of participants' experiences may well differ from their own interpretations, and indeed those of other researchers. However, my interpretations were grounded in a thorough analysis of participants' views, and participants' interpretations of their experiences were also represented in their own words through the use of verbatim extracts from their interviews and focus groups. Crucially, I also sought to understand the basis of participants' views.

A noteworthy difference in my own interpretation of participants' experiences and their own interpretations lay with the greater tendency of participants to locate their experiences at an individual rather than a structural level. This is a particularly contentious issue. Highlighting women's structural disadvantage or feminist ideas such as the way in which women's fear of sexual violence acts as a measure of social control over women, for example, may have eroded notions of power and control which participants held at an individual level. In the context of the current study, it is not difficult to imagine why acknowledging the nature, extent and impact of sexual violence within our society is perhaps an unappealing prospect for individual women to confront. My own initial experience of doing so was in many ways liberating, although it was also overwhelming and at times I wished that I was 'blissfully ignorant' to this reality. Within my research, this tension was particularly apparent when participants compared their own behaviours with that of 'other' women:

> Jessica (interview): I think some women, obviously, dress with nothing and I think that makes them more easier as a target, like maybe they're easy. I think that targets them. But I definitely wouldn't wear a short skirt and a low cut top; I'd wear one or the other. That's just the way I am.

Most participants viewed themselves as safer than other women in bars and clubs, attributing this to their personal qualities and conduct, which in turn gave them a greater level of protection and safety while they socialised in bars and clubs. Given women's heightened level of fear in public space (Stanley 1990; Tulloch 2004), behaviours and understandings that give women the sense that they are in control of their environment and their own bodies have an understandable appeal, even if this entails viewing the behaviour of 'other' women in a negative light. It can also be argued that performing 'safety behaviours' in relation to clothing and alcohol consumption is in accordance with the performance of 'appropriate femininity' and as such, it allows young women to negotiate the risk of straying beyond conventional gender norms and expectations. While some of the participants in my study may have been aware of this dynamic, for others this conclusion may simply be rejected as no more than my interpretation of their position.

Conclusion

Reflexive approaches to criminological research are characterised by an appreciation of the power dynamics inherent within the research process. Within feminist criminological research literature particular attention has been given to how women, as research subjects and as a group charac- terised by relative powerlessness, can and should be empowered through the process of participating in research. This chapter has offered a critical and reflexive account of the contradictions and challenges encountered in conducting feminist research with young female research subjects, who are conventionally positioned as powerless.

In the current study, the identity of the researcher as a feminist directly influenced the focus, conduct and interpretation of the research, yet the identity of the researcher as a feminist was not revealed to participants for fear of adversely influencing participants' responses or alienating young female participants with 'unfashionable' feminist views. Minimising the feminist identity of the researcher also extended to the discomfort of observ- ing, but not challenging, the articulation of views that discriminated against other women. As a result of these challenges, it is argued that position- ing relationships between the researcher and the researched as a binary of power and powerlessness does not adequately grasp the complexity of power dynamics within the research process.

This chapter highlights the need for a nuanced approach to understand- ing how power relations between researchers and the researched operate in practice; this relationship is by no means constant or uniform across all stages of the research process. The insights detailed in this chapter sug- gest that power of the researcher is most evident in the interpretation and presentation of findings. Ultimately, the researcher has the capacity to rep- resent participants' experiences in a way that may differ from participants' own understandings of their accounts, thus calling into question the legit- imacy of the researcher's perspective. This is arguably where the need for reflexivity on behalf of the researcher is paramount. Rather than render researchers' accounts as lacking legitimacy unless they meet the unrealis- tic criterion of being devoid of researchers subjectivities, it is imperative that the influence of researchers' understandings, experiences, values and identities are made apparent. Embracing a truly reflexive approach within criminological research requires moving beyond descriptive reflections of difficulties encountered in the research process to producing analytical accounts that examine the social processes that underpin the accounts of both researchers and research participants alike. Such an approach must also be cognisant of the fluid and multi-directional operation of power within the research process, since criminological accounts that conceptualise research participants as either 'powerful' or 'powerless' may inadvertently represent a false dichotomy.

References

Alexander, V.D. (2001) 'Analysing Visual Materials'. In N. Gilbert (ed.) *Researching Social Life*, 2nd edn, London: Sage, pp.462–81.
Carlen, P. (1983) *Women's Imprisonment*, London: Routledge and Kegan Paul.
Chatterton, P. and Hollands, R. (2003) *Urban Nightscapes, Youth Cultures, Pleasure Spaces and Corporate Power*, London: Routledge.
Day, K., Gough, B. and McFadden, M. (2004) 'Warning! Alcohol Can Seriously Damage Your Feminine Health' *Feminist Media Studies* 4(2): 165–83.
Delamont, S. (2003) *Feminist Sociology*, London: Sage.
Finch, J. (1984) 'It's Great to Have Someone to Talk to: The Ethics and Politics of Interviewing Women'. In C. Bell and H. Roberts (eds) *Social Researching: Politics, Problems, Practice*, London: Routledge and Kegan Paul, pp.343–57.
Heidensohn, F. (1985) *Women and Crime*, Houndmills, UK: Macmillan.
Hey, V. (1986) *Patriarchy and Pub Culture*, London: Tavistock Publications Ltd.
Kelly, L., Burton, S. and Regan, L. (1994) 'Researching Women's Lives or Studying Women's Oppression? Reflections on What Constitutes Feminist Research'. In M. Maynard (ed.) *Researching Women's Lives from a Feminist Perspective*, London: Taylor Francis, pp.27–48.
Lee, R.M. (1999) *Doing Research on Sensitive Topics*, London: Sage.
Letherby G. (2002) 'Claims and Disclaimers: Knowledge, Reflexivity and Representation in Feminist Research' *Sociological Research Online* 6(4): http://www.socresonline.org.uk/6/4/letherby.html
Lyons, A.C. and Willot, S.A. (2008) 'Alcohol Consumption, Gender Identities and Women's Changing Social Positions' *Sex Roles* 59(9/10): 694–712.
Mason, G. and Stubbs, J. (2010) 'Feminist Approaches to Criminological Research' *Legal Studies Research Paper* No.10/36, the University of Sydney.
Mason, J. (1998) *Qualitative Research*, London: Sage.
Maynard, M. and Purvis, J. (1994) *Researching Women's Lives from a Feminist Perspective*, London: Taylor Francis.
McRobbie, A. (2004) 'Post-Feminism and Popular Culture' *Feminist Media Studies* 4(3): 255–64.
Millen, D. (1997) 'Some Methodological and Epistemological Issues Raised by Doing Feminist Research on Non-Feminist Women' *Sociological Research Online* 2(3): 1–20.
Oakley, A. (1981) 'Interviewing Women: A Contradiction in Terms'. In H. Roberts (ed.) *Doing Feminist Research*, London: Routledge and Kegan Paul.
Oakley A. (1998). 'Gender, Methodology and Peoples Ways of Knowing: Some Problems with Feminism and the Paradigm Debate in Social Science' *Sociology* 32(4): 707–31.
Plant, M. (1997) *Women and Alcohol: Contemporary and Historical Perspectives*, London: Free Association Books.
Ramazanoglu, C. and Holland, J. (2006) *Feminist Methodology: Challenges and Choices*, London: Sage.
Riley, S. (2001) 'Maintaining Power: Male Constructions of "Feminists" and "Feminist Values"' *Feminism and Psychology* 11(1): 55–78.
Skinner, T., Hester, M. and Malos, E. (eds) (2005) *Researching Gender Violence: Feminist Methodology in Action*, Cullompton: Willan.
Smart, C. (1976) *Women, Crime and Criminology: A Feminist Critique*, London: Routledge and Kegan Paul.

Smith, D. (1987) *The Everyday World as Problematic: A Feminist Sociology*, Milton Keynes: Open University Press.

Stanley, L. (1990) *Feminist Praxis: Research, Theory and Epistemology in Feminist Sociology*, London: Routledge.

Stanley, L. and Wise, S. (1993) *Breaking Out Again*, London: Routledge.

Tulloch, J. (2004) 'Youth, Leisure Travel and Fear of Crime: An Australian Study'. In W. Mitchell, R. Bunton and E. Green (eds) *Young People, Risk and Leisure: Constructing Identities in Everyday Life*, Basingstoke, Hampshire: Palgrave MacMillan, pp.115–28.

Walby, S. (1990) *Theorizing Patriarchy*, Oxford: Basil Blackwell Ltd.

Whitehead, A. (1976) 'Sexual Antagonsim in Herefordshire'. In D. Barker and S. Allen (eds) *Dependence and Exploitation in Work and Marriage*, London: Longman, pp.169–203.

Wilkinson, S. (1999) 'How Useful Are Focus Groups in Feminist Research?' In R.S. Barbour and J. Kitzinger (eds) *Developing Focus Group Research: Politics, Theory and Practice*, London: Sage, pp.64–78.

Winlow, S. and Hall, S. (2006) *Violent Night: Urban Leisure and Contemporary Culture*, New York: Berg.

Wise, S. (1987) 'A Framework for Discussing Ethical Issues in Feminist Research: A Review of the Literature' *Studies in Sexual Politics* 19: 47–88.

Wise, S. and Stanley, L. (2003) 'Review Article: "Looking Back and Looking Forward: Some Recent Feminist Sociology Reviewed"' *Sociological Research Online* 8(3): http://www.socresonline.org.uk/8/4/wise.html

8

Power, Pregnancy and Prison: The Impact of a Researcher's Pregnancy on Qualitative Interviews with Women Prisoners

Emily Luise Hart

Introduction

This chapter explores how a researcher's pregnancy impacted on a series of qualitative semi-structured interviews with women prisoners. I will argue that the utilising of a more general feminist approach which is sympathetic to the needs of women and which has the notion of reflexivity and a commitment to less exploitative research at its centre was in the case of this research preferable to adopting a full feminist standpoint. Feminist standpoint theory reflects the view that 'women (or feminists) occupy a social location that affords them/us a privileged access to social phenomena' (Longino 1993, 201). In *Money, Sex and Power* (1983), Nancy Hartstock claimed that it was women's unique standpoint within the social world that provided the justification for feminists' claims at truth. In the research on which this chapter is based, commonality was certainly found between myself and the women prisoners in terms of both our gender and our experiences surrounding children, pregnancy and motherhood and this enhanced the research process. There were, however, other differences that our shared gender could not overcome, for example, in terms of class, power and status that meant our experiences of the social world were poles apart. I could not therefore claim to have epistemological privilege as other inequalities between us had to be considered and the approach used here therefore, while feminist in nature, stops short of a full feminist standpoint. This chapter will demonstrate how the researcher's pregnancy and reflections on this in the field led to the generation of sensitive data and access to particular insights that may not otherwise have been possible. For example, discussions around prisoners' histories of abuse may not have been divulged to a male researcher. In addition, a more equitable distribution of power between the researcher and the interviewee, a common endeavour of much feminist research, was facilitated by discussions around my visible pregnancy.

The research aimed to investigate how women prisoners, in the final months of a long-term sentence, planned and prepared for their release. For the last 9 months of the fieldwork I was pregnant with my first child. The fieldwork was undertaken over a 13-month period at a closed women's prison in England. Informed consent was secured with all the prisoners involved in the study; they were told that their accounts would be published and pseudonyms have been used in order to protect their identities. Analysis highlighted that women prisoners had significant motivation and desire to desist from crime post release but their attempts to plan for release were hindered by a responsibilisation discourse that ran throughout the prison and by a severe lack of all forms of capital (social, cultural, economic and symbolic). This resulted in many women being released with little support in place to help them achieve their aims of a crime-free life in the future. Interviews were conducted with both prisoners and members of staff; consequently the implications of my pregnancy on the research and in particular how the prisoners would respond to me had to be considered. I was anxious about the pregnancy and how its visibility would impact on the women prisoners I was interviewing as some had had children forcibly adopted away and all those who were mothers (63 per cent of women interviewed) were separated from their children through incarceration. I was worried as to how my very visible pregnancy would make them feel; however, I was surprised to discover that it had the opposite effect. Pregnancy was instead a shared experience that the women and I held. The women would compare notes and offer advice and it provided a way for them to tell me about their children and families. Reich (2003, 354–55) also had anxiety over how her pregnancy would impact on the women and families she was researching: 'I was afraid how my pregnancy body would influence my access to information whether it was cruel to be pregnant as I attended the removal of other people's children, whether it would limit me'.

The notion of reflexivity is a central element in feminist research (Gelsthorpe 1990). It is grounded in the experiences of both the researcher and the researched and having the ability to analytically look at their locations within the research process. The notion of reflexivity is grounded in the experiences of both the researcher and the researched and the 'ability to turn the analytical lens on oneself' (Mason 2002, 193). It is necessary to recognise the importance of the respondents but also the researcher's personal experiences in the data collection process, as this is central to the concept of reflexivity. The beliefs, experiences and values of those involved are an important part of the results and the recognition of the central role of issues around class, age, culture, sexuality, race, ethnicity and gender enables us to examine and study them as part of the findings.

This chapter contributes to the debates around reflexive praxis in feminist criminological research by examining the impact of pregnancy on qualitative research, an underexamined area in the criminological literature. It further demonstrates the importance of recognising the multiple experiences of both the researcher and the researched on the data construction process. Despite the overarching commitment from feminist scholarly work to produce useful knowledge that can influence material and social change, it is clear that doing feminism or more specifically feminist criminological research is not a unified endeavour.

Feminist criminologists have extensively debated the issues around feminist research methods and also the specific questions in relation to the study of women prisoners. For example, Smart (1990) takes a postmodern feminist view and argues that the study of female prisoners results in an inevitable acceptance of the ideological state definition of what it means to be a female prisoner. Others such as Daly (1997) point out that feminist researchers must recognise that the term 'woman' is culturally constructed and that it alone does not account for the variety of ways different women experience their social worlds in terms of age, culture, class, sexuality and so on. Indeed, Carlen and Tchaikovsky (1996) state that in order to make successful policy interventions with women prisoners it is vital that the differences (history of abuse, economic marginalisation, multiple mental health concerns) that shape women prisoners' and women ex-prisoners' experiences are recognised.

Furthermore it can be argued that patriarchal world views must be challenged by giving women a voice and a chance to present how they experience their social world, that they can and should be able to, when given the opportunity, speak for themselves through the utilisation of qualitative, sensitive and women-centred research methods. Giving those at the margins of society a voice and considering their views can provide a source of insight for feminist researchers (Van Wormer 2009).

Feminist research does, however, recognise the inability of the researchers to separate themselves from the social world which they study. Being reflexive, open and examining the research process and the location of ourselves within it is a key component of the feminist researcher's aim whether in criminology or the wider social sciences and it is this concept that is at the centre of this research.

The following section will discuss the reasons behind the utilisation of a more general feminist approach for this research and will outline why signing up to a full feminist standpoint was not appropriate in this instance. Following on from this I will examine the process by which a rapport was established between myself and the prisoners within the qualitative interview setting. In addition I will examine the process of developing trust between the researcher and the researched and outline the importance of this approach when interviewing on sensitive topics.

A feminist standpoint or a feminist approach?

This section will briefly outline standpoint theory but go on to discuss why this research utilised a broadly feminist approach rather than signing up to a full feminist standpoint. Feminist standpoint theory starts from the premise that that women's position in society as an oppressed group provides an epistemological vantage point from which to view women's social reality (Hartstock 1983; Harding 1986, 1987; Hekman 1997; Smith 1997). Standpoint theory begins with the notion that the less powerful in society experience a different social reality as a result of their oppression. Nancy Hartstock (1987) argued that women's lives provide a standpoint from which possibilities for overcoming oppression can be viewed. In addition some who advocate a feminist standpoint insist that connections must be made with the feminist struggle through activism, lobbying and advocacy. Cain (1990) argues that feminist researchers should engage in feminist struggles themselves in order to further their understanding of, and produce an authentic account of, a feminist standpoint.

The idea of women telling their truths is a central theme of feminist standpoint approaches. It sees the perspective of women as a standpoint – women's oppressed position in the social world provides a fuller understanding of social life rather than the potentially biased position of men can. This approach provides a 'standpoint – a morally preferable grounding for our interpretations and explanations of nature and social life' (Harding 1986, 26). It sees the feminist researcher as being able to access the real social reality as the oppressed can see the social world for what it really is. Epistemological privilege is gained not only by one's own social experience, for example, based on gender but also in relation to, for example, disability. This approach advocates that the researcher (as a woman or as a disabled person) has inside knowledge and a privileged view of the social world over others (men, non-disabled). Therefore the way women experience social life gives them a unique insight into how society works. One of the strongest criticisms levied at feminist standpoint was the notion of privileged knowledge. However, the theory has been redefined in an attempt to reconstitute it from the perspective of difference (Hekman 1997). Hekman goes on to point out that women occupy and inhabit many different realities and standpoint theory has had to accept that no one truth can explain everything. While it sees women as having certain experiences in common, it recognises that there are also significant differences between groups. Stanley and Wise (1990) argue that not all women experience the world in the same way and support the view that feminist research needs to look at different standpoints and must not attempt to provide one truth or a single set of knowledge. Instead, there should be a plurality of feminist theories emanating from the study of a variety of oppressed groups.

However, despite the arguments for it, I do not adhere to the stand-point approach that suggests my individual experience as a member of an oppressed group gives me epistemological privilege and increased knowledge and understanding over others. While there were some shared experiences with the women prisoners based on our gender, the way in which I experienced my gendered place in the social world was different than the interviewees, for example, due to differences in power and status. Harding (1987) explains in *Feminism and Methodology: Social Science Issues* that the beliefs and values of the researcher are an important part of the results and affect them no less than those of the scientific androcentric researcher. It is the fact that they are recognised and examined rather than denied, as in the case of traditional methodologies, means they can be studied and analysed as part of the evidence in criminological research. Thus, Harding argues: 'introducing the "subjective" element into the analysis in fact increases the objectivity of the research and decreases the "objectivism" which hides this kind of evidence from the public' (1987, 9). This reflexive 'turning of the lens on oneself' or, in other words, recognising the importance of my own personal experiences (in this case pregnancy) in relation to the research process, is illustrated in the following section where I describe the process by which a rapport was established with participants, how my pregnancy aided the discussion of sensitive topics and also the trust the women prisoners afforded me.

Carlen and Worrall (2004, 195) argue: 'whether or not the researcher speaks from the standpoint of her subject should depend upon the research objective'. As stated above, standpoint approaches emphasise how different women experience the social world in a variety of ways and call for a multitude of theories to explain the situation for women. My research demonstrates how, while pregnancy was a shared experience that I had with many of the women prisoners and was an experience that aided the generation of data, the way in which I experienced pregnancy was vastly different to many of those women due to differences around areas such as class, ethnicity, power and status. I was aware that the women being interviewed came from backgrounds characterised by abuse, poverty, substance misuse, below average educational attainment and many with multiple mental health concerns. I was a white, middle-class, educated woman who also held a set of prison keys (demonstrating a very literal and physical power differential). These differences had the potential to create an insurmountable barrier between myself and the women prisoners. While I may have had commonality with the women in terms of our gender and impending motherhood, this was not enough to change the other glaring differences that led to me experiencing my gendered place in society in a very different way to the prisoners. The idea that this small piece of common ground would grant me greater insight and a clearer understanding of what these women were experiencing leads to the potential devaluing of the respondents' stories. Being a pregnant woman did, however, aid the research process as discussed below and it is recognised that my gender and status enabled me to become more empathetic to the women. In addition I became aware that my views and opinions tended to 'side' with the prisoners rather than the staff.

My approach therefore is a general feminist one in that it contains the three themes outlined by Gelsthorpe (1990) that are required to make a research project feminist in nature. First, the research topic is relevant and sympathetic to the needs of women. Second, a feminist approach has a preference for qualitative methods. Lastly and crucially for this paper, a feminist approach advocates more reflexive and less exploitative research. Oakley (1981) argues that there is a distinctly feminist research method and a feminist way of conducting interviews. This involves being as open as possible with interviewees, making the research more collaborative and ensuring the interviewees were not exploited. Oakley (1981) believes that not only is this approach better for the subjects but also it allows the researcher to get closer to the viewpoints of the women she interviews. As I will outline, the trust and rapport that I was able to establish with many of the women was developed out of a shared and common experience which enabled the women to talk to me about a more personal topic. In addition, the interviews were conducted in a way that meant the interviewees had some control over the process and I, as the researcher, was as open with the women as prison regulations allowed. Reinharz (1992) argues that interviewing is consistent with the aim of avoiding control over others and developing a connection with interviewees. So, being pregnant and having (in my case impending) motherhood in common did not give me epistemological privilege, because we experienced pregnancy and motherhood in such vastly different ways, but did in fact open unexpected metaphorical doors throughout the research process, which aided the generation of rich qualitative data.

In this research the women's stories and voices were central to the findings. Their interpretations of their social world provided a moving account of the difficulties and struggles they faced. The research aimed to develop as full an understanding of and answers to the central research questions as possible. However, while the prisoners' accounts were faithfully reproduced, these descriptions alone did not answer the overall research questions. A further interpretive reading of the data was therefore made by me with the aim of going beyond description and to instead explain some of the reasons why the women found themselves in the positions they did in relation to resettlement. It is accepted that my own location within the social world had a bearing on the reading of the data and that being a (pregnant) woman myself is part of this. The standpoint approach outlined above can be useful if the aim of the research is to describe women's day-to-day experiences of prison life. The problem with this approach as far as this research is concerned is that this study aimed to go beyond a description of prison life and resettlement. It aimed to *explain* potential reasons why the women face such difficulty in their planning and the links this has to desistance via theoretical constructs. Therefore simply speaking from the standpoint of the prisoners was, in this case, not enough. A close adherence to standpoint logic could have been an obstruction to possible insights and theory drawn and developed from the data.

The impact of pregnancy on the interview experience

Rapport

I endeavoured in the interviews to create a relationship that was informal and friendly, aiming to establish a rapport with the women based on things we had in common. The topic of children and pregnancy aided this process. In her research with women awaiting trial, Wincup (1999, 121) comments on the ease with which she managed to establish a rapport with female prisoners based on things they found to have in common 'no matter how small'. Prior to the interviews I experienced anxiety about how I would manage to develop a rapport. I was apprehensive about whether I could create and nurture a friendly, informal and trusting environment in which the women would feel comfortable as the power differentials between me and the prisoners were so clear. Power differences in terms of class, education, income and of course freedom, plus the very real fact that I was in visible possession of a set of keys (I always tried to keep these as hidden as possible). However, the way in which the interviewees responded to my enquiries was helped by the fact that I was also a woman. Despite the gulf between us in terms of power and status, there was common ground to be found on the basis of our gender. The pregnancy was the most obvious example of this, but it helped in a number of ways. First, it provided an effective icebreaker at the start of the interview. I was commonly greeted by the women with enquiries after my health and questions about how I was managing with working while pregnant and when my due date was. This made the setting far more relaxed and informal than if I had been relying on my own, often stilted, attempts to start a conversation. Second, the pregnancy gave the women confidence to talk about a subject most of them had knowledge and experience of: pregnancy, birth and motherhood:

> Chanice: Oh! How many weeks are you?
> Emily: About 31. I'm feeling pretty tired.
> Chanice: Oh God, just wait 'til the last couple of weeks, I could hardly walk I was so massive. You're not really tired now... just wait until you have the baby.
>
> (Chanice, 25 years old, January 2008)

Training I had undertaken at the start of my research in the prison and advice given to me from prison staff had taught me that disclosing personal information about myself to prisoners was not good practice as it can create a security risk for both staff and prisoners alike. It heightens the risk to staff on the outside but also puts prisoners in a potentially vulnerable position as they are left open to manipulation and exploitation, as this type of information can be valuable to some. While this is reasonable, it makes not only the establishment of but also the ongoing development of a rapport with prisoners difficult, particularly when generating qualitative data where the aim is to minimise the power differences as much as possible and where a non-exploitative, feminist approach is being utilised. My pregnancy allowed me to hold a conversation about a more personal issue without divulging personal information. It enabled me to feel I was giving something of myself to the process and presenting myself as something other than a member of staff with clear power over the women:

> Jude: You gonna have it in the hospital? Best in there as it's your first one. They'll give you help with feeding and stuff before you go home.
> Emily: Yeah, I'm quite worried about labour so I thought the hospital would be best, not sure my husband would cope if I was at home!
> Jude: You're lucky to have the dad there, I was on my own, my mum was there but it's not the same...
>
> (Jude, 27 years old, September 2008)

The pregnancy enabled the women to ask me questions relating to whether I was prepared, what plans I had made for the birth, childcare, work and extended family support. All the prisoners interviewed were, however, careful to avoid more specific questions about my partner, where I lived and so on knowing I could not answer these. Overall this gave the women a degree of control and power in the interview setting making it less one sided. I was also happy to be able to reveal some things about myself that did not breach security protocol. This was an area where the women had more knowledge than me, having been through pregnancy and motherhood themselves. They offered advice on a variety of issues from brands of nappies to benefit entitlements. For example, one interviewee enquired: 'Have you had your money for fruit and veg? You know you can apply for it? Ask your midwife, I think she will have the form' (Anna, 32 years old, May 2008). This appeared to give the women a sense of self-worth as I listened and thanked them for their insights and advice. Crucially they divulged information during the interviews that I would otherwise not have been able to access had I not managed to quickly develop this kind of rapport with them.

Trust

Finch (1984) argues that qualitative methods can engender a high level of trust among interviewees and as a result researchers have a responsibility to make sure this is not abused in any way. Gaining the trust of the prisoners was key to the relationship. Indeed, Lee (1999) argues that in order to establish trust the researcher needs not only privacy and confidentiality but also a non-condemnatory attitude. It was therefore very important to support interviewees. Opportunities were provided at the end of each interview for the women to ask questions and for them to add anything else they felt they had not had the chance to say. My contact details were also left with all women and assurances given that if they wanted to talk through any further points at a later date when they had had a chance to reflect, they were welcome to do so. Again, the fact that I was a pregnant woman was relevant. Reich (2003) notes that pregnant women are not seen as threatening. While most social interactions are gendered, this is heightened when visibly pregnant as this state invokes images of soft, caring, asexual and nurturing women. While these stereotypes would anger me in everyday life, the potential they provided for the women in the field to trust me and view me as non-threatening was important. Some of the women had shocking experiences with female members of staff:

> I've been assaulted by a member of staff in November last year ... anyway I said to her I'm going, because you are getting my temper up, and I walked away. As I walked away all I can remember is her throwing me to the floor, and going into a fit and her foot being on my back, that's all I can remember. I've got epilepsy ... When I came round I was full of bruises from head to toe, I was naked, she took my clothes off me, threw me in a cell down the block, no knickers on or anything, and it was the time of the month. The room was freezing; all I had around me was a blanket ... she got charged.
>
> (Abbey, 21 years old, April 2008)

Many of the women had negative experiences with the men in their lives – from abusive fathers to violent partners and authoritarian prison officers: 'My dad used to beat us all, all the time, and my mum, she got it too. I still think about it, you know? It never leaves me' (Tracy Ann, 39 years old, April 2008). The ability of many of these women to trust a male researcher could be limited. Some women disclosed information about abusive relationships that I am certain they found less intimidating to communicate to a pregnant woman.

My pregnancy also worked in other unexpected ways that was not simply about the process of interview or the eliciting of information. For example, Christine, who had had her twins removed from her at birth and placed up for adoption, repeatedly asked me how I would feel if someone took my baby away. This clearly would have been an unlikely line of questioning with another researcher who was either (a) male or (b) non-pregnant. Again this is linked to the idea of generating shared and common knowledge and understanding between the interviewees and me. My pregnancy allowed insight into the thoughts and feeling of the women prisoners that I would not have otherwise accessed.

Sensitive topics

Gathering information about the prisoners' family life, children and personal relationships was an integral part of the results as existing research has demonstrated the central role these factors play in women's desistance (Graham and Bowling 1995; Leverentz 2006; Barry 2007). It was vital to garner as much information as possible on the past, present and future situation for these women in terms of their children, partners and family links as this was essential in gaining an understanding of the women's resettlement plans. These are sensitive topic areas and I was acutely aware of the potential to upset and distress the women in the interview setting. Lee (1999) notes that interviewing on sensitive topics can cause significant distress and needs to be managed carefully. During two interviews the interviewees became upset and I made the decision to completely change the topic under discussion. In both cases the distress was caused by talking about their children that they had been forced to put up for adoption. I personally found these instances distressing and felt guilty that the interview I had instigated had caused the women in question anguish. I had expected some of the women to become upset on occasion and I had also anticipated that my visible pregnancy would in fact make it harder for the women to disclose aspects of their own, chaotic family lives. However, the opposite appeared to be true with the women in fact referring to my ability to empathise because of my impending motherhood: 'Imagine not being able to see your baby. I've got a son aged 14 who is with my mum at the moment, he is still my baby. I've seen him once since I've been in this prison' (Sharon, 30 years old, April 2008).

While it is almost certain that many of the women found it a positive experience to have someone show an interest in their lives and to have an opportunity to talk about issues that concerned them, I did feel constant guilt that I had caused them to rake over distressing memories. However, the relationship I had developed with many of the women meant they freely disclosed information about extremely personal and traumatic events:

> I was in a domestic relationship with the father of my eldest which was violent all the way through. I took drugs to block everything out. I lost my kids because my eldest was standing at the top of the stairs and he actually booted her in the mouth at the age of two and a half so Social Services took her off me, saying I was neglecting my kids. I finished with him, then found out I was pregnant again with another baby, which he actually booted out of me, I think I was about 20 weeks and I found out the sex of the baby was a boy, which hurt me more than anything.
>
> (Abbey, 21 years old, April 2008)

I believe my pregnancy enabled Abbey to know that I understood how that would feel and that she was telling someone that could empathise with what happened to her. At the time of this interview I was around 26 weeks pregnant so not much further along than when Abbey lost her baby. I endeavoured to be as understanding and supportive as possible but found it hard to respond, as I was very aware of my limitations. I was not a trained counsellor or criminal justice professional and had to remember this when asked for reassurances by prisoners. Due to my pregnancy and the fact that I was a woman I did find myself basing my responses on topics and issues around my gender.

Conclusion: Reflections on my status and pregnancy

Pregnancy bodies are public. People feel free to comment upon, touch and advise on the pregnancy and ensuing parenthood. The behaviour of the women prisoners I interviewed was no different to people in general. While I found an uninvited hand reaching for my bump rather uncomfortable (from people in general, not female prisoners I might add), on the whole the attention focused on my changing physical state did not irritate me. In the field therefore my pregnancy allowed the women to feel more comfortable in my presence. As stated, pregnant women are not seen as threatening and the pregnancy created shared knowledge and understanding, a common experience. Letherby (2003) reflects on how her experience of miscarriage meant that the women she was interviewing found it easier to talk to her as she would understand how they felt about their own miscarriages. Being pregnant gave me an unexpected level of credibility. I was a woman who understood the complex feelings and emotions around having children and therefore would be able to empathise with and understand what the women were telling me. It was vital in establishing and developing a rapport and as outlined above, my pregnancy provided the perfect icebreaker and meant that both the interviewee and I as the researcher were more relaxed from the outset.

A general feminist approach employed in this study advocates more reflexive and less exploitative research. This chapter has therefore contributed to discussions of reflexivity in criminological research by demonstrating the importance of considering reflexivity in qualitative interviewing with vulnerable women prisoners and how the individual researcher and her personal experiences play a crucial role in the process of data generation and analysis. The utilising of feminist standpoint theory for this research was not appropriate as while I had commonality with the women in terms of gender and motherhood, these were not sufficient to surmount the other differences and inequalities that led to me and the prisoners experiencing our gendered places in society in very different ways. In particular, this chapter focuses on the impact of a feminist researcher's pregnancy in qualitative interviews, a topic that has received very little attention within criminological or social science literature. It examined how the recognition of my status as a pregnant woman by participants had to be included in the analysis, as the formation of a trusting relationship with the interviewees was influenced and enhanced by my visible pregnancy – a gendered embodiment of my status, sexuality and social roles.

Finally, this chapter has made a contribution to discussions of power/ powerlessness and reflexivity. Locating oneself as an integral part of the data generation process and recognising and analysing the impact the researcher's own social location has on the data has in the case of this study served to diminish power divides between the interviewee and interviewer. My pregnancy allowed discussions to open up based on a shared experience and gave the women a feeling of self-worth; they felt they had something to contribute not only to the interview situation but to me as a woman. They had greater knowledge and experience than me on the topics of mother-hood, pregnancy and birth which gave them an element of authority and some degree of control and ownership of the interview setting, crucial in feminist criminological research.

References

Barry, M. (2007) 'The Transitional Pathways of Young Female Offenders: Towards a Non-Offending Lifestyle'. In R. Sheehan, G. McIvor and C. Trotter (eds) *What Works with Women Offenders*, Collumpton: Willan, pp.23–39.

Cain, M. (1990) 'Realist Philosophy and Standpoint Epistemologies or Feminist Criminology as a Successor Science'. In L. Gelsthorpe and A. Morris (eds) *Feminist Perspectives in Criminology*, Buckingham: Open University Press, pp.124–40.

Carlen, P. and Tchaikovsky, C. (1996) 'Women's Imprisonment at the End of the Twentieth Century: Legitimacy, Realities and Utopias'. In R. Matthews and P. Francis (eds) *Prisons 2000: An International Perspective on the Current State and Future Imprisonment*, New York: St Martins Press, pp.201–18.

Carlen, P. and Worrall, A. (2004) *Analysing Women's Imprisonment*, Collumpton: Willan.

Daly, K. (1997) 'Different Ways of Conceptualising Sex/Gender in Feminist Theory and Their Implications for Criminology' *Theoretical Criminology* 1(1): 25–51.

Finch, J. (1984) 'It's Great to Have Someone to Talk To: Ethics and Politics of Interviewing Women'. In C. Bell and H. Roberts (eds) *Social Researching: Politics, Problems, Practice*, London: Routledge, pp.70–87.

Gelsthorpe, L. (1990) 'Feminist Methodologies in Criminology: A New Approach or Old Wine in New Bottles?' In L. Gelsthorpe and A. Morris (eds) *Feminist Perspectives in Criminology*, Buckingham: Open University Press, pp.89–106.

Graham, J. and Bowling, B. (1995) *Young People and Crime*, London: HMSO.

Harding, S. (1986) *The Science Question in Feminism*, Milton Keynes: Open University Press.

Harding, S. (1987) *Feminism and Methodology: Social Science Issues*, Milton Keynes: Open University Press.

Hartstock, N. (1983) *Money, Sex and Power*, New York: Longman.

Hartstock, N. (1987) 'Rethinking Modernism: Minority vs. Majority Theories' *Cultural Critique* 7: 187–206.

Hekman, S. (1997) 'Truth and Method: Feminist Standpoint Revisited' *Signs: Journal of Women in Culture and Society*, 22(2): 341–65.

Lee, R. (1999) *Doing Research on Sensitive Topics*, London: Sage

Letherby, G. (2003) *Feminist Research in Theory and Practice*, Buckingham: Open University Press.

Leverentz, A.M. (2006) 'The Love of a Good Man? Romantic Relationships as a Source of Support or Hindrance for Female Ex-Offenders' *Journal of Research in Crime and Delinquency* 43(4): 459–88.

Longino, H. (1993) 'Subjects, Power and Knowledge: Description and Prescription in Feminist Philosophies of Science'. In L. Alcoff and E. Potter (eds) *Feminist Epistemologies*, New York: Routledge, pp.101–20.

Mason, J. (2002) *Qualitative Researching*, 2nd edn, London: Sage.

Oakley, A. (1981) 'Interviewing Women: A Contradiction in Terms'. In H. Roberts (ed.) *Doing Feminist Research*, London: Routledge.

Reich, J. (2003) 'Pregnant with Possibility: Reflections on Embodiment, Access and Inclusion in Field Research' *Qualitative Sociology* 26(3): 351–67.

Reinharz, S. (1992) *Feminist Methods in Social Research*, New York: Oxford University Press.

Smart, C. (1990) 'Feminist Approaches to Criminology or Post Modern Woman Meets Atavistic Man'. In L. Gelsthorpe and A. Morris (eds) *Feminist Perspectives in Criminology*, Buckingham: Open University Press, pp.70–84.

Smith, D. (1997) 'Comment on Hekman's "Truth and Method: Feminist Standpoint Theory Revisited"' *Signs* 22 (21): 392–97.

Stanley, L. and Wise, S. (1990) 'Method, Methodology and Epistemology in Feminist Research Process'. In S. Wise (ed.) *Feminist Praxis: Research Theory and Epistemology in Feminist Sociology*, London: Routledge, pp.20–60.

Van Wormer, K. (2009) 'Restorative Justice as Social Justice for Victims of Gendered Violence: A Standpoint Feminist Perspective' *Social Work* 54(2): 107–17.

Wincup, E. (1999) 'Researching Women Awaiting Trial: Dilemmas of Feminist Ethnography'. In F. Brookman, L. Noakes and E. Wincup (eds) *Qualitative Research in Criminology*, Aldershot: Ashgate, pp.112–29.

9
Writing the Ethnographic Self in Research on Marginalised Youths and Masculinity

Elias le Grand

Introduction: Reflexivity and the ethnographic self

In the wake of the so-called reflexive turn in ethnographic research, researchers have increasingly reflected on their emotions, identity-work and roles during fieldwork, often through first-person accounts of their emotions, thoughts and behaviour (Coffey 1999; Lumsden 2009; Venkatesh 2013) or through the respondents' constructions of the ethnographer (Venkatesh 2002). These developments can be traced to the 1970s and onwards when feminist scholars and critical theorists critiqued the positivist notion of an impartial, objective view 'from nowhere', and instead argued that all research is made from certain standpoints, with certain preconceptions, values and interests, which fundamentally shape the process and product of research (Harding 1987; cf. Haraway 1988). In anthropology and the field of ethnographic research this led to a crisis of representation (Marcus and Fischer 1999 [1986]) as the capacity of the researcher to 'objectively' represent the culture of the researched was fundamentally questioned. This, in turn, led to a crisis of legitimation. The argument is that without any value-free standpoint from which to view the world and no way of gaining impartial knowledge about it, there is no way to legitimise the truth of one's research findings (Denzin and Lincoln 1994).

In response to this double crisis of representation and legitimation, subsequent researchers have deployed self-reflexivity as a methodological tool to account for the situated and embodied nature of knowledge production. Here writing the ethnographic self means that the fieldworker is present and visible in the analysis. This serves to increase the transparency and therefore also the legitimacy of research. It also confers responsibility on the researcher to make the analysis he/she makes (Haraway 1988). Moreover, rather than a form of narcissistic navel-gazing (a common critique of autoethnography), writing the self in ethnographic fieldwork can increase our knowledge of the social world under study (Coffey 1999; Newmahr 2008; Venkatesh 2013). In a similar way, accounting for how the respondents interpreted the researcher can also inform ethnographic understanding (Venkatesh 2002).

But despite these important developments, there is a lack of research in the field of crime and deviance incorporating the researcher's self in ethnographic research. It is only recently where the latter has been given a more central role (Venkatesh 2006; Lumsden 2009, Chapter 21 this volume; Phillips and Earle 2010; Poulton, Chapter 6 this volume). Contributing to this research agenda, the aim of this chapter is to examine how writing the ethnographic self in research on young marginalised working-class masculinity can be epistemologically productive. In so doing, I draw on ethnographic fieldwork in 'Satellite Town',[1] a deprived area located on the edges of South London.

The ethnographic self will be explored from the perspective of both the researcher and the respondents. To this end the discussion will centre on an incident involving myself and a young man and his friends. Exploring the relationship between the middle-class ethnographer and the young working-class respondents, the contention of this chapter is that the reflexive analysis of the researcher's identity-work and the roles in which he is positioned during fieldwork can contribute to our understanding of the relationship between class and masculinity among young, marginalised men.

Performing masculinity in Satellite Town

The material discussed in this chapter draws on ethnographic fieldwork in Satellite Town where I lived for five months and conducted voluntary work at two youth clubs, on and off for over a year (October 2007–December 2008). Access to the youth clubs was gained through the proprietors of both youth clubs. I presented myself as a Swedish postgraduate student doing research on British youth culture and style. During fieldwork I also regularly tried to inform youths visiting the youth clubs about my role there.

Satellite Town is located on the suburban periphery of South London and has a population of around 21,500. It consists of two large council estates, founded in the interwar period and the 1960s, respectively. Due to its geographical location and poor transport services, the area has a long history of isolation. Satellite Town is a predominantly working-class and ethnically white area, although with significant black African and Caribbean minorities. This was also the case among the respondents in the youth clubs. The area scores high on indicators of deprivation (DETR 2000) and has high rates of unemployment, low rates of economic productivity and single-parent households as well as a large proportion of council house estates (Office for National Statistics 2001). This is tied to a stigmatised place identity. Thus while the area has lower crime rates than London as a whole, in outsider's accounts (e.g. the local media) it is associated with violent crime such as stabbings and muggings (see le Grand 2014).

Such negative images were partly expressed by the young respondents during my fieldwork. Although many respondents expressed a positive sense of community in knowing 'everyone' in the area and also claimed that they felt safe there, many of them also associated Satellite Town with violence, muggings and social problems. The area was conceived as a 'rough' and dangerous place with gangs and other people 'causing trouble' or 'terrorising Satellite Town'. Or as Katie put it: 'everybody seems to have an attitude problem'. Some of the young people, particularly males, displayed the 'attitude' Katie was talking about, which can be conceptualised as different ways of putting up a 'tough' front. These were often inconsistent with common rules of propriety, such as refraining from showing deference. One way of putting up a front was to adopt a 'cool' stance, of displaying what is usually coded as distance, reserve or boredom, but as we will see, also more aggressive or hostile forms of display. During fieldwork in the youth clubs, this could involve bullying boys with lower status or challenging the authority of youth workers. In what follows I will explore such challenges of authority by discussing a series of interactions that took place during fieldwork in one of the youth clubs between me and Nicky, a 14-year-old white working-class boy.

As will become apparent, during the incident with Nicky I came to perform masculinity very much like him and other young men in Satellite Town. As a consequence, I overstepped the professional role of researcher or youth worker. This reflected a general aspect of how the fieldwork affected the ethnographic self. In some contexts I started to perform, often routinely and largely unconsciously, in some respects according to the masculinely coded behaviour prevalent in Satellite Town.

The first I remember of Nicky was during one session when I saw a boy with short-cropped dark blonde hair in a fringe, wearing a bright red hooded jumper, tracksuit bottoms, trainers and a small shoulder bag (popular among many boys at the time). He was all smiles while riding a mini bike from the entrance through to the emergency exit at the other end of the youth club. After the session, during the debrief, someone in the staff said that his name was Nicky and that he was known to be 'difficult'. I wrote this down in my fieldnotes and did not think much more about it. It was some time later that I started to notice him more. He used to come in with a few other boys in his own age group, particularly Dave, Dazza and Leon.

I have my first prolonged face-to-face interaction with Nicky before one session. I arrive early at the youth club and no one is at the staff entrance, so I go to the main entrance to ring the doorbell. Outside the entrance I see a group of five young people in their mid-teens. It's Nicky and two other boys, one of them the tall and slender boy called Dazza, and two girls, Mel and Lianne.

The youths immediately approach me, with Nicky taking the lead. But theirs are not friendly expressions of deference. Rather, they spread out around me and comment on my appearance, ask me things and joke with me in a way that surprises me by its intensity and nature. 'Are you gay?' one of the girls asks me. 'You asking me if I'm gay? Why are you so interested? Are *you* gay?' I answer, hoping to challenge and embarrass them. But they are completely unfazed and in a completely matter-of-fact tone, they provocatively say: 'Yeah, we are lesbians', then turn their faces towards each other and make a movement as if to kiss, though they never actually do so. Then Lianne recalls an evening some weeks ago when she and Mel poked me and another youth worker on the legs and behinds with pool cues (they were eventually thrown out by the proprietor): 'Didn't I poke you with a stick?' 'Yeah, you did', I answer in what I feel is an easy-going way. She and the others laugh.

I ring the doorbell, but nothing happens. I'm surprised; the doorbell should work. Dazza, who has been quiet so far, points towards a section at the wall with a neutral expression and calmly tells me: 'The door bell's there'. Easily fooled, I look to where he is pointing, searching for a door, obviously without finding one.

Meanwhile, the verbal attacks continue. Lianne asks me if I'm sore in the bum after having been poked with the pool cue. This is the moment when the jokes turn sour. I am surprised and taken aback by what to me is the malevolence of the verbal attack, and its unprovoked nature. From my original easy-going manner, I now try to maintain an adult stance, taking the role of the morally righteous youth worker. I say: 'If you don't treat others with respect, you can't expect to be treated with respect'. Hearing this, Nicky laughs and turns his face away with a mocking smile and says: 'Oh come on! Don't give me that!' as if to emphasise how hollow and pathetic my words are.

As I realise that I won't get into the youth club, I turn around to go back to the fire entrance to see if anyone with a key has arrived. 'What? You're going home?' someone says to my back as I'm about to walk out. I ignore her. 'Yeah, fuck off', Nicky says in a low voice, barely audible. I stop and turn around to face him. 'Look, maybe you shouldn't come tonight [to the youth club]', I say seriously. To my surprise, his 'mask' falls – his 'cool' and aggressive manners fail him and he mumbles, something hardly audible, like 'Yeah...', and looks down. For a few seconds it is as though a more vulnerable person underneath appears.

I walk back to the staff entrance and this time Sarah, the proprietor, has arrived. She tells me that she usually turns off the doorbell before sessions to prevent kids from abusing it. During the session, it becomes clear to me that I am Nicky's – and to some extent Lianne and Mel's – target for jokes and ridicule. This they do through sidelong glances, denigratory words said under the breath so to be just barely audible and open insults. For instance,

Nicky makes a very fast movement pointing his middle finger making a 'fuck you' sign at me. This is a skilfully accomplished performance. Made in a subtle manner, it creates a more provocative and effective way of showing disrespect and undermining my authority than if made explicitly. 'Why did you make that gesture?' I ask. 'Gesture', he mimics in a mock 'posh', high pitched voice, all the while an ironic smile plays on his lips. Again, this is skilfully executed. Making fun of my speech, this time he puts me down in a more explicit manner, showing how pathetic I appear. He makes it clear that I speak and behave in a snobbish, effeminate manner, which of course is the very opposite of putting up a tough front.

My way of getting back at him is to be a nuisance. In a low-key, non-aggressive way, I disturb him by my very presence. For instance, when he is playing PlayStation I stand close by, looking at him play. It works. 'Just go!' he says after a while. Towards the end of the evening he offers a sort of pact of mutual avoidance: 'Okay, I'll leave you alone from now on. I won't do anything to you'.

However, although initially I pay little attention to the verbal and non-verbal assaults, I gradually get more and more provoked and finally I switch from trying to maintain the professional stance of a youth worker and researcher, to someone who wants respect, who no-one is going to put down. In other words, I alter, rather unconsciously, my behaviour and start to orient my performances to the codes of interaction prevailing among many of the boys in Satellite Town. While Nicky is offering to leave me alone, I am determined not to let him get away that easily: I refuse to let him dictate the interactions that will follow. They will not be on his terms, due to his goodwill, but I will be the one to set the conditions.

Two weeks later I am back at the youth club – jetlagged, having just returned from a trip to the United States. Among the first to enter are Nicky and his friends, including Dave, Dazza and Leon. When I see Nicky it is like I am back to where we left off two weeks before. Nicky and Leon, a black boy of Nicky's age, go into the pool room, where I am standing, and they start to play. When Leon sees me, his face lights up in a grin and he greets me with an 'You alright'. He was not present two weeks ago and probably doesn't know what happened. Leon's friendly greeting may confuse Nicky as he meets my gaze and mumbles 'Alright', too. Like in our previous encounter, he suddenly displays a more vulnerable, insecure side.

I, however, want to show him that I am not going to show deference for him. Because of how he acted last time, he should not think I've got respect for him. But naively, I also thought that I had 'won', that he would not try to get back at me. That's why I was surprised at what came to happen. It begins while Nicky is playing pool, now with Dazza, and I am standing nearby (I am the staff member currently responsible for the room). Suddenly he goes and gets a table tennis bat. He uses the handle of the bat to hit the ball lying on the table. He hits the ball but the handle also smashes against the table.

He does this a few times. Shortly after, he does the same thing but uses a pool cue, hitting the ball with force. All the while, a smile is playing on his lips. Of course, he does this to provoke me. And I know that he knows that I know.

'For fuck's sake', I mutter twice under my breath, and then tell him to stop. One basic rule as a youth worker is to challenge young people's use of swearwords, and here I am swearing at one of the boys known for his 'bad language'. 'For fuck's sake', he mimics triumphantly. He knows that he is getting me where he wants, that is, provoked and angry. Then he leans closely to Dazza's ear and in a low voice says something that I can't hear. Dazza answers with a sneer. It's obviously all part of a performance to provoke me further.

I respond to Nicky's provocations by teasing him back. I stand near the pool table and fix him with my gaze. He seems to become self-conscious as he shoots a weak shot. 'Good shot', I say ironically, to mock him. 'Yeah . . .' he mumbles. Again, he displays a vulnerable, insecure side. But he is not the type to fold. A few seconds later, he has composed himself. It is as if he switches personality, and back is the seemingly self-assured boy. And he continues to wind me up in the same manner as earlier through a mix of very fine, subtle ways – small winks, gestures, glances, scornful smiles – and outright verbal taunts. And as before, he succeeds in 'winding me up'. He is winning. I try to beat him at his own game, but it is a game at which he is a master.

After a while, I decide to walk to the entrance where Diane and Annie from the staff are sitting. I tell them that I'm too angry at Nicky to remain in the pool room, so I switch place with Annie. 'Try to let it go', Diane tells me. I make an attempt and we try some small talk but I find it hard to focus on what we are talking about. Some minutes later, Nicky, Dave and Dazza pass us as they walk towards the exit. For some reason, they are left standing there. Nicky turns around and looks at me. He fixes me for several seconds with his eyes wide open and a playful smile, just to make me angrier and more upset. And this is where I 'lose the plot'. My blood boils and I look at him, furious. 'What? You angry?', he says smiling. 'Yeah', I answer, and then it all comes out: 'If you continue, I will go to jail because I will break your neck'. Nicky laughs at this, obviously not the reaction I'm after, so I say: 'No, I'm serious'. Of course, in reality, I would never do such a thing. His expression changes. He becomes very serious, even shocked. Diane tells him to leave and he goes out. Annie reappears. Outside, there is a loud commotion. Nicky is standing there with his friends and sounds upset as he says in a loud voice: 'He said he'll break my neck!' My words have sparked a scene.

Shell-shocked by my own words and by all that is happening, I rise, as if on autopilot, from the chair and walk up the stairs to the entrance and stand in front of Nicky. We square up. Dave, looking upset, warns me that I'm standing too close to Nicky. As he says this, I suddenly realise what I have caused, namely a war-like situation. In this moment, all my adrenaline and anger disappears and is replaced by sadness at what is happening. They are just boys, and I've been behaving like one of them. I turn and walk back into the youth club.

Some minutes later, I speak with Diane and Annie. I tell them I should probably not work with young people any longer and that I better go home. They tell me that it would not be a good idea to go out by myself since Nicky and his friends ran off to collect sticks to attack me. Diane adds that she and Annie took the sticks from them. Nicky also called his dad. 'They're out there, so it's not safe to go out'. I decide to remain until the end of the session, and then take the bus home. A few weeks after the incident, I was sacked and never worked at any of the youth clubs in Satellite Town again.[2]

Discussion

This incident shows how I overstepped the role of ethnographer and thus disregarded the ethical guidelines that come with such role. The unprofessionalism of such 'failed' fieldwork practice is tied to a great deal of professional and private shame. But my account serves to critique the common practice among ethnographers to sanitise and censor their fieldwork experiences so as not to look 'bad' (Fine 1993). The main point in discussing the incident, however, is to explore what it can tell us about class and masculinity. We can see how my behaviour was coded as effeminate and 'posh', and thus failed to perform according to the codes of masculinity prevalent among many of the young men in Satellite Town. Yet it also shows how I gradually appropriated such masculine codes while in the field. In response to being disrespected and feminised, I left the stance of the ethnographer or youth worker and instead started to perform tough manners like Nicky and his friends.

As a middle-class researcher and youth worker I was generally in a position of authority vis-á-vis the young respondents. But as I appropriated their codes of interaction, I entered into a game of masculinity in which they were superior. In Satellite Town putting up a masculine front through aggressive display is a cultural resource, a form of embodied knowledge of cultural codes (cf. Anderson 1999), which I had yet to fully acquire. Thus, the incident shows the contextual and spatialised nature of power between researcher and researched in face-to-face interaction. Although the structural relationship between powerful and powerless remains, in certain contexts of interaction the latter can draw on local cultural resources that can be used as a source of power or influence.

While tough displays were frequently displayed in Satellite Town, the ways in which Nicky and his friends ridiculed and 'put me down' were particular in their intensity and persistence. But we should also note how volatile and fragile Nicky's performances of masculinity were. Beneath his assured, arrogant face-work, an insecure, vulnerable child sometimes appeared. In Nicky's reputation as a serial troublemaker, there was a sense that he was going down a dangerous, self-destructive path. Sarah told me that a week after the incident Nicky was banned from the youth club after threatening another member of the staff. A youth officer I spoke with told me that if Nicky continued on this trajectory, when he became older, he would eventually encounter other institutions such as the police.

Thus while Satellite Town is a relatively marginal space, Nicky's situation seemed particularly insecure. As a response he performed a form of protest masculinity. Connell (2005 [1995]) argues that protest masculinity is formed in volatile situations characterised by poor prospects, economic marginality and a lack of cultural resources. In these circumstances, performances of self in social interaction, often through spectacular display, become a source of value. This is why concerns with face and keeping up a front become so important. In Nicky's case this could be observed by his impression management in front of his friends. Nicky knew that I was not literally going to break his neck, but since he was playing to an audience of his friends, he had to respond as if this public threat should be taken literally. I had challenged him, and he had to protect his honour. Similarly, his friends reacted to the threat posed to one of the members in their group. By threatening Nicky, I threatened the entire group.

In the context of protest masculinity, Nicky's tough performances and bullying should be interpreted, not so much as classed resistance against a Bourgeoisie social order (cf. Willis 1977), but as bound up with a quest for recognition. As few sources for value and recognition were available for Nicky, the ability to put up a tough front was a way to gain respect and status. This reflects a more general pattern regarding the relationship between worth and marginalisation in deprived working-class areas such as Satellite Town (Anderson 1999; Hemmings 2002). In this context, to denigrate and ridicule a youth worker was part of the quest of respect and recognition. Here Nicky defined his own masculine identity by drawing boundaries against my effeminate, 'posh' performances. And this was far from an isolated event. Members of the staff told me that Nicky had bullied a former youth worker for an extended period, among other things repeatedly calling him 'gay'. By devaluing and feminising the performances of others, he enhanced his own worth and sense of manliness. Similar dynamics are identified in Willis' (1977) seminal ethnography of the 'counter school culture' among a group of white working-class boys in a Midlands school as well as in Mac an Ghaill's (1994) study of the 'rasta boys', a group of Afro-Caribbean working-class boys. The latter taunted academic black boys in their school, referring to them using the homophobic term 'batty men'.

Conclusion

This chapter has contributed to discussions of reflexivity in criminological research by showing how an analysis of the researcher's self can increase our ethnographic understanding of how young marginalised masculinity is performed. To this end I show how the ethnographer, as an embodied, visible and situated actor in the fieldwork setting, both influences and is influenced by the respondents' performance of masculinity. In particular, it is through accounting for the interactions between the middle-class researcher and the young working-class respondents that the classed dynamics of masculine performances becomes visible. The chapter contributes to discussions of power/powerlessness and reflexivity by addressing the contextual nature of hierarchy and power between the researcher and researched. In conclusion, the lessons that can be learned for future research on crime and deviance are greater acknowledgement of the benefits in incorporating the researcher's self in ethnographic analysis and of the situated nature of power in research relationships.

Notes

1. All names of individuals and locations have been anonymised.
2. Although a youth worker may be allowed to continue working after such an incident, the problem was that I was not registered with the Criminal Registration Bureau (CRB), which is compulsory for all youth workers. But since I was a volunteer, I was allowed to start working even while still not registered. After the incident, however, such an exception could no longer be made and I was forced to quit. While I stopped visiting the youth club where the incident took place, I continued my fieldwork at the second youth club, though no longer in the capacity of youth worker but rather as a friend 'dropping by to say hello'.

References

Anderson, E. (1999) *Code of the Street: Decency, Violence, and the Moral Life of the Inner City*, New York: Norton.
Coffey, A. (1999) *The Ethnographic Self: Fieldwork and the Representation of Identity*, London: Sage.
Connell, R.W. (2005 [1995]) *Masculinities*, 2nd edn, Berkeley: University of California Press.
Denzin, N.K. and Lincoln, Y.S. (1994) *Handbook of Qualitative Research*, London: Sage.
DETR (2000) *Index of Multiple Deprivation*, London: Department of the Environment, Transport and the Regions.
Fine, G.A. (1993) 'Ten Lies of Ethnography: Moral Dilemmas of Field Research' *Journal of Contemporary Ethnography* 22(3): 267–94.
Haraway, D. (1988) 'Situated Knowledges: The Science Question in Feminism and the Privilege of Partial Perspective' *Feminist Studies* 14(3): 575–99.
Harding, S.G. (ed.) (1987). *Feminism and Methodology: Social Science Issues*, Bloomington: Indiana University Press.
Hemmings, A. (2002) 'Youth Culture of Hostility: Discourses of Money, Respect, and Difference' *International Journal of Qualitative Studies in Education* 15(3): 291–307.
le Grand, E. (2014) 'Class, Community and Belonging in a "Chav Town"'. In P. Watt and P. Smets (eds) *Mobilities and Neighbourhood Belonging in Cities and Suburbs*, Basingstoke: Palgrave Macmillan, pp.164–81.

Lumsden, K. (2009) '"Don't Ask a Woman to Do Another Woman's Job": Gendered Interactions and the Emotional Ethnographer' *Sociology* 43(3): 497–513.

Mac an Ghaill, M. (1994) 'The Making of Black English Masculinities'. In H. Brod and M. Kaufman (eds) *Theorizing Masculinities*, London: Sage, pp.183–99.

Marcus, G.E. and Fischer, M.M.J. (1999 [1986]) *Anthropology as Cultural Critique: An Experimental Moment in the Human Sciences*, 2nd edn, Chicago: University of Chicago Press.

Newmahr, S. (2008) 'Becoming a Sadomasochist: Integrating Self and Other in Ethnographic Analysis' *Journal of Contemporary Ethnography* 37(5): 619–43.

Office for National Statistics (2001) *Census: Aggregate Data (England and Wales)*. URL (accessed 12 August 2013): http://infuse.mimas.ac.uk

Phillips, C. and Earle, R. (2010) 'Reading Difference Differently?: Identity, Epistemology and Prison Ethnography' *British Journal of Criminology* 50(2): 360–78.

Venkatesh, S.A. (2002) '"Doin' the Hustle": Constructing the Ethnographer in the American Ghetto' *Ethnography* 3(1): 91–111.

Venkatesh, S.A. (2006) *Off the Books: The Underground Economy of the Urban Poor*, Cambridge, MA: Harvard University Press.

Venkatesh, S.A. (2013) 'The Reflexive Turn: The Rise of First-Person Ethnography' *The Sociological Quarterly* 54(1): 3–8.

Willis, P.E. (1993 [1977]) *Learning to Labour: How Working Class Kids Get Working Class Jobs*, Aldershot: Ashgate.

Part III

Researcher Identities, Subjectivities and Intersectionalities: Race and Ethnicity

Editors' Introduction

Karen Lumsden and Aaron Winter

This section of the book, the second of two on *researcher identities, subjectivities and intersectionalities*, focuses on *race* and *ethnicity*. As outlined in the introduction to this collection, there have been calls for work on race and ethnicity, particularly in the field of criminology, to engage in reflexive critiques, research and analysis. Responding to such calls and important work by sociologists of race and ethnicity and criminologists that has come before it, the chapters in this section examine a wide range of subject matter, issues and levels of reflexive analysis. They examine and go beyond analyses of identity, subjectivity, subject position and privilege to examine and interrogate a range of issues related to criminological research on race and ethnicity. Such issues include the role of researcher as an institutional agent, knowledge production, access, trust, ethics, funding, representation, the dangers of complicity, the labelling, stigmatisation or oppressive treatment of marginalised groups by authorities, or as members of such groups, and the role of objective, subjective and political research. The authors focus on a range of research subjects and participants in different subject positions and with different identities and experiences, as well as diverse contexts. While the focus of this part of the book is on race and ethnicity, some of the authors examine the ways in which it can overlap and intersect with other sites of identity, subjectivity, inequality and powerlessness, most notably sexuality and gender.

In Chapter 10, David Glisch-Sánchez discusses his work on hate crimes against lesbian, gay, bisexual, transgender and queer (LGBTQ) Latinas and Latinos and examines the power relationship between researcher and research participant. He also looks at and interrogates the mechanisms that create criminological scholars as agents of the state and academic discipline and institutions and how reflexive practices are commonly reduced to the indexing of differences across various categories of identity, such as race, ethnicity, sexuality and national origin. In Chapter 11, Breea C. Willingham provides a reflexive account of being an African American woman with male relatives incarcerated in the American penal system and thus having a relationship with and sharing an overlapping social position with the powerless, as opposed to being an institutional agent of the state and criminal justice system. In Chapter 12, Meghan E. Hollis outlines her experiences of researching minority police officers in the United States and the difficulties assessing the experiences of the non-white and/or female police officers, and the possible role of her identity and subject position in this. In Chapter 13, Monish Bhatia discusses his research on the UK's immigration policies and procedures on asylum seekers and 'illegal' migrants and examines the role of emotional reflexivity in research and the ways in which it can serve as tool for researchers, driving critical criminological knowledge and exposing state and structural violence, and injustice against them. In Chapter 14, Clare E. Griffiths discusses a research project that sought to capture the perspectives of an established local community and a transient immigrant community in England on crime and disorder and reflects on researching 'hidden' populations. In Chapter 15, Michael Wearing, focusing on research on child sexual assault in remote Aboriginal communities in Northern Australia, examines how qualitative criminology helps to frame 'law and order' agendas of state surveillance and can legitimise false constructions of the 'other'.

10
From 'Hate Crimes' to Social Harm: Critical Moments and Reflexive Practice

David Glisch-Sánchez

Introduction

Reflexive practice is a difficult enterprise to embark upon because it is a methodology and area of criminological and sociological debate that is imbued with ethical, political and pragmatic considerations. Such considerations make efforts to identify effective reflexive practices difficult because the power dynamics and dominant epistemologies and ontologies that reflexivity seeks to identify, critique and ultimately upend have created a social world and academic disciplines that are infinitely complex and nuanced in their reification and reproduction of social inequalities. This essay does not have at its core, neither the intention to eschew the ethical, political and pragmatic issues within reflexive discussions, nor the desire to present my own reflexive process as unencumbered from the complex web that is created by racism, patriarchy, heterosexism and capitalism. Rather, it seeks to present and understand two moments, in particular, during my dissertation research where despite my stated commitment to socially responsible criminological research with an eye towards the power dynamics between the researcher and participant, I continued to make powerful and subtle assumptions about the phenomenon I am attempting to empirically understand. This chapter explores not just the 'what' and 'why' of the assumptions, but considers the process through which the *critical moment* of recognition occurs. That is, what enables the recognition of a researcher's a priori epistemologies and ontologies as such.

The site for this reflexive analysis is research on the experiences of social harm (Hillyard et al. 2004) by transgender, lesbian, gay, bisexual and queer (TLGBQ) Latinas/os in the United States. This study relies on 30 life story interviews conducted with TLGBQ Latinas/os ranging in ages from 18 to 66 years residing in the state of Texas. During the interviews, I asked participants to reflect upon specific periods of their life and speak to 'challenges

[they] faced during this time? Were [they] ever harmed in some way?' Additionally, I asked questions regarding 'when [they] felt secure and safe?' or 'when [they] were fearful or scared?' These interviews were designed to help understand *how* TLGBQ Latinas/os were experiencing various forms of social harm and *what* their beliefs are surrounding *why* they experienced these social harms. My analysis presented here, therefore, places in conversation the development of my research project with details of my own biography and social location as a Cuban American gay male doctoral candidate in a US-based sociology programme. In short, this chapter seeks to outline what Wendy S. Pillow (2003) refers to as 'reflexivities of discomfort' that resist simple and 'comfortable' patterns of reflexive reasoning.

Drawing upon Bourdieu and Wacquant's (1992) ideas, I define reflexivity as a range of practices scholars employ to ascertain the moments and ways their research, and research in general, is shaped and constructed by their socialisation within and in relation to groups, institutions and the profession. It is to render visible – and to the degree possible, knowable – those components and processes within the intellectual and scholarly enterprise that are invisible, taken for granted and seemingly natural; or as Bourdieu states it is the pursuit of identifying those 'unthought categories of thought which delimit the thinkable and predetermine the thought', which masks to near perfection the critical assumptions we all make at the very outset of any project (cited in Wacquant 1992, 40). For this reason, building upon Bourdieu's conceptualisation of reflexive practice, Wacquant (1992) argues that reflexivity is a requirement of sociological work, because, as Bourdieu points out, not only does bias stem from the habitus formed in one's fields of social origin (such as class and ethnicity), but also it is formed in the field of academia writ large and the various disciplinary and interdisciplinary fields specifically (such as criminology). Bourdieu and Wacquant emphasise the bias inherent in the very tools we take for granted in the undertaking of scholarly endeavours. This point cannot be stressed enough: the reason reflexivity must become a requirement of sociological and criminological work is because a part of the problem is rooted in the everyday practices of what it means to be a criminologist; the solution must be collective because the problem is. It stands to reason that if we are collectively reflexive and not as isolated individuals we have a better chance of observing within the empirical methods and hegemonic theories of criminological research the embedded assumptions about how the very phenomena we strive to 'objectively' measure and observe operate and manifest themselves. It is for this reason, why anthologies, such as this, and special issues of academic journals, and conference sessions dedicated to the continued development of reflexivity within criminology are so important.

The range of activities that constitute various forms of reflexivity are numerous (Nelken 1994; Chan 2000; Pillow 2003; Alvesson and Sköldberg 2009); however, in this chapter I would like to focus on one particular practice, the previously mentioned *critical moment(s)* of recognition. Although I will go into greater detail later, by *critical moment(s)* I refer to the potential – realised or not – that is produced in the moment where an individual or group of researchers identifies the possibility of understanding, either empirically or theoretically, any phenomenon under investigation outside of the intellectual traditions of their field of study. While these events are 'critical' because they create the possibility of resistance to the traditional or orthodox epistemologies and ontologies within a given discipline or sub-discipline, it does not presuppose that an individual or group of researchers will act upon the realisation or recognition of this 'new' knowledge. It is my contention that utilising the philosopher Eckhart Tolle's (2005) ideas around 'identification' would aid criminology's efforts to capitalise on these critical moment(s) and continue the process of implementing effective reflexive praxis.

Institutional socialisation and the research process

My dissertation project at its inception was concerned with the experience of 'hate crimes' whose targets were Latina/o TLGBQ people. More broadly, I wanted to better understand how identities and violence shaped the day-to-day experiences of TLGBQ Latinas/os. At the time I believed the socio-legal language and concept of 'hate crime' was the most appropriate framework and body of literature to base my dissertation. I believed this because at the time I was completing a Master's degree in public policy, which built upon my undergraduate degree that is also in public policy studies. Central to public policy programmes, at least in the United States, is the core belief that law and governmental regulation are the appropriate and even necessary venue for addressing and understanding the intersecting issues of violence and identities. Through my socialisation at the undergraduate and graduate levels I agreed wholeheartedly with this approach. I believed that preventing and addressing violence once it occurs were classic examples of appropriate intervention by the state. Even though the very establishment of a 'hate crime' within the US federal and state statutes was decidedly controversial (Jenness and Broad 1997), the unanimous decision by the conservative US Supreme Court in *Wisconsin v. Mitchell, 508 U.S. 476* (1993) that declared the constitutionality of punitive 'hate crime' statutes solidified the role of law and public policy in addressing this particular form of violence. Additionally, it should be noted that the very first 'hate crime' legislation passed by the US federal government – the Hate Crimes Statistic Act of 1990 – was only concerned with the collection of 'hate crime' statistics, which I would argue has had a profound impact on the scholarly investigation of 'hate crimes' since the initial investment by the national government was the collection of data. In addition to the socialisation I received from my formal educational training, between my undergraduate and Master's degree programmes, I was a lobbyist and grassroots organiser for two years working for the United Council of University of Wisconsin Students, Inc.[1] (United Council). While at United Council I worked on issues related to access to higher education, focusing on tuition and financial aid policy, and campus safety, with a focus on sexual violence and racially motivated and anti-TLGBQ violence. My work during this period consisted entirely of attempting to pass all necessary policy changes regarding economic access and campus safety through the governing board of the university system. This merely cemented my absolute belief in the necessary role of government in solving most, if not all, social problems and inequalities. To say that I decided, which would imply a conscious decision, to use the concept of 'hate crime' would not be accurate, because I could not conceive at that time of an alternative way of studying identity and violence, especially in the contemporary United States. At the time, 'hate crime' was an object, a noun and not a contested social formation.

At the beginning of my research project, during a pilot study and before I formally declared my dissertation topic, one of my primary objectives was simply to document the various kinds of 'hate crimes' my research participants experienced since there existed little to no scholarship within the 'hate crime' literature concerning Latinas/os in the United States (Ituarte 2009), not to mention US Latinas/os who are TLGBQ. In 2009, the US Congress tasked the National Institute of Justice (NIJ) with conducting a study to evaluate the trends of 'hate crime' violence that targeted immigrants, people perceived to be immigrants and Latina/o-Americans. This represents the single largest effort to have been undertaken to understand the trends and underlying causes of 'hate crimes' targeting immigrants and Latinas/os.[2] Although this effort is undoubtedly welcomed and admirable, two problems plague the project from the outset: (1) not all Latina/o victims of 'hate crimes' are targeted specifically for their ethnoracial identity or immigration status, especially when we are talking about the experiences of TLGBQ Latinas/os, thus it is likely their experiences are left outside of the data collected and (2) the NIJ relies on statutory language for its definition and criteria of what is and is not a 'hate crime', a major problem I explore later on in the chapter. There was a specific set of central facts and categories of information I initially desired to collect through in-depth interviews. I wanted to understand the social factors influencing the decisions of Latinas/os to report or not report the 'hate crimes' they experienced. I wanted to catalogue the various types of perpetrators and locations where these 'hate crimes' occurred. If they decided to report, I wanted to understand what were their experiences of police, victim services and prosecuting attorneys. I especially wanted to understand the kinds of programmes or interventions TLGBQ Latinas/os wanted in order to prevent 'hate crimes' from happening.

Designing a recruitment strategy, in particular language for recruitment flyers, e-mails and posters, was challenging. First, I am studying a very specific population – TLGBQ Latinas/os – that rarely has formalised spaces (e.g. community organisations and commercial establishments) specifically established for its needs. Usually, spaces are designated as either predominantly Latina/o *or* TLGBQ (and within that category primarily gay and lesbian), and the racial and heteronormative politics that often structure these social environments alienate TLGBQ Latinas/os. Second, I was afraid of using 'have you ever experienced a hate crime?' as an eligibility question, because some potential participants may have thought they needed to report any events to law enforcement or needed law enforcement to confirm a bias motivation in order to respond affirmatively to the question. I could have stipulated that they did not need to have reported the incident, but that still would not have addressed the problem that 'hate crime', as a legal concept, has always been difficult to determine which events are appropriately labelled such while others do not merit such a determination. We know law enforcement agents have difficulty in applying 'hate crime' charges (Levin and McDenitt 2002; Bell 2003; Chakraborti and Garland 2009), so I had very real concerns on whether prospective TLGBQ Latinas/os would self-select themselves out of the study. Additionally, I was interested in opening up the participant pool to those individuals whose primary language is Spanish, not just English. I could have easily directly translated the language I had first developed in English to Spanish, but I began to worry whether the meanings, and not just the words, would translate. The very term, 'hate crime', arises out of a very specific socio-historical formation in the United States; and even in the United States there are great debates regarding what language to use to label the violence that has come to typify what many refer to as 'hate crime' (Perry 2005). Even stating what a 'hate crime' legally consists of can be a difficult task because variation and important difference exist between jurisdictions in the United States (Petrosino 2003). However, despite these differences there are some key similarities: (1) all 'hate crime' statutes in the United States contain protected classes of people[3] and (2) are prosecuted either as stand-alone criminal offenses or as penalty enhancements. Barbara Perry's (2005) article, 'A Crime by Any Other Name: The Semantics of "Hate"', served as a lightening rod when I first read it because it ignited an important question and struggle within my own research: what was I exactly signalling through the use of 'hate crime' to participants and recipients of this research? Once I began questioning what the most effective recruitment and selection criteria for interviewees would be, I started to realise that I was already making a basic assumption that all English-speaking Latina/o TLGBQ people would relate to the term 'hate crime' in a similar, if not the same, way. Thus, I decided to use a more flexible phrasing of the question, in both English and Spanish, when recruiting participants; instead of saying 'have you ever experienced a hate crime?' on recruitment materials, I asked 'have you experienced some type of harm/violence because of who you are?' This new language helped me address my greatest fear at the

time, which was a self-selection bias among eligible Latina/o TLGBQ people. The structure of the new eligibility question allowed for greater variety
and diversity in the language TLGBQ Latinas/os use in narrating their own
experiences with harm/violence as it connects, intersects or relates to their
identities. Potential recruits are already primed to think of identity because
the two proceeding eligibility questions ask if they are of Latin American
descent and whether they are transgender, lesbian, gay, bisexual or queer.

Even though I had begun to question the language I used, I limited this
moment to concerns about effectiveness in communication and its potential effect on selection bias. At no point did I question what the effect the
language I used would have on epistemological concerns, and therefore on
knowledge production. In short, I had as of then not attempted a reflexive
practice and analysis. I had not yet come to the realisation that 'hate crime'
was one of those 'unthought categories of thought' Bourdieu had warned
us about (Wacquant 1992). In fact, during both the pilot study and several
of the first interviews of the dissertation project, I still wanted to categorise
people's experiences as 'hate crimes', unless they expressly said they did not
think an event was a 'hate crime'; I was determined to use 'hate crime',
I was not willing to give up on its utility. Eventually, the logic of categorising
people's experiences as a 'hate crime' regardless of how they themselves identified the event(s) collapsed under the mounting evidence of 'hate crime' as
a sociopolitically constructed category, and therefore a contested conceptual space within the law, the application of laws and academic and public
discourses. It became clear that 'hate crime' meant many different things,
to many different people (Perry 2005; Chakraborti and Garland 2009). The
meaning of 'hate crime' was not a given; some participants did in fact categorise their experience as being a 'hate crime' while most interviewees
rejected the application of the term for various reasons. One rationale being
the belief that their experiences did not meet the legal criteria for a 'hate
crime'; another, that labelling their experiences as 'hate crimes' would invite
police or state intervention, something they vehemently wanted to avoid.
Others resisted the label 'hate crime' because of the everyday and common-
place nature of 'hate violence', a pattern identified in my interview data
through the aid of Iganski's *'Hate Crime' and the City* (2008), where he advocates a victim-centred approach that recognises the actual ubiquity of 'hate
violence' in society that stands in contrast to the media's representation of
'hate crime' as rare and exceptional.

As I was collecting the life story data that contradicted my research
objectives to study, analyse and ultimately theorise Latina/o TLGBQ experiences of 'hate crimes', a dilemma arose. To continue labelling participants'
experiences as 'hate crimes' would have assigned a meaning to a social phenomenon that they themselves did not give, and in some instances refused
the categorisation for very specific reasons. If I continued to do this, I would
have effectively colonised the narratives of my research participants, people

who trusted that I would rigorously and faithfully represent what they said and identify my beliefs and resulting analysis as my own and not pass it off as theirs. Such actions would have only served to harm Latina/o TLGBQ people and maintain the racism and heteropatriarchy that keep them at the margins of academia or exclude them altogether. Yet, it was undeniable, I was convinced of the utility of 'hate crimes' to my dissertation project. It was not until a reflexive moment was presented through the dual works of Iganski (2008) and Basia Spalek (2008) that I began to seriously question for *whom* did 'hate crime' hold utility. Iganski (2008) stressed the absolute need for a victim-centred approach to criminological research, and Spalek (2008) stressed that there was space to conduct research that did not rely on socio-legal concepts steeped in the social dynamics of identities and power, such as 'hate crime', but still honoured Latina/o TLGBQ accounts of profound harm. Through Spalek, I was introduced to the work of Hillyard et al. (2004) and their role in developing *social harm* or zemiology as an alternative to formalised socio-legal categories of crime. For me, a reflexive turn was made possible through the written works of others, for other scholars it could be through conference sessions, article/book peer-review processes or informal encounters. Regardless, of how the reflexive turn comes about, I would argue that most, if not all, contain what I refer to as a *critical moment* wherein reflexivity's ethical and intellectual potential are not yet realised but stand upon the precipice of coming to fruition. I now turn to an exploration of the critical moment produced during the course of my research and what I now believe is a major feature structuring this psycho-social space.

Critical moments and over-identification in criminology

Critical moments arise from what many may describe as the cognitive dissonance found in the moment(s) when what we thought we knew or how we knew it comes into question under the pressure of new and/or persistent information. This information can be presented in many forms, such as through the reading of scholarly articles and books, formal and informal feedback by peers and senior scholars, community accountability and/or through the data itself. The production or happenstance of critical moments is necessary to the process of reflexivity because they are those events that draw out the presence and contours of our habitus; in effect, I term 'critical moments' as those events where we are made aware of our taken-for-granted knowledges, epistemologies and ontologies. My taken-for-granted epistemology and ontology resulted in my desire to retain the use of 'hate crime' as a category of analysis. I lived for 12 years, through academic training and professional experiences, where public policies were discussed as both problem and solution. I approached most social problems through this framework that foregrounded questions about what current policies existed, why were these public policies ineffective and what policies would rectify the situation. Even as I write this, I recall that in secondary school, I participated during all four years in policy debate competitions. Taking inventory of all this biography and taking stock of the various fields I was embedded in and how they were shaping my habitus, one could argue that it was all but predetermined that I chose the policy-related category of 'hate crime' to study the interrelatedness of violence and identity for TLGBQ Latinas/os.

Critical moments, however, are not overdetermined events; their occurrence does not mandate or necessitate a reflexive outcome. Critical moments merely provide an opportunity and offer up the chance to make a decision that fulfils the goals and potential of reflexivity. The larger ethical and political project of reflexivity is to eschew orthodoxy in disciplinary methods and theories; to understand and correct for, as best as possible, the fields of power that produce these orthodoxies and shape individual habituses, which construct and constrict the knowledge-making process within criminology and other areas of study. Therefore, once a critical moment presents itself, the scholar or scholars that are given this opportunity must decide whether they will follow the line of reflexive analysis wherever it may lead. It is the juncture of the decision to engage or not in reflexivity that merits further understanding, because if we understand, at least in part, the psycho-social factors that influence the outcome of this decision we then may be able to institute social changes that support reflexive activities. I should stress that the need for cataloguing both the social and psychological factors that influence the decisions we make during critical moments stems from the fact that Bourdieu's (1992) conceptualisation of the habitus acknowledges the role of social fields and human memory (or psychology) in the construction of one's own epistemological and ontological orientations. Thus, any theories and practices of reflexivity must acknowledge and address these factors.

The purpose of this chapter is not to itemise and explore every single psycho-social factor; rather, I would like to focus on a psychological phenomenon relevant to the choice inherent in critical moments *and* the social forces that complement the work being done by this psychological phenomenon in developing our habitus. The phenomenon I am referring to is the development of the ego through a process of over-identification. I am not using ego as a euphemism for arrogance or a vain sense of superiority, although that could very well be a particular manifestation of the ego. Neither am I referring to the psychological understanding of the ego as one of the key structures of the human psyche. Rather, I am drawing on notions of the ego as described by the philosopher Eckhart Tolle (2005). His conceptualisation of the ego can best be understood as a false sense of self that is created by the mind; in short, it is often the stuff we say about ourselves when answering the question: who am I? Tolle (2005, 35) writes:

> One of the most basic mind structures through which the ego comes into existence is identification. The word 'identification' is derived from the Latin word *idem*, meaning 'same' and *facere*, which means 'to make'. The

same as what? The same as I. I endow it with a sense of self, and so it becomes a part of my 'identity'.

Tolle (2005) argues that the practice of identification is formed early on in childhood, starting with learning about the idea of possession through the teaching of children that their clothes and toys *are* theirs, are an extension of who they are. As we develop through adolescence and adulthood, those toys and clothes become entertainment systems, technology, cars and so on. The problem with identification, Tolle explains, arises because the objects with which we imbue a sense of self are finite, temporary and/or fleeting; thus, our sense of self is continuously being undermined. I would extend Tolle's analysis of identification with physical objects and include identification with *immaterial* objects as well, like ideas.

On one hand, it would seem understandable why people, especially criminologists and other academics, would come to identify with our ideas. They do, in fact, come from our minds and the primary currency of criminology and any scholarly field is ideas. This is not to say that our ideas have no relationship at all to who we are, but rather to caution against an *over-identification* with our ideas as representing all, most or a lot of who and what we are as human beings. It is this over-identification or over-placement of self into our ideas that structures a vast swath of our professional lives. However, I argue, this is not by happenstance because criminology as a field (in the Bourdieuian sense of field), like all fields, contain its own specific modes of power and authority that replicates and maintains the dominance of particular methods and theories. An example is as follows: many criminologists, based upon our research projects and interests, need access to law enforcement agencies, penal institutions, court systems and prosecutorial offices. It is not unheard of within criminological research networks to hear how these institutions limit or deny access to personnel, inmates or documents if there is a (perceived) threat or fear that a project's outcomes may yield critical results. Independent foundations and governmental institutes constitute the primary sources of financial support for criminological research. These financial institutions function in effect as gatekeepers, not just to basic financial capital but capital in the form of designating a project as 'legitimate' and worthy of the finite financial resources of a discipline. Through these mechanisms (and others), many criminologists are socialised into dominant epistemologies that then form the foundation of our ideas with which we often are over-identified and as a result hold to and defend vigorously.

Conclusion

Over-identification is inimical to reflexive praxis because critical moments and the reflexivity they portend by definition ask criminologists to consider whether they are in error, and possibly in error in a fundamental way.

The mechanisms of power in operation within the field of criminology provide every social and material incentive to maintain fidelity with the hegemonic epistemological order, and our over-identification with our ideas and epistemologies that creates a sense of one being undermined or even attacked supplies the psychological motivation to adhere to dominant methods and theories. Therefore, the challenge before all scholars committed to a reflexive criminology will be to create new modes of power and authority that does not promote the practice of over-identification and rewards occasions when critical moments do occur. Some of this work has already been done and forwarded by feminist and critical criminologists in the last 40 years; however, the fact that we must still label such efforts as *feminist* and *critical* and thus denote a difference from the practices of criminology writ large indicates there is yet much to be done. Work that this anthology helps in doing.

This chapter owes a great deal to the research that inspired the critical moment and reflexive turn in my own scholarship with a shift from 'hate crime' to social harm, in particular the works of Perry (2005), Iganski (2008), Spalek (2008) and Hillyard et al. (2004). Their respective works documenting the meaning of 'hate crime' as contested terrain, the necessity of victim-centred approaches that understand the everyday nature of 'hate violence' and the proliferation of social harm as a valuable tool provided enough intellectual space for me to reflect upon my habitus, participants' life story accounts and the knowledge being produced by both. It is important to note that effective collective reflexive practice can occur in various forms. It can occur within feedback shared between colleagues in an academic department, comments provided in a public forum such as conferences and colloquia and as my previous comments suggest through the reading of scholarly works that provoke new ways of knowing or, more likely, rendering old ways of knowing visible and not taken for granted. However, to do so we must continue to embrace critical moments and actively resist processes of over-identification.

Notes

1. United Council of University of Wisconsin Students, Inc. is a statewide student organisation dedicated to increasing access to higher education in the University of Wisconsin System. It also has a stated commitment to improving student experiences on campuses in order to increase retention and ultimately graduation rates, especially of underrepresented social groups like students of colour and TLGBQ students. It is the oldest statewide student organisation in the United States, having been established in 1965.
2. The NIJ study is now in its second phase; no preliminary findings are as of now available.
3. The most common protected classes are race, ethnicity, religion and national origin; however, gender, sexual orientation, disability and veteran status are also

frequently included. It is important to note that under US law, group member-ship is not a criterion for 'hate crime' applicability. For example, the prosecution of an individual or group for a race-based 'hate crime' does not depend on whether the victim(s) are racial minorities, rather they can be charged with a 'hate crime' as long as race was the motivating factor. Thus, people can, and have, been prosecuted for targeting white people for violence.

References

Alvesson, M. and Sköldberg, K. (2009) *Reflexive Methodology: New Vistas for Qualitative Research*, 2nd edn, London: Sage.
Bell, J. (2003) 'Policing Hatred: Police Bias Units and the Construction of Hate Crime'. In B. Perry (ed.) *Hate and Bias Crime: A Reader*, New York: Routledge, pp.427–38.
Bourdieu, P. (1992) *The Logic of Practice*, Palo Alto, CA: Stanford University Press.
Bourdieu, P. and Wacquant, L.J.D. (eds) (1992) *An Invitation to Reflexive Sociology*, Chicago: University of Chicago Press.
Chakraborti, N. and Garland, J. (2009) *Hate Crime: Impact, Causes, and Responses*, Thousand Oaks, CA: Sage.
Chan, J. (2000) 'Globalisation, Reflexivity, and the Practice of Criminology' *The Australian and New Zealand Journal of Criminology* 33(2): 118–35.
Hillyard, P., Pantazis, C., Tombs, S. and Gordon, D. (eds) (2004) *Beyond Criminology: Taking Harm Seriously*, London: Pluto Press.
Iganski, P. (2008) *'Hate Crime' and the City*, Bristol, UK: Policy Press.
Ituarte, S. (2009) 'Legitimized Anti-Latino Sentiment: Breeding the Prejudice That Per-petuates Violence'. In B. Perry (ed.) *Hate Crimes: Vol. 3. The Victims of Hate Crime*, Westport, CT: Praeger Publishers, pp.45–64.
Jenness, V. and Broad, K. (1997) *Hate Crimes: New Social Movements and the Poli-tics of Violence*, Social Problems and Social Issues Series, Piscataway, NJ: Aldine Transactions.
Levin, J. and McDevitt, J. (2002) *Hate Crimes Revisited: America's War Against Those Who Are Different*, Boulder, CO: Westview Press.
Nelken, D. (1994) 'Reflexive Criminology?' In D. Nelken (ed.) *The Futures of Criminology*, London: Sage, pp.7–42.
Perry, B. (2005) 'A Crime by Any Other Name: The Semantics of "Hate"' *Journal of Hate Studies* 4: 121–37.
Petrosino, C. (2003) 'Connecting the Past to the Future: Hate Crime in America' Crime'. In B. Perry (ed.) *Hate and Bias Crime: A Reader*, New York: Routledge, pp.9–26.
Pillow, W.S. (2003) 'Confession, Catharsis, or Cure? Rethinking the Uses of Reflexivity as Methodological Power in Qualitative Research' *International Journal of Qualitative Studies in Education* 16(2): 175–96.
Spalek, B. (2008) *Communities, Identities, and Crime*, Bristol, UK: Policy Press.
Tolle, E. (2005) *A New Earth: Awakening to Your Life's Purpose*, New York: Penguin.
United States Supreme Court (1993) *Wisconsin v. Mitchell, 508 U.S. 476*, Washington, DC.
Wacquant, L.J.D. (1992) 'Toward a Social Praxeology: The Structure and Logic of Bourdieu's Sociology'. In P. Bourdieu and L.J.D. Wacquant (eds) *An Invitation to Reflexive Sociology*, Chicago: University of Chicago Press.

11
Prison Is My Family Business: Reflections of an African American Woman with Incarcerated Relatives Doing Research on Incarcerated African American Fathers

Breea C. Willingham

Introduction

As an African American female prison researcher with incarcerated relatives, I make no pretence at objectivity when researching the impact of incarceration on black families. My standpoint is a reflexive one that attempts to account for the fact that I cannot separate the research from my personal experiences. This position presents a compelling paradox: my personal connection to the research adds a valuable and constructive context as my position creates opportunities, not limitations. It also puts me in a unique outsider within position that Michelle Fine (1998, 135) refers to as 'working the hyphen' – 'probing how we are in relation with the contexts we study and with our informants ... revealing far more about ourselves and far more about the structures of Othering'. In addition, sociologist Linda Carty argues that a researcher's racial and gendered identities should be embraced during the research process, not ignored:

> Feminist epistemology grants us the legitimacy to claim all the identities we have been taught to deny as real knowledge, and we have since learned that the impersonal, so-called objective approach is incapable of doing justice to this kind of work.
>
> (Carty 1996, 139–40)

As some feminist criminologists argue, researchers cannot avoid their background influencing or shaping their studies:

Regardless of how objective researchers like to believe themselves to be, they cannot help but be influenced by values, personal preferences, and aspects of the cultural setting and institutional structures in which they live and work. Feminists challenge themselves and fellow researchers to explicitly acknowledge the assumptions, beliefs, sympathies and potential biases that may influence their work.

(Renzetti 2013, 11)

Using a feminist reflexive approach, this chapter examines how my race, gender and experiences with incarcerated relatives presented unique challenges when conducting research on how prison impacts the relationship between incarcerated African American fathers and their children.

I began doing prison research eight years ago when I wrote an editorial for *USA Today* newspaper in October 2005 about my perspective of the tenth anniversary of the Million Man March – an American modern civil rights movement that called for African American men to make a vow of solidarity to become better men – as an African American woman with a father and brother in prison. In the editorial I discussed how incarceration severely impacted my relationship with my father and brother. My brother was three years into his life sentence when I wrote the essay and remains incarcerated. One of my nephews is also serving a life sentence. My father, who served more than a decade in prison, has since been paroled. As I half-jokingly say, 'prison is my family business'.

My editorial received a tremendous amount of feedback from incarcerated fathers from across America describing their stories of the pain of not being able to see their kids or their own contentious relationships with their fathers. The men's stories illustrated how incarceration is not just about the people behind bars. It is also about the mothers who cry for their sons, the siblings who have to bond with their brothers through prison walls and the children who grow up without a father. The families left behind are constant reminders of the true tragedy that prison families like mine face: the societal ramifications, largely immeasurable, of a nation that warehouses so many people.

I naively thought I could remain objective as I began researching incarcerated fathers. I did not realise that even in my *USA Today* editorial, I had already begun to practice reflexivity, in part, by connecting my personal story to a national historical event. For instance, when I wrote about my brother I noted:

I get to visit Rodney only a couple of times a year, but when I was a reporter I used to see my brother just about every day. Every time I was in court covering a case and I saw a young black man standing before the judge in an orange jumpsuit with shackled hands and feet, I thought about Rodney. Or when I'd see a young child watching the judge sentence her father to prison, I'd think about my 16-year-old nieces, the daughters my brother had to watch grow up in pictures.

(Willingham 2005, 13A)

Some feminist criminologists argue that reflexivity in research strengthens the research process by 'promoting greater honesty and awareness of the limitations and bias inherent in our research. Furthermore, reflexivity encourages us to think about the relationship between ourselves as researchers and the people who agree to be our research subjects' (Flavin and Desautels 2006, 20). The line between researcher and research had already begun to blur for me.

African American fatherhood arrested

The American prison population has grown from 300,000 in the 1970s to 2.3 million today. America incarcerates more of its population than any other country in the world: it makes up just 5 per cent of the world population, but comprises 25 per cent of the world prisoners. African Americans comprise nearly one million of the country's total prison population and men are most disproportionately impacted. African American males are six times more likely to be incarcerated than white males and 2.5 times more likely than Hispanic males. There are more African American men imprisoned or on probation/parole today than were enslaved in 1850 (Alexander 2010). Furthermore, it is estimated that one of every three African American males born today can expect to go to prison in his lifetime compared to one of every 17 white males (Mauer 2013). Racial disparities in arrests, trials and sentences contributed to this mass incarceration of African Americans and helped create this new racial caste system – much like Jim Crow and slavery – whose main function is to oppress and control African Americans (Alexander 2010).

The war on crime, the war on drugs, mandatory drug sentencing laws and the belief that society has become dangerously more punitive have all been blamed for the exponential rise in the American prison population. The cause of the increase centres on the primary argument that the solution to stopping crime is to build more prisons. Radical scholars and prison activists argue that racism and profit-driven tactics are behind the rising incarceration rates. Liberals have traditionally believed that people will commit fewer crimes if the root causes of crime – poverty and poor education, for example – are addressed. Those on the right accuse the liberals of being dangerously naïve in their approach to crime and called for a tougher, lock them up and throw away the key approach. Radical scholars and activists argue that harsh drug sentencing policies set during the Reagan–Bush drug wars of the 1980s – not an increase in crime rates – contributed to the increasing incarceration rates and exacerbated the racial disparities in incarceration.

For instance, possession of five grams of crack cocaine would result in a mandatory minimum five-year sentence whereas possession of 500 grams of powdered cocaine triggered the same sentence, a disparity of 100 to 1. These policies resulted in the excessive incarceration of nonviolent offenders, most of whom were poor African Americans and Hispanics. Once prisons became overcrowded as a result of the get tough on crime era, private prison corporations began to promote and profit from the idea that creating more prisons was necessary to fixing the overcrowded prison problem. Politicians in favour of the tough crime policies were able to appear competent because they were able to 'look tough on crime and fiscally conservative at the same time' (Greene 2003, 100).

African American children are paying the steepest price for the booming incarceration rates. Black children are eight times more likely to have a parent in prison than white children. The Bureau of Justice Statistics reports an estimated 809,800 people in American prisons are parents to 1,706,600 minor children (BJS.gov 2008). Among fathers in state and federal prisons, more than four in ten were black, compared to three in ten white and two in ten Hispanic fathers. The separation of father and child due to incarceration remains a major issue for African American families. Many of these men supported their families financially prior to incarceration, thus 'massive incarceration deprives thousands of children of important economic and social support' (Roberts 2001, 1017). Children of incarcerated parents also experience such traumas as separation anxiety, survivor guilt and aggression (Johnston 1995).

Based on these harrowing statistics – which includes my family – I proceeded with my research asking two primary questions: 'What is the meaning of fatherhood for incarcerated black fathers?' and 'How does incarceration influence the relationship between black fathers and their children?'

The incarcerated fathers' study

I had already built a rapport with some of the men in the study following the publication of my editorial so recruiting research participants was not too big a challenge. I mailed 30 questionnaires to the men I had been communicating with and asked them to distribute the questionnaires among other men incarcerated in their facility. The questionnaire consisted of 13 questions including, 'What does being a father mean to you and how is that role compromised by your incarceration?' It is important to note that doing prison research by mail is not an ideal method and is recommended primarily for researchers who do not have sufficient time to spend in the field. As such, research by mail presents its own set of issues. It limits the control the researcher has over the information gathering process, and there is the possibility the researcher will not get a response. Questions may be misinterpreted, resulting in answers the researcher is not looking for and unable to use. This method also restricts the researcher from asking follow-up questions on the spot and, because the inmate mail is inspected by prison personnel, the questions and answers may be compromised (Bosworth et al. 2005).

Despite the challenges, mailing the questionnaires was the best option for me primarily because of time and financial limitations. I received 15 completed surveys from men incarcerated in North Carolina, Texas, Georgia and Florida. Of the 15 men who responded, four are incarcerated for murder, five for aggravated robbery or armed robbery, five for drug offences and one for possession of stolen property. The respondents range in age from 26 to 50. One of the overwhelming themes that resulted from the questionnaires was the men's desire to be better fathers. Being a father and able to parent from prison is the hope that keeps many of the fathers surviving in a hopeless environment, but many of them simply do not know how to be the father they want to be, mainly because they did not have good father role models. They also experience a sense of powerlessness when trying to establish or maintain a relationship with their children because of the obstacles working against them, for instance mothers who will not allow the children to visit their father or children who simply do not want to have anything to do with their father.

Older children seem less interested in mending and maintaining relationships with their father, as in the case of Keith Barbour who has been incarcerated in Texas for 16 years. Barbour has two grown daughters who were 25 and 30 at the time of the study. He has been able to maintain an amicable relationship with his older daughter, but his relationship with the younger daughter has been volatile, at best. In a letter she wrote to her father in 2006, the younger daughter expressed her disinterest in having a relationship with her father. She wrote:

> I feel like the past year or so that we've been somewhat keeping correspondence has been a charade. I feel as though I've simply been going through the motions of trying to establish some sort of a relationship that doesn't exist. Though I may honor you and I harbor no ill will towards you, this does not mean that I owe you a relationship. I don't know how to feel about you because I've never had any conception of what it is to have a father. I don't know that I'll never want a relationship with you; I just know that at this moment I don't see the point. You've never been here and I've been fine. I don't see how you deserve to know me. You didn't try to establish yourself in my life when you should have.

In his response, Barbour tells her: 'I'm well aware the apologies I owe could fill a couple of more life times, but what good are 70 million if you won't accept one sincere one?' Barbour refers to his younger daughter as 'The

Blaze' because of her fiery tone. The relationship between Barbour and his younger daughter is also an example of a father/child relationship that was already damaged prior to his incarceration, which only exacerbates the problem.

Barbour's oldest daughter seems to be more forgiving than her sister. In her letter, she talks about the pain of having to see her father – for the first time in more than 13 years – through a glass partition in the prison visiting room. She wrote:

> Ever since I came to see you, my heart has been hardened, not from anything that you've done though. My heart has been broken…not being able to touch you or have you hold me was excruciating…I love you. I forgive you for being young and dumb. I don't fault you for anything. I don't underestimate the love that you have for me. Over the years in your letter I have sensed your growth and maturity, and it's never too late.

Barbour said his mission is to get his daughters to forget the boy that abandoned them and 'acknowledge the man who now fights for them. I don't know their definition of a real man, but I know the man I can offer'.

Barbour's relationship with his daughters reminded me of the relationship with my own father, described in my essay as on again/off again:

> I used to believe that any fantasy I ever had of having a father/daughter relationship with my dad was dead, but I had hope after I went to visit him in April. It was the first time I had seen my father in eight years, and the first time we had spoken in five years. We had a candid heart-to-heart conversation about why our relationship had become so estranged and agreed to find a way back into each other's lives.
>
> (Willingham 2005, 13A)

The visit went well, but the relationship with my father was severed again after he read the essay. He was not happy with what I had written about him. It would be another five years before we would speak again.

Fathers like Byron Gamble, who is serving a 51-year sentence in Texas for aggravated robbery with a deadly weapon, take pride in giving advice to their children. At the time of the study, Gamble had not seen his 12-year-old son for three years, but explains how he is still able to communicate with his son:

> I write my son approximately twice a month in order to dissuade him from following in my footsteps and to encourage him in any possible way by explaining all the negativity that surrounds me and letting him know that my mistakes are not genetic and as long as he continues to

perform well in school, sports, church, he can succeed in becoming a well-rounded, responsible man. Being a father means to provide love and support no matter the circumstances. I can always provide love because love isn't limited to a physical presence. However, I compromise my role of father in that it's almost impossible to support my son without actually being there.

Gamble represents an interesting paradox: he acknowledges the limitations of this style of parenting, yet embraces it and is proud to be able to do it. Michael McCoy, a 30-year-old father serving a 75-year sentence in Texas for a drug-related offense describes how it feels to be a father to his five sons, aged 6–12, while incarcerated. He writes, 'I can actually and honestly say it is definitely painful. There's a void that has been placed on me and my sons, and it cannot be filled until I am there physically'. Other men described parenting from prison as disappointing. Larry Jackson, who is incarcerated in Texas, said being an incarcerated father means 'I am not a parent'. Those five little words illustrate the extreme limitations the prison places on the men's parenting abilities, rendering them powerless fathers. Many of these men feel they cannot be a parent because they are in prison. Michael Carter, a father in North Carolina who has four children, said he was very interested in filling out the questionnaire, 'then I realised I wasn't the good father I thought I was'. He described how the love and support he got from his father influenced the father he is. 'I never felt left out or mistreated by my father, and through our many differences he still got my back despite my many shortcomings. From my examples of a father, how could I not be the best at fatherhood?' Dino Lowe, incarcerated in Louisiana at the time of the study, described establishing and maintaining a relationship with his son through telephone and mail. It had been nearly ten years since Lowe held his son. He writes in his response:

I've made the best of it by being positive, encouraging, understanding and extremely loving. Over the years we've gotten as close as can be regarding the situation.... At this point I tell him to make me proud by working hard to be the best in his class, to always obey his mother and never make the same decision and choices I made to come to prison.... It's hurtful and stress-filled to know I can't be there with him but at the same time I have to be strong and to make sure all my choices and future decisions are predicated upon what I want for my only child. It's rough being away but I look at it as a chance to mature & understand the power of choice, a chance to embrace virtues and be responsible so that I can teach my son and others by example.

Similarly, Andre Mays, a father of six who is incarcerated in Georgia, describes how parenting from prison has given him an opportunity to get to know his daughters:

> For any man in prison who sincerely cares about his children, maintaining a relationship with them is very important. At times it may get somewhat rough on father and child. My 16-year-old daughter wrote me a letter and talked about the pain she has to live with knowing her father is in prison.

I was able to interview Mays' oldest daughter, Jasmine, in 2007 when she was a senior in high school. She was approximately four years old when she last saw her father prior to his incarceration and described how hard it was to see other children with their fathers:

> I don't want that prison to be his life. Now that I'm getting older it doesn't hurt as much as when I was younger, but now it hurts because he can't see me go to the prom and he can't see me graduate.
>
> (Jasmine Mays, telephone interview 2007)

Surprisingly, Jasmine said it was not that hard to maintain a relationship with her father. In fact, she found it was easier to confide in him sometimes because she knows he would not get mad like her mother would, and he is not able to punish her like her mother can:

> He's a good father. Even though he's in jail, he tells us to do the right thing, to stay out of trouble and that it's more than the ghetto life out there.
>
> (Jasmine Mays, telephone interview 2007)

In sum, the fathers in this study acknowledge the difficulty of parenting from prison but they make the best of it because it is the only connection they have to their children. Though the odds are stacked against them, they want to be good or better parents to their children and do not want to be seen as criminals who give up on their children once they are incarcerated. More importantly, they want to break the cycle of incarceration in their families by setting an example of what not to do.

Reflexivity and objectivity: Challenge of the research

The biggest challenge of this study was the suspicions some of the fathers had about my motives for doing the research. My researcher status did not help to establish trust with the men as quickly or easily as

I thought it would. Several of the fathers expressed some reservations about my project. When Johnie Erwin – incarcerated in North Carolina and father to a daughter – returned his questionnaire he included a letter that said:

> This place breeds so much negativity and negative thinking that … I was surprised & shocked to hear their response. One guy told me that you were/are using me as a guinea pig for your own personal gain; another said I'm being used as a test dummy.

Barbour, the father of two grown daughters, passed along similar sentiments from other fathers:

> I have passed the questionnaire around to as many conscious brothers as I have come in contact with. They all, from the jump, asked me what is your motivation and agenda and though I am vague, they trust me simply because I am extending my trust to you.

One criticism of using reflexivity in criminological research is the concern some feminists have of the potential 'objectification and exploitation of subjects, particularly when information is gained through interviews or surveys' (Flavin 2004, 82) because it fosters a distance between research and subject. As Flavin (2004) explains,

> [o]bjectification occurs when it is assumed that a radical difference exists between the roles of scientist and subject. While conventional criminology assumes that scientific detachment requires emotional detachment, the quest for neutrality and objectivity can be a disadvantage when so much emphasis is placed on 'maintaining distance' that context and recognition of the individual humanity of the subjects are stripped away.
>
> (Flavin 2004, 82)

Applying this critique to my research, though it was not my intention to objectify the fathers in my study that is what I did when I refuse to share details about my relationship with my father. Erwin asked what impact the research was having on my relationship with my father and whether I planned to seek reconciliation with him. 'What steps are you taking to bridge that gap? Maybe I can use the same steps to reach my daughter.' Erwin asked legitimate questions, but at the time I did not think it was appropriate for me to share personal information with my research participants. I avoided what Renzetti (2013) refers to as reciprocity – instead of establishing distance from participants, researchers self-disclose by answering participants' questions. In my quest to remain objective, I was 'stripping away context and the humanity of the research participants' (Flavin and Desautels 2006, 20) by insisting on maintaining a neutral and objective stance. Erwin eventually withdrew from the study, in part because I would not self-disclose.

I was then questioned about my motives for incorporating a self-reflexive standpoint in my work when I presented my research during a faculty luncheon at the university where I was teaching in 2008. In an email I received from the former associate director of campus ministries, she suggested I separate the personal from the research. She wrote:

> Because you not only freely disclosed your personal struggles, you incorporate it into your paper comparatively to the youth and children you mention, I am concerned that when you present it again you may be discounted as someone who doesn't know how to roll with the academic discourse setting. I would tone down the self-disclosure in the paper, perhaps having it closer to the end rather than the beginning. Remember, it is your experience as a journalist that legitimizes you for this paper, not the fact that you are one of the walking wounded.
>
> (Field Research Journal, 2007)

These comments reflect a more positivist view that does not take into account that a personal connection to the research is precisely what adds value to it. Linda Carty contends that this type of sociological scientific view

> argues against researchers placing ourselves in any personal relation to our subject of study. In other words, we are to separate ourselves from what we know and what we investigate if we wish to produce legitimate sociology.
>
> (Carty 1996, 137)

Likewise, Leon Pettiway (1997) argues in *Workin' It: Women Living Through Drugs and Crime* that attempts to make criminology more scientific have overlooked the worth of reflexivity. He writes:

> For the most part, criminology is unreflective. While conscious that researchers should not bring their prejudices to the research table, many criminologists, in their search for neutrality, fail to consider their own identity in their investigative enterprises. Perhaps this is the aftershock of attempting to impose the strictures and methods of the physical sciences on criminology in our effort to make it more scientific. Therefore, armed with proper scientific rigor that ensures replication, some criminologists so distance themselves from their hearts and souls and from the context and fabric of their subjects, that they assume they are the objective

observers of 'criminals' and the conduit through which others understand the activities of 'deviants'.

(Pettiway 1997, xv–xvi)

Using reflexivity in my work has forced me to accept the fact that it is impossible for me to be objective when doing prison research. In fact, any attempts at being objective would be a disservice to the research. Being an African American woman with incarcerated relatives who is researching incarcerated African American fathers and other prison issues not only guides and informs my research, but forces me to see my research participants as people, not just subjects to be studied. Adopting a feminist reflexive approach has become more than just a way of doing research; it is a mirror image of me because when researching people in prison, I am researching my life. As Fine (1998) suggests, in qualitative research, 'self and other are knottily entangled':

> This relationship, as lived between researchers and informants, is typically obscured in social science texts, protecting privilege, securing distance, and laminating the contradictions. Despite denials, qualitative researchers are always implicated at the hyphen. When we opt, as has been the tradition, simply to write about those who have been othered, we deny the hyphen. When we opt, instead, to engage in social struggles with those who have been exploited and subjugated, we work the hyphen, revealing far more about ourselves, and far more about the structures of othering. Eroding the fixedness of categories, we and they enter and play with the blurred boundaries that proliferate.
>
> (Fine 1998, 135)

Working the hyphen for me includes negotiating my role as an African American woman with incarcerated relatives critiquing the system that is profiting off my family's pain.

Conclusion

This chapter contributes to discussions of power/powerlessness and reflexivity by analysing how a reflexive approach allows researchers to give voice to the voiceless and legitimises the experiences of incarcerated people. This chapter also contributes to discussions of reflexivity in criminological research by illustrating how the value of reflexivity and using a reflexive standpoint create opportunities for researchers to tell powerful stories of the oppressed. However, when the researcher is also a member of an oppressed group similar to the people in the research, reflexivity becomes more than a research method and cannot be reduced to an academic exercise. Even with its limitations and criticisms, future researchers should understand that reflexivity can actually be an advantage to criminological research. As such, reflexivity should be explored, not stifled. Though the researcher may struggle with navigating the hyphen between researcher and research, the struggle presents challenges that should be viewed as possibilities and not obstacles.

References

Alexander, M. (2010) *The New Jim Crow: Mass Incarceration in the Age of Colorblindness*, New York: The New Press.

BJS.gov (2008) *Bureau of Justice Statistics Parents in Prison and Their Minor Children*. URL (accessed 9 September 2013): http://www.bjs.gov/content/pub/press/pptmcpr.cfm

Bosworth, M., Campbell, D., Demby, B., Ferranti, S.M. and Santos, M. (2005) 'Doing Prison Research: Views from Inside' *Qualitative Inquiry* 11(2): 249–64.

Carty, L. (1996) 'Seeing Through the Eye of Difference: A Reflection on Three Research Journeys'. In H. Gottfried (ed.) *Feminism and Social Change: Bridging Theory and Practice*, Urbana: University of Chicago Press, pp.123–42.

Fine, M. (1998) 'Working the Hyphens Reinventing Self and Other in Qualitative Research'. In N. Denzin and Y. Lincoln (eds) *The Landscape of Qualitative Research Theories and Issues*, Thousand Oaks, CA: Sage, pp.130–55.

Flavin, J. (2004) 'Feminism for the Mainstream Criminologist'. In P.J. Schram and B. Koon-Witt (eds) *Gendered (In)Justice: Theory and Practice in Feminist Criminology*, Long Grove, IL: Waveland Press, Inc., pp.68–92.

Flavin, J. and Desautels, A. (2006) 'Feminism and Crime'. In C. Renzetti, L. Goodstein, and S. Miller (eds) *Rethinking Gender, Crime and Justice*, New York: Oxford University Press, pp.11–28.

Greene, J. (2003) 'Entrepreneurial Corrections: Incarceration as a Business Opportunity'. In M. Mauer and M. Chesney-Lind (eds) *Invisible Punishment: The Collateral Consequences of Mass Imprisonment*, New York: The New York Press, pp.95–113.

Johnston, D. (1995) 'Effects of Parental Incarceration'. In K. Gabel and D. Johnston (eds) *Children of Incarcerated Parents*, New York: Lexington Books, pp.59–87.

Mauer, M. (2013) 'Report of the Sentencing Project to the United Nations Human Rights Committee: Regarding Racial Disparities in the United States Justice System'. URL (accessed 2 December 2013): http://sentencingproject.org/doc/publications/rd_ICCPR%20Race%20and%20Justice%20Shadow%20Report.pdf

Pettiway, L. (1997) *Workin' It: Women Living Through Drugs and Crime*, Philadelphia: Temple University Press.

Renzetti, C. (2013) *Feminist Criminology*, Abingdon: Routledge.

Roberts, D. (2001) 'Criminal Justice and Black Families: The Collateral Damage of over Enforcement' *University of California-Davis Law Review* 34: 1005–28.

Willingham, B. (2005) 'Millions Just Like Me'. *USA Today*, 12 October, 13A.

12

Accessing the Experiences of Female and Minority Police Officers: Observations from an Ethnographic Researcher

Meghan E. Hollis

Introduction

The focus of policing research is typically on the perspective and experience of the white, male police officer (Holdaway and O'Neill 2006a). It is often difficult for researchers to access and assess the experiences of female and/or minority police officers. This difficulty comes about as a result of the under-representation of females and non-whites in the police occupation. It is exacerbated when these areas are not the focus of research. If those who carry out research of the police are not actively seeking out female and non-white research participants, the research findings presented will frequently neglect to reflect these experiences. This failure to include a diversity of experiences is not intentional, yet it may influence the findings that are presented.

This chapter seeks to examine this (often un-intentional) neglect of the female and non-white police officer populations. Of particular importance is the inability to examine the reflexive nature of race and police culture as well as assessment of gender and police culture. This chapter develops a reflexive perspective on the researcher's experiences during a three-year ethnographic study of a police department in an attempt to understand the difficulties in accessing and assessing the experiences of female and/or non-white police officers. The chapter will start by exploring the policing literature to provide a foundation of research experiences that have examined the experiences of females and non-white police officers. The focus will then shift to an examination of the researcher's experience in the ethnographic study with explanations regarding difficulties in access and assessment provided. Finally, the implications of the researcher's position as a white female on access and fieldwork will be discussed with a focus on whether the experiences in the field changed the researcher or if the researcher's presence changed that which was observed.

Fielding (1994, 46) states: 'The archetypal police perspective is hard-bitten, cynical and drawn to rigid in-group/out-group distinctions. Until recently, the relationship between these cultural values and gender has passed unremarked outside feminist thought'. The policing occupation continues to be dominated by white males (Heidensohn 1992; Fielding 1994; Walklate 2000; Brown 2007; Loftus 2008; Manning 1997, 2010), and this domination exists both in the United Kingdom and the United States. Furthermore, research has indicated that the values of female officers bear a marked resemblance to those of the dominant male culture in the policing occupation (Brewer 1991; Fielding and Fielding 1992; Fielding 1994). Fielding (1994, 47) describes the police culture as 'an almost pure form of "hegemonic masculinity"' outlining four key features that are highlighted by this culture. These four key features include (1) a focus on aggressiveness and physical action, (2) emphasis on competitiveness and 'preoccupation with the imagery of conflict', (3) an emphasis on heterosexual orientations (often including use of misogynistic terminology and patriarchal views of women) and (4) clear and strict in-group/out-group distinctions (Fielding 1994, 47). Waddington's (1999) examination of the police 'canteen culture' finds that the behaviours and interactions that occur in the canteen (backstage area of interaction) involve expressive talk which is used to indicate the meaning of different (and potentially problematic) police experiences. These behaviours have been portrayed as encouraging racist and sexist 'canteen banter' in previous work (Waddington 1999). Brewer and Magee (1991) highlight the heavily masculine occupational culture and how it contributes to differential treatment of female police officers.

Taking this argument further, the literature is indicative that policing is not only a masculine culture, but that it is dominated by a white, heterosexual, masculine perspective. Loftus (2008, 756) used data from an ethnography of police culture to examine 'how the extension of recognition for previously marginalised groups has shaped the *interior* culture by examining the ways in which such developments resonate within the informal ideologies of officers working within the organization'. She found that there were two dominant perspectives that emerged. The first perspective was held by the heterosexual, white, male officers and involved resentment towards institutionalised diversity, while the second perspective (held by female, minority, ethnic, gay and lesbian officers) indicated that there was a persistent imperious, white, male, heterosexist culture. Loftus (2007) also used this ethnographic study to assess class-based influences on police culture. She found that poor and low-status white males carried out the majority of the organisation's workload in practice. Loftus (2010) also indicated that these deeply ingrained (orthodox) views and practices continue to influence police culture and the police organisation.

Holdaway and O'Neill (2004) examined the relationship between the development of black police associations in England and Wales and the articulation of race and race-based perspectives in police organisations. They indicated that these associations were representative of a new articulation of race as well as indicative of a need for a new approach to police management. This new approach would require response to the organised demands of these formal organisations. Despite this, Holdaway and O'Neill (2006b) indicated that institutional racism continued due to an institutional memory of racism within the various constabularies. This is likely attributable to the dominant white, heterosexual, male culture that persists in police organisations.

Loftus (2008) was able to assess female and non-white officers' experiences; however, her research was *designed* to do so. In other words, the focus was on these differing experiences directly. For those researchers who are studying policing more broadly (for instance Waddington 1993; Manning 1997, 2010; Hollis 2013), there is often no intent to purposefully seek out the experiences of non-white and female officers. Furthermore, as noted by Loftus (2007), when the majority of the practical workload is carried out by white males this can create additional constraints on researchers in assessing the experiences of the non-white and female officers.

Holdaway and O'Neill (2006a, 496) indicate that research on ethnic differences in police experience is a neglected area of research. They further indicate that the literature has ignored notions of work/employment and organisational cultures around work and employment as contexts which influence conceptualisations of ethnicity. It is possible that this lack of attention has developed, at least in part, as a result of difficulties in access with respect to those outside of traditional white, male police roles. This is indicative of a need to reflect on the research experience in an effort to understand this lack of access and assessment.

The police department and the study site

In the metropolitan city where the ethnography was conducted (see Hollis 2013 for a full description of the study, methodology, study site and findings), there were a total of 205 sworn police officers at the time of the study. This included 1 police chief, 5 captains, 15 lieutenants, 27 sergeants and 157 patrol officers at the time of the study. The department also employed 38 full-time civilian personnel. There are several special units in the police department, including detectives, a drug unit, a vice unit, a community policing unit, Drug Abuse Resistance Education (DARE) officers, school resource officers, a marine/scuba unit and K-9 officers. This department receives around 60,000 calls for service per year, and they make around 2000 arrests per year. The police officers in this department are mostly white males (see next section). These officers typically come from middle-class backgrounds, and the majority are from families that have been in the city for generations. There are many officers whose parents and other relatives were officers in the police department (and some still are). For example, the police chief's son was hired as a police officer recently. Many of the officers have some college education, and some have graduate degrees.

The coastal New England city where this research was conducted is one of the ten largest cities in the state. It has a population of just over 90,000 individuals in approximately 38,000 households. This city covers 26.9 square miles, with 16.9 square miles of land and about 10 square miles of water. There are approximately 27 miles of shoreline included in the city limits. The population of the city is nearly 80 per cent white, 15 per cent Asian, and 2 per cent black; however, nearly 20 per cent of the population is foreign born. Approximately 49 per cent of the residents own their homes, and the median household income is $47,121 with 7 per cent of residents living beneath the national poverty threshold. There is a subway line that runs through the city connecting it to the nearby metropolitan hub. Most of the residents are commuters who travel to the nearby metropolitan city for work.

Differences in accessing and assessing female and non-white police officer experiences

The distribution of officers by race and sex is informative. Of the 205 sworn police officers, only 12 (5.85 per cent) are females. The city has a population of 93,027, and 52.1 per cent of those residents are female. Clearly the representation of females on the police force is not reflective of the distribution of females in the population. Of the 205 officers, there are no Hispanic officers (0 per cent), 10 Asian officers (4.88 per cent) and 1 black officer (0.49 per cent).

The distribution of the population in the city with respect to race/ethnicity as of the year 2000 census was 78.4 per cent white (non-Hispanic), 15.4 per cent Asian, 2.2 per cent black, 0.2 per cent American Indian/Alaskan Native and 2.1 per cent Hispanic/Latino. Comparing this to the more recent 2010 census is helpful in understanding the dynamic of the city in recent years. As of the 2010 census, 65.5 per cent of the population was white (non-Hispanic), 24.0 per cent Asian, 4.6 per cent black, 0.2 per cent American Indian/Alaskan Native and 3.3 Hispanic/Latino. This is indicative that the city is continuing to see shifts in the makeup of the population. The percentage white (non-Hispanic) has decreased by 12.9 per cent. The percentages of Asian, black and Hispanic/Latino residents have increased. The percentage of residents who are Asian has increased by 8.6 per cent. The percentage of residents who are black has increased by 2.4 per cent, while the percentage of Hispanic/Latino residents has increased by 1.2 per cent.

The changing population suggests that there should be (ideally) a related change in the number of officers hired representing the different races. While there have been more Asian officers hired over the past decade, the other racial and ethnic groups have not seen similar increases. The economic downturn and budgetary restrictions (and related hiring freezes) may have had an impact on this; however, the most recent hires (within the past year) have not included any individuals representing these groups. There was one female officer hired in the past year (she recently graduated from the police academy and is now in field training). There is a disparity between the distribution of different racial/ethnic groups in the city and their representation in the department.

The minority police officer's experience

Given the under representation of these groups in the police department (11 non-white officers and 12 female officers), it is not surprising that it was difficult (near impossible) to assess the experiences of these individuals in the ethnographic research. The one black police officer on the force worked the midnight shift (from midnight until 8 am). Most of the ethnographic research was carried out during the day (8 am until 4 pm) and evening (4 pm until midnight) shifts. There were a limited number of observations and 'ride-alongs' conducted with the midnight shift, and during that time there was only one interaction with the black police officer. This interaction occurred when passing each other in the hallway of the station.

The interactions with the Asian officers were slightly less limited as there were Asian officers who worked during both the day and evening shifts. These interactions involved some conversations while in the station as well as some limited interaction when these officers would respond to the same call as the officer that I was in the cruiser with. Unfortunately, there was no interaction beyond this superficial level. Given the limited interactions and limited *opportunities* for interaction with the non-white officers, the majority of the findings cannot be generalised to this group of officers. Furthermore, the white officers did not discuss the non-white officers with me or reference them in stories that were told.

This lack of information and access with respect to the non-white police officer's experience is concerning. Most of the research on policing has focused on the white male police officer's experience. These difficulties raise important empirical questions: Does the non-white police officer's experience differ from that of the white police officer? Do non-white officers' perceptions of the work differ from that of the white police officer? Do non-white police officers' perceptions of people, places and events encountered as a result of the job differ from white officers' perceptions? Some research (as discussed previously) has made progress in examining differential perceptions of organisational culture based on race, but more research is needed in this area as well.

The female police officer's experience

Interactions with the female officers were limited as well. There were limited opportunities while inside the station to interact with female officers, and there were a small number of calls where a female officer also responded to an incident that the officer that I was riding along with responded to. This combined with the low number of female officers to limit the opportunities for observations and data collection that involved the female police officers. These limitations on opportunities for interactions and observations with female officers also indicate that the findings cannot be generalised to the female officers.

Further complications with studying female officers and their experiences arose from the influence of the white male-dominated police culture. Female police officers are often sensitive to perceptions of their male colleagues. As a result, many female officers feel they have to work harder, emphasise what are determined to be desirable masculine characteristics and constantly have to make efforts to 'prove themselves' to be seen as good police officers and to be accepted by the male-dominated organisational culture. Unfortunately, observations and conversations were limited, therefore it is possible that this is a limited perspective.

Male perceptions of female officers were classified in one of two ways. These two perceptions were frequently discussed with me when female officers were a topic of conversation. Males either saw female officers as 'butch' or 'lesbians' who were good police officers only because they possessed masculine attributes or as 'whores' or those females they believe only have their position because of a sexual relationship with someone (or a superior's desire for a sexual relationship). The latter were often portrayed as 'bad' police officers who were not capable of doing the job. It is possible that these perceptions combined with the desire to prove themselves made it less likely that the female officers would talk to me or interact with me as much – particularly since I am a female as well.

The lack of information and access with respect to the female police officer's experience is, similar to the previous discussion regarding non-white police officers, concerning. As mentioned previously, much of the policing research has focused on the white male police officer's experience. Some important empirical questions that this raises include the following: Does the female police officer's experience differ from that of the male police officer? Do female officers' perceptions of the work differ from that of male police officers? Do female police officers' perceptions of people, places and events differ from male officers' perception? Do female police officers' experience with and perception of the organisational culture differ from that of male officers? While some research has examined these and other questions related to the female police officers' experience, much more research is needed in this area.

The researcher's role

The researcher's role in policing research needs to be examined as well. One key question that should be addressed further related to my role as a white, female researcher – more specifically, what was the relationship between my status as a white, female researcher and that observed. I find that those observed changed me as a researcher, but simultaneously I likely changed the behaviours that I was observing. The level of access may have been higher due to my status as a female researcher, for example. As a female, my perception was often that I was seen as less of a threat than a man would be. The police officers also often took on standard patriarchal roles in relation to me. Further discussion of the research experience highlights these observations.

Female researchers in the field of police studies have documented important observations on the relationship between observer characteristics and that which is observed. Hunt (1984) indicates that the personal characteristics of the researcher have an important effect on their research practice. Furthermore, she indicates that being a female researcher brings unique problems to the field; however, it also can increase 'female penetration' into the field. Brewer and Magee (1991) highlight specific concerns with treatment of female researchers when studying a male-dominated occupation, including experiences with sexual hustling, fraternizing and paternalistic attitudes. Women may be treated as 'acceptable incompetents' (Lofland 1971, 180 see also Brewer and Magee 1991).

My experiences in the research project discussed here highlight some of these concerns. I was frequently subjected to sexual harassment and innuendo. For example, one night after eight hours of observation (a ride-along with an officer during his shift) I was invited to go with the officers to the bar. As we were sitting in the bar talking, one of the officers asked me: 'So, what do women really think of porn?' This occurred early on in my research (about six months after I started my fieldwork). I realised that this was (in some ways) a test of my trustworthiness and acceptability in the group, therefore I knew that my response would shape my access, and the level of trust with these officers in the future. At the very least, these types of situations required strategic responses.

Other experiences highlighted the paternalistic attitudes of some of the officers. In one such instance, as I was sitting in the communications room prior to going on a ride-along, the communications sergeant asked me: 'Are you sure you want to go out in a cruiser? The things police do are really dangerous for a girl'. He followed this with the statement that he wasn't 'trying to treat me with "kid gloves" but wanted to make sure [I knew] what [I was] getting [myself] into'. The sergeant further indicated that the officers I rode along with couldn't baby me or babysit me as they had jobs to do. It is important to note that I had already been doing ride-alongs and observations for a month at this point. This sergeant continued to act in this paternalistic (and almost condescending, at times) manner throughout the time that I engaged in my research with the police department. These experiences were similar to those of other researchers mentioned previously.

Despite these challenges, I was successful in navigating access difficulties in the research. There were several research decisions that I made that may have enhanced my access over the course of the study. I willingly wore the bullet-resistant vest that the department asked me to wear during ride-alongs and observations. When officers ran after subjects, I kept up with them and proved that I would not be a burden. During my observations with the Marine Unit (on the boats), I pitched in with the rest of the team when loading and unloading the boats and preparing for missions. I openly engaged in conversations with the officers, and I frequently answered questions about my perspectives and experiences in a form of reciprocity (Mauss 1990). I also reacted to stressful and unusual situations in a manner that resulted in increased acceptance by the officers.

There are several examples of stressful and unusual situations where my reactions increased my level of acceptance and access in the research; however, I will highlight two here. In one instance, I was riding with one of the patrol sergeants and we were dispatched to a call for a medical assist. As we were driving to the location (with lights and sirens on), the sergeant asked me if I had a strong stomach. I responded that I did, and he indicated that they typically only dispatch a sergeant to those types of calls when there is a potential death. When we arrived at the location, there was an older man (probably mid- to late 60s) who was (indeed) dead. It appeared that the man rolled off of the bed in his sleep, hit his head against a stool that was next to his bed and broke his neck. As we walked into the room, the first thing that I saw was the deceased man on the floor next to his bed naked. I was aware that the officers present were watching me for my reaction, so I reacted in a way that is common for the police officers in uncomfortable situations, by making a joke, 'I guess that is why you shouldn't sleep naked'. The officers chuckled and went about their work as usual. After that incident I was accepted more by the officers and my level of access increased.

Another fieldwork experience involved my ability to stay calm and act appropriately in a potentially dangerous situation. There was a dispatch that came over the radio for 'all cars' to respond to a fight at a popular club (on a Saturday night at closing time). We were on the opposite side of town, and the officer drove with lights and sirens on at a speed of nearly 80 miles per hour at times to get there quickly. On our way more information was provided by the dispatcher, and we found out that there was a fight where some people were using knives of 'approximately 100 people'. As we got close to the club, the officer I was riding with indicated that when we arrived he needed me to stay close behind him as it could be more dangerous for me to stay in the cruiser by myself. He drove right up to the crowd, ordered me to follow him and jumped out of the car with his can of pepper spray out. I followed close behind him as he ran into the centre of the crowd and sprayed a cloud of pepper spray on those around him. As he did this, I ended up being sprayed with pepper spray as well. The officers quickly got the crowd to disperse, made some arrests of those individuals who continued to be disorderly and assisted the paramedics in providing medical attention where necessary. The officer realised that I stayed close behind him even after I had been sprayed and asked if I needed him to drive me home or if I needed to go to the hospital. He seemed surprised that I had followed his orders and stayed with him. I indicated that I would be fine, but needed to know what to use to wash out my eyes. He got me a bottle of saline from the trunk of the cruiser and helped me wash out my eyes and nose. He gave me instructions for showering that night and washing my clothes so I did not end up with more problems (as water reactivates the spray). I continued my ride-along for another four hours after this incident. The officers were increasingly likely to talk to me and accept me as one of the group after this incident, and my level of access increased dramatically.

The experiences in the field also changed me as a researcher. I think many of those changes were a result of those being the experiences of a white, female researcher. In many ways as the research progressed, I began to take on some of the subjects' characteristics such as a stance similar to the police officers, surveillance habits that they often engage in (referred to as 'head on a swivel' by many of the officers) and constantly checking which street I am on and what the nearest cross street is when I am driving. I also had to learn new ways of responding to comments and actions that I would normally consider offensive in order to be accepted by the male officers.

Related to notions of where a researcher stands on the participant-observer continuum (is the researcher more participant as observer, observer as participant or something in the middle) are questions of how much the researcher changes that which is observed. In the study discussed here, the key question relates to how much the presence of a white female researcher changes that which was observed. In other words, how might the findings have differed if the researcher had been a white male, minority male or minority female. Those who are studied also can have an impact on the researcher. The subjects in ethnography often change the ethnographer in key ways. This can also further change that which is noticed or observed as the ethnographer becomes more attuned to certain aspects of that which is observed. My experiences in the field changed me in many ways, including the development of a type of hyper-vigilance, a different manner of carrying myself and a new understanding of police communication and the policing occupation and culture. This is a natural part of the ethnographic process in many ways.

Conclusion

This chapter has contributed to discussions of reflexivity in criminological research in two ways. It first examined the relationship between race/ethnicity/gender and police culture. This discussion examined difficulties in assessing whether the race and gender of the police officer impact their assessment of culture or whether the dominant culture impacts the impression management of the individual officer. The chapter then examined the researcher's role. This included discussions of whether the researcher changes that which is observed in ethnographic research, or if those observed change the researcher. Its contribution to discussion of reflexivity (focusing here on the intersection of class, race, gender and researcher experiences) is related to the typical underrepresentation of minorities and females in the police force. This discussion involved an examination of difficulties in assessing and understanding the female and/or minority police officer's experience. The discussion further highlighted the experiences of an atypical police ethnographer – a female ethnographer. Although the number of females doing this type of research is growing, much of the key literature comes from male researchers. This chapter further develops this work by reflecting on the difficulties that are faced by policing scholars when attempting to assess the experiences of non-white and female police officers.

This chapter also examined the unique challenges faced by a female ethnographer in studying a male-dominated occupation. Research experiences were used to highlight the unique obstacles that I faced as well as my approach to handle those obstacles. I was subjected to sexual harassment and, to some degree, a level of role confusion as police officers often pushed me more into a role of participant in interactions and further away from an observer role. Officers also treated me as a 'fragile creature' they had to care for in some instances. This changed the process of negotiating access. This is consistent with experiences of other female police ethnographers (see, e.g. Hunt 1984; Brewer and Magee 1991; Marks 2004). Trust tests and a requirement that you can 'prove yourself' in a hyper-masculine atmosphere form a common thread in these research experiences.

The lessons that can be learned for future researchers are related to the need for further research in this area as well as a conscious attempt to be more inclusive when doing ethnographic research. Further research needs to examine the relationship between race/gender and experiences and perceptions of police culture. Is it the individual's gender or race that impacts their perception and experience of the police culture, or does the culture itself impact the impression management carried out by members of different racial, ethnic and gender classifications? Could it be both acting in a reflexive manner? Researchers also need to make a more conscious attempt to include observations of female and non-white officers when doing more general policing research (that research that does not look to compare experiences or focus solely on the experiences of non-white and female officers). Finally, researchers – particularly ethnographic researchers – need to continue to reflect on the experiences in the field to build the methodological literature regarding researcher impact. The researcher both impacts and is impacted by those studied in ethnographic (and other) research.

References

Brewer, J. (1991) 'Hercules, Hippolyte and the Amazons – or Policewomen in the Royal Ulster Constabulary' *British Journal of Sociology* 42(2): 231–47.
Brewer, J.D. and Magee, K. (1991) *Inside the RUC: Routine Policing in a Divided Society*, Oxford: Clarendon Press.
Brown, J. (2007) 'From Cult of Masculinity to Smart Macho: Gender Perspectives on Police Occupational Culture'. In M. O'Neill, A. Singh and M. Marks (eds) *Police Occupational Culture: New Debates and Directions*, Oxford: Elsevier, pp.205–26.
Fielding, N. (1994) 'Cop Canteen Culture'. In T. Newburn and E.A. Stanko (eds) *Just Boys Doing Business: Men, Masculinities, and Crime*, New York: Routledge, pp.46–63.
Fielding, N. and Fielding, J. (1992). 'A Comparative Minority: Female Recruits to a British Constabulary Force' *Policing and Society* 2: 205–18.
Heidensohn, F. (1992) *Women in Control: The Role of Women in Law Enforcement*, Oxford: Oxford University Press.
Holdaway, S. and O'Neill, M. (2004) 'The Development of Black Police Associations: Changing Articulations of Race Within the Police' *British Journal of Criminology* 44(6): 854–65.
Holdaway, S. and O'Neill, M. (2006a) 'Ethnicity and Culture: Thinking About "Police Ethnicity"' *British Journal of Sociology* 57(3): 483–502.
Holdaway, S. and O'Neill, M. (2006b) 'Institutional Racism After MacPherson: An Analysis of Police Views' *Policing and Society* 16(4): 349–69.
Hollis, M.E. (2013) *Defining Crime: An Analysis of Organizational Influences on Police Processing of Information*. Doctoral dissertation, Northeastern University. Criminology and Justice Policy Dissertations, Paper 18. URL (accessed 1 October 2013): http://hdl.handle.net/2047/d20003245.
Hunt, J. (1984) 'The Development of Rapport Through the Negotiation of Gender in Fieldwork Among the Police' *Human Organization* 43: 283–96.
Lofland, J. (1971) *Analyzing Social Settings*, Belmont, CA: Wadsworth.
Loftus, B. (2007) 'Policing the Irrelevant'. In M. O'Neill, M. Marks and A. Singh (eds) *Police Occupational Culture*, Oxford: Elsevier Press, pp.181–204.
Loftus, B. (2008) 'Dominant Culture Interrupted: Recognition, Resentment, and the Politics of Change in an English Police Force' *British Journal of Criminology* 48: 756–77.
Loftus, B. (2010) 'Police Occupational Culture: Classic Themes, Altered Times', *Policing and Society* 20(1): 1–20.
Manning, P.K. (1997) *Police Work: The Social Organization of Policing*, 2nd edn, Prospect Heights, IL: Waveland Press.
Manning, P.K. (2010) *Democratic Policing in a Changing World*, Boulder, CO: Paradigm Publishers.
Marks, M. (2004) 'Researching Police Transformation: The Ethnographic Imperative' *British Journal of Criminology* 44: 866–88.

Mauss, M. (1990) *The Gift: The Form and Reason for Exchange in Archaic Societies,* New York: W.W. Norton.
Waddington, P.A.J. (1993) *Calling the Police,* Brookfield, VT: Ashgate.
Waddington, P.A.J. (1999) 'Police (Canteen) Sub-Culture: An Appreciation' *British Journal of Criminology* 39: 287–309.
Walklate, S. (2000) 'Equal Opportunities and the Future of Policing'. In F. Leishman, B. Loveday and S. Savage (eds) *Core Issues in Policing,* 2nd edn, Essex: Pearson Education, pp. 191–203.

13
Researching 'Bogus' Asylum Seekers, 'Illegal' Migrants and 'Crimmigrants'
Monish Bhatia

Introduction

Both immigration and criminal laws are, at their core, systems of inclusion and exclusion. They are designed to determine whether and how to include individuals as members of society or exclude them from it, thereby, creating insiders and outsiders (Stumpf 2006). Both are designed to create distinct categories of people – innocent versus guilty, admitted versus excluded or, as majority would say, 'legal' versus 'illegal' (Stumpf 2006). Viewed in that light, perhaps it is not surprising that these two areas of law have become inextricably connected in the official discourses. When politicians and policy makers (and also law enforcement authorities and tabloid press) seek to raise the barriers for non-citizens to attain membership in society, it is unremarkable that they turn their attention to an area of the law that similarly functions to exclude the 'other' – transforming immigrants into 'crimmigrants'.[1] As a criminological researcher one then has to rise up to the challenges of disentangling these so-called officially constructed (pseudo) realities, and breaking free from a continued dominance of authoritative discourses, and developing an alternative understanding of 'crimmigration' by connecting the processes of criminalisation and 'othering' with poverty, xeno-racism and other forms of social exclusion (see Institute of Race Relations 1987; Richmond 1994; Fekete 2001; Bowling and Phillips 2002; Sivanandan 2002; Weber and Bowling 2004).

Criminology has to constantly strive for an inclusionary vision that is connected to debates in human rights, democratic accountability and social justice (Barton et al. 2007). To facilitate this, alternative methodologies such as peace-making, feminist, activist and participatory action research (to list a few) have emerged, offering a counter-discourse and challenging the status quo. They are increasingly employed to uncover state and structural violence, human suffering and inequalities of marginalised and oppressed groups. While considerations of these methodologies are not new, their (re)emergence within criminology strongly coincides with the sixth and seventh moments of qualitative inquiry (Denzin and Lincoln 2000; Yuen 2011; Bhatia 2014), and emotions are given prime importance within these moments.

This chapter has two aims. It not only draws upon emotions to demonstrate how it can provide a navigation tool for researchers, drive critical criminological knowledge and help in exposing state brutality and injustice against crimmigrants; but it also outlines the ethical and methodological dilemmas faced while conducting sensitive qualitative research with marginalised and vulnerable groups. The chapter offers rigorous and in-depth analysis of my field experiences and of my emotions. I have extensively drawn upon the *research journal* (from now on referred to as RJ) to aid clarity in reflections.[2]

Why turn to emotional reflexivity?

> Forty years ago there seem to have been more scientists; now there appear to be more selves.
>
> (Mintz 1989, 793)

The use of the academic 'self' in the data collection process brings the researcher close to the real-life experiences of vulnerable participants, and it also helps in capturing the multidimensionality and intricacy of such experiences (Rew et al. 1993). The (sub)conscious attempt to establish a connection with the participants for data collection purposes results in the researcher developing an empathetic lens, which enables the visualisation of the world from the insider's point of view. However, this type of close and regular engagement with participants in the field settings raises both practical and ethical challenges related to the issues of blurring boundaries (Watts 2008). Becoming exposed to the raw words and vulnerability of participants can also make it difficult for the researcher to act as an 'omnipotent expert', who is expected to be in control of the 'passive' research subjects and the research process. Further, the role of the 'self' in field settings (for instance the traditional understanding of the academic self) as an impartial outsider, detached, distanced, freed of personality and bias might become difficult to sustain when confronted with injustice, pain and human suffering, which affect the researcher emotionally. Instead of disguising or blocking these emotions, and considering it as a threat to objectivity, one must actively acknowledge its role in the research process and production of knowledge. As Hochschild (1983, 31) suggests, emotions have a 'signal function' just as hearing and seeing, which acts as clues 'in figuring out what is real'.

Similarly, while highlighting the link between knowledge production and emotions, Wilkins (1993, 94) argues that '...our emotional responses constitute key cognitive and analytic resources in the "here and now" of the research setting and are capable of yielding important sociological insights'. She also mentions that such responses may aid sophisticated sensibility in two ways:

> Firstly, properly understood, they have a sensitising, cognitive function which alerts us to the meanings and behaviours of others. They make possible a sensitive attunement predicated on our capacity to empathise, which in turn depends upon our personal and emotional resources. Secondly, a sophisticated sensibility, grounded in our emotional responses, has an important interpretive function. It is a medium through which intuitive insight and inchoate knowledge arise, and this in turn depends on the availability of similar emotions and/or experience...
>
> (Wilkins 1993, 96)

While an emotional way of knowing may be contrasted with an 'objective', 'scientific' approach, it is more appropriate to perceive our emotional and cognitive functioning as inseparable (Hubbard et al. 2010).

Since research is part of an evolving process and not just a finished product, it entails reflecting on and learning from field experiences, being able to analyse/re-evaluate our roles critically, and perhaps our emotions, which can induce self-discovery, insights and new hypothesis about the research questions. It may also help us 'confront seriously and thoroughly the problems that these topics pose' (Lee and Renzetti 1993, 10). Keeping this in mind, this chapter focuses on emotionality, ethical problems that arose during various stages of the fieldwork and my position to those who were researched. First however, the following section provides information about my research.

My research

My thesis titled *Resisting 'Bare-Life'? Impacts of Policies and Procedures on Asylum Seekers and 'Illegal' Migrants* examined the impacts of the United Kingdom's immigration policies and procedures on asylum seekers and 'illegal' migrants. It draws upon their experiences of living in the empty bureaucratic space and shows the ways in which they have used their agency to 'resist' and overcome the controls that render them as 'bare-life'. The study narrated their experiences of the British criminal justice and immigration systems, the treatment they received in hands of the authorities, the violence and abuse they endured in detention centres and while getting forcefully deported from the United Kingdom and the travesty of justice they received from courts. I employed qualitative methodologies and in-depth interviews with 22 asylum seekers and six specialist practitioners. By embedding myself as a volunteer support worker with three refugee organisations over a period of

18 months, I was able to access research participants and interact with state authorities, and gathered a rich qualitative data set. The following sections offer narratives of my field experiences.

On the fine line of academic boundaries

The most challenging aspect of the research was adopting the role of a volunteer worker. The role helped in capturing a kaleidoscopic image of the world. It required a commitment, perseverance and a great deal of patience. I had no experience of the asylum system or working with the asylum seekers, and it was somehow difficult to anticipate the outcomes of being in an environment that extensively assists these individuals. There was a constant fear of 'whether this role would obstruct my data collection process and make me go native' (RJ 11/09). As I progressed further with the role, the amount of time spent on the casework directly contributed to my understanding of the system; however, it also triggered a feeling of frustration and exhaustion, and on one occasion the clash of roles resulted in *severe confusion*. During January 2010, I was assisting Bukola[3] (pseudonym), who had seven days to complete a form and present it to the *Court of Appeal*. She did not have any legal assistance, funds or time to go through the referral process. I agreed to assist her, as noted in the RJ:

> I was extremely worried of the consequences and that she might get detained [again]...she kept crying and reminding me of her 20 week old premature baby...to some extent I was also feeling obligated, as she trusted me with her story and kept saying repeatedly 'you are like my brother – help me please!'...she also mentioned about the feeling of embarrassment and emotional exhaustion that she encountered by repeatedly telling various organisations details of her situation [including the time she was forced into prostitution and raped]...and then being turned down and refused help...the researcher side of me kept insisting to protect such vulnerable subjects...The compassionate side of me wanted to offer unconditional help...I had to take advantage of my position as a volunteer to overcome this dilemma and anxiety...
>
> (RJ 02/10)

However, due to my lack of knowledge and experience of the appeal process, I had to forward this case to the senior caseworker. This legal instrument was beyond his expertise as well and he therefore advised me to contact the Immigration Law Centre and make an urgent referral. Some of the staff members at the Law Centre were aware that I was a doctoral researcher. On calling the Law Centre, I explained the case and difficulties encountered in filling the form.[4] The confusion of my volunteer and research roles spilled over in the conversation. Also, the communication was greatly affected due to excessive background noise at the drop-in session, and the Law Centre staff assumed that I (as a doctoral researcher) was attempting to submit an important legal instrument which could have serious repercussions for the asylum seeking woman and her premature baby. The Law Centre staff member discussed this issue with a colleague at the University (who also happened to be her friend) without first discussing the matter with me, which would have enabled me the opportunity to provide an explanation. The colleague then raised her concerns directly to senior members of the department, with the effect of escalating the situation. I was called for a meeting and confronted regarding my ethical practices. Further, concerns were raised that I was getting in 'too deep' and crossing my academic boundaries. All those involved had to be provided with a detailed explanation/clarification of the circumstances/situation (including the Law Centre staff).[5]

A few days after the incident I had an opportunity to reflect and analyse my emotional reactions and record it in my journal:

> absolutely horrifying...I was scared that the issue will reach the ethics committee...and my practices will be subjected to scrutiny...having just initiated the interview process, this was the least thing I was expecting...I was baffled to see the number of people who got involved due to the confusion caused by the lack of clarity in my roles...those who agreed to offer help were surprised by the intensity of the situation...and the fact that the ethics on the ground can be challenging and totally different to what we mention on the forms...and sympathised with me, i.e. a PhD student, who had to take tough decisions in precarious and unexpected situations...on one hand my mind was filled with fear...that my research will get paused and I will have to make a fresh application to the ethics committee...on the other hand I was just stressed finding ways to resolve this problem...I had over a week of an emotional roller coaster...the pressure of dealing with people...panic and anxiety...which in the end affected my confidence...making me think negatively and encouraging pessimistic thoughts.
>
> (RJ 04/10)

At this stage it turned absolutely necessary to disentangle the academic and volunteer roles, without neglecting the assistance requests made by vulnerable participants. Therefore, to solve the ethical dilemma, I decided to adopt a *binary strategy* and started getting involved in the capacity of a secondary case worker. The lead case/social worker owned the case, and responsibilities were equally divided between us (or vice versa). Interviewees were referred back to the lead (or secondary) case/social workers, if they had any problems or presented any issues at all that could interfere with my role as a researcher. Nevertheless:

memory of this entire incident left me feeling paranoid...whenever I encountered a difficult situation, finding a solution turned twice as challenging and stressful...until last month I found it difficult to trust social worker A and B...and had a strange feeling that I was being observed...and assumed they were skeptical of my practices...Both of them later made me aware of my strengths, capabilities and problem solving skills....

(RJ 07/10)

This incident was discussed during the debriefing sessions at the University Occupational Therapist, with an aim to restore my optimism and confidence.

Becoming a co-victim of suppression

The rapport-building process created a trust-based relationship and closeness with the participants, encouraging disclosure during the interview; however, this relationship occasionally positioned me on the edge of academic boundaries and made me feel like a *bystander* who observes the victims of injustice, but keeps walking without immediate intervention. For instance, Gracie (pseudonym) was facing mental health deterioration due to the electronic tag, which was attached to her leg for longer than six months. She had a four-year-old son and was not able to leave the house for 8–12 hours or go to public places without worrying about the tag getting visible and/or being judged. She mentioned being called a 'paedo' by a group of teenagers, when the tag was accidently visible. After the interview I really wanted to help, as noted in the RJ:

> After the interview, I really felt that something needs to be done, as the punishment was unfair and not justified...she kept asking for help...I wanted to write a strongly worded letter to the security company and UKBA officials requesting to remove this tag...but I could not stop thinking about the consequences of crossing the boundaries of a researcher...I referred her to the social workers...I was later told that RCOs cannot write letters requesting to reduce such a punishment...there was a constant fear that if at all individuals abscond, RCOs could be held liable by the UKBA...however, on the participants request, the social worker wrote a letter highlighting that the 'organisation had no legal expertise' and the letter was written 'on behalf of the client explaining her current situation'...(RJ 04/10)...eventually the letter was not considered by the UKBA...and eight weeks on, she still remained tagged with a hope to hear back from the authorities...(RJ 06/10).[6]...she requested me for assistance [again] and I referred her to the legal advisor and a mental health charity...the circumstances made me feel trapped in

the victim-bystander cycle, where being a bystander was making me feel like a co-victim of suppression... and this just added to my on-going feeling of frustration and powerlessness [written 1 week prior to commencing the debriefing sessions].

(RJ 07/10)

Each time when I felt that stress and discomfort was of a higher intensity than usual, I pulled myself out from the interviewing process and rescheduled future interviews. Such a delay helped to significantly minimise the cumulative effect of facing too much data and too many emotions at any one point. This also created extra time for reflection, increasing the depth of the analysis as opposed to a brief cursory examination because of the emotional pain.

On one occasion my reaction was completely opposite to the one faced above. I had interviewed two female asylum seekers during the month of May 2010, both single mothers, who had completed their prison term. However, at the same time, I was doing case work with other asylum seekers – as noted:

today was the first time I did not get affected by clients' emotions... and instead of feeling glad, I am getting concerned... when she cried [referring to a client] I gave her a tissue and kept writing preliminary case notes... until my conscience started to sting... and then I offered her a brew with a big smile... I did not feel what I usually feel... and that smile was not very real... now I am thinking of that incident... it is making me feel very uneasy, and perhaps very guilty. I really hope what I have built so far is not collapsing... my empathy threshold must not turn weak... it is impossible to research sensitive topics... if you are not sensitive to the individuals you encounter... being sensitive is a pre-requisite quality... and perhaps mandatory, when conducting research with this group... I must not turn into a robot that collects 'facts'...

(RJ 05/10)

I discussed this incident with my colleague and decided to indulge in social activities for couple of days (what she described as 'clear your head').

I felt confinement!

My preparation with regard to the fieldwork largely involved planning and constructing strategies to protect the research participants from harm. The research methodology literature does not fully address the emotional impacts on the researcher of prolonged contact with this particular group and I was uncertain of the intensity and depth of suffering, and the extent to which such disclosures could affect me as a person. Throughout the fieldwork it was noted that those who interacted with the AS on a regular basis faced a surge of emotions[7] when confronted with extreme suffering; for instance, Mariam (RCO manager at organisation A; Pseudonym) once mentioned:

> ...did you see his sad eyes? It was just painful to listen what he is going through...I have been doing this for 7 years and can't do it any-more...my blood pressure is always high and the doctor keeps prescrib-ing me tablets for anxiety...I should switch it off, but it is hard!...I am going part-time very soon, maybe 1 day a week...can't do it – just can't do it anymore (crying)....
>
> (RJ 03/10)

Whereas, social worker Beth (pseudonym) mentioned that:

> I feel jaded and worn out...I feel about 10 years older...sometimes I just sit in my garden and think about my cases and what they have gone through...not that I want to, but sometimes it's your brain which does not give up on the thinking.....
>
> (RJ 01/11)

After the initial five months in the field, I started to experience a similar lack of ability to 'switch it off', as thinking, reflecting, acting, planning and analysing were crucial aspects of the research process, and these elements advanced when the data collection process gained a momentum.

On one occasion I was following social worker Anita (pseudonym) on a home visit and to conduct health assessment of a male asylum seeker called Iqbal (pseudonym). The purpose of the visit was to assess his health condition and to implement suicide prevention and well-being strategies.[8] I decided not to interview the participant, as he was suffering from active suicidal thoughts and had to recourse to the Crises Team after a failed sui-cide attempt, and in-depth qualitative interview had a potential to cause further emotional distress. However, I was granted access for the observation purposes. As I entered the property,[9]

> I saw a poorly looking man, wearing a soiled track suit bottom and old jumper, standing around the door (not entirely outside) to wel-come us...he pushed the door slowly and gently to let us in...he was weak and frail...as I walked in, I was overwhelmed by the smell...there were unwashed clothes hanging on rusty metal hooks...there was a bro-ken refrigerator in one corner...on top of the refrigerator there was a microwave and on top of the microwave there was a small old television and on top of the television there was an old 1980s style radio...all of which were covered in dust and not in active use...that tiny space was his living room, bed room and kitchen...On the other corner was Iqbal's

bed...beside his bed was a small table, where he kept a cocktail of anti-depressants and pain killers...I was sitting on a damp chair, opposite to his bed...I could see a carton of smelly curdled milk, rotten banana and dried pomegranate lying on the floor...room was dark even with a tube light switched on...social worker Anita started asking few procedural questions so as to establish his mood and whether he was exhibiting any active suicidal thoughts. He replied back to every question after a 30 second pause...he stated in a low voice *'sometimes voices ask me, they ask me to end my life and it is very difficult to control!'* His eyes were on the floor while replying to the questions...occasionally when he made an eye contact, his eyes started to water immediately...he mentioned about severe lack of interest in outdoor activities and that he hasn't left those four walls in weeks...in past he was taken to the Crises Team twice due to suicide attempts...on both the occasions doctors increased the strength of his medication and granted discharge the same day...and he continues to exhibit suicidal thoughts and has no interest in life or living...he repeatedly asked about the asylum case and whether social worker heard anything back from the solicitor or UKBA...he kept mentioning that it has been too long and he wants decision on the case...it became apparent from the conversation...only thing mattered to him the most was becoming recognised as a refugee and having a 'legal' status in the UK... he mentioned about being full of life and happy in the past...and now being reduced down to a corpse like state...after the initial 15 minutes, I began to experience stomach discomfort and wanted to vomit...this was not triggered due to the overpowering smell or the conversation about death and dying or state of the room...It was due to the fact that I *felt* his confinement and the feeling was extremely powerful. I was not in a detention centre, I was not in a prison and I was not physically confined to a space against my will...but as he started talking about asylum case and pointless existence...I felt his pain, I felt his suffering, I felt his frustration, I felt his helplessness, I felt his hopelessness, I felt his lifeless existence, I felt the dark empty space – I felt confinement, without becoming physically confined.

(RJ 09/11)

As soon as we left the premises, I had a debriefing chat with social worker Anita in order to 'break free'. As a criminologist, it opened up a new area for analysis and a curiosity to know ways in which the system confines asylum seekers – one which goes beyond physical imprisonment or detention.

Ethnic identity and trust

Throughout my fieldwork I repeatedly questioned myself as to why participants (on most occasions) willingly and openly disclosed sensitive details about their past, present and future. I often reduced every trusted revelation as an outcome of being able to empathise. However, the dynamics behind forming strong rapport and trust-based relationship were far more complex:

> it was very hard to understand the dynamics of rapport building...and what was making me trusted? Was it because I was a volunteer worker, who had knowledge and understanding of the problems they face?...was it because I was a student who strongly believes in human rights and that makes individuals feel morally obligated to bestow me with their trust?...was it because of my personality and body language...or because of my colour and ethnic origins...or merely due to me turning into a 'known face'...whom they encountered every week same time-same place? To become trustworthy, one has to prove his worth and integrity...and throughout the course of fieldwork...I have been analysing ways in which this can/has been proved...
>
> (RJ 04/10)

There were times when I was left stunned by the responses from the participants and clients who approached me for assistance, but nevertheless such responses unveiled the various positions in which they saw me. For example, a male asylum seeker from Iran once asked me:

> Participant: Where are your parents from?
> Researcher: India
> Participant: You been living here for long?
> Researcher: Yes, close to 10 years
> Participant: As long as me then [smile]. Do you have Indefinite Leave to Remain?
> Researcher: [after 30 second pause] Nope [smile]
> [Participant then pats my back, gives me a vague look, smiles and walks away]
>
> (RJ 11/10)

After this incident, the participant made regular visits to the organisation and always initiated a friendly conversation (both of which he never did before). He often shared troubles and occasionally asked for assistance. After organisation A closed, I encountered him on a few occasions while walking to the University, and each time he made a point to stop and strike a friendly conversation about the research and life in general. To be honest:

> initially this incident made me feel very uncomfortable...I was not sure how to react...I was not ready or willing to disclose any aspect of

my personal life with the participants... and certainly did not feel the need for a pat... and still not sure what that look meant... however, during the course of the research I realised that a certain amount of disclosure was necessary to balance the power relations... and help them [referring to participants] locate something in common with the researcher... I also realised that, just the way I was uncomfortable with disclosures... participants might be going through similar feelings while disclosing their vulnerabilities... and hoping that researcher... will not judge them... if one is expecting truth and authenticity from the participants... and hoping that... they will be honest in their self-portrayal... then one has to follow a similar principle... and not be afraid of getting judged... also [with regards to the legal status], I found it necessary to be honest as most of them either assumed that I was born in Britain or a refugee... on more than few occasions I revealed my legal status as a tool for neutralising power... empowerment... and gaining access as an insider... and their trust...

(RJ 05/11)

This cultural identity, on a rare occasion, made me strongly connect with one participant. I happened to be introduced to a young Afghani man at a community centre, who was as mentioned by one of the asylum seekers as being 'in need of help'. Initially I was not sure of the ethical implications of initiating one such (un-invited) conversation as a researcher or voluntary worker:

but then I was told that he is only 15... He looked really young and lost... just felt like talking to him and check whether he is doing ok... it would have been unethical to refuse to initiate such a conversation... I decided to introduce myself as a PhD student... and hoped that he will talk.

(RJ 01/10)

During the chat he mentioned the asylum case, which had been recently refused. He also stated that social services have wrongly assessed his age as 19. When I asked him about the accommodation, he replied: 'sometime with one friend... sometime with other... sometime when I get work, I sleep in garage' (RJ 01/10). When I questioned him regarding work, he replied 'rubbish work'. After a 10-minute chat he drifted away and got back to me when I was sitting alone. He requested me to call the social services and arrange for a re-assessment of his age. I was '... in a situation where refusal was not an option any more... not that he would have felt let down... but I couldn't do it... he was wrongly considered as an adult by the Department of Social Services and wanted me to arrange for an appointment' (RJ 01/10). On calling the Department of Social Services and explaining the situation, an employee said:

Employee: Have we assessed his age as 19 (?)...

Researcher: Yes. Ok, but he is not 19...He certainly does not look 19...Could you not re-assess his age?

Employee: May I ask what makes you think he is under 16...?

Researcher: This underage lad is Asian and I am Asian, so it is easy for me to figure out whether he is under 16 or not...Sorry, but he does not agree to this age...says he is 15...I would support your decision, but firmly believe that he is under 16 years of age.

Employee: ...we use robust interviewing techniques to determine age... If the senior social workers have assessed him as 19, then he is 19!

Researcher: Can you not connect me to one of your senior social workers? I am not saying their judgement is wrong...but there could be an error with this one...? Can you let me know how to go about with this?

Employee: We have had this problem in the past. See, they have to prove their age prior to accessing any sort of child support...and they don't carry a passport or birth certificate with them...I understand what you are saying, but we have made this decision. If at all you want to raise this matter further, I suggest that you follow the complaint procedures mentioned on our website.

Researcher: I just want to let you know that he is very vulnerable and homeless...

Employee: As I said, if you have evidence of his age then write to us and we will re-assess him.

Researcher: Can they not send him for a medical examination or something? I am sure doctors could help in making such difficult decisions?

Employee: As far as I know, they [referring to the doctor] give us an age range and then we have to do the interview again to determine the exact age...

Researcher: So unless he gets evidence of the right age, he will be considered as an adult? Can you please...please...help him out on this one...? I can't explain you over the phone, but he is very vulnerable.

Employee: Sorry, if I knew how to conduct an age interview, I would do it for you. But this decision is not in my hands...

(RJ – date unknown)

During the 18 months of fieldwork, I observed three unaccompanied minors who went through the age determination process and were considered as adults. In two of the cases (including the current one), I *felt* that the individuals were under the age of 16, but had been placed in the adult asylum system. All the three asylum cases were refused even before these 'pseudo' children had a chance to contest their age via legal means. My reactions to this case were noted in the RJ:

during the conversation he was sitting on a small table fidgeting with a pen and a piece of paper...drawing random faces...he spoke in a very squeaky voice...I sensed straightaway that he is young and nervous...and felt that it would be better if I give him space...but after 30 minutes or so...he started talking...it was really shocking to hear the places that he visited in an attempt to sell sex...most of the times such attempts were unsuccessful...and he was afraid to go ahead...other times individuals refused, as he looked underage...those who were willing...questioned his age...and he mentioned the one determined by the social services...I [reluctantly] asked him regarding the types of activities he is involved in...and he refused to answer...had no idea as to what is HIV, STD or STI...and had never seen a GP...a 'pseudo child' who accepted the pseudo identity given by the state authorities...and now using this new pseudo identity for survival...it had only been 5–6 weeks since he started this work...and attended 3 clients...I was experiencing this very unusual protecting instinct...one that an elder brother would experience...and worst, my first attempt to protect him failed...eventually I booked him an appointment with the GP and insisted to see social workers and visit a local charity organisation...since his legal age was determined 19...he was outside the child protection framework...

(RJ 01/10)

After a few weeks he called me[10] to inform that social workers had signposted him to a solicitor. The solicitor appealed against the UK Border Agency (UKBA) decision, which was successful, and he was eventually accepted as a 16 year old after re-assessment. They provided him with a room in a shared house and he is now waiting for a decision. He also mentioned about not pursuing sex-work any further.

My position in this situation was exclusive. The fact that participant called from a 'withheld number', and made a request that his mobile number should not be noted (if it was displayed at all), indicated a lack of trust. Further, he refused participation in the interview, which according to me, was due to his lack of acceptance of me as an insider. While I got slightly carried away due to a combination of factors (i.e. the age of the participant, his ethnicity and vulnerability), this relationship was not entirely reciprocal. Very strangely:

when I introduced myself as a PhD student...and then got tangled up in brotherly feelings...I started believing that...he will agree to further participation...and assumed...'trust' has somewhat been achieved...I was not being selfish or manipulative...but making a default (and rather faulty) assumption...that all the people of colour will trust me...as we have something in common...which will make us understand each other well....

(RJ 03/10)

Conclusion: Is my research 'scientific' enough?

Emotional connectedness to process and practices of fieldwork is normal and appropriate. It should not be denied or stifled. It should be acknowledged, reflected upon and seen as a fundamental feature of well executed research. Having no connection to the research endeavour, setting or people is indicative of a poorly executed project.

(Coffey 1999, 159)

When we get emotionally affected by daily events in the field, we become aware of not only our own selves, but also others who surround us. By acknowledging the emotional responses, I largely became alert to the world surrounding me, which also induced a sense of curiosity and a craving for knowledge and truth. Since emotions had become epistemologically relevant, almost like a navigation system, it was difficult to keep them hidden in a box with a fear of becoming rated as 'unscientific':

every tear... and every shiver meant something... and I used this to the betterment of this research... at times it felt as if I am 'objectifying' my emotions... and doing exactly what I was escaping from... however, not reflecting on emotions deeply... and thoughtfully... would have rendered a threat to this research... and perhaps ruin the 'scientific' value, credibility... and quality of the data....

(RJ 01/11)

In this chapter I have shown how emotions can be connected to the processes and practices in the fieldwork, in order to make a well-executed and rigorous criminological research. I have also raised ways in which they can assist a researcher in understanding and uncovering state crime, structural violence and oppression of marginalised and excluded groups. Finally I have addressed ways in which emotions can inform critical criminology and challenge the mainstream positivist agenda, which over the years has continued to establish itself on an obnoxious claim that this form of research is 'scientific' and 'value free':

How and why does hiding emotions and subjectivities make a research 'scientific' and acknowledging it makes a research 'unscientific'? It is like saying... being honest and subjective is bad... and being dishonest and objective is good? I rather turn into an 'unscientific' but honest academic... rather then turning into an 'objective' robot, collecting 'facts', pretending to lack emotions... Emotionally intelligent humans are far more superior then those having so-called high IQ levels. I have proved it!

(RJ 09/12)

Notes

1. This term was first used by Juliet Stumpf in the article: *The Crimmigration Crisis: Immigrants, Crime, and Sovereign Power* 56 AM. U. L. REV. 367 (2006).
2. For further discussion on the use of research journal, see Bhatia (2014).
3. I had previously assisted Bukola in writing a complaint to the accommodation provider regarding an electrical problem. A few days later and after a few conversations, an interview session was arranged. During her visit in February 2010, she precisely mentioned about 'feeling exhausted' of talking to people about her problems and repeatedly being ignored. I was requested to act as a middle-man, due to having detailed knowledge of the case and her personal circumstances (obtained during case work and followed by an interview). I was given the consent to discuss the case with the senior case worker and relevant external organisations.
4. I was requested by the senior case worker not to mention his name while making this referral (for reasons unexplained). He also insisted that I do not include the organisation's name; however, I turned down this request. The lack of clarity of the situation and roles made it difficult for me to convey the information in a consistent manner.
5. The Law Centre staff refused to provide assistance, as they were facing shortage of staff. A senior case worker was requested to write a letter to the court requesting for extension of the time limit, which was eventually granted. The client was referred to several other agencies who offered her support and assistance, as organisation A had reduced service provisions.
6. Ali, Rizwan, Ikeoluwa were tagged. All the respondents were carrying copies of letters written by their respective GPs and immigration solicitors. None of these letters were acknowledged by the UKBA.
7. This is also termed as 'soul sadness' (Niederland 1081, 420) and it is often faced by the therapists (or those involved in human services) who regularly work with trauma victims or those suffering from depression.
8. The social workers at charity organisation employed several individualised techniques so as to reduce the risk of self-harm among asylum seekers. These techniques include (but not limited to) helping them secure voluntary employment in their area of expertise and skills, allotment projects, walks in park, tea meetings, home visits and befriending, language class and in some cases helping them seek access to trained psychologists.
9. Iqbal was a destitute asylum seeker. However, a member of a refugee community provided him with space to live in his family home. The room appeared to be a storage space converted into a bedroom, which is one reason why it was compact, effectively outside of the house and guarded by a metal gate and a door.
10. He requested that his name and mobile number should not be noted.

References

Barton, A., Corteen, K., Scott, D. and Whyte, D. (eds) (2007) *Expanding the Criminological Imagination: Critical Readings in Criminology*, Willan Publishing, Cullompton.

Bhatia, M. (2014, forthcoming) 'Emotional Reflexivity in Immigration and Crime Research' *Journal of Qualitative Inquiry*.

Bowling, B. and Phillips, C. (2002) *Racism, Crime and Justice*, Longman, London.

Coffey, A. (1999) *The Ethnographic Self: Fieldwork and the Representation of Identity*, London: Sage.

Denzin, N.K. and Lincoln, Y.S. (2000) 'Introduction: the Discipline and Practice of Qualitative Research'. In N.K. Denzin and Y.S. Lincoln (eds) *Handbook of Qualitative Research*, Thousand Oaks, CA: Sage, pp.1–28.

Fekete, L. (2001) 'The Emergence of Xeno-Racism' *Race and Class* 43(2): 23–40.

Institute of Race Relations (1987) *Policing Against Black People*, London: IRR.

Hochschild, A.R. (1983) *The Managed Heart: Commercialisation of Human Feeling*, Los Angeles, CA: University of California Press.

Hubbard, G., Backett-Milburn, K. and Kemmer, D. (2010) 'Working with Emotion: Issues for the Researcher in Fieldwork and Teamwork' *International Journal of Social Research Methodology* 4(2): 119–37.

Lee, R.M. and Renzetti, C.M. (1993) 'The Problems of Researching Sensitive Topics'. In C.M. Renzetti and R.M. Lee (eds) *Researching Sensitive Topics*, London: Sage.

Mintz, S. (1989) 'The Sensation of Moving, While Standing Still' *American Ethnologist* 16(4): 786–96.

Rew, L., Bechtel, D. and Sapp, A. (1993) 'Self-as-Instrument in Qualitative Research' *Nursing Research* 42(5): 300–01.

Richmond, A.H. (1994) *Global Apartheid: Refugees, Racism and the New World Order*, Oxford: Oxford University Press.

Sivanandan, A. (2002) 'The Contours of Global Racism'. Speech presented at *Crossing Borders: The Legacy of the Commonwealth Immigrants Act 1962*, 15–16 November, London. URL (accessed 15 December 2013): http://www.irr.org.uk/2002/november/ak000007.html

Stumpf, J. (2006) 'The Crimmigration Crisis: Immigrants, Crime, and Sovereign Power' American University Law Review URL (accessed 15 January 2014): http://www.wcl.american.edu/journal/lawrev/56/stumpf.pdf

Watts, J.H. (2008) 'Emotion, Empathy and Exit: Reflections on Doing Ethnographic Qualitative Research on Sensitive Topics' *Medical Sociology Online* 3(2): 3–14.

Weber, L. and Bowling, B. (2004) 'Policing Migration: a Framework for Investigating the Regulation of Global Mobility' *Policing & Society* 14(3): 195–212.

Wilkins, R. (1993) 'Taking It Personally: A Note on Emotion and Autobiography' *Sociology* 27(1): 93–100.

Yuen, F. (2011) 'Embracing Emotionality: Clothing My "Naked Truths"' *Critical Criminology* 19(1): 75–88.

14
Researching 'Hidden Populations': Reflections of a Quantitative Researcher in Understanding 'Established' and 'Immigrant' Groups' Perceptions of Crime and Social (Dis)Order

Clare E. Griffiths

Introduction

Reflexivity is often considered a 'vital counterpoint... to the positivist, quantitative agenda' (Jewkes 2012, 69). The aim of this chapter however is to provide a critical and reflexive account of a quantitative research project, that used supplementary qualitative methods, in order to demonstrate the value of reflexivity in quantitative and mixed methods research.

For Steier (1991), the importance of reflexivity is in adopting a constructionist stance, in recognising that social worlds are constructed by researchers. This is often the starting point in much qualitative research which challenges 'objectivist and rationalist views of inquiry' (Steier 1991, 1). The recognition of subjectivity, partisanship and selectivity in the research process has been discussed in depth in qualitative accounts. However, these terms are deemed to sit uncomfortably among quantitative researchers who should instead seek for objectivity and randomness in pursuit of uncontaminated results that reflect the 'truth' and 'reality' of the social world. Due to this epistemological stance, quantitative researchers are often accused of presenting a sterile account of the methodology adopted in a hope to portray such objectivity. However, as Sampson (2012, 71) suggests, the inevitable 'twists, turns and compromises' are often ignored. This chapter seeks to argue that in certain types of quantitative research (particularly those with 'hidden' and 'hard to reach' populations), being reflexive can in fact add value to the criminological research endeavour.

In order to do so, the chapter presents a research project that sought to capture and compare the perspectives of both an established local community and a transient immigrant community on crime and disorder in their local neighbourhood after a period of rapid social and demographic change through immigration. It reflects on incidents that raised questions for the random and objective principles of a quantitative research project and shows how special considerations are needed when researching such a contentious topic that involves minority immigrant communities *and* majority established communities. The chapter discusses the challenges faced, and compromises made, throughout the research process, focusing particularly on negotiating access and sampling difficulties.

Adopting a mixed methods approach in community research

The main aim of my research was to explore the consequences of, and responses to, a recent wave of migration of Polish nationals that settled in a small working-class town in the North West of England. It sought to capture and compare the perceptions and experiences of both the established local residents and the new Polish migrants living in the town on issues relating to crime, insecurity and community cohesion. There is a wealth of literature investigating indigenous residents' attitudes towards immigration and its perceived association with a disrupted social order (Skogan 1990; Sampson 2009). The majority of this research, however, fails to gain the perspectives of *both* groups within the neighbourhood – local residents *and* new immigrants.

Following Elias and Scotson (1965, 167) in their seminal study *The Established and the Outsiders*, the methods adopted in the research therefore directly reflect the 'interdependencies' of groups living within the same neighbourhood and how, in order to fully understand social order, exploring and comparing both established local residents' and new Polish migrants' experiences and perceptions of their current neighbourhood are essential. The project thus attempts to break away from the longstanding tradition of research on immigration and neighbourhood social order, most of which has adopted either an ethnographic approach (Suttles 1968; Thomas and Znaniecki [1918–1920], 1996) or has instead provided statistical analyses at a macro level exploring the links between immigration and crime (Martinez and Lee 2000). In recognition of Phillips and Bowling's (2003, 270) plea to reconcile 'criminological data with the "lived experiences" and subjectivities of minorities', a combination of bilingual survey design and a sequence of quantitative and qualitative methods and analyses was instead considered the appropriate strategy in researching neighbourhood change in this small town.

To compare the two groups' attitudes, perceptions and experiences, a bilingual survey was designed, translated and administered to local and migrant populations throughout the selected neighbourhood via a 'random walk' sampling design. In response to the difficulties inherent in gaining an adequate sample of a migrant population, however, and to provide a more interpretative account and 'flesh out' (Brannen 1992, 25) groups' perceptions and experiences, additional qualitative-oriented techniques were incorporated. This first involved a 'targeted' sampling strategy, whereby a number of relevant sites were selected to gain access to the migrant community, such as local Polish food shops and the local Catholic Church; a field diary was kept during the sampling procedure; focus groups were held with local and migrant inhabitants; and expert interviews were carried out with key institutional gatekeepers.

Therefore, although a quantitative survey was at the centre of this research project, a range of other more informal qualitative approaches were also essential due to the 'hidden' and 'hard to reach' nature of some of the research participants. This brought with it a greater element of subjectivity, of challenges, obstacles, decisions and compromises that I had to overcome. The chapter now turns to reflect on some of the incidents experienced when trying to negotiate access and sample respondents.

A contentious topic: Gaining access

Immigration and its perceived consequences for crime, insecurity and community cohesion are contested issues that are widely covered in the local and national media. An awareness of the sensitive and contentious nature of the topics investigated in the research was thus required at all times and had potential implications for the data collected. As Phillips and Bowling (2003, 271) recognise, there exists a

> dilemma of engaging with debates about minority victimization and offending and contributing to the creation of false pathologies which might then serve to naturalize and reify images of certain minorities as inherently criminal.

As a researcher, I therefore felt I had a duty to report the findings not only in an objective way, but also in a responsible manner with considerations regarding how the results could be misinterpreted due to the research's politically attractive nature (Sieber 1992). I was conscious therefore of the need and potential difficulty of striking this balance early on. This also raised challenges in gaining access to respondents and key gatekeepers to participate in the research. Having received a great deal of support from local agencies previously, by the time data collection was due to begin the response became much more cautious. Part of this came from the rather negative press that the area was beginning to receive regarding Polish immigration and a reported increase in crime and conflict. This was also not helped by other reports of the area being dangerous for researchers. There was an emphasis on the importance of me representing my research in more positive tones. Rather than stating my research was interested in the connection between immigration and crime, for example, I reworded the focus to be on immigration and its consequences for community integration. The decision to reframe the purpose of my research to respondents and potential gatekeepers could be viewed as being steered and influenced by the officials in the town who were keen to portray a positive image of the area. However, reflecting back, this small change in how I presented my research could have had important consequences. Community tensions are often a concern in this type of research and so using terms such as 'Polish immigration' and 'crime' could have escalated any existing conflict in the area. It may also have discouraged residents from taking part. Even with this change in wording, I did nevertheless experience one incident of tension with an established resident during sampling which I noted in my field diary:

> While I was collecting questionnaires today, I was approached by a local woman who lived in the area who was rather aggressive, accusing me of being racist. I did manage to diffuse the situation and explain that the research project was interested in the recent changes to the neighbourhood and was certainly not racist or intended to offend. She still refused to complete the questionnaire however.
>
> (Fieldnotes, September 2008)

Although the only situation of its kind, it did bring to light the contentious nature of the project and how some people are uncomfortable and wary regarding issues of immigration.

It is often a stereotype in this type of research that conflict and community tensions would be present in the neighbourhoods under study, a situation that could be inflated by the research being carried out (Jamieson 2000; Lee-Treweek and Linkogle 2000; Hancock 2001; Oliver 2003). In fact, I was 'warned off' sampling the neighbourhoods by another researcher who had apparently experienced threats to personal safety while researching immigration in the area. Thankfully, conversations with local police contacts, who strongly disputed such myths about the area being a dangerous place, allayed any concerns, and such stereotypes did not generally come to fruition during the time spent there by myself and the research team. Following the more positive reports that came from the police on the consequences of Polish immigration in the area, and from my own experiences during sampling (discussed below), the focus of my research did in fact seem to shift to one that sought to dispel many of the myths associated with immigration, deprivation and crime. While trying to maintain objectivity in the analysis and representation of results, my own values and attitudes as a researcher perhaps inevitably had a role to play in this. Being conscious early on about not inflating any existing tensions in the area, or playing up to stereotypes of immigration and crime, perhaps helped influence this shift in focus and the way in which I represented my findings. Being open and honest about how our own views as researchers may influence the research process, even one with a quantitative design, is a crucial part of being reflexive, however.

Looking back, the wariness of other researchers and certain agencies in the town to help with my research could have been a blessing in disguise. Hancock (2000), for example, similarly discusses this negotiation of access in a community setting. For her, it was important to speak to the community residents first before going to the various agencies with vested interests in the community. This was to try and avoid any association or identification with such agencies. Although such caution and warning off by certain officials in the town, as well as other researchers, caused me a great deal of anxiety and fear at the time, it did allow me greater independence in my research project and opened up other avenues for gatekeepers during the sampling process.

The sampling process

The term 'field work' and discussions about time spent 'in the field' are the kinds of terminology used in qualitative research and not typically found in quantitative accounts of the data collection process. My research, although predominately survey focused in nature, did not involve an arm-chair sampling strategy, where researchers typically post out questionnaires to randomly selected addresses and sit waiting for them to come trick-ling back in. Rather, I entered the field and personally distributed and collected questionnaires by 'going around the houses' (Hancock 2000, 382) with a small research team, whereby questionnaires were distributed via a 'drop-collect' method, that is, the questionnaires were self-completed by the respondents and subsequently collected at a later arranged date. The deci-sion to adopt this sampling strategy rather than a more traditional distanced approach was in an attempt to improve the response rate and to improve my familiarity with the area. Sampling in this way allowed me to keep a field diary of any observations or conversations I had with people while out and about in the area, which added depth and richness to the quantitative data. Of course, there were also some drawbacks to this approach, particularly for some of the traditional principles of quantitative research. These challenges and their implications will now be discussed.

The research team: The importance of 'cultural insiders'?

A small research team was recruited to aid with the distribution and collec-tion of questionnaires. This included three bilingual students with Polish as a first language, two of which lived in one of the selected neighbourhoods of interest, and thus were invaluable in their knowledge and experience of the local area and in helping to provide contacts. Birman (2006, 171) contends that 'ethical research cannot be conducted across cultures without involvement of members of the community being studied'. Shared cultural background and language between migrant respondents and 'ethnically matched' (Phillips and Bowling 2003, 275) individuals in the research team are therefore suggested to help build the trust and rapport of migrant respondents. The benefits and necessity of recruiting 'cultural insiders' (Birman 2006, 156) into the research team became evident throughout the sampling process:

> On my first day of sampling, I noticed that the Polish members of the research team were entering migrant respondents' households. When I asked about why they were entering people's houses, I was told that this is a traditional custom in Polish culture and it is typically considered impolite to refuse entry. This created a dilemma for me as I was concerned about ensuring the safety of the research team as recommended by the research ethics committee and it was also taking up quite a lot of time. I therefore spoke to the research team about it and suggested that they do not enter a respondent's house but explain politely that this is a requirement of the University's safety procedure, so as to avoid appearing discourteous.
>
> (Fieldnotes, September 2008)

This one example effectively demonstrates the importance of involving 'cultural insiders' in the data collection process, as ignorance of certain cultural customs could otherwise alienate migrants from taking part in the research.

Although including Polish 'cultural insiders' in the research team certainly seemed beneficial for encouraging Polish migrants to fill in a questionnaire, it occurred to me that it also had the potential to be less effective at encouraging the local established residents to do so. As the research was interested in Polish migration and community cohesion, I was aware that there was potential for community conflict, particularly by having Polish speakers distributing the questionnaires to local residents. This begins to show the more complex nature of community research with diverse populations and of including 'cultural insiders' in the project. One of the main findings that came out of my research, however, was that social relations between Polish migrants and local residents were in fact very positive (see Griffiths 2013). Instead, the main area of conflict that I did find existed within segments of the Polish migrant community themselves. Although the use of so-called 'insiders' in such a research project is typically presented in a positive way, reflecting back on my research process in the light of my main findings demonstrates how this is much more nuanced than originally assumed. The way in which groups are constructed as 'insiders', 'outsiders' or 'others' is indeed rather complex and was an aspect that my research was interested in exploring. The use of so-called cultural 'insiders' therefore should be reflected on more critically by researchers. Naples (1997) similarly argues against such a reductionist stance on the 'insider/outsider' standpoints, showing instead the complexity of this and their continuously shifting nature.

A 'random' walk?

It was originally planned to obtain an overall sample of approximately 400 respondents for the survey, including a random, but not proportionate, sample of 200 respondents from the Polish community and 200 respondents from the local community living within the selected neighbourhoods. However, the practice of sampling is not comparable to its theory, and it soon became apparent throughout the sampling stage that this would be an unachievable target.

According to Kemper et al. (2003, 273), '[n]early any complex research question requires more than one sampling technique and often involves both probability (i.e. representative) and purposive sampling techniques'. Supporting this, the sampling techniques in my project were diverse and involved two sweeps: a 'random walk' procedure, followed by an additional purposive sample of the migrant population. As Hoffmeyer-Zlotnik (2003, 206) notes, random walk sampling involves a number of different sampling strategies, or 'multilevel selection processes' as the author terms it. This first required a purposive and strategic selection of neighbourhoods; second, a systematic random sample of households nested within these neighbourhoods via the random walk, selecting every fifth household; and finally, a random sample of a household member to take part in the survey.

Although the method chosen to distribute questionnaires was labour intensive and time-consuming for a lone researcher with limited funds and time, I considered it the most appropriate method to use for my research, as it allowed me to gain first-hand experience of the area, more so than if any other method of sampling had been used. A particular beneficial consequence has therefore been an intense familiarity with the neighbourhoods sampled, right down to the individual streets within the neighbourhoods; having the opportunity to speak to many different people living in the neighbourhoods; and being able to observe first-hand the physical appearance of the areas, for example, and how people live their lives. The below account from my field diary provides one example of this:

> On some evenings during sampling, people had their doors wide open. Tonight there were Polish children playing down one of the streets and the Polish families had their doors open; some were out on the street talking to each other, it was a very vibrant atmosphere. As I walked around certain streets, I heard many Polish accents. Although these streets are considered poorer areas and I did initially feel nervous about going into these areas during the evenings due to other researchers warning me

off, I enjoyed spending time there and did not once feel threatened. Throughout the evening, I had short informal conversations with some of the residents. An elderly local woman tonight for example told me about a time when she was walking to the supermarket and it began to rain heavily. She told me how a Polish woman hurried across and escorted her with an umbrella to the supermarket. The Polish woman did not speak any English but the two women have since met on the street in their neighbourhood and have smiled and said 'hello' to each other.

(Fieldnotes, September 2008)

These conversations turned into invaluable sources of data that helped me to interpret and make sense of the quantitative results. Sampling in this way was certainly an emotional process that was tiring and rather unfulfilling at times. It was very hard work, expensive and time-consuming in comparison to the number of questionnaires I received back. Despite this, I feel I have lived and experienced the area much more than if I had adopted a different method of sampling. This has provided some richness of data that is not typically present in quantitative accounts.

Despite these definite benefits to my sampling strategy, there were some drawbacks. For example, I am able to see how I, as a researcher, had the potential to impact on the objectivity and random nature of my sampling strategy. Just one account from my field diary again provides an example of this:

I turned up a little early this evening to begin sampling with my research team so I parked in a lay-by to wait for the others. As I was sitting there, a man walked past my car with a rather vicious looking dog and stopped and stared at me. I felt very intimidated and uncomfortable. A few minutes later, he returned on the street with a group of other men with dogs who began to hang around close to my car. When the others in the research team arrived (all of us young females), they similarly felt uncomfortable and were not happy to sample in this area. We therefore decided to leave and begin sampling in a different street. I reflected on this experience later that evening. As a group of young females, we made the decision not to sample an area based on our instincts, based on judgments of the appearance of an area and the behaviour and appearance of the people hanging around on the streets. It went against all of the principles of quantitative criminological research, which should be objective, scientific and random. This situation and the way in which I reacted caused problems for all of these principles – it was emotional, subjective, and based on instinct. This resulted in an entire area not being included in the sample.

(Fieldnotes, September 2008)

This incident occurred relatively early on in the sampling stage, and I spent a long time agonising over the decision. Part of being reflexive, however, is to recognise and admit to the ways in which I as a researcher was part of the social world in which I was studying (Brewer 2000). Reflecting back on the sampling process demonstrated how as a young, inexperienced female researcher, my own perceptions, preconceptions, culture and biases played a part in the sampling procedure. This therefore gives an insight into how knowledge is constructed by showing who is studied and who is potentially ignored (Hertz 1997). Another example of this comes from the way in which the Polish migrant community was sampled.

Accessing a 'hidden' migrant population

During the random walk, it became apparent that insufficient numbers of the Polish questionnaires had been distributed. Due to time and financial pressures, I made the decision to discontinue sampling the local population and solely target the Polish migrant population. This initially involved a snowball sampling method, whereby the streets known to house many Polish migrants were directly targeted and migrants were asked where their Polish neighbours lived. Dahinden and Efionayi-Mäder (2009, 6) similarly suggest that once traditional sampling methods are saturated when attempting to access minority populations, snowball sampling methods are a viable alternative, whereby 'respondents are reached through referrals, i.e. through people they already know, persons out of their personal networks'. As Dahinden and Efionayi-Mäder (2009) similarly experienced, however, this method was saturated very quickly as many Polish migrants did not know their Polish neighbours.[1] It became apparent that in order to obtain an adequate sample of the migrant population living in these neighbourhoods, I would need to adapt to the situation in order to take 'advantage of circumstances and events as they arise while undergoing the data collection process' (Kemper et al. 2003, 283). Faugier and Sargeant (1997) similarly stress the need for a mixture of methods to be used when researching 'hidden populations' where no sampling frame exists. An opportunistic or 'targeted' sampling method was thus further used to maximise the number of Polish migrants taking part in the study. Targeted sampling typically involves the recruitment of respondents at sites identified as salient from 'ethnographic mapping' (Watters and Biernacki 1989; Heckathorn 1997, 175). Through the time spent in the area, the background research carried out with key institutional gatekeepers and informal contacts made with members of the target population, a number of sites were selected in an attempt to gain access to the migrant community. Along with a Polish-speaking member of the research team, I placed myself at these sites for the remainder of the sampling period. These sites initially included a recruitment agency known to employ a large number of Polish migrants in the town and a popular local Polish food shop located along a main busy street. At these sites, individuals were approached and were invited to take part in the research. However, the decision as to which sites to select also proved rather problematic:

> Today I visited a recruitment agency that are known to have employed many of the Polish migrants in the town. I stayed there for a while inviting Polish people to fill in the questionnaire. It became clear that most individuals visiting the agency were there to make a complaint though and so I decided to leave and to not use this as a form of recruitment as I was concerned about being associated with the agency.
>
> (Fieldnotes, September 2008)

Although initially pleased that the recruitment agency was happy to help with my research and act as a gatekeeper, it soon became apparent this was not necessarily an appropriate way to gain access. There was potential for research participants to associate me with those in a powerful position who were viewed as acting in an unethical and exploitative manner towards new migrants.

The final sampling approach resulted from a chance meeting with a crucial gatekeeper to the migrant community and was in the end the most successful strategy adopted. In the light of the difficulties experienced, I approached the Polish social club in the town for help. This social club was originally established by the first-generation Polish community who arrived in the town after the Second World War. More recently, it has been taken over by the newer Polish migrants who hold Polish evenings there. Once at the social club, I and a Polish member of the research team were introduced to the local Polish priest who was at the club by chance. This chance meeting proved to be the break I was looking for and was a critical turning point in accessing the Polish migrant population. The priest offered to make an announcement to his congregation at the next Polish mass held at a local Roman Catholic Church about the research project and to explain what help was needed. We attended mass that Sunday and many members of the congregation expressed their interest in the research and were incredibly forthcoming in completing a questionnaire.

It was through this method that the largest number of questionnaires were distributed and collected, demonstrating how credible and 'facilitative' gatekeepers (Hammersley and Atkinson 2007, 58) are invaluable in providing access to a minority or migrant population. Further to this, it highlights how being flexible and willing to revise the targeted sampling plan is crucial for any research seeking the perspectives of a migrant population. As Watters and Biernacki (1989, 427) stress, '[t]his flexible approach provides a systematic means for addressing some of the more vexing research problems associated with sampling hidden populations'.

Difficulties in sampling a migrant population are inevitable and compromises need to be made and solutions sought. This is a price to pay when researching such populations, which does have implications for the general-isability of results. Language difficulties and accessing a migrant population, adequately tapping into their perceptions, together equate to a difficult task. It is an expensive research exercise, whereby translation and interpreta-tion are constantly required. The research process, when trying to access such a population, thus becomes a balancing act between pressures on time and financial resources and obtaining an adequate sample. This in the end resulted in smaller numbers than anticipated and required alternative non-probability sampling strategies to be adopted, which is a potential source of bias in the current migrant sample. Although the questionnaire distributed was a highly structured research instrument completed by the respondent without the researcher being present, the way in which the sample itself was collected can nevertheless contaminate results. Understanding this and being honest about the sampling procedure is a crucial step in the research process, one that quantitative researchers can be guilty of ignoring.

Conclusion

Research does not often follow the path that was intended. As Davies and Francis (2011, 282) note, 'even the best laid plans and designs have to be actualized in social, institutional and political contexts which can have a profound effect on the outcome of research'. This is particularly the case when researching those that are transient and 'hidden' in various respects, which can help explain why such populations are underrepresented in quan-titative research (Deakin and Spencer 2011, 141). This chapter has attempted to provide a reflexive account of a quantitative research project that explored established residents' and new Polish migrants' experiences and perceptions of crime and social (dis)order after a period of social and demographic change. Reflecting on the research process – on the challenges faced and decisions made – is an important aspect of criminological research as it demonstrates what factors have contributed to the social construction of knowledge (Davies and Francis 2011, 281). Davies and Francis (2011, 284) suggest, for example, that the main purpose of providing a reflexive account of the research process is to allow for the validity of research findings to be assessed based on the decisions, and trade-offs, made throughout the research process.

Such a 'methodological self-consciousness' (Finlay 2002, 210) is typically not presented among quantitative researchers, however. This chapter aims to break away from this tradition by showing how sampling in particular is rarely a straightforward and objective process, particularly when researching a sensitive topic with 'hidden' populations. By reflecting on my own values and my identity as a young, inexperienced female researcher, this allowed me to understand the ways in which I inevitably influenced the research pro-cess, even if unknowingly at the time. This had implications for the way in which I represented my research and its main findings, by trying to balance objectivity with a responsibility not to contribute to existing stereotypes of immigration and crime. It also had implications for the 'random' nature of my sampling strategy. Rather than seeing this as a limitation, it has been suggested that recognising and being honest about how researchers influence their research is a vital process that should be undertaken (Devine and Heath 1999). This chapter has demonstrated how providing such a reflexive account in quantitative or mixed methods research can in fact enrich the data and the conclusions drawn. This allows for readers to make their own conclusions of the research findings and how this knowledge has been socially constructed by the researcher. It is also hoped that lessons can be learned from this chapter for future researchers about the special considerations that are needed when researching a contentious and politically attractive topic that involves minority immigrant communities *and* majority established communities. While the methods outlined in this chapter certainly have their limitations, the alternative is for researchers to continue to ignore such minority and 'hidden' populations. The result is that such voices continue to go unheard, that we know little detail about such populations and that stereotypes continue to be relied upon.

Note

1. This came as a surprise to me and was an interesting observation in itself, as it provides insight into the types of social interactions between Polish migrants in this town.

References

Birman, D. (2006) 'Ethical Issues in Research with Immigrants and Refugees'. In J.E. Trimble and C.B. Fisher (eds) *The Handbook of Ethical Research with Ethnocultural Populations and Communities*, Thousand Oaks: Sage, pp.155–78.

Brannen, J. (1992) 'Combining Qualitative and Quantitative Approaches: An Overview'. In J. Brannen, (ed.) *Mixing Methods: Qualitative and Quantitative Research*, Aldershot: Ashgate Publishing, pp.3–37.

Brewer, J.D. (2000) *Ethnography*, Buckingham: Open University Press.

Dahinden, J. and Efionayi-Mäder, D. (2009) 'Challenges and Strategies in Empirical Fieldwork with Asylum Seekers and Migrant Sex Workers'. In I. Van Liempt and V. Bilger (eds) *The Ethics of Migration Research Methodology: Dealing with Vulnerable Immigrants*, Eastbourne, UK, Sussex Academic Press, pp.98–117.

Davies, P. and Francis, P. (2011) 'Reflecting on Criminological Research'. In P. Davies, P. Francis and V. Jupp (eds) *Doing Criminological Research*, 2nd edn, London: Sage, pp.281–86.

Deakin, J. and Spencer, J. (2011) 'Sensitive Survey Research: An Oxymoron?' In P. Davies, P. Francis and V. Jupp (eds) *Doing Criminological Research*, 2nd edn, London: Sage, pp.139–60.

Devine, F. and Heath, S. (1999) *Sociological Research Methods in Context*, Basingstoke: Palgrave.

Elias, N. and Scotson, J.L. (1965) *The Established and The Outsiders: A Sociological Enquiry into Community Problems*, London: Frank Cass.

Faugier, J. and Sargeant, M. (1997) 'Sampling Hard to Reach Populations' *Journal of Advanced Nursing* 26: 790–99.

Finlay, L. (2002) 'Negotiating the Swamp: The Opportunity and Challenge of Reflexivity in Research Practice' *Qualitative Research* 2(2): 209–30.

Griffiths, C. (2013) 'Living with Aliens' *Criminal Justice Matters* 93(1): 26–27.

Hammersley, M. and Atkinson, P. (2007) *Ethnography: Principles in Practice*, London: Routledge.

Hancock, L. (2000) 'Going Around the Houses: Researching in High Crime Communities'. In R.D. King and E. Wincup (eds) *Doing Research on Crime and Justice*, Oxford: Oxford University Press, pp.373–84.

Hancock, L. (2001) *Community, Crime and Disorder: Safety and Regeneration in Urban Neighbourhoods*, Basingstoke: Palgrave.

Heckathorn, D.D. (1997) 'Respondent-Driven Sampling: A New Approach to the Study of Hidden Populations' *Social Problems* 44(2): 174–99.

Hertz, R. (1997) 'Introduction: Reflexivity and Voice'. In R. Hertz (eds) *Reflexivity and Voice*, Thousand Oaks: Sage, pp. vii–xviii.

Hoffmeyer-Zlotnik, J.H.P. (2003) 'New Sampling Designs and the Quality of Data'. In A. Ferligoj and A. Mrvar (eds) *Developments in Applied Statistics*, FDV, Methodoloski zvezki, Ljubljana, pp.205–17.

Jamieson, J. (2000) 'Negotiating Danger in Fieldwork on Crime: A Researcher's Tale'. In G. Lee-Treweek and S. Linkogle (eds) *Danger in the Field: Risk and Ethics in Social Research*, London: Routledge, pp.61–71.

Jewkes, Y. (2012) 'Autoethnography and Emotion as Intellectual Resources: Doing Prison Research Differently' *Qualitative Inquiry* 18(1): 63–75.

Kemper, E.A., Stringfield, S. and Teddlie, C. (2003) 'Mixed Methods Sampling Strategies in Social Science Research'. In A. Tashakkori and C. Teddlie (eds) *Handbook of Mixed Methods in Social and Behavioral Research*, Thousand Oaks: Sage, pp.273–96.

Lee-Treweek, G. and Linkogle, S. (2000) 'Putting Danger in the Frame'. In G. Lee-Treweek and S. Linkogle (eds) *Danger in the Field: Risk and Ethics in Social Research*, London: Routledge, pp.8–25.

Martinez, R. and Lee, M.T. (2000) 'On Immigration and Crime' *Criminal Justice* 1: 485–524.

Naples, N.A. (1997) 'A Feminist Revisiting of the Insider/Outsider Debate: The "Outsider Phenomenon" in Rural Iowa'. In R. Hertz (eds) *Reflexivity and Voice*, Thousand Oaks: Sage, pp.70–94.

Oliver, P. (2003) *The Student's Guide to Research Ethics*, Maidenhead: Open University Press.

Phillips, C. and Bowling, B. (2003) 'Racism, Ethnicity and Criminology: Developing Minority Perspectives' *British Journal of Criminology* 43: 269–90.

Sampson, R.J. (2009) 'Disparity and Diversity in the Contemporary City: Social (Dis)order Revisited' *The British Journal of Sociology* 60(1): 1–31.

Sampson, R.J. (2012) *Great American City: Chicago and the Enduring Neighborhood Effect*, Chicago: The University of Chicago Press.

Sieber, J.E. (1992) *Planning Ethically Responsible Research: A Guide for Students and Internal Review Boards*, Newbury Park: Sage.

Skogan, W.G. (1990) *Disorder and Decline: Crime and the Spiral of Decay in American Neighbourhoods*, New York: The Free Press.

Steier, F. (1991) *Research and Reflexivity*, London: Sage.

Suttles, G.D. (1968) *The Social Order of the Slum: Ethnicity and Territory in the Inner City*, Chicago: University of Chicago Press.

Thomas, W.I. and Znaniecki, F. [1918–1920] (1996) *The Polish Peasant in Europe and America: A Classic Work in Immigration History. Edited by Eli Zaretsky*, Urbana and Chicago: University of Illinois Press.

Watters, J.K. and Biernacki, P. (1989) 'Targeted Sampling: Options for the Study of Hidden Populations' *Social Problems* 36(4): 416–30.

15

'Coming In from the Cold': Constructing Qualitative 'Criminality' in Australia's Penal-Welfare State

Michael Wearing

Introduction

The uncertainty in 'speaking for the other' raised by poststructuralist philosophers such as Deleuze (1976, 41) also raises the core issue of reflexivity in qualitative criminology research – how complicit are qualitative researchers in translating 'lived experience' into constructions and representations of 'the other' (Van Maanen 1990; Clandinin and Connelly 2000). How complicit are qualitative criminologists in rationalising and legitimising the subjectivities of research participants as victims, perpetrators or bystanders of crime? How ethical is the qualitative research product as a usable policy resource for knowledge building and a commoditised-like resource atomised and disembodied from its subjects in a market-based economy? The two key contemporary criminological works I rely upon to understand the political bias and influence of qualitative criminology are Howard Becker and David Garland. Becker (1963, 1967) in the early days of qualitative deviancy research alerts us to the lack of social understanding of deviance and the 'blaming and labelling' of these people and asks the researchers an ethical and political question in relation to the powerful and the powerless as to 'whose side are we on?' (Cohen 2011). Garland (1985, 1990, 2002) argues, following Foucault, that 'penal welfare practices embodied a style of "social" governance that relied upon forms of social expertise and techniques of rule that were characteristic of welfare state societies' (Garland 2002, 49). This argument frames the possibilities that qualitative criminological research is part of such penal-welfare strategies and is explored in greater detail in the examples below.

Do qualitative criminological researchers contribute to (welfare) state-based surveillance and thereby long-distance social control or governance of populations (Law 1986; Webster 2012)? This chapter will focus on the state's role and raise issues of power, knowledge and constructed identity in criminological research with powerless and vulnerable people, notably Australian Aboriginal communities. I initially raised issues of state surveillance and research in my doctoral research on homeless and marginalised people who were 'edge-living' in Sydney and heavily reliant upon poverty relief resources (Wearing 1990, 1991; Law et al. 2011). To illustrate my arguments I will use the example of the Northern Territory (NT) intervention into remote and regional Aboriginal communities initiated by the 'Little Children Are Sacred' Report in 2007.

There is a powerful qualitative account on the first page of the Overview of this report that sets the 'alarmist' tone for the emergency response as a national moral panic, a political and policy response that would in part be settled under the burden of overwhelming 'evidence' of child sexual assault in these communities following the release of the report. Cohen (2011, 241) has recently characterised such widespread moral panics as 'anti-denial movements' where 'previously denied realities' such as paedophilia and child sexual assault 'must now be brought to public attention, their dangers exposed, their immorality denounced'. Against this silence and denial came a wave of official, expert and eventually public concern for these denied realities as criminogenic behaviours based in causative factors such as intergenerational sexual violence and resultant psychosocial developmental issue in these Aboriginal communities. The alarm was sounded in the very first quote of the report:

> He was born in a remote Barkly (NT) community in 1960. In 1972, he was twice anally raped by an older Aboriginal man .... In 1993 he annaly raped a 10 year old girl and, in 1997 an eight year old boy (ZH). In 2004, ZH anally raped a five year old boy in the same community. That little boy complained. 'ZH fucked me'. Who will ensure that in years to come that a little boy will not himself become an offender.
>
> (NTG 2007, 12)

How are Australian Aboriginal subjectivities and criminality being constructed in this qualitative account? Is such intergenerational abuse and sexual violence only happening in this way in the 'criminalities' of Aboriginal communities? Given the trauma experienced by such sexual assault what government interventions could hope to stop, heal and overcome the effects of such sexual violence? Such reflexive questions and their ties to policy raise issues of the inextricable link between power and knowledge in social and criminological research, and the use of qualitative research as un/ethical product. In particular it raises questions based on Foucault's (1988) incomplete project on 'technologies of self' (Garland 2002; Rose 1999) around the textual constructions of qualitative 'criminality'. In a practical way, the focus on reflexivity in the making of qualitative criminology is about a situated ethics and understanding the political effects of research by taking one step back and asking 'what do we know?' and then another step back asking 'how do we know this?' (Gullemin and Gillam 2004).

This reflexivity also requires a deeply personal approach to 'knowing or not knowing the other' in the researcher's lived experience. A personally reflexive point I would make here, having grown up in the NT in the late 1960s, is that I witnessed as a child a similar anal sexual assault between boys of 7–10 years. This traumatic memory drives my intellectual and social justice commitment in this chapter to understand the links between qualitative research knowledge and power/discourse as governing the constructions of criminality as part of the intersections of oppression among marginalised people notably Aboriginal Australians (Wearing 1991; Stringer 2007; Baird 2008; Yuval-Davis 2011). Such criminalising selves are framed with what Garland has called penal-welfare strategies for crime control (Garland 2002) as well as critical indigenous issues of decolonising 'white man's' research (Smith 1999). The issues of reflexivity in qualitative research as they apply to postmodern, critical indigenous and critical theory research methodologies are fully addressed by others (Smith 1999; Denzin et al. 2008; Alvesson and Sköldberg 2009). The following will illustrate this in remote and rural areas where Aboriginal people's own recognition and belonging can challenge commodified university-based and governmental research and further white assumptions in the writing and use of qualitative research (Parker and Lynne 2002; Anthony and Blagg 2012).

The 'Northern Territory Interventions' begun under the Howard government in 2007 ostensibly to target child sexual abuse in remote communities and have been continued in earnest by the Rudd–Gillard (2007–2013) Labor Governments. Income management as case managing up to 50–70 per cent of pensions and benefits is used by Centrelink in remote and rural Aboriginal communities and has also been piloted in other lower socio-economic communities around Australia including Sydney (ACOSS 2010). These interventions from the start have used qualitative material to justify increased moral regulation and surveillance of such communities as well as intruding deeply into the lives of Aboriginal people's beyond acceptable legislative powers. In-depth interviewing and other qualitative data were used as information and 'evidence' to justify these 'law and order' policies, which itself is called into serious question no matter the craft of this enterprise (Kvale and Brinkmann 2008; May and Berry 2011).

Among qualitative researchers in criminology there is agreement that neither positivism nor naturalism provides the answers to dealing with issues of political bias, values and neutrality. Noaks and Wincup (2004), for example, show how political knowing can influence the agendas of criminology research. This is possible through understanding research impact including the agendas and outcomes set by topic, theory, funding and timing of research. I have demonstrated this with the 'moral panic' as an anti-denial movement surrounding the NT interventions in Australia above (Stringer 2007; Howe 2009). Central to this is reflexivity, which these authors propose is an awareness 'of the ways in which the political context shapes our research' (Noaks and Wincup 2004, 35). Qualitative criminological research that is used to enhance state powers to criminalise, normalise and re-integrate is no exception to a focus on governmental rulings as delivering technologies of self.

Qualitative research as domestic liquid surveillance

This brings us back to the core reflexive questions – are qualitative researchers agents (directly or indirectly) of state surveillance and control? 'Control' appears in John Le Carré's (1963) *The Spy Who Came in from the Cold* as a malevolent figure in charge of post-war British spying wanting his operatives to 'come in from the cold' and divulge 'intelligence information'. Control, perhaps more so than an Orwellian 'Big Brother', is the archetypal authority of British surveillance and control in post-war literature: a cool, calm, calculated, manipulative, authoritarian and frighteningly real figure.

To suggest that the qualitative researcher engages in spy-like and covert activities to collect data for an unseen controller seems at odds with the humane, relational and ethical intent of such research. Qualitative researchers will often have the intent to go deeper into the life worlds of 'the other' and their networks and provide an understanding of these social worlds. Nonetheless, the road to deeper understanding itself is 'paved with good intentions that go wrong' or become complicit themselves in power structures, governmental documentary rulings and relations of domination (Smith 1984). Are qualitative criminologists becoming part of the long-distance 'drones' – in the military sense of being controlled from long distances and unethical 'hollowed out' sense – of government and/or contracted research?

The use of research as state-based interventions and surveillance work for governments is aptly illustrated in the pre-ordered research that justified the post 2007 NT interventions. At one level, we can interrogate some of the key research and 'risk discourse' that have contributed to such interventionist strategies. Several researchers in Australian criminology have made significant inroads in understanding the link between Aboriginal culture and white law in areas such as children's welfare, sexual assault, community and family support and driving offences (Baird 2008; Howe 2009; Sherwood 2010). At another level, there is what Bauman (Bauman and Lyons 2013, 97) argues about liquid surveillance in modernity that risk discourse is replaced by collateral discourse. Those criminalised and marginalised in these new social processes are the collateral damage of the penal-welfare state (Rodgers 2008; Muncie 2009; Bauman 2011).

Such collateral discourses help to excuse and justify the damage, hurt and impact of such heavy-handed interventions, that is, re-moralising the heavier regulation and residualising of income management, criminalising and policing interventions in such communities (cf. Anthony and Blagg 2012). This reaches into the unintended consequences of qualitative criminological research. Once written up, albeit the participants are de-identified for research ethics clearance, it is not known as to what ends such writing for governmental normalising or re-education of the sample populations of this research will be put. The liquidity of life, subjectivities and modernity makes it such at least for the more vulnerable: 'Old moorings are loosened as bits of personal data extracted for one purpose are more easily deployed in another. Surveillance spreads in hitherto unimaginable ways, responding to and reproducing liquidity' (Bauman and Lyons 2013, 2–3). This is how secondary and primary data in qualitative research can be used for normalising and criminalising purposes for entire sub-groupings and populations of 'the constructed other'.

These constructions are not however 'a one way street' in terms of power relations. In the NT intervention example, and in others, qualitative research can be read as a 'double edged sword'. One edge, as a necessary part of state governance and dominance reinscribing 'law and order' agendas over Aboriginal communities; the other as offering subordinate and counter-possibilities and spaces for reflexivity, decolonising and resistance to punitive state control and the rulings of elite and powerful others (Smith 1999; Stringer 2007; Howe 2009; Sherwood 2010). This counter-discourse to neoliberal agendas in research that involve normalising, commodifying and objectifying non-white others can oppose, resist and challenge some of the 'collateral damage' for vulnerable and disadvantaged groups in social policy.

It takes little stretch of the imagination to see how the penal-welfarism of the state dominates in this kind of fluid but hierarchical modernity and the surveillance and control measures of research and monitoring subject populations within this modernity. This is commensurate with Garland's (2002, 48) double-edged arguments that Anglo welfare states such as Australia are defined as hybrid 'penal-welfare states' that combine 'the liberal legalism of due process and proportionate punishment with a correctionalist commitment to rehabilitation, welfare and criminological expertise'. This penal-welfarism has been focused on a carceral and imperialist gaze that renders gender relations, subjectivities, space and time within a social system that is underpinned by western culture, knowledge making and values (Baird 2008; Denzin et al. 2008).

Several questions are raised by the analysis of the NT interventions example. First, how is qualitative research complicit in penal-welfare strategising and policy content, for example, when discursively deployed with terms such as 'evidence based research' and 'policy reform'? Second, to what degree has qualitative criminological research become part of the state's liquid surveillance of 'risk filled' marginalised populations notably in new punitive 'risk discourse' and 'collateral discourse' that helps to criminalise the disenfranchised other (Beck 1992; Rodgers 2008; Webster 2012)? Finally, are there any independent modes of qualitative research and inquiry that can be defined as spaces of 'researcher-participant' agency that might act reflexively and resist the initiatives of such governmental policies (Gillian and Monahan 2012)?

Constructed qualitative 'truths' as penal-welfare knowledge

How does qualitative criminology contribute to new agendas for penal-welfare arrangements and crime control? A new age of crime control that primarily aims to manage the impact of residual social policy and the criminalisation of select populations focused on the powerless as 'risky' and tagged 'at-risk' subjects. The qualitative criminological research text is an ensemble of social representations of those subject to its mode of assessment. The text is partly useful in getting 'to know' through statistical aggregation or getting to know sub-groupings or cultures usually associated with crime and welfare. In qualitative research the criminological expert is engaged in specialised forms of reflexive monitoring of 'the different other' as risky individuals. Such research practices can intensify risk and collateral discourse in dealing with crime and social policy (Beck 1992; Wearing 2001, 2012). On the boarders of crime and social policy there are those engaged in 'edge living', where space and territory is governed by financial and social survival (Hannah-Moffat and O'Mally 2007; Rodgers 2008; Webster 2012).

Applying reflexive analysis to the lives of the marginal and powerless enables policy communities to begin to scrutinise their own and others research texts for ill-informed and possibly politically prejudiced representations of the other. This involves a folding back of knowledge building to include those who construct criminalising and normalising identities in the text and talk of criminal justice administrative and crime research documents (Wearing 1991; Walters 2003; Noaks and Wincup 2004; Muncie 2009).

One recent example that represents the mainstream use of qualitative data in criminology is from the US Ohio Life Course Study of delinquent youth to illustrate the complexity of intergenerational transmission of crime and abuse. These youths (16–18 years old) have subjectivities enabled and rendered by the author as knowing and resisting their parental influence as in a case with an alcoholic mother – '"shit", you know, I think I am going to be like her. I just think that I might slip and fall' or as feeling trapped in criminalising social networks – 'wrong place, wrong time, wrong people, wrong crowd... I was picked up for forging... for drug paraphernalia... and... criminal trespassing' (Giordano 2010, 169, 190). The key textual triggers for these youth to escape a life of crime triggers are imagined by the author as based both in 'resilience' as a psychosocial strategy and, further, in the longer term commitment to faith or family values that give push factors to move away from criminal activities. There is heuristic and justice imperatives in developing narrative and life course approaches of this type in criminology notably in pointing to 'freedom practices' for such youth. Nonetheless such methodologies and analysis have major limitations when shaped as humanistic realism in that they are not necessarily generalisable even to a very limited cohort of diverse young offenders nor does such research provide any concrete answers for change.

This intergenerational narrative and logic is also heavily influential in the 'Little Children Are Sacred' Report in the major themes of Aboriginal children and youth needing to escape the systemic intergenerational abuse and sexual violence in communities (NTG 2007). Data sources for this report included significant qualitative data such as written submissions, qualitative PhD theses, journal articles and other narrative forms such as transcript from interviewing elders, adult residents and children in remote NT Aboriginal communities. Chapter 4 of the report in particular concentrates on the nature of sexual abuse in these communities and uses qualitative 'evidence' extensively. The repertoire of intergenerational offending is being used again to emphasise the possibilities of it influencing filial and kinship offending. Space precludes a detailed analysis but a few points can be made and depth analysis is available elsewhere (Stringer 2007, Howe 2009). The quotes of perpetrators and children in this report arrange subjectivities within a frame that is complex but when sourced multiply or even given the uniqueness of many cases tends to be inconsistent in generalised constructions of qualitative analysis and evidence about the other. The approach to the use of evidence is commonly realist humanist in such official report writing and sometimes horrific and quasi-scientific at least in governmental writing as a cataloguing of expert researchers' claims about sexual offending.

A reflexive position on knowledge and power in criminology research acknowledges all documentation of children, youth and adults crime and especially powerless people will exercise long-distance forms of social control – whether conducted in life course research, qualitative research, welfare files, welfare interviews, policy research, policy consultation or sociological research (Law 1986, Latour 2005). Hence, the political bias of the researcher is implicated in this documentation and its possible use, as official data and evidence needs reflexive subversion to maintain a voice/s for the other. Becker (1967) defined the relationship between qualitative research and political bias in his request that researchers need to ask 'Whose side are we on?' notably based upon his own subversive research into drug users and juvenile offenders. Becker (1967, 241) proposed that qualitative research participants are commonly subordinate in the political order. Participants and their subject populations are also potentially at risk of political and legal reprisal if they speak up or even if qualitative researchers do on their behalf. Those who make their problems and 'life-worlds' known in voicing their daily struggles against power, deviance as social difference and identity definition itself are also at risk of suppression of their struggles. By giving up information on themselves their subjectivities are at risk of being co-opted and incorporated into the systems of power and thereby official and legal governance. The governance of the research participant is thus captured by expert and official discursive forms that make up the hierarchical institutions of power and control in modern society (Foucault 1991, Garland 2008).

Whose side are we on? – translating, inscribing and resisting

University-based crime prevention research is one example where contracts and tenders have been set by government agendas to crack down on 'crime' and perceived related law and order issues such as border protection, sexual offending and substance abuse to create a security state (Walters 2003). Out of such an emphasis qualitative criminology researchers are faced with set of technical, political and ethical questions about the social utility and ethicality of their research. These uncertainties in the viability of their knowledge building and representations of the other have formed against the backdrop of Garland's penal-welfare strategies and researchers' complicities in orienting individuals back to the rule of law: 'The effectiveness of the penal-welfare agencies, depended, in large part, upon the capacity of civil society to control individuals and channel their activities in law abiding directions' (Garland 2002, 49).

Part of a critical interpretive method is that qualitative analysis does not claim to be definitive in translating all the forms of control exercised on a population group. Beginning the research process with a strategy and methodology that is reflexive allows the researcher to apply critical interpretation to a range of socio-legal and social settings and the discourse that circulates in the documents of these settings. While we might not end this process with an entirely clear picture of what is actually going on, our interpretations can potentially re-position contests over the conceptual spaces of and social assumptions about the subjects of research.

Becker (1967, 123) defined the question in qualitative research relating political bias to a research strategy in qualitative research as simply, 'Whose side are we on?' The postmodern research strategy hinges on a more uncertain question, 'How do you know you're on that side?' Coincidentally, this is a question that Stan Cohen had recently revisited and addressed in terms of the hidden agendas of moral panics theory (Cohen 2011). Such a reflexive question opens up analysis of the positioning of the researcher and other evaluators as agents or translators involved in surveillance and control practices (Silverman 2003; Guillemin and Gillam 2004).

Qualitative criminology and the new crime control

John Le Carré's (1965) novel *The Spy Who Came in from the Cold* provides a critical literary point in the mid-20th century for the turning back into domestic policy of internationalised and covert powers of surveillance and control where criminology research starts to mimic the power struggles and tools of the spy trade (as Le Carré characterises it). The reflexive internal surveillance mechanisms as part of an epoch of interventionism are part of Garland's penal-welfarism that developed in the years post Second World War around welfare state goods and services notably in the disciplines of social administration and social policy and slightly later in Anglo empirical criminology all heavily reliant on their theoretical roots in Anglo-American sociology. Such mechanisms for social welfare including rehabilitation and penology were sanctioned by the deliberations of university-based and professional researchers involved in the monitoring and breaking down of the 'collateral damage' of those most on the margins: those who pose a threat to the social order because of their social difference and also create unprecedented fear in media and governmental policies as 'collateral discourse' (Garland 2008; Bauman 2011; Bauman and Lyons 2013).

This is why the author's narrative in qualitative research needs to be placed under the ethical and political microscope by researchers themselves. Their independence from 'the Leviathan' of the state's trajectories needs to be questioned and re-positioned. This reflexivity then forms part of the basis for the critical interpretive and reflexive method proposed to open up subjugated voices in modernity. Presentation of qualitative data in an interpretive and critical approach is not to accept what is said by the subjects of research as realism or to spruik such myth-making to the powers that be. The presentation of this material is selectively based not only on the bias of the researcher but also upon the imaginations and textual simulations of the social reality of the researched. The gestures to experience a reflexive critique would at least partially acknowledge that neither the researched nor the researcher can know the truth of this social reality if in fact there is one that is known.

Reflexivity offers the potential to warn researchers that their writings also potentially exercise liquid surveillance and authoritative discourses that themselves position subjects (see also Becker 1967; Walters 2003; Gilliam and Monahan 2012). The point of reflexivity is to reflect back over penal-welfare strategies and cultures, sub or submerged cultures and their effects in legitimating identities and in counter-discourse of political resistance and everyday resistance. In modern conditions of liquid surveillance subjectivities are often captured and deployed to bring about negative and unproductive policies. For example, policy directed at maintaining law and order rather than nurturing or caring for low-income and marginalised communities as illustrated by the NT interventions.

As Garland (2002, 204) has argued the costs of not acknowledging the dangers of qualitative constructions of 'criminality' remain rooted in modern penal-welfare strategies where the crime complex is now dispersed in civil society and also more politicised. The problems with more vigilante crime control and alarmist 'anti-denial' panics if unchecked are that their fall out can lead unchecked into more authoritarian crime control and rulings by the state. This contributes significantly to a rigid social order where the discursive construction of 'criminality' itself becomes collateral damage for that order.

Conclusion

To conclude this chapter, questions of ethical and political reflexivity in qualitative criminology underline the need for greater sensitivity and political robustness in our research practice. The chapter owes a debt to the classic studies by Becker (1963, 1967) on labelling of deviance as 'the marginal other' and the work of Garland (1985, 1990, 2002) on the nature, histories and politics of the modern penal-welfare strategies of governance. These authors have provided me with inspiration, a contextualising and a political critique of my own qualitative research and how I might comprehend political and ethical complicities in the construction of 'criminality' in such research. Crime and welfare measures coalesce in the penal-welfare state in anti-prevention policies that commonly overstep their own legal systems of rule exemplified in the secretiveness of say privatised prisons and heavy-handed surveillance and globalise control of vulnerability in public spaces using CCTV.

References

Alvesson, M. and Sköldberg, K. (2009) *Reflexive Methodology: New Vistas for Qualitative Research*, 2nd edn, London: Sage.
Anthony, T. and Blagg, H. (2012) *Addressing the 'Crime Problem' of the Northern Territory Intervention*, Canberra: Criminology Research Grants (CRG 38/09–10).
Australian Council of Social Services (2010) *Compulsory Income Management: A Flawed Answer to a Complex Issue*. URL (accessed 26 May 2013): http://acoss.org.au/images/uploads/ACOSS_analysis_income_management.pdf
Baird, B. (2008) 'Child Politics, Feminist Analysis' *Australian Feminist Studies* 23(57): 291–305.
Bauman, Z. (2011) *Collateral Damage*, Cambridge: Polity.
Bauman, Z. and Lyons, D. (2013) *Liquid Surveillance*, Cambridge: Polity.
Beck, U. (1992) *The Risk Society*, London: Sage.
Becker, H. (1963) *Outsiders*, New York: Free Press.
Becker, H. (1967) 'Whose Side Are We On?' *Social Problems* 14(4): 239–47.
Clandinin, D.J. and Connelly, F.M. (2000) *Experience and Story in Qualitative Research*, San Francisco, CA: Jossey-Bass.

Cohen, S. (2011) 'Whose Side Are We On? The Undeclared Politics of Moral Panics' *Crime Media and Culture* 7: 237–43.

Deleuze, G. (1976) *Negotiations*, New York: Columbia University Press.

Denzin, N.K., Lincoln, Y. and Smith, T.H. (eds) (2008) *Handbook of Critical and Indigenous Methodologies*, London: Sage.

Foucault, M. (1988) 'Technologies of Self'. In L.H. Martin, H. Gutman and P.H. Hutton (eds) *Technologies of the Self*, Amheist: University of Massachusetts Press, pp.16–49.

Foucault, M. (1991) 'A Question of Method'. In G. Burchell, C. Gordon and P. Miller (eds) *The Foucault Effect*, Chicago: University of Chicago Press, pp.73–86.

Garland, D. (1985) *Punishment and Welfare*, Aldershot: Gower.

Garland, D. (1990) *Punishment and Modern Society*, Oxford: Clarendon.

Garland, D. (2002) *The Culture of Control*, Chicago: Chicago University Press.

Garland, D. (2008) 'On the Concept of Moral Panic' *Crime Media Culture* 4: 9–30.

Gilliam, J. and Monahan, T. (2012) 'Everyday Resistance'. In K. Ball, K. Haggerty and D. Lyon (eds) *Routledge Handbook of Surveillance Studies*, London: Routledge, pp.410–28.

Giordano, P.C. (2010) *Legacies of Crime*, New York: Cambridge University Press.

Gullemin, M. and Gillam, L. (2004) 'Ethics, Reflexivity, and "Ethically Important Moments" in Research' *Qualitative Inquiry* 10(2): 261–80.

Hannah-Moffat, K. and O'Mally, P. (2007) *Gendered Risks*, New York: Routledge Cavendish.

Howe, A. (2009) 'Addressing Child Sexual Assault in Australian Aboriginal Communities – the Politics of White Voice' *Australian Feminist Law Journal* 30: 41–61.

Kvale, S. and Brinkmann, S. (2008) InterViews: *Learning the Craft of Qualitative Research Interviewing*, London: Sage.

Latour, B. (2005) *Reassessing the Social*, Oxford: Oxford University Press.

Law, A., Harrington, M. and Wearing, M. (2011) 'Out of Work, Out of Leisure, Out of Place' *The Greek Review of Social Research* 131(3): 63–78.

Law, J. (1986) 'On the Methods of Long Distance Control'. In J. Law (ed.) *Power, Action and Belief*, Henley: Routledge, pp.234–63.

Le Carré, J. (1963) *The Spy Who Came in from the Cold*, London: Penguin Books.

May, T. with Berry, B. (2011) *Social Research and Reflexivity*, London: Sage.

Muncie, J. (2009) *Youth and Crime*, 3rd edn, London: Sage.

Noaks, L and Wincup, E. (2004) *Criminological Research: Understanding Qualitative Methods*, London: Sage.

Northern Territory Government (NTG) (2007) *Ampe Akelyernemane Meke Mekarle 'Little Children are Sacred'*, Report of the Northern Territory Board of Inquiry into the Protection of Aboriginal Children from Sexual Abuse, Darwin, Northern Territory Government Publishing.

Parker, L. and Lynne, M. (2002) 'What's Race Got to Do with It?' *Qualitative Inquiry* 8: 7–22.

Rodgers, J. (2008) *Criminalising Social Policy*, Cullompton, Devon: Willan.

Rose, N. (1999) *Inventing Our Selves*, New York: Cambridge University Press.

Sherwood, J.M. (2010) *Do No Harm: Decolonising Aboriginal Health Research*, Unpublished PhD Thesis, University of New South Wales, Sydney, Australia.

Silverman, D (2003) *Interpreting Qualitative Data*, 3rd edn, London: Sage.

Smith, D. (1984) 'Textually Mediated Social Organisation' *International Social Science Journal* 99: 59–75.

Smith, L. T. (1999) *Decolonizing Methodologies*, London: Zed.

Stringer, R. (2007) 'A Nightmare of the Neocolonial Kind: Politics of Suffering in Howard's Northern Territory Intervention' *Borderlands* 6(2): 13.
Van Maanen, M. (1990) *Researching Lived Experience*, Albany, NY: State University of New York Press.
Walters, R. (2003) 'New Modes of Governance and the Commodification of Criminological Knowledge' *Social & Legal Studies* 12(1): 5–26.
Wearing, M. (1990) *The Documentation of the Poor: Surveillance and Control in Welfare Agencies*, Unpublished PhD, University of New South Wales, Sydney, Australia.
Wearing, M. (1991) 'Legal-Administrative Repertoires: Official Accounts of Black Deaths in Custody' *Journal of Social Justice Studies* 4: 133–60.
Wearing, M. (2001) 'Risk, Human Services and Contractualism' *Law in Context* 18: 129–53.
Wearing, M, (2012) 'Demonizing Non-White Identities in the Global Security State'. In D. Petty and C. MacFarland (eds) *Citizenship*, New York: Nova Science, pp.121–38.
Webster, C.W.R. (2012) 'Public Administration as Surveillance'. In K. Ball, K. Haggerty and D. Lyon (eds) *Routledge Handbook of Surveillance Studies*, Hokoben: Routledge, pp.313–30.
Yuval-Davis, N. (2011) *The Politics of Belonging*, Los Angeles, CA: Sage.

Part IV
Risk, Ethics and Researcher Safety
Editors' Introduction
Karen Lumsden and Aaron Winter

Part IV focuses on *risk, ethics and researcher safety* in criminological studies in the United Kingdom and South America. Risk and issues of researcher safety are magnified in many forms of criminological research, including most evidently those investigations which involve spending time with 'deviant' or 'criminal' groups including prisoners, offenders, deviant subcultures and other risky behaviours. The risks and dangers of conducting research with deviant or criminal groups, or in dangerous settings, have long been reflected upon in sociology, anthropology and criminology. Notable examples include Becker's (1963) study of jazz musicians and research on delinquent gangs (Thrasher 1927; Fleisher 1998), hustlers (Polsky 1985[1967]), high steel ironworkers (Haas 1977) and drug users (Adler 1985; Jacobs, 1998; Weisheit 1998). Additional risky research settings have included policing and the 'troubles' in Northern Ireland (Sluka 1990; Brewer and Magee 1991) homelessness (Arrigo 1998), security staff (Winlow et al. 2001), bicycle messengers (Fincham 2006) and the shipping industry (Sampson and Thomas 2003; Belousov et al. 2007).

Ethical guidelines in many countries such as the United Kingdom and North America mean that gaining approval for many criminological studies is now more difficult and nigh impossible if these involve the researcher being directly confronted with issues or situations which impact on their physical, psychological and/or emotional well-being. These issues are further exacerbated and brought to the fore in instances where the researcher's identity (such as gender) magnifies such risks (see Lee-Treweek and Linkogle 2000; Sampson and Thomas 2003).

In Chapter 16, Ruth Armstrong, Loraine Gelsthorpe and Ben Crewe candidly describe the ethical compromises of a UK postgraduate conducting ethnographic work with prisoners and ex-prisoners in the United States. They question whether being ethical is synonymous with following ethical protocols to the letter or whether taking risks might respect the values that underpin ethical regulations more than trying to rule out these risks entirely. They also reflect on the discomfort of undertaking and supervising these risks and describe the importance of trust, honesty and 'ethical sensibility' in the process of fieldwork and research reporting. Then, in Chapter 17, Stephanie C. Kane provides an account of the gendered cultural process through which crime affectively circulates in the community, beyond victims, perpetrators and agents of social control through widening spheres of social relations. She shows how reflexive methods clarify the contingent process of knowledge production and amplify criminology's cultural imagination. A knife assault witnessed on a globally popular beach in Salvador da Bahia, Brazil, illuminates the 'political unconscious' of crime and its dynamic relationship to place. Serendipitously in the scene of a crime, a distressingly mundane act of violence enhances communicative trust between co-witnesses, the ethnographer and her interlocutor.

References

Adler, P.A. (1985) *Wheeling and Dealing*, New York: Columbia University Press.
Arrigo, B.A. (1998) 'Shattered Lives and Shelter Lies? Anatomy of Research Deviance in Homeless Programming and Policy'. In J. Ferrell and M.S. Hamm (eds) *Ethnography at the Edge*, Boston: Northeastern University Press, pp.65–85.
Becker, H.S. (1963) *Outsiders*, New York: Free Press.
Belousov, K., Horlick-Jones, T., Bloor, M., Gilinskiy, Y., Golbert, V., Kostikovsky, Y., Levi, M. and Pentsov, D. (2007) 'Any Port in a Storm: Fieldwork Difficulties in Dangerous and Crisis-Ridden Settings' *Qualitative Research* 7(2): 155–75.
Brewer, J.D. and Magee, K. (1991) *Inside the RUC*, Oxford: Clarendon Press.
Fincham, B. (2006) 'Back to the "Old School": Bicycle Messengers, Employment and Ethnography' *Qualitative Research* 6(2): 187–205.
Fleisher, M.S. (1998) 'Ethnographers, Pimps and the Company Store'. In J. Ferrell and M.S. Hamm (eds) *Ethnography at the Edge*, Boston: Northeastern University Press, pp.44–64.
Haas, J. (1977) 'Learning Real Feelings: A Study of High Steel Ironworkers' Reactions to Fear and Danger' *Work and Occupations* 4(2): 147–70.
Jacobs, Bruce A. (1998) 'Researching Crack Dealers: Dilemmas and Contradictions'. In Jeff Ferrell and Mark S. Hamm (eds) *Ethnography at the Edge*, Boston: Northeastern University Press, pp.160–77.
Lee-Treweek, G. and Linkogle, S. (eds) (2000) *Danger in the Field*, London: Routledge.
Polsky, N. (1985[1967]) *Hustlers, Beats and Others*, Chicago: University of Chicago Press.
Sampson, H. and Thomas, M. (2003) 'Lone Researchers at Sea: Gender, Risk and Responsibility' *Qualitative Research* 3(2): 165–89.
Sluka, J. (1990) 'Participant-Observation in Violent Social Contexts: Managing Danger in Fieldwork' *Human Organization* 49(2): 114–26.
Thrasher, F. (1927) *The Gang*, Chicago: University of Chicago Press.
Weisheit, R.A. (1998) 'Marijuana Subcultures: Studying Crime in Rural America'. In J. Ferrell and M.S. Hamm (eds) *Ethnography at the Edge*, Boston: Northeastern University Press, pp.178–203.
Winlow, S., Hobbs, D., Lister, S. and Hadfield, P. (2001) 'Get Ready to Duck: Bouncers and the Reality of Ethnographic Research on Violent Groups' *British Journal of Criminology* 41: 536–48.

16
From Paper Ethics to Real-World Research: Supervising Ethical Reflexivity When Taking Risks in Research with 'the Risky'

Ruth Armstrong, Loraine Gelsthorpe and Ben Crewe

Introduction

In real-world research, ethics are not fixed. Ethnographic researchers require flexibility to negotiate the ambiguities of ethical compromise and honour ethical values. Indeed, in what has been termed a 'reflexive turn' (Brewer 2000), it is now more common than previously for researchers to engage reflexively with the fieldwork process, acknowledging knowledge production as both situated and partial (Lumsden 2012) and emotional (Ruby 1980; Israel and Hay 2006; Jewkes 2011). Less common is expressed reflexivity regarding the ethics of particular studies, acknowledging how the implementation of ethical safeguards is also situated, partial and sometimes compromised in the field (but see McGraw et al. 2000; Guillemin and Gillam 2004). This is especially taboo because of the heightened ethical concerns of work with 'vulnerable populations' in the field of criminology. This chapter considers how powerful institutions can utilise ethical procedures designed to both define and protect 'the vulnerable' to inhibit research that aims to encounter these individuals within the risky realities of their lives. We deliberate on what Israel and Hay (2006) outline as the two difficulties facing social scientists: (i) the need to engage in ethical conduct while (ii) also ensuring regulatory compliance. We argue that researchers seeking to conform to ethical review procedures can design methodological safeguards that, in practice, may numb their ethical sensibilities and discourage honest engagement in and reflexive deliberation of 'ethically important moments' (Guillemin and Gillam 2004).

This chapter is the product of the shared reflections of its three authors. Ruth Armstrong (RA) writes from her perspective of the ethical dilemmas of both access and encounter in her ethnographic work with male convicts[1] in prison and during the first year post-release. Loraine Gelsthorpe (LG) and Ben Crewe (BC) write from their perspectives as RA's academic supervisors. Our collective aim is to take the reader 'back stage' (Tunnell 1998), to show the underside of the research process (Gelsthorpe 2007), to expose ethical vulnerabilities and thereby permit accurate reflection of the ethical rigour of the research described here. In candidly describing the ethical compromises of a UK postgraduate conducting ethnographic work with prisoners and ex-prisoners in the United States, we question whether being ethical is synonymous with following ethical protocols to the letter and ask whether taking risks might respect the values that underpin ethical regulations more than trying to rule out these risks entirely. We reflect on the discomfort of both undertaking and supervising these risks and describe the importance of trust, honesty and 'ethical sensibility' in the process of fieldwork and research reporting. Finally, we outline how, in this case, the academic supervision process both facilitated reflexivity and made a safe space for the ethical manoeuvrings of a novice researcher discovering the realities of ethnographic fieldwork.

Negotiating access to the powerless through the powerful

The research described in this chapter was conducted in the United States with participants selected from a pre-release prison programme. In total, 51 prisoners fell within the pre-defined release period and were eligible to participate. Permission to carry out the research was sought and granted by the director of the voluntary sector agency responsible for programming in the pre-release prison, who also arranged initial access to the prison. Eligible prisoners were approached and 48 agreed to participate. However, on the second visit to the prison, the director highlighted access problems. He could not authorise the use of recording equipment in the prison and could only arrange for limited access to prisoners. The obvious route to gain broader access was to get authorisation for the research from the state Department of Corrections (DoC). However, academics in the United States warned that this would be a lengthy process, likely to derail a Ph.D, which is meant to be completed within a three-year period within the United Kingdom, and unlikely to be authorised due to a perceived reluctance to permit independent external research and the difficulty of getting ethnographic research with 'vulnerable populations' past the requisite institutional review boards (IRBs). As leading American criminologist Professor Mark Hamm has noted: 'In America it is harder for a criminologist to get into prison than it is for a convict to break out of one'.[2]

The ethical dilemma faced in this instance was that the study already had ethical approval from the ethics committee of a leading UK university, and the participants had already agreed to take part. Would subjecting the study to further review by an IRB and by the administrators of the participants' captivity help to protect participants' autonomy – one of the foundational principles of ethical review processes in the United States? Would 'respect for persons' – a second core principle – be better safeguarded by avoiding further access scrutiny? Might not restrictions on prisoners' and ex-prisoners' freedom to choose to communicate their experiences violate the third principle – that of beneficence?

The 1991 Federal Policy for the Protection of Human Subjects, known as the 'Common Rule', sets out the special conditions for research on 'vulnerable populations' defined as 'persons who are relatively or absolutely incapable of protecting their own interests'. They include children, foetuses and pregnant women, the terminally ill, students and employees, comatose patients and prisoners. As a vulnerable group of humans, research involving prisoners is therefore subject to 'special regulations ... that *restrict* the involvement of prisoners in research'.[3] The Common Rule defines prisoners as 'any individuals involuntarily confined or detained in a penal institution'. This does not include persons on probation or parole. The state DoC in this study defines research projects requiring their authorisation as 'any external empirical analysis of the practices and proceedings of the department involving offenders under supervision in the criminal justice system'. It applies to all people supervised by the DoC before, during and after incarceration. Part of the DoC external research approval process is IRB approval.[4] The role of IRBs as ethical review boards in the United States grew from recognition of the need to protect human subjects from potentially risky medical and behavioural research. However, IRBs have been criticised for 'mission creep' (Gunsalus et al. 2006; Whitney et al. 2008) on the basis that rather than protecting human participants from biomedical and behavioural research experiments, they have come to regulate human interactions (Gunsalus 2004, 369 emphasis added). Gunsalus (2004, 381) argues this situation has 'undermined respect for important ethical oversight' because ethical review has come to be understood as 'pro forma compliance as opposed to review of fundamental ethical issues' (Gunsalus 2004, 373).

At worst, the 'protections' offered to prisoners as 'vulnerable populations' can provide a legalistic mechanism to censor external research, ironically denying vulnerable persons the autonomy to participate in research concerning their conditions of captivity. Other ethnographers have argued that, in reality, official 'protection of human subjects' paperwork does little to safeguard the dignity and interests of socially vulnerable research subjects and is more often used to safeguard institutions from lawsuits (Bourgois and Schonberg 2009). In this project, care had been taken to ensure participants' informed consent. The obligatory forms had been ethically reviewed, the research had been clearly explained, as had the freedom to refuse to participate (chosen by three potential participants), to withdraw at any point (later chosen by one participant), to moderate participation as desired and the independence of the research from the criminal justice system and its internal processes. In this light, it felt uncomfortable to request further DoC authorisation to engage in a conversation with an ex-prisoner about their experiences post-release or that IRBs should have authority to regulate 'two people talking situations' (Gunsalus 2004). Experienced US academics advised that the best way to 'officially' navigate this situation was to present the research as an 'evaluation' of the third sector programme which did not 'empirically analyse the practices and proceedings of the department' in order to safeguard against criticism for choosing to circumvent the DoC authorisations. But these informal understandings about how to frame research in order to avoid bureaucratic hurdles so as to access 'vulnerable' populations inhibit academics from writing in an honest way about what they have actually done, and why.

Several options for ethical access were considered, including only contacting the participants once released. However, because DoC research authorisation is required to speak to people who are in the community but still subject to parole supervision, this strategy did not erase the ethical dilemmas. Instead, access was facilitated through volunteering for the pre-release programme within the prison. This approach enabled researcher's presence in the prison, but prohibited recording equipment other than a field notebook and printed questionnaires. This contact pre-release proved very important to establishing relationships of trust between the researcher and the participants which translated into a very low attrition rate.[5] Voluntary status overcame a bureaucratic hurdle and got researcher access through the gate, but within the prison it was known that the researcher's role was both altruistic and academic. The director of the pre-release programme was keen to discuss the research with officials, and the researcher talked about her work with the DoC audit team, the Executive Director of the DoC and the Director of Parole. A special trip was made to DoC headquarters to discuss the research with the DoC Head of Volunteer Services. What the project lacked in formal compliance it gained through relational legitimacy. Despite this, what the warden of the prison knew, or thought, or preferred not to know, was never made explicit. However, it was not necessary to be dishonest in order to be discreet. If deciding not to seek official authorisation was engaging in a form of deception, then it was a deception that Tunnell (1998, 212) suggests is 'central to the sociology of crime... deceiving those whose positions of official power... allow them to adversely affect participants, researchers, and researchers' work'. This research did not engage in 'conflict methodology' (Tunnell 1998); the epistemology was person centred, not anti-institutional. In order to learn from 'fellow mortals' one must approach them as such.

Taking risks in person-centred 'edgework' with 'the risky'

Lyng (1998, 221) argues that '[m]any important empirical and theoretical problems taken up in the social sciences can be thoroughly and honestly studied only by placing oneself in situations that may compromise safety and security in a normative or corporeal sense'. Ex-prisoner re-entry studied 'from below' is one such problem (Wacquant 2010). The document drafted to secure ethical approval for this study included strategies to safeguard against imagined risks to both participants and researcher and stated its overriding consideration as safeguarding participant well-being. One way to safeguard participant well-being as the overriding consideration was through authentic encounter in supportive and validating social interactions, but facilitating this meant minimising the power differentials between researcher and participant through coming alongside participants in the risky realities of their lives.

In line with the proposed methods drafted pre-fieldwork and approved by the ethics committee, interactions with released prisoners began through pre-arranged meetings with participants in public places and in locations selected by the researcher. The methods proposed involved safeguards such as not travelling with participants alone and not letting participants know the home address of the researcher. However, it became evident very quickly that sticking to some of these 'safeguards' would result in a failed fieldwork project. Tunnell (1998) suggests that in order to experience 'backstage behaviours' researchers must take a 'backstage approach'. His argument is practical rather than ethical and is persuasive. However, in this re-entry study, engagement in 'experiential anarchism' through 'edgework' (Lyng 1998, 1990) was not merely for practical reasons, but was grounded in ethical concerns. These fieldnotes capture the dilemma:

> The individuals I want to meet with are not used to moving around the city and are not particularly motivated to spend their newly found free time with me [RA]. As such, in order to engage my participants I need to make it as easy as possible for them to meet with me, that is, I need to do it on their terms where possible.

> However, this approach to fieldwork is not merely a pragmatic decision in order to ensure a good follow up rate. In no small way it comes from the theoretical underpinnings of the study developing through my time with the men. It feels incongruous to nod and smile and encourage these men to tell me everything about their lives, to hear how individuals who believed in their goodness helped to enable that goodness, but to insist we meet in a public place of my choosing, unspoken, yet understood, to ensure my security.[6]

Bottoms (2007, 83) calls for a dialogical relationship between theory and empirical observations as researchers navigate the 'rough waters' of data collection. Liebling (2001) also argues that attention to synthesis is required in empirical research. Reconciling the dialogue between desistance theory, data and ethical methods required a methodological re-orientation towards the participants and towards interaction. Methodologically prioritising the personhood of participants involved both embracing risk and trusting instincts. Sticking to methods designed to avoid risk entirely would have limited opportunities to encounter the realities of ex-prisoners' lives, whereas prioritising personhood permitted close-range encounters with the realities of re-entry: visiting where participants lived, meeting their families and friends, feeling the public stigma and constraints of electronic monitoring, racing back from excursions to comply with curfews, sensing participants' frustrations when we 'arrived' at their chosen venue to find that their old haunts had long since disappeared. One participant proudly acted as chauffer to show off his newly purchased vehicle, but was then frustrated and embarrassed, heavy in the atmospheric stigma of the label 'murderer', when he took a wrong turn and found he was headed towards a dead end on a country lane at midnight in an area he claimed he 'used to know like the back of [his] hand'. These experiences, and others, provided knowledge of the re-entering prisoners' mortification in the mundane – the sense of dislocation in finding they no longer belonged in the place they thought they were from.

Approaching participants on the basis of their present personhood rather than their past convictions permitted trust to grow and authenticity to flourish. This involved frequenting forgotten neighbourhoods, carefully following instructions of the route out and warnings not to stop; picking a way through a ransacked house, not yet cleared up following a revenge burglary; celebrating homecomings with home-made food and extended family; and watching prostitutes walk the street while rocking on the porch holding the hand of a mother sobbing for her drug-addicted son. This non-judgmental approach meant that participants felt able to share struggles as well as success. When Morris[7] moved out of a halfway house at 3 pm, with only an hour to get across town to a homeless shelter before intake closed at 4 pm, he called for a lift. He would never have made it on public transport and of course had no money for a cab. Arriving with moments to spare, he submissively and successfully negotiated his bed in the hostel. When Elijah was released from the city jail at 4 am, due to 'round-the-clock' release policies to deal with overcrowding,[8] he called to ask for a lift home, providing insight into jail release procedures that see hundreds of men released in the dead of every night onto the empty streets, little money and no way to get home. Compliance with risk protocols now embedded in ethics guidelines would not have permitted appreciation of such predicaments, nor provided the opportunity to speak to participants in such moments, such as asking Elijah about his few days back inside and what might come next in his life. This involvement helped with the development of appropriate questions for subsequent meetings and provided the platform of trust from which they could be asked. Ethnographic solidarity created a safe environment in which difficult realities were shared and discussed and discrepancies between explanations and experiences could be challenged. In other words, taking risks provided a vista to the realities of participants' lives and provided a receptive forum in which participants could both speak and be heard.

Being person centred and taking risks do not eschew the need for imposing safeguards when it seems prudent. When David requested a 5 am pick up to take him to a rehab centre, it seemed sensible to arrange for another ex-prisoner who knew him, but was not a participant in the research, to chaperone the dawn foray. David was living on the streets. He was thin and dirty, addicted to crack cocaine. Picking him up alone at 5 am with few people around involved risks both for the researcher's safety and for the participant, by providing an easy target for a robbery that could supply the proceeds for a quick drug fix. However, requesting a chaperone also involved ethical compromise in terms of participant confidentiality. Ravaged by drugs, sleeping rough, not having eaten for three days and without transport to get from rehab to parole to change his address and back again before intake closed, David would not have got into rehab without the help of a belligerent foreign white woman with a penchant for persistence. This experience brought home how with all the will in the world bureaucratic structures can block avenues of assistance for those seeking a way out. One situation also made it questionable whether withholding the home address was an ethical way to proceed. Casey had secured himself a job working away, and, proud of his achievement, he wanted to send a postcard, responding to the many he had received from England during his participation in the research. Perceiving the need to justify such revelations to an imaginary ethical police, RA's fieldnotes recall:

> I didn't want to say no to him. I felt like saying no would detract from his humanity. I am not concerned about what he will do with it, but rather, how I can account for giving it to him if I should be 'discovered'.

The account is thus: that in order to describe re-entry one must understand it, that 'depth of understanding' is 'related to the degree of co-presence' between researchers and participants (Lyng 1998, 225), that to get this understanding requires the 'honesty and openness' of participants, and facilitating this 'cannot be a one way process... to ask for these things generates obligations' (Liebling 2011, 520). On this occasion, withholding the address would have involved complicity in a pejorative power differential. These examples of interactions with David and Casey show how the imposition of safeguards is not always antithetical to expressing trust and facilitating authenticity, whereas pre-ordained risk management strategies can over-regulate the research process, curtail spontaneity (through encouraging researchers to avoid situations involving ethical compromise) and consequently numb researchers' ethical sensibilities. Taming the research process through legalistic adherence to ethical protocols could have damaging consequences for both ethical practice and research outcomes: it could result in researcher withdrawal from difficult and hidden areas of social life or encourage dishonesty about the realities of this work. In research with 'the risky', taking some risks may be part of a researcher's ethical obligations.

Guillemin and Gillam (2004) outline the value of reflexivity in providing both a 'language' and an 'approach' that can assist researchers in dealing with the 'ethically important moments' that arise in research. They distinguish between 'procedural ethics', drafted for ethical review boards pre-research, and 'ethics in practice' which are negotiated in situations that are 'difficult, often subtle, and usually unpredictable' (Guillemin and Gillam 2004, 262). A researcher's 'ethical competence', they argue, is only tested in practice through showing a willingness to recognise and acknowledge ethical dimensions in the 'micro-ethical' dimension of their work and to think through ethical issues and respond appropriately. While they therefore suggest that 'procedural ethics cannot in itself provide all that is needed for dealing with ethically important moments in qualitative research' (Guillemin and Gillam 2004, 262), and that 'arguably, procedural ethics has little or no impact on the actual ethical conduct of research' (Guillemin and Gillam 2004, 269), they posit a continuity between procedural ethics and ethics in practice. As the examples in this chapter show, however, there is a danger that the perceived need to adhere to pre-determined 'paper ethics' can undermine the fundamental principles on which ethical review is based, through suppressing researchers' willingness to engage in – and then honestly recount – the messy ethical dilemmas of ethnography. In the following section, we reflect on the role of open, honest and high-trust supervision in nurturing 'ethical sensibility'. We discuss how such an approach could be utilised by ethical review boards to facilitate reflexivity in 'ethics in practice' and help safeguard the ethical values that good researchers aim to uphold.

Supervising risk in research with 'the risky'

As Guillemin and Gillam (2004, 276) write, it is important to have or be able to develop 'a means of addressing and responding to ethical concerns if and when they arise in the research (which might well include a way or pre-empting potential ethical problems before they take hold)'. As supervisors, we are duty bound to ensure that research students are aware of ethical guidelines for the discipline (in this case criminology) and, indeed, for the university, to conduct a 'risk audit' for anyone planning to undertake fieldwork. One of us (LG) has chaired a professional ethics committee for many years as well as undertaking fieldwork in a variety of criminal justice contexts, and teaches 'ethics' as part of a social science methods programme – all the while promoting the exercise of 'ethical muscles' and reflexivity, while the other (BC) has extensive experience of conducting prison-based research with all the complexities and concomitant concerns regarding access that involves. In our dealings with senior gatekeepers, there has always been an understanding – sometimes explicit – that some creative (but careful) interpretation of formal research guidelines may be a prerequisite for meaningful research. Senior practitioners have expressed faith in our ability to make decisions in the field that are sensible and defensible, with defensibility defined in relation to the spirit more than the letter of ethical frameworks. In other words, we are trusted to know what the rules are and how to use them. In supervising students, we try to generate the same relationship and the same understanding of what it means to undertake ethical research. This requires an ethical sensibility that is broader in scope, and deeper in spirit, than can be assured through simple compliance with ethical protocols. Part of our preparation work with students is to point out the limitations of codes of ethics. We also seek to reproduce the relationship of mutual trust that we ourselves have experienced as researchers, despite the insecurities that result from it, because it is only under conditions of trust that truly helpful discussions can take place about the context-specific ethical dilemmas that they confront.

We had all along anticipated ongoing contact with Ruth during the fieldwork, well aware that ethical issues might arise in the process. Certainly, there was no belief that codes of ethics hold all the answers, or that ethics committees know what the realities of fieldwork might be like. Moreover, we have become increasingly conscious of the fact that institutional ethics committees sometimes confuse safety, security and ethical practice and have criticised increased regulatory controls over research under the guise of 'ethics' in our teaching (Israel and Hay 2006). But there is a difference between questioning the meaning of 'ethical practice' in the classroom and addressing it in practice. Thus engagement in Ruth's ethical dilemmas renewed concern to think about the values which underpin research and how new regimes of regulatory ethical control can limit rather than facilitate 'value-led' research. Doing qualitative research is by nature a reflective and recursive process of course (Ely et al. 1991, 179) but somehow direct engagement with Ruth's dilemmas brought it all closer to home and we needed to be reflexive in relation to the ethics of her research.

As we see it, the process of reflexivity is an attempt to identify, do something about and acknowledge the limitations of research: its location, its subjects, its process, its theoretical context, its data, its analysis; and recognise that the construction of knowledge takes place in the world and not apart from it. For us, being reflexive in doing research is part of being honest and ethically mature in research practice, and we would certainly endorse any steps which require researchers to 'stop being "shamans" of objectivity' (Ruby 1980, 154).

One of the immediate reactions when learning of the complexities of Ruth's research – both in terms of her access and her ongoing practices – was to think defensively: How could she ensure safety, and how could we ensure her safety – at great distance? Would the research be compromised? Would our institution's reputation be compromised if anything were to go wrong? Thus classroom debates became a pressing reality. We either had to trust the person we knew, and who was close to the ground, or compromise her research ourselves, by insisting upon formal rather than substantive compliance with official practices and procedures. We were thus prompted to think about the differences between 'procedural ethics' and 'ethics in practice' (Guillemin and Gillam 2004).

Our faith in Ruth's judgment and maturity, and our recognition that she was street smart, was crucial here. It made it easier to leave decisions in her hands, even though this meant living with a degree of nervousness about the potential for things to go wrong. (The fact that both the country and criminal justice system in which she was working were relatively unknown to us, and were far away, perhaps made it easier to live with our nerves.) With other students we have supervised, we would have been considerably more reluctant to give such latitude. Indeed, we might well have drawn upon official guidelines to dissuade a student from making such decisions or, even, to pull the plug on some aspects of the study. In this respect, formal protocols were potentially a shield behind which we could all withdraw. In this case, it made more sense to offer ourselves as sounding boards for Ruth in precisely those moments when she found herself in situations which could not possibly be covered by formal research guidelines, when her insecurities were likely to be their greatest. Ruth's constant candour about the edgework in which she was engaging was an edgy experience for us, as supervisors. But we came to recognise more forcefully than hitherto that it was more valuable for her to expose (us to) the messy negotiations and risky practices inherent in her research than for her to avoid them, deal with them alone or tidy them away in the writing up of her research. Had she done any of these, not only would her research have suffered, but so too would her development as an ethically sensitive researcher.

Conclusion

This chapter has argued that reflexivity is an important mechanism through which ethical rigour can be maximised. It builds on the previous work on reflexivity and ethics to suggest that legalistic adherence to existing forms of ethical safeguards might not always protect the values we hope they will. We have argued that ethical supervision, in the form of capacity for honest discussion of ethical compromises in an atmosphere of trust contemporaneous with fieldwork, could help to promote such reflexivity. Israel and Hay (2006) argue the researcher's job is to ensure both ethical conduct and ethical compliance. Reflexivity in this project has forced us to question whether this is always possible. The concern is that, all too often, human research participants might be underprotected or disempowered as academics engage in broad and bland research proposals, solid enough to survive the ethical review process, but elastic enough to permit pragmatic research. These concerns are heightened in criminological research where powerful state institutions can evade an independent academic gaze behind paternalistic determinations and oversight of how to protect 'vulnerable' people from 'risky' interactions.

Dequirez and Hersant (2013) describe the 'virtues of improvisation' in ethnography: it gives researchers the freedom to adapt and to be inventive which is beneficial for both knowledge production and analytical frameworks. In this chapter, we have argued such flexibility might also lead to more ethical research and develop more ethically sensitive researchers who report the realities of their labours candidly. Essentially, the research has to be ethically 'good-enough' (Winnicott 1973). Within policing, Bowling (2009) argues 'good-enough' means being clear about fundamental values and transparent about the means and the ends. The same holds true for research. This experience of trying to do a 'good-enough' ethnography (Scheper-Hughes 1989) suggests to us that it might be possible for ethical regulatory bodies to oversee ethnographic research in politically sensitive areas in a way that permits transparency about ethical improvisations while upholding ethical values. This would involve movement towards a more social scientific standard of rigour where research is not judged by the absence of ethical ambiguities, but by evidence of ethical sensibilities through practices that return us to the heart of the matter – respect for autonomy, beneficence and justice.

Notes

1. This term was preferred by participants, as it distinguishes them from others on the basis of their conviction, rather than offending behaviour.
2. Personal communication.
3. See the US Department of Health and Human Services, Human Participant Protections Education for Research Teams, Nov 2002: p. 22.
4. While the study had approval from the ethical review committee of a leading UK university, US academics thought this was unlikely to satisfy the requirement for IRB approval because the UK university's ethical review committee did not include either an ex-prisoner or prisoners' representative on the panel, a requirement for an IRB deciding the ethicality of research involving prisoners.
5. RA lost contact with just six participants during the course of the study.
6. For reasons of confidentiality the date and location of this fieldwork note is not included. It was recorded within the first month of the first prisoner participant's release, as Ruth began to realise why and how her data collection strategy was inappropriate both practically and theoretically.
7. All names used are pseudonyms.

8. A recent bill to mandate release from jails only during daylight hours did not pass
   through the legislature.

References

Bottoms, A.E. (2007) 'The Relationship Between Theory and Empirical Observations in
   Criminology'. In R.D. King and E. Wincup (eds) *Doing Research on Crime and Justice,*
   Oxford: Oxford University Press, pp.75–116.
Bourgois, P. and Schonberg, J. (2009) *Righteous Dopefiends,* Berkeley, CA: University of
   California Press.
Bowling, B. (2009) 'Fair and Effective Policing Methods: Towards "Good-Enough"
   Policing' *Journal of Scandinavian Studies in Criminology and Crime Prevention* 8:
   17–32.
Brewer, J.D. (2000) *Ethnography,* Buckingham: Open University Press.
Dequirez, G. and Hersant, J. (2013) 'The Virtues of Improvisation: Ethnography
   Without an Ethics Protocol' *Current Sociology* 61(5/6): 646–60.
Ely, M., Anzul, M., Friedman, T., Garner, D. and McCormack Steinmetz, A. (1991)
   Doing Qualitative Research: Circles Within Circles, London: the Falmer Press.
Gelsthorpe, L. (2007) 'The Jack Roller: Telling a Story?' *Theoretical Criminology* 11:
   515–42.
Guillemin, M. and Gillam, L. (2004) 'Ethics, Reflexivity, and "Ethically Important
   Moments" in Research' *Qualitative Inquiry* 10(2): 261–80.
Gunsalus, C.K. (2004) 'The Nanny State Meets the Inner Lawyer: Overregulating While
   Underprotecting Human Participants in Research' *Ethics and Behaviour* 14: 369–82.
Gunsalus, C.K., Bruner, E.M., Burbules, N.C., Dash, L., Goldberg, J.P., Greenough, W.T.,
   Miller, G.A. and Pratt, M.G. (2006) *The Illinois White Paper: Improving the System for
   Protecting Human Subjects: Counteracting IRB 'Mission Creep',* Illinois: The Centre for
   Advanced Study.
Israel, M. and Hay, I. (2006) *Research Ethics for Social Scientists,* London: Sage.
Jewkes, Y. (2011) 'Autoethnography and Emotion as Intellectual Resources: Doing
   Prison Research Differently' *Qualitative Inquiry* 18(1): 63–75.
Liebling, A. (2001) 'Whose Side Are We On? Theory, Practice and Allegiances in Prisons
   Research' *British Journal of Criminology* 41: 472–84.
Liebling, A. (2011) 'Being a Criminologist: Investigation as Lifestyle and Living'. In
   M. Bosworth and C. Hoyle (eds) *What Is Criminology?* Oxford: Oxford University
   Press, pp.518–30.
Lumsden, K. (2012) '"You Are What You Research": Researcher Partisanship and the
   Sociology of the "Underdog"' *Qualitative Research* 13(1): 3–18.
Lyng, S. (1998) 'Dangerous Methods: Risk Taking and the Research Process'. In
   M.S. Hamm and J. Ferrell (eds) *Ethnography at the Edge: Crime, Deviance, and Field
   Research,* Boston: Northeastern University Press, pp.221–51.
McGraw, L., Zvonkovic, A. and Walker, A. (2000) 'Studying Postmodern Families:
   A Feminist Analysis of Ethical Tensions in Work and Family Research' *Journal of
   Marriage and the Family* 62(1): 68–77.
Ruby, J. (1980) 'Exposing Yourself: Reflexivity, Film and Anthropology' *Semiotica*
   30(1/2): 153–79.
Scheper-Hughes, N. (1989) 'Death Without Weeping: Has Poverty Ravaged Mother
   Love in the Shantytowns of Brazil?' *Natural History* 98: 8–16.
Tunnell, K.D. (1998) 'Honesty, Secrecy, and Deception in the Sociology of Crime: Con-
   fessions and Reflections from the Backstage'. In M.S. Hamm and J. Ferrell (eds)

Ethnography at the Edge: Crime, Deviance, and Field Research, Boston: Northeastern University Press, pp.206–20.

Wacquant, L. (2010) 'Prisoner Re-entry as Myth and Ceremony' *Dialectical Anthropology* 34: 605–20.

Whitney, S.N., Alcser, K., Schneider, C.E., McCullough, L.B., McGuire, A.L. and Volk, R.J. (2008) 'Principal Investigator Views of the IRB System' *International Journal of Medical Sciences* 5: 68–72.

Winnicott, D.W. (1973[1964]) *The Child, the Family, and the Outside World*, London: Pelican Books.

17
Armed Robbery and Ethnographic Connection in Salvador da Bahia, Brazil

Stephanie C. Kane

Introduction

Note on reflexive ethnographic method

Grounded in dialogue, moving through openings between systematicity and serendipity, ethnography is inherently reflexive. Yet for reflexivity to matter, to influence the understanding of human being and action in cross-cultural context, the ethnographer must explicitly analyse and articulate the way that particular people socially interacting in specific settings co-produce both objective and subjective knowledge about the world, and also, how such knowledge (re)shapes culture. Story-telling – presenting criminology as the story of encounter – is a classic method of conveying ethnographic analysis and pulling in theoretical interventions that deepen and expand the meanings entailed in a fieldwork project. An armed robbery on a Brazilian beach, witnessed by the ethnographer and a woman who, by virtue of this shared, albeit indirect, trauma, became her trusted interlocutor, is the point of departure for this discussion of how trust emerges – unplanned yet mobilised in the flow of field experience.[1]

Sideline criminal encounters

A stretch of national coastline – historically the heart of the slave trade and culturally still the heart of Afro-Brazil – becomes fieldwork terrain for observing how globalisation extends, embeds and creates opportunities for crime. In the process of such transformations, the sandy edge becomes a stage. Like its other inhabitants and visitors, the ethnographer enters into the beach's gendered cultural ecology of pleasure, fear and trust. Vaguely eyeing fishing boats bouncing colourfully against a blue-green horizon, bathing-suited bar-restaurant clientele enjoy the sun, pulsating music, beer, sugar cane rum (*cachaça*) and fried food. For those who look persistently, the 'false pretense of eroticism' (Veissière 2008) can erode the cheerfulness. Nevertheless, the spectacle of racialised tropical encounters continues to be encoded and circulated in seductive images that attract globe-trotting tourists, connecting this beach to the world. Together with the working, middle and upper class clientele from up the block and down the coast, all participate in recreating the enduring myth that is Bahia. But it is the flow of international tourist dollars in particular that fuels the real estate, financial and beverage industries. These industrial interests increasingly appropriate the beach, often illegally or quasi-legally, thereby undermining the legal status of the coastline as public trust and the ecological balance of the natural environment.

The urbanisation of the nation's coast creates establishments for people with money to spend. This is set beside neighbourhoods with varying degrees of 'irregularity' (a euphemism for relative poverty and insufficient infrastructure). The juxtapositions create both desired and despised concatenations of sociality and anti-sociality which become ethnographically accessible in an oddly reflexive moment of violent encounter on Itapuã's Lighthouse Beach in Salvador.[2] Itapuã, a former fishing village, offers only meagre opportunities for, as one bar-restaurant owner puts it, 'young men to be human'. The crimes some of these young men commit are violent but basically sidelined: they are performed in coordination with (although by no means in cahoots with) hotel, condo and restaurant businesses. Participating and observing the entrenched and transitory inhabitant networks, my gaze is drawn to crime scenes even as my analysis is drawn to the often hidden and mundane forces and conditions that combine to produce them. Focusing on one event and its ramifications, this chapter illuminates the discursive and relational productivity of crime. It fleshes out Durkheimian theory of crime's societal function by illuminating how crime can open and diversify new forms of relationship and interaction, even as it can close others down.[3] I show how one violent beach crime (a variant of 'street crime') can generate gendered fear-based forces of cohesion that can lead to new, positive social relationships that spin off from their fearful origins.

In the scenes to follow, I do not focus analysis on the character and motivations of those who actually commit armed robbery: I do not refer here to crime's utilitarian functions, its seductions (Katz 1988), carnivalesque aspects (Presdee 2000) or the amplifying spirals of crime and culture mediated by the Internet (Ferrell et al. 2008), although these, too, are worthwhile approaches. My goal is more aligned with a reflexively engaged feminist criminology: I am interested in forms of trust and empathy that arise out of witnessing violent crime by those who live and work face-to-face on the beach.[4] A reflexive approach to participant observation allows for real-time analysis of these processes.

Cross- and intra-cultural understanding is made possible when personal emotions and social prejudices combine in the aftershock of being a victim of, or a witness to, violent crime. The Brazilian concept of *confianza* refers to a quality of trust that can be invested in certain persons and places. Confianza may be extended as a result of sharing a direct or narrated experience of crime. Confianza is a theme and social interactional strategy that citizens and foreigners employ to create a somewhat illusory protection from crime – a form of politeness, a small comfort, a concerned consideration for others, if you will. In this case, the ethnographer becomes part of the unfolding of the crime itself, part of local dramas that vividly demarcate those who are, and those who are not, *de confianza* (trustworthy). Through the lens of confianza, I examine coping mechanisms that generate understanding rather than blame. The chapter explores the communicative potential and limits of co-witnessing in the context of a fairly typical Brazilian urban beachside wherein hyper-mobile and culturally diverse elite nationals, foreign transients (tourists) and semi-transients (retirees, investors and this North American ethnographers) collide and collaborate with a mostly darker-complexioned resident majority that includes a decisive segment of hyper-*im*mobilised young men.

The beach as assaultive landscape

The narrow strip of beach is lined with *Barracas* – restaurant-bars that range from improvised thatch huts (increasingly uncommon, but technically legal) to overly developed, internationally financed and run cement and stone structures (increasingly common and technically illegal).[5] Barracas serve alcohol and food to sets of clientele differentiated by class, cultural affinity and national origin. I live directly behind the beach in a condo located within a parallel strip of other condos, private homes and hotels. With revelations of assaults and thefts involving residents and people they know increasing steadily in intensity during my stay, crime invades my original, ethnographic project on urban water ecology and social justice. Being open to events that do not necessarily fit into one's plans is an important dimension of reflexive methods because it entails a willingness to engage, to move with and attend to unfolding dynamics of social interaction.

In this chapter, I focus on an event in which the ethnographer is drawn into the scene of the crime itself. I describe crime as an intrusion into the frame of the everyday (a woman and I chat as we gaze at the sun setting over the Atlantic) and how the singular intrusion puts us in dialogue with the chain of beach crimes extending into the past and future. I build on the analysis of the gaze from its roots in feminist media criticism to explore a gendered (rather than explicitly sexual) context in which women's active gazing, though disempowered by crime, nevertheless enhances ethnographic insight.[6] My purpose here is to contribute to two areas of inquiry, one general and one place based: (1) to suggest how analytic attention to mundane events helps us get an angle on crime's template in the 'political unconscious' (Jameson 1981, 75–76) and (2) to show

how the process of 'imagining crime' (Young 1996) is shaped in and by the spatiotemporal characteristics and cultural character of a popular beach.

The social bonds of witness

A day after moving in, I leave the condo in bathing suit and *Haviana* flip flops, key around my neck, and head for the beach, a small square of which I can see through my kitchen window. That first time doing what became a daily exercise, I stop at the first *barraca* at the end of the street and stick the flip flops inconspicuously between a tree and the cement platform of the barraca, a step above the tables on the sand filled with a lively clientele. Chico, the fisherman whose wife owns and runs the business, warns me that they would surely be stolen if left there, that I should give them to the woman inside the hut for safekeeping. That is how I meet Gloria and her family. After that, I chat a little every day, leaving my flip flops inside the door, and waiting for opportunities to talk in the midst of their busy work schedule. If I go out for my walk close to dusk, they warn me sternly that assault is a real threat. I would laugh, saying I have nothing with me anybody would want. Until one day:

> [w]itnessed an assault on the beach. Went to talk to the beach-shack owners near my house, they were closing up, and we were chatting and she said, 'Look, they are assaulting that man', and we watched two young guys point their knives at a man by the rocks on the shore. Right in front of us, then they ran up the street, one fumbled and dropped something, the other ran back and then they both ran up our street. Then a friend of theirs came out of the shadows to the group of us, who obviously saw exactly what went down, meaning to be intimidating I suppose but acting like he was our friend. High-fived Chico, who did lightly comment on what went down, saying something like it wasn't good for business. Right before he came over, I was talking to Gloria, asking, 'Why don't you tell the police?' and Chico warned us under his breath that one of them is coming over. My friend was practically crying. Damn! She said they come every 'Santos', all the time, and they feel that they cannot do anything about it. The one that came over is 'with them', though he was not directly involved in pointing the knives. Gloria said the man lost his sandals and a cell phone. I don't know how she knew.
> (Twilight, Friday evening, 26 January 2006)

When I came into the gate of the condo, Adrian and Sergio were sitting chatting. I told them about what I had just seen and they said that you cannot go on the beach at this hour, even though it still wasn't quite dark. Sergio said that his woman with her little girl left the condo about this hour and were standing right across the street in front of the Colegio waiting for friends to pick them up to take them to church when she was assaulted at knife point.

(Twilight, Friday evening, 26 January 2006)

Another Assault: First I talked to Chico [saying] that I was sad about the assault the other day, how they did it right in front of us as if we didn't matter and then (the one) came over to threaten us. Chico said that it happens all over, that it happened on the street the other day, and that they live in fear and that only God will help. I asked, 'what about the police?' He said that if they report an assault to the police, it is always after the fact. They [the witnesses] end up spending two hours doing paperwork, leaving all heated, with nothing to show, the robbers have already gone.

(Sunday afternoon, 28 January 2006)

Then I sat down with Gloria. She said yet another assault: a friend of theirs, a fellow barraca-manager was robbed at his barraca at two or three o'clock in the afternoon! She asked about my work and we started talking...

(Sunday afternoon, 28 January 2006)

This moment of shared witness, the feelings of outrage, sadness and frustration at our powerlessness, created an emotional bond between Gloria and me that grows into a meaningful ethnographic exchange in a series of subsequent interviews and interactions. Before she points out the assault in-progress I was admiring the sunset over the rocky outcrop and sea. She pulls my line of sight into the criminal tableau with her words. I see the glint of the knife and the tourist man's little fat belly, his coveted objects pass in the too-small space between him and his attackers. All of this is happening barely ten feet away. And then, my questions, spoken too loudly. Chico's warning of the third man who was tucked away, watching us; the watcher threatens us with his approach and dares us to exert any form of social control. We do not challenge. Even if he, they, could not hurt us at this moment, Gloria and Chico and their family, including the little ones, are too easily targeted as they try to earn their living day by day. I have stepped into their time series: these same young men, at the same spot in front of their barraca, have robbed beach-goers before and will again. In one of our post-incident conversations, Chico basically agrees with Juvená: one simply cannot expect young men to avoid crime when legitimate educational and employment opportunities are systematically denied to them.

Police power: Two tableaus

No one I spoke with believed that the police could or would do anything effective to curtail the problem of assault on lighthouse beach. Offenders who are arrested stay in jail only two or three days and are then released. Police are as much a part of the cultural ecology of beach crime as victims, perpetrators and witnesses. Their lack of effective crime control contributes to the perpetuation of assault as a mode of livelihood. With the intention of gathering statistics on assault and homicide rates, I head off to the local civil police station on 23 February 2006, having waited for things to calm down post-Carnaval. Following information shared by the morning secretarial staff, I return at two o'clock this afternoon, passing through the front office and climb the back stairs to find that the statistician had already left for the day. The woman at the desk sends me instead to see the titular, the titled one, a.k.a. the police chief, the imposing man responsible for the approximately 500,000 souls of the 12th district of Itapuã (as well as others passing through).

He is delighted to meet me it seems, asking about my work and ideas, and happy to have me wait while he deals with various questions and interruptions from staff and one long phone conversation that sounds like a cop who had gotten in trouble and to whom he suggests, with much repetition and patience, an excellent lawyer with experience defending cops. One staff person comes running and proceeds to relay the news of yet another heinous crime. Speaking so excitedly makes it difficult for me to understand but her tale is accompanied by much illustrative gesturing. Not one, but two guns were aimed at either side of the head of a woman who was related to her next-door neighbours. The gun-wielding man, who it turns out had already killed the neighbours, told the woman that she was a worthless piece of shit and then allowed her to run away. (Gun to the head is a common motif used in robbery in the street and at home, in car-jacking and sometimes ending in murder. A gun was held to the head of our landlord once in the very condo above ours, although it would not be he who tells us that little unsettling detail.)

During this long waiting period, every time I figure I might as well split and start to get up from the chair facing his desk, the chief motions, 'stay, stay'. And as it is not uninteresting and there are those stats that could be useful, I continue to observe. Finally, there's a lull and he turns to me and asks a string of questions which on their face seem designed to pigeon-hole me: Why do you think people commit crimes? What should we do about it? Do you believe in capital punishment? After a decent interval of listening, he declares that he believes that it all boils down to a lack of love. Given the extreme circumstances of people in his district, I cannot believe that he is sincere, but there is no facial expression indicating whimsy or religious fervour. Then he takes me on a tour of the statistics room and the jail.

The jailer, a tall dark-complexioned man (in local parlance, a *preto*), reins over a tiny domain in the back of the station. Like many jails, this one, meant to be a temporary holdover for a small handful of men, is punishingly overcrowded. It is a tiny concrete non-air-conditioned space packed with shirtless men, several of whom are playing cards on the wet floor. They all squeeze forward to the barred entrance when the chief and I approach. To my surprise I'm suddenly burdened by the chief's arm around my shoulders and he's telling me in front of them, enacting the hierarchy of power, that I have his permission to come back any time and interview the prisoners (something I have not requested), in addition to getting my data when the statistician comes back on Monday. Anxious to depart, I extend my hand, which he ignores I presume to allow me the opportunity to indulge the standard Brazilian gesture of arrival and departure – a peck on each cheek; instead he brushes my mouth.

On Friday, the chief said that when I return I should speak to him before meeting with the statistician. When I do return on Monday, my husband is kind enough to accompany me to clarify my standing and mitigate further sexualisation of the ethnographic encounter. We are ushered into his office and offered the couch off to the side while we wait. He is speaking to a woman in her 50s or 60s who is accompanied by a younger woman, probably her daughter. The older woman is crying and begging obsequiously. Her hand is stretched out across the wide desk, holding his. She is stroking the hand imploringly and he is telling her that 'It is in God's hands' and 'yes, we will help'. I am astonished to watch as she gets down on her hands and knees before his feet as the chief remains seated behind his desk. Her request is that he locate the assassin responsible for the death of a family member. It seems to have something to do with a cheque that was left on a table that should have been paid to someone but was not, but again, it is difficult to understand the chaotic rush of words referring to a story whose details had been revealed before we arrived. When the women leave, the chief turns his attention to us, making a big deal about my husband looking like his brother (as these Afro-Brazilian and Afro-American men have complexions of similar shade). Dispatching us quickly, he tells the statistician to give us everything we need. These statistics cannot meaningfully unpack the systematic chaos of assaultive and murderous intention, yet they do reflect the categories and distribution of reported crimes. Unsurprisingly, none of them include environmental crimes, my area of primary interest.[7]

Some days later, Gloria and Chico hear that one of the trio assaulters we witnessed had attacked another tourist, who coincidently bumped into his attacker on the beach again after which the victim went to the police and described him [sk: How?] Skinny, 17–18 years old, etc. [sk: But how could the police know where to go from that little info?] All these guys already have multiple citations (*queixas*), they tell me. So the police went to the address they had on file: his mother's house. And there was the camera, under the house. She didn't want them to arrest her son, but they did. [sk: How can the police handle all these arrests? I saw the tiny, unsuitable place where they put them.] They let them go after two or three days. Their mothers sell the TV or refrigerator to pay for a lawyer to go over and get them out of jail. On my last night in town, I bump into Gloria and Chico walking home clearly exhausted from a long day at work. She says again that she watched the same trio of lads assault a client on the beach. The one who had been caught with the tourist's camera had been let out a few days after his arrest only to re-enact the assaultive repertoire with his team. And so danger maps, knife-wielding gestures and inter-locking gendered gazes repeat: attackers, victims and witnesses join their listeners in the discursive shadows, entering their fears and alliances into archives of popular memory (cf. Taylor 2003).

Confianza and coercion

A young Japanese-Brazilian woman sitting next to me on the flight from Brazil to Argentina tells me the story of her family's maid, who when she first arrived in São Paulo lived in one of its poorest and most crowded favelas.[8] After shootings, as the banditos quickly dragged the bodies away before the arrival of police, they would call the women out of their homes and into the narrow streets and alleys in order to clean up blood that had drained from the victims. The gendered character of confianza here is telling, the women washing the bloodied streets complicit even though coerced in a form of community confianza that outwits even the pretence of police protection.

The feeling of coerced confianza, of being a part of something that you abhor and that traps you at the same time, recalls (albeit in a much weaker way) the emotional tension of the assault Gloria and I witnessed on Itapuã's Lighthouse Beach, and also the mixed emotions of the mother of the young man who does not want the police to take her son to jail for stealing the tourist's camera and stashing it under her house, who like other mothers would, if she had to, sell her refrigerator to free him. Brazilians living in poverty undeniably suffer a greater degree of violence, of crime perpetrated by individuals and by gangs, police and banditos, as well as the structural violence perpetrated by the system (Goldstein 2003; Scheper-Hughes 1992). However, for better or for ill, violent crime and its witness feed a cultural and emotional current that links favela to working class and upscale beach neighbourhoods, poor to rich, locals to outsiders. This current shadows the sexual, racial, musically seductive mixture of Brazilian culture celebrated as '*brasilidade*'. Even so, the ecology of fear and trust on the beach includes humanity's festive and tragic dimensions.

Brazil is a place that you cannot help having *saudades* (longing) for, despite the undeniable swashbuckling plunder of its beautiful beaches, inhabitants and visitors. Fieldwork long over, writing about the relief of escaping Itapuã conjures many saudades. In my experience as witness, I find that co-observation of a knife assault and participation in its discursive shadow deepens communication channels, quickening this stranger-ethnographer's move towards insider status, to being *uma pessoa de confianza* (a person of/in confidence). Co-observing the beach assault (and other incidents) enhanced my ability to generate data from participant observation because the event enmeshed me in the complicated structural forces and feelings characteristic of place. Beyond the boon that serendipity can bring to the systematic researcher, however, a stronger emphasis on witnessing as a coerced and complicit form of social engagement can, I suggest, provide an alternative focus in the study of law and crime more generally. A shift away from traditionally hyper-vigilant engagement with perpetrators, punishers and victims, or better said, an expansion of analytic horizons or addition of analytic angles, can open up pathways through the vast uncharted social spaces between the sureties and abominations of law and crime. Where causes, motives, boundaries, transgressions and methods of control do not segment easily into pre-assigned categories, scholars may find ways to read otherwise and elsewhere.

Conclusion

This chapter shows the way in which reflexive analysis and writing can create criminological insight – not, in this case, about the perpetrator or victim, the police or courts – but insight about how an act of co-witness can enhance fieldwork in the lived landscape of crime. The place-based evocation of inter-personal experience provides a window into the general and gendered cultural process through which crime affectively circulates through widening spheres of social relations. Building on the work of feminist, cultural and critical criminologists who continue to experiment with a multiplicity of perspectives, I offer this chapter as an instantiation of socially situated thought, acknowledging, following Stephen Pfohl (1994, 405), that the 'form and content are partial, provisional, and reflexively open to ongoing historical modifications'.

In fieldwork as in life, there are crucial moments when aspects of identity intersect fluidly, shifting their meaning in context. Crime drives this dynamic. On Lighthouse Beach, co-witnessing the knife assault weakened the difference in social power that, as is so often the case, had been an obstacle to trusting communication between me and my would be interlocutor. For better or worse, this is *crime's power* (Parnell and Kane 2003): it both disrupts and perpetuates patterns of exclusion and inclusion, creating a mix of coercion and confianza, powerlessness and potential, that push ethnographers beyond the parameters of planned observation. Analytically open to chance, used on their own or in combination, reflexive methods clarify the contingent process of knowledge production and amplify criminology's cultural imagination.

Notes

1. Acknowledgements: Fulbright Hays provided funding for field research and writing was supported by a sabbatical from Indiana University. An early version of this essay was presented at the international conference on 'Ethnographies of Gender and Globalization', Netherlands Association for Gender and Feminist Anthropology (LOVA), Amsterdam, 3–4 July 2008. Thanks to the folk in Salvador who participated in this project and to C. Jason Dotson, project videographer.
2. This chapter is part of a multi-sited port city water project in Brazil and Argentina (Kane 2012a). For analyses of how violent crime transforms socio-natural spaces see Kane (2010 and 2012b).
3. On reworking Durkheim see Young (1996, 1–26) and Greenhouse (2003).
4. For scholarship on empathy and crime see Brydon and Greenhill; and Mark; in Parnell and Kane (2003).
5. See Kane (2013) on legal controversy over beach shacks.
6. See Kuhn (1985, 27–28) for analysis of dynamics of power and the gaze in pornography. See also analysis of the gaze in an experimental piece on stigma in the ethnography of prostitution (Kane 1998).
7. Crime statistics, organised and distorted by contested racial categories and the calendar of festival activities, vary dramatically by neighbourhood. For state crime statistics, see websites of the military police, www.pmba.ba.gov.br and the Secretary of Public Security, www.portalssp.ba.gov.br.
8. Fieldnotes, 5 March 2007. In her ethnography of life in a Rio de Janeiro favela, Goldstein (2003, 174) mentions an instance where a man "was shot in the head eight times, his blood running along the lanes beside the shacks [the ethnographer] knew so well. The victim's *compadre* cleaned the blood-stained before the authorities arrived and adhered to the favela's 'law of silence'". Caldeira (2000) analyses the feelings of powerlessness that witnesses feel when they do not have protection from, and hence cannot report crime to, the police (e.g. case narrative pp.187–88).

References

Brydon, A. and Greenhill, P. (2003) 'Representations of Crime: On Showing Paintings by a Serial Killer'. In P. Parnell and S. C. Kane (eds) *Crime's Power: Anthropologists and the Ethnography of Crime*, New York: Palgrave Macmillan, pp.145–72.
Caldeira, T.P.R. (2000) *City of Walls: Crime, Segregation, and Citizenship in São Paulo*, Berkeley: University of California Press.
Ferrell, J., Hayward, K. and Young, J. (2008) *Cultural Criminology*, Los Angeles, CA: Sage.
Goldstein, D.M. (2003) *Laughter Out of Place: Race, Class, Violence, and Sexuality in a Rio Shantytown*, Berkeley: University of California Press.
Jameson, F. (1981) *The Political Unconscious: Narrative as a Socially Symbolic Act*, Ithaca, NY: Cornell University Press.
Kane, S.C. (1998) 'Reversing the Ethnographic Gaze: Experiments in Cultural Criminology'. In J. Ferrell and M.S. Hamm (eds) *Ethnography at the Edge: Crime, Deviance and Field Research*, Boston: Northeastern University Press, pp.132–45.
Kane, S.C. (2010) 'Beach Crime in Popular Culture: Confining the Carnivalesque in Salvador da Bahia, Brazil'. In M. Deflem (ed.) *Popular Culture, Crime, and Social Control*, Bingley, UK: Emerald Group, pp.243–62.

Kane, S.C. (2012a) *Where Rivers Meet the Sea: The Political Ecology of Water*, Philadelphia: Temple University Press.

Kane, S.C. (2012b) 'The Art of Torture and the Place of Execution: A Forensic Narrative' *Political and Legal Anthropology Review (PoLAR)* 35(1): 53–76.

Kane, S.C. (2013) 'Coastal Conflict: Implementing Environmental Law in Salvador da Bahia'. In N. South and A. Brisman (eds) *Routledge International Handbook of Green Criminology*, New York: Routledge, pp.379–93.

Katz, J. (1988) *The Seductions of Crime: Moral and Sensual Attractions in Doing Evil*, New York: Basic Books.

Kuhn, A. (1985) *The Power of the Image: Essays on Representation and Sexuality*, London: Routledge and Kegan Paul.

Mark, V. (2003) 'Hear No Evil, Read No Evil, Write No Evil: Inscriptions of French World War II Collaboration'. In P. Parnell and S. C. Kane (eds) *Crime's Power: Anthropologists and the Ethnography of Crime*, New York: Palgrave Macmillan, pp.245–68.

Parnell, P. and Kane, S.C. (eds) (2003) *Crime's Power: Anthropologists and the Ethnography of Crime*, New York: Palgrave Macmillan.

Pfohl, S. (1994) *Images of Deviance and Social Control: A Sociological History*, 2nd edn, New York: McGraw Hill.

Presdee, M. (2000) *Cultural Criminology and the Carnival of Crime*, London: Routledge.

Scheper-Hughes, N. (1992) *Death Without Weeping: The Violence of Everyday Life in Northeast Brazil*, Berkeley: University of California Press.

Taylor, D. (2003) *The Archive and the Repertoire: Performing Cultural Memory in the Americas*, Durham: Duke University Press.

Veissière, S. (2008) 'Gringos in Bahia; Mulatas in Milan: the Transnational Political Economy of Violence, Desire and Suffering in Brazil and Italy'. Paper presented at the International Conference of LOVA, 3 July 2008.

Young, A. (1996) *Imagining Crime*, London: Sage.

Part V

Power, Partisanship and Bias
Editors' Introduction
Karen Lumsden and Aaron Winter

This section highlights the role of *power, partisanship and bias* in research involving those typically seen as occupying *powerful* positions in society, such as legal professionals, courts, criminal justice agencies, politicians, the police and the media. As Hughes (2000, 235) observes: 'All social science has a political dimension, in the non-party-political sense. All aspects of research necessarily involve the researcher in both the analysis and practice of power and, in turn, have the potential to generate conflicts of interest between a whole host of interested parties'. In Chapter 18, Gemma Birkett describes her research with criminal justice professionals in the British government. She addresses the distinct issues involved in interviewing female policy elites and considers the difficulties encountered in the dissemination of political research findings. In Chapter 19, Kate Fitz-Gibbon also focuses on her research experiences with powerful groups. She argues that a time when academia is increasingly recognising the importance of policy application and the transfer of research into practice, interviews with legal practitioners provide an opportunity for criminologists to validate and support research findings with the experiences of those working within the field. In Chapter 20, Vanina Ferreccio and Francesca Vianello observe how their research in prisons in Italy and Argentina involved a balancing exercise between the strategies developed and implemented by the institutional actors of the prison with the aim of influencing and directing research and the existing possibilities for the researcher to resist and construct a space of partial autonomy within the research field. In Chapter 21, Karen Lumsden then reflects on her experience of conducting research with both the powerless – boy racers, and powerful groups including the police, local council and authorities, politicians and media. She focuses on the role of bias and partisanship in the study of boy racers, and the tendency for sociologists of deviance to side with the powerless. She also draws attention to how we 'give voice' to our research participants, focusing on her interactions with the media.

Reference

Hughes, G. (2000) 'Understanding the Politics of Criminological Research'. In V. Jupp, P. Davies and P. Francis (eds) (2000) *Doing Criminological Research*, London: Sage, pp.234–48.

18

Politics, Power and Gender: Reflections on Researching Female Policy Elites in Criminal Justice

Gemma Birkett

Introduction

Most qualitative researchers will attempt to be aware of their role in the (co)-construction of knowledge (Finlay 2002a, 11) which is of critical importance when researching the vulnerable. But what about those with *powerful* participants? Elite research raises 'a particular set of issues and dilemmas which have important implications for the methodology, mode of interviewing and the process of analysis and interpretation' (Ball 1994, 97). Researching political actors, those criminal justice professionals in the UK government, Whitehall[1] and beyond, introduces specific power dynamics between the researcher and the researched, particularly if political partisanship or personal agendas are at play. Based on the fieldwork experience of researching an elite network of individuals working on the reform of women's penal policy, this chapter will provide a reflexive account of the research process and will critically reflect on matters of gendered power and partisanship. In addressing these specific issues, it will also consider some of the ethical difficulties encountered when disseminating political research findings of this kind. It is clear that cautious balance needs to be afforded to the interests of competing political groups and individuals, an issue better addressed by other disciplines and one which criminology has remained largely silent on. This chapter will argue that by engaging in a process of reflexivity or 'methodological self-consciousness' (Finlay 2002a), criminologists are well positioned to uncover and report on the nature of power dynamics in research encounters involving female elites.

The research

Reflexivity can be defined as thoughtful, conscious self-awareness (Finlay 2002b, 532) and often begins 'pre-research'. At the embryonic phase of

233

planning an investigation, it can be necessary to reflect on both the topic of research and one's own relationship to that topic (Finlay 2002b, 536). It is important to appreciate that the individual biography of the qualitative researcher has a major impact on a research project, shaping its methodological and theoretical foundations, and as a result, the final analysis (Oakley 1981; Edwards 1993; see also Arendell 1997; Finlay 2002b; Broom et al. 2009, 51). As past experience greatly influences my own area of research it is important to make explicit at the outset. Developing an interest in criminal justice policy development (and in penal reform more specifically) while working as a researcher in the UK Parliament, over the course of several years I had the opportunity to visit prisons, a women's community centre 'one-stop-shop' and attend various All-Party Parliamentary Groups and Palace of Westminster (the seat of the UK government) receptions. Despite this position, it would be erroneous to label myself as an 'insider'. I had not worked in the criminal justice policy sphere, and nor did I have any direct contacts. My advantage, however, was that I had operated in the same 'Westminster village' as many of the participants. As an 'informed outsider' I was able to watch live debates, attended events, read documents (sometimes restricted to Members of Parliament) and follow the work of key individuals with great interest. Such knowledge of the policy 'network' provided inspiration for future research projects.

The research discussed in this chapter examined the strategies employed by political actors working on the reform of women's penal policy in England and Wales. It sought to investigate the different approaches – the public (or indeed private) 'messaging structures' employed by such actors to influence others in their policy 'network' (see Rhodes 1990, 1997; Marsh and Rhodes 1992), politicians, the media and the public. Participants comprised of various political and policy elites from across the spectrum, the majority of whom were public figures: chief executives and directors of organisations working on women's penal reform, former Home Office and Justice Ministers, former senior civil servants, several members of the House of Lords, 'state' officials including a Crown Court judge and a former prison governor, high-profile academics and a number of journalists reporting on crime and home affairs. While not all participants were female, the majority were, and such encounters provide the focus of this chapter.

Feminist empiricism challenges the notion that the identity of the researcher has no effect on the quality of their findings (Harding cited in Sarantakos 2005, 57) and seeks to include the researcher as a 'person' (Reinharz 1992). Adopting a liberal feminist standpoint, my endeavours therefore remained faithful to the underlying reflexive principle that the researcher 'must be placed within the frame of the picture that she attempts to paint' (Harding 1987, 9). Feminist research is by its nature politically value laden and critical (Sarantakos 2005, 56) and part of its agenda must entail a serious acknowledgment and analysis of the '*micropolitics*' of research projects (Conti and O'Neil 2007). This final element should not be an afterthought, but must be central to the documentation and dissemination of the research (Conti and O'Neil 2007). As highlighted by Duke (2002, 44), there is consequently a strong tradition among feminist researchers of providing analyses on the nature and practice of conducting research (e.g. Roberts 1981; Stanley and Wise 1983) and a growing body of work emerging in criminology (Jupp et al. 2000; King and Wincup 2008). While such work has undoubtedly helped to highlight and politicise debates about the conduct of research (Duke 2002, 44), the majority of guidance remains firmly focused on researching the vulnerable and more work needs to be published on the research experiences of feminists studying 'up'.

A short note on studying 'elites'

Punch stated in 1986 that social researchers have 'rarely penetrated the territory of the powerful', with field studies traditionally focused on the deviant or marginalised. This is certainly true in the field of criminology, yet in the last few decades social scientists have increasingly turned their research endeavours to the actions of the elite members of society and the power that they yield. Such developments have led to a small but growing body of literature that exposes the specific challenges of investigating this group. While expanding scholarship has led to a wide recognition that there is no universal definition of the term 'elite', such actors have variously been described as 'those with close proximity to power' (Slote Morris 2009, 209), or with particular expertise (Burnham et al. 2004). Some have expressed unease with the term and its 'connotations of superiority' and Reisman (cited in Smith 2006, 645) in particular was dissatisfied that he had found 'no other term that is shorthand for the point I want to make, namely that people in important or exposed positions may require VIP interviewing treatment on the topics which relate to their importance or exposure'. Recognising attempts to problematise the classification, the research adopted Slote Morris' (2009) distinction to include those in positions of [or close proximity to] power (as described above). Burnham et al. (2004, 205) characterised elite interviewing as 'a situation in which the balance is in favour of the respondent' and this can lead to additional challenges in the participants' natural tendency to *take control* of the agenda (Burnham et al. 2004; Bygnes cited in Slote Morris 2009). The next section will critically reflect on this issue in relation to the negotiation of research space involving female policy elites.

Negotiating female policy elites: Issues of power and partisanship

Power

Traditional elite research has tended to concentrate on a 'linear orientated conception of power' (Neal and McLaughlin 2009, 695), where authority is statically defined as 'residing in the explicit structural positions of *either* the researcher *or* the research participant'. Such structural accounts often assume that the power associated with people through their professional positions will transfer directly onto the interview space (Smith 2006, 645). Having worked with political elites and conducted elite research, it is easy to appreciate why social scientists have tended to provide these descriptions. As fieldnotes highlight:

> [w]hen she arrived after about ten minutes she extended her hand for me to shake and went to the other side of a very large table. She was pretty intimidating. She didn't really answer any of the questions and spent the majority of the time giving me a history of her career. Her power and status was ever-present, and despite the fact that she gave me an hour she controlled the whole thing. I'm not sure if I've gathered the information I want and I'm annoyed at myself for not drilling further into certain issues, but it just didn't seem a possibility...
>
> (22 September 2012)[2]

Despite the undoubted frequency of such accounts, some have critiqued traditional interpretations of power as inflexible to the reality of social inquiry and have instead advocated the application of a 'poststructuralist filter' to the analysis of elite power. Smith (2006, 645) in particular stressed 'the idea that elites can be neatly defined and treated as consistently powerful is a view which relies on a rather simplistic idea that there is a dichotomy between powerful elites and powerless others', arguing that 'such an outlook ignores the preposition that power exists in a variety of modalities... that these modalities of power can be negotiated and... that elites may change over time'.

While feminist versions of reflexivity (Reinharz 1992; Wilkinson 1998) have sought to address concerns about unexamined power balances between participants and researchers (Finlay 2003), this has often focused on the researcher as the powerful one in the relationship. It is clear, however, that feminists researching female public figures require different skills to negotiate the dynamics of this particular research space. Attempting to understand the power dynamic between researcher and elite informant is crucial, because it not only shapes the interview process, but also *defines how knowledge is created* (Conti and O'Neil 2007, 67 emphasis added). Echoing the case presented by Smith, Neal and McLaughlin (2009, 703) who describe the 'untidy and emotional research encounters in which power moved in mobile ways across interview landscapes' during their fieldwork with elite participants. My experience with elite females complements their understanding:

> When she approached she told me off for being in the wrong place and said that she had pretty much given up on our meeting. I am certain

that I was in the right place, but I couldn't question her as I have been desperate to meet for so long. We set off to the interview location. It was clear she wasn't that interested in small talk. I seriously wondered how I was going to turn this round. We sat in a really inappropriate place for an interview, but again I couldn't question. During the interview she was fairly brusque, but at points divulged some personal information. She was pretty emotional at one stage. She didn't really look at me at all. I am really confused ...

(27 November 2012)

As well as that of 'space', power in the research context can also relate to interview *location* and *length*. All venues were selected by participants, with some clearly unsuitable for the purposes of political research. Elwood and Martin (2000) highlighted how interview location has a clear effect on the length and tone of conversation, arguing that researchers have tended to ignore 'the power dynamic constituted by the interactions among interviewer [and] participant *in particular interview sites*' (2000, 651 emphasis added). This is an important consideration in elite research where the researcher lacks control of the situation. My experience confirmed that in some busy public spaces – in this case a variety of cloakrooms, hotel lobbies, cafes and bars, open plan offices and noisy benches in the House of Lords[3] – it simply was not appropriate to ask politically sensitive questions. While private offices were clearly more suitable in terms of privacy, conducting interviews in grand office suites could also be an intimidating experience.

As well as location, most participants also controlled the interview length. While this was understandable given their status and demanding agendas, consistent with the experiences of others it required me to 'quickly prioritise questions at the same time as asking them, editing the schedule as the interview proceeded' (Fitz and Halpin 1994, 47). One recurring issue, highlighted by Walford (2011, 3), is that elite participants have a tendency to 'just talk' and not answer the specific questions asked.[4] It is therefore up to the researcher to try and steer answers back to the interview guide while often working within a tight timeframe. Body language (such as looking at the door or clock) would demonstrate when my participants were anxious to get away, and during most interviews I felt compelled to say 'only a couple more questions' as I was acutely aware of the time, or even boredom, however long the interview lasted. On many occasions I left the interviews dissatisfied with the amount of information that I had gathered, and this had obvious implications for the final analysis.

Partisanship

Related to issues of 'power' is the requirement for researchers to possess 'sufficient cultural and social awareness to know how to play the game well enough to remain in the field' (Fitz and Halpin 1994, 48). Those studying elites must quickly understand the individuals and personalities – the 'micropolitics' – within their chosen 'network' and behave accordingly. As my previous career had prepared me, learning to 'tread carefully' is by no means an afterthought, as 'individuals... communicate with each other, about you and your research. Staying in is often dependent upon not making mistakes' (Fitz and Halpin 1994, 39). It is no surprise, therefore, that those investigating this field (which routinely involves ideologically opposed participants) have determined that 'political interviews are themselves highly political' (Ball 1994, 97). It has been said that elites use an interview to 'present themselves in a good light... to convey a particular version of events, to get arguments and points of view across (and) to deride or displace other interpretations and points of view' (Ball 1994, 97–98). On many occasions I was asked 'who else are you talking to?' and explained that my research involved interviews with members of the main political parties and directors of major campaign organisations (who may also have a public political allegiance). Having worked in politics, I understood that the vast majority of my participants spoke with a political agenda of some kind and prepared for interviews with an appreciation that this would be the case.

Of particular difficulty in elite interviews is the methodological necessity to ask probing questions. As highlighted in the previous section, 'probing' elites can be difficult enough due to their tendency to control the research 'space', but an added consideration in political inquiry is that researchers may never get to the 'whole truth'. While all would endeavour to get to the 'bottom line' of their chosen topic, those studying elites may find that they have to satisfy themselves with the 'official' or 'party' line. As someone who had been previously tasked with devising such 'positions', I was aware that my participants would be very unlikely to divulge 'secrets' to someone who was talking to their 'competitors'. Recounting their experience of interviewing senior bureaucrats in Whitehall, Fitz and Halpin (1994, 40) recalled an 'imposed reality' that was 'highly constrained'. Researching an area shrouded in secrecy, they glimpsed 'an unfamiliar world that was only ever partially revealed' (Fitz and Halpin 1994, 40). Experiencing similar frustrations during the interview process I was aware on several occasions that I was simply being fed what was already 'on the record'. At the same time I was acutely aware that my participants had given their time 'altruistically' and on the presumption that they would not be aggressively questioned or contradicted. While several academics have called for researchers to be more confrontational in situations like these (see Mickelson 1994; Walford 2011), this was certainly not my approach and is not the approach universally adopted by feminists.

It is clear, therefore, that 'handling' an elite interview can be a very complex business (Lilleker 2003, 210), and it is easy to see why there is a 'defeatism' among social scientists in their dealings with the powerful (Mungham and Thomas cited in Williams 1989, 254). Of concern is the fact that few researchers have been prepared to discuss the 'issues and dilemmas' that are faced when studying elites (Lilleker 2003) and there is a clear require-ment for more first-hand accounts of 'political' interviews, particularly those involving women.

Interviewing female policy elites: 'A sisterly exchange of information?'

The age, ethnicity and *social status* of women being interviewed has been shown to be influential in the power relations between women in the inter-view setting (Riessman 1987; see also Cotterill 1992; Reinharz and Chase 2001; Broom et al. 2009, 53). While a fundamental principle of feminist research has been to *minimise* the power disparity in research settings, working with political elites who also happen to be women can result in considerable anxieties: 'on the one hand, political actors are well known for trying to control discussion and manage the topic schedule, (yet) at the same time, a feminist researcher working with female subjects should be try-ing to give some control to her interviewees' (Ross 2001, 164). Feminists usually favour the researcher being a 'supplicant' (McDowell 1992, 1998), and this approach has been recommended for women interviewing women so as not to 'objectify our sisters' (Finch cited in Desmond 2004, 265). While such guidance is rightly aimed at those researching vulnerable populations and giving voice to the 'powerless', little commentary exists for those inter-viewing female elites. One reason for this may be because the term 'elite' is more widely associated with men, or simply because there are substantially fewer females in positions of power. As such, very little consideration has been given to feminist research situations where the researcher lacks control over the interview (Puwar 1997, 2.4) and there is consequently a paucity of commentary on the negotiation of space while conducting interviews with female political elites – those who are simultaneously an 'elite' and a woman (Puwar 1997, 4.2).

Oakley (1981) painted a picture of 'sisterly interaction' between women interviewing women; however, the female researcher studying 'up' may not always enjoy such a rosy encounter. Puwar (1997, 1.1) described her experience of interviewing female MPs as 'not always a cosy, friendly exchange of information' and concluded that 'the whole power asymmetry is *reversed* when researching women elites' (Puwar 1997, 1.1 my emphasis). Desmond's (2004) experience of interviewing women elites was distinctly similar. Female participants were found to be 'tough, brusque and offi-cial' and Desmond (2004, 265) concluded that 'it is a mistake for female researchers to assume a feminist solidarity exists'. As a feminist researcher operating on the assumption that interviewing women would be a positive experience, it was unfortunate that a great many of my research encounters echoed the descriptions above. One fieldnote highlights this disappointment:

> I had looked forward to meeting her and so I was pretty nervous on the way to the interview. She did give me an hour, but it wasn't anything new. I wasn't comfortable probing her, probably due to her eminence. I felt that she was bored with my questions and skipped quite a few towards the end. I know I should feel extremely grateful for even five minutes of her time, and I am, but I feel pretty deflated. I'm not sure what I should have expected....
>
> (2 September 2011)

Such anecdotes highlight why some feminists have warned against a 'delusion of alliance' (Stacey 1991, 116) for those researching women elites. While my female participants would have undoubtedly labelled themselves as 'feminists' (some very high profile), my research encounters were not necessarily consistent with the traditional 'feminist' interview. Despite such experiences, it would be erroneous to describe all encounters with women as difficult. Many participants were professional and helpful, and interviews that I dreaded turned out to be incredibly encouraging and positive experiences:

> As she had ignored my emails for over a year I wondered what sort of person she would be. I walked into the office with a slight feeling of unease. When I opened the door she was instantly warm and directed me to the kitchen to make myself a tea. We went and chatted in a quiet room and she answered all questions with consideration. She was warm and funny and inspirational. One of the best interviews, loads of great information...
>
> (1 November 2012)

It is therefore too simplistic to conceptualise the research relationship between elites and researchers as a one-dimensional hierarchy (Duke 2002, 52). Adopting a poststructuralist conception of power, my experiences complement those of Puwar (1997): that at times the research echoed Ann Oakley's (1982, 55) description of interviewing women as a friendly exchange of information, while at other times it related more to Ball's (1994, 113) description of elite interviews as 'events of struggle'. On reflection I had inadvertently taken to adopting what Rice (2010, 70) referred to as the 'elasticity of positionality' as a 'field strategy' to help negotiate the often unpredictable and unequal power relations I encountered (see also McDowell 1993; Duke 2002).

Publishing political research findings: A reflexive approach

My experiences add weight to the claim that qualitative research can be uncomfortable and challenging (Finlay 2002b). Fieldwork is certainly a process of discovery, and Lilleker's (2003, 213) assertion that 'whether you love or hate your interviewees, the experience of meeting them gives colour to your writing' is undoubtedly relevant to a great number of research projects. Yet many qualitative researchers continue to refrain from reporting on the host of influences in the data collection process (Broom et al. 2009). For some, telling 'the whole story' is of lesser importance, while for others (myself included) it is a crucial element of the research process. Reflexivity can be understood as a 'confessional account of methodology' (Finlay 2002a) and revealing its intersubjective elements can only serve to improve the integrity of qualitative data, while providing others with further insight into the environment within which the information emerged (Broom et al. 2009, 63). That does not mean, however, that reflexivity comes without its own myriad dilemmas and decisions, mainly focused around the extent to which researchers should 'come clean' (Duke 2002). As Finlay has warned, engaging in reflexivity can be akin to 'negotiating the swamp' (2002a) and while social scientists should expect to get 'the seats of their pants dirty by real research' (Park cited in Burgess 1982, 6), those engaged in political investigations must appreciate the real possibility of dirtying their own reputation in the process.

Those walking the tightrope of political research routinely face a series of dilemmas when deciding on what information to put 'out there'. While a great deal of literature discusses the ethics and importance of protecting the vulnerable when publishing research findings (Jupp et al. 2000; Liamputtong 2007), there can be a similar tendency to 'protect' the elite, albeit for different reasons. Notwithstanding their ability to instruct legal proceedings, the fact that participants are powerful (and in my case public figures) can lead to self-censorship (Walford 2011, 4). Woliver (2002) described the dilemma of being told things in an interview that would be damaging to the respondent were they published, and this was certainly my experience. Marshall (1984, 236) believed that researchers in policy settings encountered either 'ostriches' – people who obfuscated or avoided them – or 'pussycats' who were delighted to relate 'secrets'. While it is undoubtedly more rewarding to feel the thrill of uncovering something new (as opposed to being fed the 'official line'), decisions about the subsequent use of this data can be difficult for researchers. I left several interviews having learned a great deal of 'inside' information, knowing full well that I could not use it for ethical reasons.[5]

For feminist researchers the act of *representing* people is a very personal and moral activity (King and Horrocks 2012, 138), and this includes taking accountability for the political and ethical implications of knowledge production (Ramazanoglu and Holland 2002, 11). As Josselson neatly summarised: 'I have taken myself out of a relationship with my participants...to be in a relationship with my readers. I have, in a sense, been talking about them behind their backs and doing so publicly' (1996, 70). While such reflections may routinely relate to vulnerable participants, researchers studying elites have similar moral dilemmas when deciding what politically sensitive information to include or expel in their publications – the stakes perhaps even higher when publishing accounts of public figures.

My own research developed into a publication that was heavily self-censored, despite the fact that my participants talked to me 'on the record'. This 'over-censorship' could perhaps be viewed as a method of self-protection, but as a feminist researcher my overriding loyalty was to my participants (whether I liked them or not). Ultimately, I did not wish to be obstructive, yet neither did I wish to publish a wholly 'sanitised' account of my research encounters. Reflexivity enabled me to discuss my research experiences while at the same time 'protecting' my participants. It also enabled me to take a critical stance towards my impact on the research and the context in which it took place (King and Horrocks 2010, 126). It would be erroneous to assume that my gender, past experience and political stance did not have an impact on the finished result – indeed feminist research *aims* to be both contextual and emotional. It is therefore important to critically reflect on and 'accept our subjectivity, our emotions and our socially grounded positions [rather] than to assume some of us can rise above them' (Ramazanoglu cited in Westmarland 2001, para 21).

Conclusion

This chapter has contributed to discussions of reflexivity in criminological research by demonstrating that through engaging in reflexive practice criminologists are better positioned to scrutinise the sometimes unsettled nature of power dynamics in research encounters involving criminal justice policy elites. Oakley (2005, 217) once stated that 'interviewing is rather like marriage: everybody knows what it is, an awful lot of people do it, and behind each closed front door there is a world of secrets'. Reflexive stories (such as the anecdotes highlighted in this chapter) show that it is possible for criminologists to open a window on areas that in other research contexts would remain concealed from awareness (Finlay 2002b, 541).

Contributing to discussions of power and reflexivity, this chapter has highlighted the sometimes complex power symmetry that emerges when researching *female* elites in this field. It has been argued that the traditional feminist conception of power can be *reversed* in such circumstances, and it is easy to see why some argue this to be the case. While acknowledging the relevance of structural accounts, it may be more sensible to adopt a *poststructural* conception to the analysis of power in such settings, allowing a more flexible analysis to be applied to the sometimes murky emotional complexities of female elite research. As a *feminist* researcher, I believe we need more published reflections and 'confessional accounts' from those undertaking both elite and gender studies in criminology. However, as an *elite* researcher I veer towards self-censorship and continue to debate internally the extent to which I should 'come clean' (Duke 2002). It is therefore easy to see why Finlay labelled the process of engaging in reflexivity as 'perilous, full of muddy ambiguity and multiple trails' (2002a, 212).

Yet as knowledge expands, valuable lessons for future research can be learned. *Whatever* the experience of interviewing female elites, we must continue to provide accounts that are 'just as diverse and rich as the wide range of accounts to be found when the researcher is the privileged one in the relationship' (Puwar 1997, 111). As with all forms of feminist research, 'coming out' through reflexive analysis is ultimately a political act. But although fraught with ambiguity and uncertainty it has the potential to spur others towards a more radical consciousness (Finlay 2002b, 544). It is equally important that academics are not deterred from engaging with elite members of society (political or otherwise) in the quest for expanding criminological knowledge. Loader and Sparks (2011, 18) have called for criminologists engaged in such research to develop an understanding of the 'circumstances of politics' (Waldron 1999, 106) and cultivate a 'qualified tolerance' towards those who practice politics as a vocation (Swift and White 2008, 64). My own experiences would suggest this to be a judicious way forward.

Notes

1. Whitehall is recognised as the heart of the UK government, and is a street in Westminster lined with many Ministries and Departments. The term is often used as a metonym for the general UK government administration.
2. As the policy network under discussion is restricted to a small number of high-profile individuals, I have chosen to grant anonymity to my research subjects. Divulging their profession may also reveal their identity, so this information has similarly been omitted.
3. The House of Lords is the Upper House of the UK Parliament. It is independent from, yet complements, the House of Commons. Lords help make and shape laws and hold the government to account. However unlike the elected House of Commons, most new members are appointed (membership of the House of Lords was traditionally hereditary).
4. Perhaps, according to Ostrander (1995), not simply down to self-centredness, but an accurate reflection of their position in power.
5. Other social scientists have discussed self-censorship in terms of protecting future access (Fitz and Halpin 1994; Kogan 1994; Walford 1994; Ostrander 1995; Sabot 1999; Lilleker 2003), and this is clearly an important consideration.

References

Arendell, T. (1997) 'Reflections on the Researcher-Researched Relationship: A Woman Interviewing Men' *Qualitative Sociology* 20(3): 341–68.

Ball, S. (1994) 'Political Interviews and the Politics of Interviewing'. In G. Walford (ed.) *Researching the Powerful in Education*, London: UCL Press, pp.96–115.

Broom A., Hand K. and Tovey, P. (2009) 'The Role of Gender, Environment and Individual Biography in Shaping Qualitative Interview Data' *International Journal of Social Research Methodology* 12(1): 51–65.

Burgess, R.G. (ed.) (1982) *Field Research: A Source Book and Field Manual*, London: Allen & Unwin.

Burnham, P., Gilland Lutz, G., Grant, W. and Layton-Henry, Z. (eds) (2004) *Research Methods in Politics*, Basingstoke: Palgrave Macmillan.

Conti, J. and O'Neil, M. (2007) 'Studying Power: Qualitative Methods and the Global Elite' *Qualitative Research* 7(1): 63–82.

Cotterill, P. (1992) 'Interviewing Women, Issues of Friendship, Vulnerability, and Power' *Women's Studies International Forum* 15: 593–606.

Desmond, M. (2004) 'Methodological Challenges Posed in Studying an Elite in the Field' *Area* 36(3): 262–69.

Duke, K. (2002) 'Getting Beyond the "Official Line": Reflections on Dilemmas of Access, Knowledge and Power in Researching Policy Networks' *Journal of Social Policy* 31(1): 39–59.

Edwards, R. (1993) 'An Education in Interviewing'. In C.M. Renzetti and R.M. Lee (eds) *Researching Sensitive Topics*, London: Sage.

Elwood, S. and Martin, D. (2000) '"Placing" Interviews: Location and Scales of Power in Qualitative Research' *Professional Geographer* 52(4): 649–57.

Finlay, L. (2002a) 'Negotiating the Swamp: The Opportunity and Challenge of Reflexivity in Research Practice' *Qualitative Research* 2(2): 209–30.

Finlay, L. (2002b) '"Outing" the Researcher: the Provenance, Process and Practice of Reflexivity' *Qualitative Health Research* 12(4): 531–45.

Finlay, L. (2003) 'The Reflexive Journey: Mapping Multiple Routes'. In L. Finlay and B. Gough (eds) *Reflexivity*, Oxford: Blackwell, pp.3–22.

Fitz, J. and Halpin, D. (1994) 'Implementation Research and Education Policy: Practice and Prospects' *British Journal of Educational Studies* 42(1): 53–69.

Harding, S.G. (1987) 'Introduction: Is there a Feminist Method?' In S.G. Harding (ed.) *Feminism and Methodology: Social Science Issues*, Bloomington, IN: Indiana University Press, pp.1–14.

Josselson, R. (1996) *The Space Between Us: Exploring the Dimensions of Human Relationships*, Thousand Oaks, CA: Sage.

Jupp, V., Davies, P. and Francis, P. (eds) (2000) *Doing Criminological Research*, London: Sage.

King, E. and Wincup, R. (eds) (2008) *Doing Research on Crime and Justice*, Oxford: Oxford University Press.

King, N. and Horrocks, C. (2010) *Interviews in Qualitative Research*, London: Sage.

Kogan, M. (1994) 'Researching the Powerful in Education and Elsewhere'. In G. Walford (ed.) *Researching the Powerful in Education*, London: UCL Press, pp.67–80.

Liamputtong, P. (2007) *Researching the Vulnerable: A Guide to Sensitive Research Methods*, London: Sage.

Lilleker, D. (2003) 'Interviewing the Political Elite: Navigating a Potential Minefield' *Politics* 23(3): 207–14.

Loader, I. and Sparks, R. (2011) 'Criminology's Public Roles: A Drama in Six Acts'. In M. Bosworth and C. Hoyle (eds) *What is Criminology?* Oxford: Oxford University Press, pp.17–34.

Marsh, D. and Rhodes, R.A.W. (eds) (1992) *Policy Networks in British Government*, Oxford: Clarendon Press.

Marshall, C. (1984) 'Elites, Bureaucrats, Ostriches, and Pussycats: Managing Research in Policy Settings' *Anthropology & Education Quarterly* 15(3): 235–51.

McDowell, L. (1992) 'Doing Gender: Feminism, Feminists and Research Methods in Human Geography' *Transactions of the British Institute of Geographers* 17: 399–416.

McDowell, L. (1998) 'Elites in the City of London: Some Methodological Considerations' *Environment and Planning* 30: 2133–46.

Mickelson, R.A. (1994) 'A Feminist Approach to Researching the Powerful in Education'. In G. Walford (ed.) *Researching the Powerful in Education*, London: UCL Press, pp.83–94.

Neal, S. and McLaughlin, E. (2009) 'Researching Up? Interviews, Emotionality and Policy-Making Elites' *Journal of Social Policy* 38(4): 689–707.

Oakley, A. (1981) 'Interviewing Women: A Contradiction in Terms'. In H. Roberts (ed.) *Doing Feminist Research*, London: Routledge and Kegan Paul, pp.217–32.

Oakley, A. (2005) *The Ann Oakley Reader: Gender, Women and Social Science*, Bristol: Policy Press.

Ostrander, S. (1995) 'Surely You're Not in This Just to Be Helpful: Access, Rapport and Interviews in Three Studies of Elites' *Journal of Contemporary Ethnography* 22(1): 7–27.

Punch, M. (1986) *The Politics and Ethics of Fieldwork*, Beverly Hills: Sage.

Puwar, N. (1997) 'Reflections on Interviewing Women MPs' *Sociological Research Online* 2(1): http://www.socresonline.org.uk/2/1/4.html (accessed 1 December 2013).

Ramazanoglu, C. and Holland, J. (2002) *Feminist Methodology: Challenges and Choices*, London: Sage.

Reinharz, S. (1992) *Feminist Methods in Social Research*, Oxford: Oxford University Press.

Reinharz, S. and Chase, S.E. (2001) 'Interviewing Women'. In J.F. Gubrium and A. Holstein (eds) *Handbook of Interview Research: Context and Method*, Thousand Oaks, CA: Sage, pp.221–38.

Rice, G. (2010) 'Reflections on Interviewing Elites' *Area* 42(1): 70–75.

Riessman, C. (1987) 'When Gender Is Not Enough: Women Interviewing Women' *Gender and Society* 1(2): 172–207.

Rhodes, R.A.W. (1990) 'Policy Networks: A British Perspective' *Journal of Theoretical Politics* 2 (3): 293–317.

Rhodes, R.A.W. (1997) *Understanding Governance: Policy Networks, Governance, Reflexivity and Accountability*, Buckingham: Open University Press.

Roberts, H. (ed.) (1981) *Doing Feminist Research*, London: Routledge and Kegan Paul.

Ross, K. (2001) 'Political Elites and the Pragmatic Paradigm: Notes from a Feminist Researcher – In the Field and Out to Lunch' *International Journal of Social Research Methodology* 4(2): 155–66.

Sabot, E.C. (1999) 'Dr Jekyl, Mr H(i)de: The Contrasting Face of Elites at Interview' *Geoforum* 30: 329–35.

Sarantakos, S. (2005) *Social Research*, 3rd edn, Basingstoke: Palgrave Macmillan.

Slote Morris, Z. (2009) 'The Truth About Interviewing Elites' *Politics* 29(3): 209–17.

Smith, K. (2006) 'Problematising Power Relations in "Elite" Interviews' *Geoforum* 37: 643–53.

Stacey, J. (1991) 'Can There Be a Feminist Ethnography?' In S. Berger Gluck and D. Patai (eds) *Women's Words: The Feminist Practice of Oral History*, New York: Routledge, pp.111–19.

Stanley, L. and Wise, S. (1983) *Breaking Out: Feminist Consciousness and Feminist Research*, London: Routledge.

Swift, A. and White, S. (2008) 'Political Theory, Social Science and Real Politics'. In D. Leopold and M. Stears (eds) *Political Theory: Methods and Approaches*, Oxford: Oxford University Press, pp.49–69.

Waldron, J. (1999) *Law and Disagreement*, Oxford: Oxford University Press.

Walford, G. (1994) *Researching the Powerful in Education*, London: UCL Press.

Walford, G. (2011) 'Researching the Powerful' *British Educational Research Association*. URL (accessed 28 March 2013: www.bera.ac.uk/system/files/Researching%20the%20powerful.pdf)

Westmarland, N. (2001) 'The Quantitative/Qualitative Debate and Feminist Research: A Subjective View of Objectivity' *Forum: Qualitative Social Research* 2(1): http://www.qualitative-research.net/index.php/fqs/article/view/974

Wilkinson, S. (1998) 'Focus Groups in Feminist Research: Power, Interaction, and the Co-Construction of Meaning' *Women's Studies International Forum* 21(1): 111–25.

Williams, F. (1989) *Social Policy: A Critical Introduction*, Polity Press: Cambridge.

Woliver, L. (2002) 'Ethical Dilemmas in Personal Interviewing' *PS: Political Science and Politics* 35(4): 677–78.

19

Overcoming Barriers in the Criminal Justice System: Examining the Value and Challenges of Interviewing Legal Practitioners

Kate Fitz-Gibbon

Introduction

In 'Transparency and Participation in Criminal Procedure', American Professor of Law and Criminology Stephanos Bibas (2006, 911) describes the gap between those within the criminal justice system and those outside of it:

> A great gulf divides insiders and outsiders in the criminal justice system. The insiders who run the criminal justice system – judges, police and especially prosecutors – have information, power and self-interests that greatly influence the criminal justice system's process and outcomes. Outsiders – crime victims, bystanders, and most of the general public – find the system frustratingly opaque, insular and unconcerned with proper retribution.

This description by Bibas aptly captures the problematic 'gulf' that exists between those working within, and those outside of, the criminal justice system. This dichotomy can also be referred to as the gap between 'the powerful' – the practitioners who make decisions, impose the law and undertake judgment in the courts – and the 'the powerless' – those who are at the behest of the law and who must place their confidence in the hands of those who administrate it. For the 'outsider' the criminal justice system can be viewed as 'hidden behind closed doors, and cloaked in jargon, technicalities, and euphemism . . . and more concerned with efficiency and technicalities than with justice' (Bibas 2006, 913). This perception is amplified by media reporting of crime and justice that can serve to decrease public confidence in the processes of justice and the decisions made by those working with the criminal courts.

Within this dichotomy, the criminological researcher arguably moves between insider and outsider status depending on the stage of the research, the success of gaining access to those within the legal system and the quality of the rapport developed once access is attained. Consequently, recognition of the 'great gulf' that exists between those within and those outside of the justice system highlights the inherent value of research that successfully penetrates these barriers. Such research provides a unique insight into the decisions and experiences of those working within the criminal justice system as well as valuable empirical research for government bodies and policy stakeholders to draw from when undertaking review and reform of the criminal law and the administration of the criminal justice system.

This chapter examines the benefits and difficulties of undertaking interviews with legal practitioners. This analysis is undertaken by reflecting on the author's own experiences interviewing those most powerful within the criminal justice system. Between 2010 and 2013, over 100 in-depth interviews were conducted with members of the English and Australian criminal justice systems as part of an internationally comparative analysis of divergent approaches taken to reforming the law of provocation in Australia and the United Kingdom.[1] These interviews were conducted across three criminal jurisdictions – Victoria (Australia), New South Wales (NSW, Australia) and England (UK) – with a range of criminal justice professionals, including members of the judiciary, prosecutors, defence counsel, police officers and relevant policy stakeholders. The interviews sought to gain insight into legal practitioners' experiences with the partial defence of provocation, their perceptions of the divergent approaches that have been taken to reforming the law of provocation as well as their reflections on the operation of this law in practice.

In reflecting on the process through which this research was undertaken, this chapter considers the value of interview data that provides a direct insight into the experiences of those charged with the daily implementation of the criminal justice system as well as the difficulty of accessing legal populations. In the second half of the chapter, ethical issues arising from interviews with legal practitioners as well as the need for qualitative research to be reflexive are also considered.

The view from the inside

The value of interviews and consultations conducted with legal practitioners is well recognised in criminological and legal inquiry (Davis 2005; Partington 2005; Nelken 2010; Flynn 2011). Interviews with legal practitioners undoubtedly provide an additional layer of insight into the operation of the criminal justice system and offer a unique opportunity for criminologists to go beyond the pages of trial transcripts, sentencing judgments and legislation to gain valuable insight into the operation of the criminal courtroom from those who operate within it (Flynn and Fitz-Gibbon 2011). In this respect, interviews with legal practitioners are important in terms of illuminating the experiences, motivations and attitudes of those working within our criminal justice system. As Nelken (2010) argues, discussions with key actors within the criminal justice systems allow research to better understand and make sense of legal trends and observations.

This is particularly important given the proliferation of negative imagery surrounding those who work in the legal profession (Mackenzie 2005; Posner 2008). As noted by Mackenzie (2005, 1) 'judges are often portrayed as harsh, unfeeling and somehow distanced from the community in which they live. The reality, however, is far from the case'. In countering this populist image, Mackenzie's (2005, 12) research, and indeed other research that draws on interviews with members of the judiciary, is important in terms of providing a 'human face' to judging and the sentencing process.

The benefits of conducting interviews with members of the legal system to inform criminological research have also been recognised by government bodies, law reform commissions and parliament inquiries. These bodies regularly draw on the results of targeted consultative processes with legal practitioners and key stakeholders to inform discussion papers, final reports and the drafting of legislative reform (see, e.g. Law Commission 2003, 2005; Victorian Law Reform Commission 2004; Sentencing Advisory Council 2007, 2009; Ministry of Justice 2008). As Davis (2005, 156) notes:

> Face to face consultations remain a key consultative strategy . . . Direct meetings allow the agency and those it consults to talk much more freely about the topics of interest; to explain and amplify their views or the reasons behind them; or to apply nuance where this is inevitably harder to do in writing . . . Little is as valuable as an understanding of how the law and its institutions operate in practice.

Reflecting on his experience as Law Commissioner for England and Wales, Martin Partington (2005, 139) adds that consultation with relevant stakeholders can be used to 'fill gaps in knowledge by deliberately engaging with people or other agencies or groups with special knowledge or experience in the current operation of the law and how it might develop'.

Interestingly, however, despite these recognised benefits consultation processes often stop with the publication of a Commission or Inquiry's final report. Consequently, such consultations fail to examine how legal practitioners respond to the reforms introduced, what practitioners experience in their interactions with the law in the period immediately following the reform's implementation and what effects the reforms have in practice from the perspectives of those charged with the daily operation of the law. These are vital areas of criminological inquiry, particularly in the light of research that recognises the diverse impacts that the application of the law can have on marginalised and vulnerable populations, such as battered women and indigenous defendants (Stubbs and Tolmie 2008; Sheehy et al. 2012a, b). Consequently, by conducting interviews with legal practitioners in the period following the implementation of law reform, criminological research can offer particularly valuable insights into the operation of the criminal court system in practice. This is vital research for governments to draw upon when seeking to conduct a review of reforms implemented after a set period of time (an evaluation process that is often built in to the implementation of a law reform package and typically scheduled to occur 5–10 years following the introduction of the reform package).

Engagement with legal professionals following the implementation of law reform is also particularly important in the light of an increasing body of research which recognises the dissonance between the intent of legislation and the actual application, interpretation and (in some cases) manipulation of that law in practice (Flynn and Fitz-Gibbon 2011; Wells and Quick 2012; Fitz-Gibbon 2013a, 2014). This is illustrated with reference to the recent operation of the new partial defence of loss of control in England and Wales. Implemented by the British government in October 2010 this defence effectively replaced the controversial partial defence of provocation and was formulated to overcome the injustices that had arisen in its operation (Fitz-Gibbon 2013a, 2014). With this intent in mind, the new loss of control defence was drafted to include a specific provision that a defendant could not raise this partial defence and evade a conviction for murder, where he/she had killed in response to allegations or an occurrence of sexual infidelity (*Coroners and Justice Act 2009* s.55[6][c]). However, less than two years following the implementation of the loss of control defence, in a 2012 decision this restriction was reinterpreted by the Court of Appeal in a way which has again opened the English law of homicide up to manipulation by jealous and controlling men who kill their female intimate partners (Quick and Wells 2012; Fitz-Gibbon 2013a, 2014). Consequently, and as noted by Flynn and Fitz-Gibbon (2011, 909), interviews with legal practitioners permit research to 'capture the variation between what should happen according to internal policy and what does happen in practice'. This is an important outcome in the light of the value of gaining an understanding of the subtleties, nuances and varied interpretations of the law from those operating within it.

Researching an 'open and transparent' system of justice

The value of interviews that transcend the barriers of the criminal justice system is also emphasised when considered in the context of the need for justice to be open and transparent. By their very nature Westminster criminal justice systems are based on principles of open and transparent justice. However, over the last ten years several legal practices and decision-making processes have emerged that serve to threaten and undermine the transparency of the criminal justice system. This trend away from transparency represents a turn towards a system of justice where key decisions are made out of mind, sight and analysis of those outside the criminal justice system. Such a shift highlights the increasing importance of undertaking research with those working within the criminal justice system – research that can gain an insider perspective into an increasingly closed-off system.

This trend away from open and transparent justice is evident in Western criminal justice systems, including Australia, the United Kingdom and the United States where under the auspices of upholding national security and the need for increased efficiency, justice systems are increasingly adopting decision-making processes that occur outside of the 'open and transparent' publicly accessible courtroom. A key example of this in respect to efficiency is plea bargaining. Plea bargaining involves the process whereby a negotiated resolution is achieved between the prosecution and the defence outside of the bounds of a 'transparent' courtroom (Bibas 2006; Flynn 2012). Through plea bargaining important decisions relating to culpability and the guilt or innocence of an accused are decided 'in private negotiating rooms and conference calls; [while] in-court proceedings are mere formalities that confirm these decisions' (Bibas 2006, 912). Consequently, as a researcher of the criminal court system it is increasingly difficult, if not impossible, to discern the motivations underpinning important legal decisions that occur behind closed doors, such as negotiated resolutions.

This can, however, be countered with research involving interviews with legal practitioners, or indeed observational research is also valuable in this respect. By adopting such methods insight can be gained into what motivates a prosecutor to seek a negotiated resolution, why a defence counsel may advocate for their client to accept a 'plea bargain' and what benefits and limitations legal practitioners perceive that this has for the key parties involved. Such research has been conducted in Victoria examining the effects of plea bargain on victims (see Flynn 2012) and the use of plea bargaining in the post-law reform context (see Flynn and Fitz-Gibbon 2011).

More recently in the United Kingdom, the implementation of the *Justice and Security Act 2013* (UK) provides a clear example of decreasing transparency in criminal justice decision-making in the name of national security. Introduced in April 2013, the Act permits closed hearings (also referred to as 'secret courts') to be used in intelligence-related cases (Bowcott 2013; Zaiwalla 2013). While the merits of individual legal practices, such as closed hearings and plea bargaining, are open to debate what is clear is that the gradual movement away from a system of open and transparent justice to secretive and closed-off decision-making highlights the increasing powers bestowed upon those within the criminal court system and, consequently, the apparent importance of research that engages with legal practitioners. More so than previously such research is essential to ensuring that the application of the law in practice, its impacts and the experiences of those working within the court system are understood by legal scholars, considered in criminological research and scrutinised by those seeking to reform the system.

Issues of access

Alongside recognition of the importance of attaining the views of those within the criminal justice system is a body of research by law and criminology scholars that considers the obstacles encountered when a researcher endeavours to access traditionally closed legal populations, such as members of the judiciary, legal counsel and policy representatives (Ashworth 1995; Mackenzie 2005; Baldwin 2008, Flynn 2011). As Flynn (2011, 49) argues there is often a reluctance within adversarial criminal justice systems 'to engage with outsiders, particularly those analysing legal conduct'. Acknowledgement of the difficulties that have traditionally arisen in academic pursuits to interview legal practitioners has often led to a stronger focus in criminology research on the experiences and views of the outsider or the 'powerless'. As Richards (2011, 68) describes, criminological research has consequently tended to focus on 'the views of those controlled by the criminal justice system rather than those who control it'.

This is not to say that criminology and legal scholarship have been entirely unable to engage legal practitioners in research interviews, this has been done to varying degrees over the past three decades (see, e.g. Bartels 2009; Erez and Rogers 1999; Fionda 1995; Fitz-Gibbon 2012, 2013a, 2013b, 2014; Flynn 2012; Mackenzie 2005; Mulcahy 1994; Washington 1998). The importance of this body of research as well as the difficulty of gaining access to participants is aptly captured by English Law Professor, Andrew Ashworth (1995, 263):

> Research into why judges and magistrates do what they do has long been advocated as a prerequisite of the successful development of sentencing policy, but sentencers in many countries seem to resist research. Apart from the irony that judges sometimes berate academics for not understanding practice when it is the judges who bar the way to research by means of observation and interview, the social importance of sentencing is a powerful argument in favour of careful research. More ought to be known about the motivation of judges and magistrates. Such knowledge would assist in the formation of sentencing policy.

As such, while barriers may at times appear impenetrable, it is important that criminological inquiry continues to move between the legal 'insider' and 'outsider' given the significant benefit of research that elicits first-hand accounts of the law's operation.

Recognition of the difficulties that researchers encounter when attempting to research the legal insider also highlights the importance of reflecting on research that has overcome these barriers. In conducting interviews on legal practitioner's perceptions of the effects of homicide law reform in three criminal jurisdictions (Victoria, New South Wales and England) throughout 2010 and 2012, I encountered few 'access' barriers. In this respect, I undoubtedly benefited from the currency of the topic. Over the period of my interviews in all three jurisdictions – Victoria, NSW and England – the specific government and/or law reform body were reconsidering, reviewing and active in reforming the law of homicide. This provided a key 'hook' for legal practitioners to engage with the research which sought to provide insider accounts of how the law was operating in practice, what approaches to reform were favoured by legal practitioners and what effects of the reforms were evident or anticipated in practice. On reflection in successfully accessing over 100 legal practitioners over this three-year period it would appear that the interest of those working within the field to the focus of the research was essential in attaining access to target participants.

In 'enticing' legal practitioners to engage with, and become actively involved in a research interview, I also sought to interview only practitioners who had direct experience with the law of homicide in the period immediately prior to, during or following the reforms. This level of experience of all legal practitioners interviewed (whether in the role of judge, prosecutor or defence counsel) allowed an examination of homicide law reform to be informed by those most closely connected to its application. This method of participant selection also had the double benefit in that the richest interview data undoubtedly emerges from interviews with practitioners who are interested, engaged and invested in the very issue that is under study, thus highlighting the value and importance of targeted participants in criminological research.

Ethical considerations when interviewing the powerful

Conducting research interviews with the 'powerful' as opposed to the 'powerless' inevitably engenders less conversation about ethical dilemmas and perceived risk to the researcher. However, regardless of the status of the participant, issues relating to participant anonymity and confidentiality are important factors. While, Australian-based criminological research has suggested that legal practitioners 'may justifiably want their contribution [to the research] to be acknowledged' (Richards 2011, 73) the decision to name a participant or offer anonymity is an essential consideration in the design of any qualitative research interview and the subsequent publication of that data.

Allowing a respondent confidentiality and anonymity has benefits in terms of the individual's willingness to participate in the research and the freedom of discussion (Fitz-Gibbon 2012, 2013b; Fitz-Gibbon and Pickering 2012). As Fitz-Gibbon and Pickering (2012, 161) observe in their analysis of homicide law reform in Victoria by ensuring confidentiality to legal participants, the research 'accessed a broader and more senior sample of legal stakeholders who have traditionally not contributed publicly to discussions about law reform or the operation of the law in practice'. However, these benefits must be weighed up against the limitations of not being able to list the calibre of legal practitioners that have engaged with the research. Additionally, a researcher may be faced with the prospect of having to omit valuable interview data that would identify the participant, such as a practitioner's reflections on their involvement in a specific case.

The importance of reflexivity when interviewing the powerful

Even in research where confidentiality and anonymity have been granted to interview participants, a significant responsibility bestows the qualitative researcher who in disseminating their interview findings presents the views, perceptions and experiences of those working within the criminal justice system. At this point of the research, the participant is at the behest of the researcher in trusting that the resulting analysis will not take their opinions out of context and will capture the sentiment and essence of their experiences. The responsibility of the researcher is captured in the reflections of Australian criminologist, Kelly Richards (2011, 73), who when analysing interviews with key legal stakeholders commented that:

> I quickly realised that my initial thoughts – that since the interview consisted of participants' own words, they were ultimately responsible for what they said and therefore how they were portrayed in my research – were misguided. While interviews may consist of participants' own words, they are constructed and constrained by the parameters of the interviewer's research and the questions researchers ask.

For this reason, reflexive practices are essential during the interview, data analysis and dissemination phases of research that involves interviews with the powerful or, indeed, the powerless. Reflexivity is explained by Gobo (2011, 22) as:

> the self-aware analysis of the dynamics between researcher and participants, the critical capacity to make explicit the position assumed by the observer in the field, and the way in which the researcher's positioning impacts on the research process.

The value of using reflexive practices in criminological research has been noted in previous studies, particularly in relation to critical criminology and feminist criminology (Davis and Francis 2001; Skinner et al. 2005; Stubbs 2008). While reflexivity can be achieved through a range of divergent practices (Finlay 2002), within the context of this discussion the practice of intersubjective reflection is particularly useful. Finlay (2002, 215) defines this as a process whereby researchers 'explore the mutual meanings emerging within the research relationship'.

Within the context of analysing interviews undertaken in Victoria, New South Wales and England on approaches to homicide law reform the need for reflexive analysis was particularly important given my own expressed views on the viability of divergent approaches favoured by several justice systems to reforming the law of provocation. This was particularly evident during the NSW interviews conducted in 2012, where prior to the interview phase of the research I had given evidence and provided two submissions to the *NSW Parliamentary Inquiry into the Operation of the Partial Defence of Provocation* recommending abolition of the controversial partial defence. While during the interviews I used open-ended questions to prompt legal practitioners from the NSW Supreme Court judiciary, Office of the Director of Public Prosecutions and Public Defender's Office to discuss their own views on the operation of provocation, its viability as a partial defence to murder and preferences for its reform, it was still important during the analysis phase of the research to undertake intersubjective reflection to consider how knowledge of my own opinion on the topic of provocation (which undoubtedly several practitioners were aware of at the time of interview) may have influenced the responses elicited from those interviewed.

Reflexivity is also important in terms of regaining your 'outsider' status following the interview phase of the research and critically analysing not only the extent to which your role as an outside 'researcher' impacted upon the responses elicited from interview participants but also how any of your own assumptions, beliefs and biases may have inadvertently influenced the direction of interview discussions and the opinions expressed by participants (Skinner et al. 2005). In this respect, it is naïve to consider that when one is interviewing the 'powerful' they do not exert some influence over the direction, emphasis or opinions elicited during a semi-structured or open-ended interview. As noted by Davis and Francis (2001, 279), a 'vital' part of the research process involves an analysis of the 'factors which have contributed to the social production of knowledge'.

Conclusion

While significant barriers confront qualitative researchers who seek to give voice to the perspectives and experiences of those working within the criminal justice system, the returns for those who gain access are high. At a time when academia is increasingly recognising the importance of policy application and the transfer of research into practice, interviews with legal practitioners provide an important opportunity for criminologists to validate and support research findings with the experiences of those working within the field. In the context of homicide law reform, the dissemination of research that has engaged the experiences of those within the courtroom is essential to providing illustrative and practitioner 'road-tested' analyses of the effects of homicide law reform in practice. This has clear value not only in terms of contributing knowledge to the administration, management and reform of the criminal justice system but also in terms of illuminating the practices, experiences and perceptions of those operating within the criminal justice system while critically analysing the influential role of the legal 'insider'.

Note

1. The findings from these interviews have been published in Fitz-Gibbon (2014, 2013a, 2013b, 2012), Fitz-Gibbon and Pickering (2012) and Flynn and Fitz-Gibbon (2011).

References

Ashworth, A. (1995) 'The Role of the Sentencing Scholar'. In C.M.V. Clarkson and R. Morgan (eds) *The Politics of Sentencing Reform*, Oxford: Clarendon Press, pp.251–65.

Baldwin, J. (2008) 'Research on the Criminal Courts'. In R.D. King and E. Wincup (eds) *Doing Research on Crime and Justice*, 2nd edn, Oxford: Oxford University Press, pp.375–98.

Bartels, L. (2009) 'Suspended Sentences – A Judicial Perspective' *Queensland University of Technology Law and Justice Journal* 9: 44–63.

Bibas, S. (2006) 'Transparency and Participation in Criminal Procedure' *New York University Law Review* 81(3): 911–66.

Bowcott, O. (2013) 'What Are Secret Courts and What Do They Mean for UK Justice?' *The Guardian*, 14 June.

Coroners and Justice Act 2009 (UK).

Davis, I. (2005) 'Targeted Consultations'. In B. Opeskin and D. Weisbrot (eds) *The Promise of Law Reform*, Sydney: The Federation Press.

Davis, P. and Francis, P. (2001) 'Reflecting on Criminological Research'. In P. Davis, P. Francis and V. Jupp (eds) *Doing Criminological Research*, 2nd edn, Los Angeles, CA: Sage, pp.281–86.

Erez, E. and Rogers, L. (1999) 'Victim Impact Statements and Sentencing Outcomes and Processes: The Perspectives of Legal Professionals' *British Journal of Criminology* 39(2): 216–39.

Finlay, L. (2002) 'Negotiating the Swamp: The Opportunity and Challenge of Reflexivity in Research Practice' *Qualitative Research* 2(2): 209–30.

Fionda, J. (1995) *Public Prosecutors and Discretion: A Comparative Study*, Oxford: Clarendon Press.

Fitz-Gibbon, K. (2012) 'Provocation in New South Wales: The Need for Abolition' *Australian and New Zealand Journal of Criminology* 45(2): 194–213.

Fitz-Gibbon, K. (2013a) 'Replacing Provocation in England and Wales: A Partial Defence of Loss of Control' *Journal of Law and Society* 40(2): 280–305.

Fitz-Gibbon, K. (2013b) 'The Mandatory Life Sentence for Murder: An Argument for Judicial Discretion in England' *Criminology and Criminal Justice: An International Journal* 13(5): 506–25.

Fitz-Gibbon, K. (2014) *Homicide Law Reform, Gender and the Provocation Defence: A Comparative Perspective*, Basingstoke: Palgrave Macmillan.

Fitz-Gibbon, K. and Pickering, S. (2012) 'Homicide Law Reform in Victoria, Australia: From Provocation to Defensive Homicide and Beyond' *British Journal of Criminology* 52(1): 159–80.

Flynn, A. (2011) 'Breaking into the Legal Culture of the Victorian Office of Public Prosecutions'. In L. Bartels and K. Richards (eds) *Qualitative Criminology: Stories from the Field*, Victoria: The Federation Press.

Flynn, A. (2012) 'Bargaining with Justice: Victims, Plea Bargaining and the Victims' Charter Act 2006 (Vic)' *Monash University Law Review* 37(3): 73–96.

Flynn, A. and Fitz-Gibbon, K. (2011) 'Bargaining with Defensive Homicide: Examining Victoria's Secret Plea Bargaining System Post Law Reform' *Melbourne University Law Review* 35(3): 905–32.

Gobo, G. (2011) 'Ethnography'. In D. Silverman (ed.) *Qualitative Research*, 3rd edn, Los Angeles, CA: Sage, pp.15–34.

Justice and Security Act 2013 (UK).

Law Commission (2003) *Partial Defences to Murder: Summary Paper*, Consultation Paper No 173, London: The Law Commission.

Law Commission (2005) *A New Homicide Act for England and Wales? Consultation Paper No 177*, London: The Law Commission.

Mackenzie, G. (2005) *How Judges Sentence*, Sydney: The Federation Press.

Ministry of Justice (2008) *Murder, Manslaughter and Infanticide: Proposals for Reform of the Law: Consultation Paper CP19/08*, London: Ministry of Justice.

Mulcahy, A. (1994) 'The Justifications of "Justice": Legal Practitioners' Accounts of Negotiated Case Settlements in Magistrates Courts' *British Journal of Criminology* 34(4): 411–30.

Nelken, D. (2010) *Comparative Criminal Justice*, London: Sage.

Partington, M. (2005) 'Research'. In B. Opeskin and D. Weisbrot (eds) *The Promise of Law Reform*, Sydney: The Federation Press.

Posner, R.A. (2008) *How Judges Think*, Cambridge: Harvard University Press.

Richards, K. (2011) 'Interviewing Elites in Criminological Research: Negotiating Power and Access and Being Called "Kid"'. In L. Bartels and K. Richards (eds) *Qualitative Criminology: Stories from the Field*, Victoria: The Federation Press, pp.68–79.

Sentencing Advisory Council. (2007) *Sentencing Indication and Specified Sentencing Discounts*, Melbourne, VIC: Sentencing Advisory Council.

Sentencing Advisory Council. (2009) *Maximum Penalties for Sexual Penetration with a Child under 16: Consultation Paper*, Melbourne, VIC: Sentencing Advisory Council.

Sheehy, E., Stubbs, J. and Tolmie, J. (2012a) 'Defences to Homicide for Battered Women: A Comparative Analysis of Laws in Australia, Canada and New Zealand' *Sydney Law Review* 34: 467–92.

Sheehy, E., Stubbs, J. and Tolmie, J. (2012b) 'Battered Women Charged with Homicide in Australia, Canada and New Zealand: How Do They Fare?' *Australian and New Zealand Journal of Criminology* 45(3): 383–99.

Skinner, T., Hester, M. and Malos, E. (2005) 'Methodology, Feminism and Gender Violence'. In T. Skinner, M. Hester, and E. Malos (eds) *Researching Gender Violence: Feminist Methodology in Action*, Portland, OR: Willan Publishing.

Stubbs, J. (2008) 'Critical Criminological Research'. In T. Anthony and C. Cuneen (eds) *The Critical Criminology Companion*, Annandale, NSW: Hawkins Press, pp.6–17.

Stubbs, J. and Tolmie, J. (2008) 'Battered Women Charged with Homicide: Advancing the Interests of Indigenous Women' *Australian and New Zealand Journal of Criminology* 41: 138–61.

Victorian Law Reform Commission. (2004) *Defences to Homicide: Final Report*, Melbourne, VIC: Victorian Law Reform Commission.

Washington, L. (1998) *Black Judges on Justice: Perspective from the Bench*, New York: New Press.

Wells, C.K. and Quick, O.L. (2012) 'Partial Reform of Partial Defences: Developments in England and Wales', *Australian & New Zealand Journal of Criminology* 45: 337–50.

Zaiwalla, S. (2013) 'Secret Courts: Justice Conducted Behind Closed Doors Is Not Justice at All' *The Guardian*, 19 August.

20
Doing Research in Prison: How to Resist Institutional Pressures

Vanina Ferreccio and Francesca Vianello

Introduction

Most methodological issues you encounter when entering the field of prison as a researcher are common to other settings for research on institutionalised so-called 'deviants' (like hospitals, therapeutic communities and identification centres). The first problem is access to the field. As Goffman (2010 [1961]) argues, the world of inmates (as well as that of staff) is a world that is protected by physical and psychological barriers which make it particularly difficult for external subjects to access the field. It is no coincidence that the researchers who first studied prisons were in some way involved in the management of the institution (e.g. Clemmer, as a clinical sociologist). Freedom of movement, in an environment which has been designated to limit freedom, and access to personal data, which are considered sensitive, are resources that are not easily made available to outsiders. Conversely, research as an inside observer involved in the running of the institution has considerable limitations and consequences, related to occupational pressures and moral dilemmas (cf. Marquart 1986). A cultural variable can be added to this, that is to say the different countries' recognition of the value of scientific research, criminological research in particular: some countries are interested in or at least willing to have their institutions undergo constructive assessment and constant monitoring; others are somewhat reluctant to open the doors to their prisons. The long time that it takes to acquire the necessary authorisations, often months of waiting, does not help as it separates the researcher from the field and the subjects of the research. On obtaining permission, a standing presence is required of the researcher, concentrated in limited time spans, which is difficult to reconcile with other academic activities.

The chapter is the product of joint discussions. The first, third and fourth sections were written by Francesca Vianello, whereas the second and fifth sections were written by Vanina Ferreccio.

Aside from the difficulties in accessing the field, another common issue related to the study of deviant contexts and biographies, which is particularly prominent in the study of prison and prison careers, is the hierarchy of socially recognised credibility (Becker 1967; cf. Liebling 2001). This relates to the different weight given to the declarations and affirmations of the prison population. The external researcher, disoriented in face of the unknown world of the prison, risks instinctively seeking reassurance by relying on those who run the institution, their considerations and representations of that reality. They share with the researcher a socially recognised status and the reassuring illusion of being on the side of justice.

This social proximity is likely to influence not only perceptions, but also the ability to withstand the pressures that inevitably the administration will try to exercise on the researcher's work. It is suggested that sociologists of deviance, criminologists and in particular ethnographers are naturally inclined to sympathise with their subjects (cf. Becker 1967). This is advantageous particularly if the interview is chosen as a tool, since a horizontal relationship should be sought, with no diffidence or judgment on either side. But what most threatens the researcher's freedom is not so much the difficulty of taking sides between the often conflicting representations offered by the subordinates/prisoners and their controllers.[1] It is not the socially dominant vision of the officials which is disputed, but rather the ideology of prison, which risks permeating the reading of both sides, as it does for the normal citizen and each one of us.

In this chapter we will analyse different strategies used by the prison administration and inside workers in an attempt to influence and direct criminological research. Following our research experiences,[2] we will suggest some possible forms of resistance to be taken in order to manage pressures and carry on independent research work, mainly focusing on prison as a field and promoting horizontal relationships. Finally, we reflect on the need to take distance from the research environment without sacrificing empathy towards the individuals who inhabit it.

The prison strategies

The rehabilitative logic pervades the whole prison, giving sense to the time spent in prison in the case of the prisoners and to daily work in the case of prison staff. It is, then, a working tool and, also, an element which legitimises how the institution works. This can create considerable problems for the researcher which can spill out in both the writing phase and in the reflexive recovery of the gathered material. Here we will concentrate on the consequences that a researcher's explicitly critical stance can have on their interactions with the various actors within the prison world, particularly when this contrasts drastically with the dominant ideology of the prison as an institution. Goffman (2010, 94) describes a 'widespread feeling, among inmates, that time spent in the institution is time wasted, taken from one's life; it is always a question of time that has to be cancelled; something which has to be "overcome", "marked", "accelerated" or "slowed down"'. However, representing one's time inside as a phase of life destined for rehabilitation or the internalisation of norms, which individuals believe they did not know before entering prison, is a particularly important tool for justifying the time that one spends inside an institution and, even more so, for organising their future 'once they are out'. Interaction with researchers who do not attribute this aim to prisons, or who do not consider it useful with respect to the time spent in prison, can prove to be destabilising for both the prisoners and the staff.

In such contexts, not explaining one's own critical position about the institution in order to avoid prisoners having doubts about their detention time is a paternalistic attitude carried by the researcher, who considers the prisoners unable to accept ideas about the prison, which are different from his/her ideas. For prison staff, however, rehabilitation and/or interventions which aim at a subsequent re-socialisation are so much a part of the every-day routine of prison work that, with the exception of few rare moments which could even be considered institutional crises, these objectives are never discussed, nor are they considered an object of reflection. Within this context it is interesting to identify the strategies deployed by the institution, through its various actors, to attract research into the net of the correctional paradigm.

'Trade Unionist' strategy

The 'Trade Unionist' strategy is carried out by the staff who seek to take advantage of the research as an opportunity to highlight the adverse con-ditions (in particular the limited time available) in which the treatment of prisoners is carried out. The description of a typical moment of a research study will serve to help readers understand what we call the 'Trade Unionist' strategy. The investigation we will address in this section is part of the author's research for their doctoral thesis which was conducted in two pris-ons in the Santa Fe province in Argentina. Participant observation was employed and in-depth interviews with detainees and their relatives dur-ing visit days. The first part of the fieldwork consisted of archive research in the correctional offices of both prisons. The organisation of the work within the prison makes these offices a nerve centre, not only due to the permanent transit of staff and prisoners who are in an 'advanced phase' of their term and, for this reason, usually take on the cleaning and upkeep of these spaces, but also because this is where the dossiers of all the people hosted in the institution can be found. The interactions that take place here involve dif-ferent actors of the prison since this is a necessary stop for operators before they enter the wings, where they consult the prisoners' dossiers – known inside the institution as the 'criminal records' – and also it is the area where new arrivals are admitted. The research objective was to reconstruct the life stories of the prisoners through the successive reports drawn up by prison staff and collected in these dossiers. While working on these dossiers, there were different opportunities whereby the staff – in particular social workers and psychologists – would spontaneously collaborate with the research by suggesting dossiers which, in order to refer to a specific typology of inmate, could serve as a paradigmatic example of what the staff considered to be the object of the research.

Two issues emerge here: first, the *translation* effect of the treatment lens on the research objectives, expecting to make them serve the institutional project. Second, the need to show, through the identification of the 'more interesting' cases, extensive knowledge of the personal and family situations of the prisoners, thus dismantling the classic accusation of institutional indifference of prison workers. Precisely, when it comes to researching the perspective of the treatment staff regarding the life stories of the prisoners, a rift, which is generally difficult to bridge, opens between the staff interviewed and those doing research in the prison space. This rift can be attributed to a professional identity – absorbed by a strong sense of charity which the staff unsuccessfully try to escape from – which has been damaged by the speed with which they are expected to respond to requests from the prison. This situation is disclosed to the researcher who, on the contrary, seems to benefit from having the time needed to listen and analyse, time that the staff would like to have. In this scenario, *lack of time* to think of the cases and design effective intervention strategies is often invoked. What the researcher *has to* observe is not the correctional aim which clearly emerges from the prisoners' 'dossiers'. On the contrary, the prison worker *suggests* the failure of this succession of interventions *has to be observed* through the lens of immediacy or of the speed which constrains prison work.

In this way, and adopting the form of a *union complaint*, the staff assigned to treatment on the one hand questions the utility of scientific research, the results of which require a long process of analysis, in contrast with the immediacy which governs the prison space. On the other hand, the staff attribute the failure of correction or future re-socialisation to the prison's demand for immediacy. If they had as much time as the researcher, success would be guaranteed:

> If I could dedicate a whole morning to a dossier, like you do ... the results would be different, lots of things could be done ... !
>
> (Social worker, prison treatment group)

Accessing and selecting research participants

In some prisons, however, the suggestion of the prison staff with regard to the reading of prisoners' dossiers takes on the nature of a (hidden) censorship through selection:

(...) look, these are the *ideal* reports for you to get an idea of what you want to research.

(Psychologist, prison treatment group)

After saying this, the social worker, psychologist or occupational therapist takes the dossiers into their arms and into their study and indicates, with great precision, which pages should interest us: that in which the prisoner's impressive criminal record is detailed or the failed attempts of the prison staff to involve the family in the correctionalist treatment and, in particular, the page where the infinite disciplinary sanctions have been registered. This selection, which was not requested by the researcher, brings with it the difficulty of filtering the material one has access to and, in some way, determining the way in which relations with the treatment staff are established. In Cicourel's words (2011, 31) 'observing and/or recording the daily practical and organizational activities always has a cost. Getting data from the environments studied requires demanding observations at the same time as one is negotiating delicate interpersonal relations'. And it is precisely this simultaneity between accessing important information and establishing relationships which will be key for the continuation of the research, which risks trapping the researcher in the regulatory schema of the institution.

However, these should not be considered as attempts to manipulate or even less to adulterate the information provided. In general, it is none other than the need of those who interact with the *stranger* – that is the researcher – to translate and simplify objectives and interrogatives that the research poses and which are incompatible with the daily running of the prison. In fact these techniques can serve alternatively as filters and as corridors. In the first case, the researcher will have access to a certain group of prisoners while the rest will remain inaccessible. A similar thing occurs when working on material produced by the prison: from the beginning we know that certain documents will not be made available to us. And these two 'reserve fields' tend to meet when the 'protected' documents – or directly subtracted from the researcher's glance – refer to the prison treatment of prisoners who also escape our field of accessibility. In this way, one filter reinforces the other, deleting from the field of research a group, whose constitution is variable (which can be differently made up depending on the prison, or rather on the decisions of the prison administration) and of whom we cannot even have a rough estimate. In the second case, the collaboration of staff[3] reduces the research, leading it towards certain spaces where the prison's correctional paradigm is displayed.

The situation is slightly different when the prison staff use the excuse of the researcher's safety to impede both observation and interviews. As Rostaing (2006) warns with reference to the interview, the sociologist who intends to work in the prison environment will have to get used to not having access to common tools which any other sociologist can use. Similarly, the will to continue with research in contexts that are marked by violence escapes the researcher's decisional space since it is the guard who decides to block access on the basis of the researcher's protection. This situation certainly needs to be further explored, which is not the scope of this chapter. However, it is important to highlight the (paradoxical) distinction between the *protection of the re-socialisation project* (and consequently, the subtraction of the spaces and people who do not serve to illustrate it in its ideal type) and the *protection of the researcher* (and consequently, their removal from spaces of violence which, on the other hand, are constituent of the prison universe). This brings us to the challenges faced when interviewing the prisoners.

Restrictions of the prisoners

The interview, together with observation, is still one of the most commonly used methods for studying the prison experience. However, the closed nature of the space is a heavily conditioning factor, illustrating the delicacy of 'research in the prison field (...) in the extent to which the tools that the sociologist usually has access to are not usable for reasons of security or individual respect' (Rostaing 2006, 37). These special conditions derive from the multiple filters which cross prison research and the physical limitations of the interviewees who depend on the prison guards to be able to arrive at the venue for the interview. In particular when the research involves interviews with inmates, the successive filters we mentioned above circumscribe access to both the spaces and the persons. At the beginning of the research at least, these people will be those who have some form of 'premiums' within the prison: first of all, those who are towards the end of their terms; then, those who have a certain 'freedom' of movement within the prison; and finally, those who have been 'beneficiaries' of 'easy' jobs or much appreciated by the prison population like, for example, in the Argentinian situation at least, the kitchen or cleaning the offices nearest the road and far from the centre of the prison.

With regard to these initial contacts, Cicourel, citing Benjamín Paul (2011, 83), considers it important to take a distance from the characteristic attitude of the:

> novice who wants to be completely accepted by the natives and for fear of not being welcomed, sometimes avoids the 'regional emissaries'. However, it is not very useful being welcomed by the natives if this causes problems with the authorities assigned to follow the movements of the foreigners. [...] Their support for the project can be decisive and also useful for conveniently establishing relations.

If we extrapolate Cicourel's affirmations to the prison context and replace 'natives' with 'prisoners', while the 'authorities' will be the 'prison governors' and also the 'inmate leaders', it would appear that the researcher should privilege relations with the latter as a way of assuring the continuity of their research and the multiplication of contacts. The reflection on prison research, however, leads us to a further level: that which regards the meaning and the value, though this can be only negative, of a stance which privileges contact with the 'regional' authorities (whether these are members of the prison staff or the inmate leaders). It means going beyond the choice of favouring contact with one or other part of the actors of the prison space and also studying the reflections that this tension (contacting the authorities and through collaboration with them interviewing prisoners or trying to generate a network of trust which spreads through the prisoners the desire to take part in the research) will have at the moment of setting up the sample and afterwards, when embarking on the analysis of the material.

Following the line of reflective analysis of this pseudo-option (or of this form of freedom of choice which the researcher is offered) can reveal the depth with which the correctional paradigm permeates the institutional dynamics. The contacts that our first interviewees indicate to us will be other prisoners who have reached the same levels of prison treatment. In this way, the correctional paradigm transforms itself – not only symbolically but also materially – into a sort of circle which selects (or determines) the first chances of contact and also those which will be obtained during the research study. The problem looks different but it responds to the same logic. It pervades to such an extent that the selection made by the prisoner responds to the same reasons as those which determine the prison staff's selection.

The strategy which we initially called 'Trade Unionist' occurs also in the selection made by the staff (both guards and those assigned to treatment) of the prisoners they consider 'interviewable'. These will be the prisoners who, in some way, represent the re-socialising attempt, thus justifying the work that is done in prison. Although it may seem ridiculous, it is almost identical reasons which push the prisoners to choose, from their peers, those who 'give a good impression' (Inmate, 32 years old), who are not 'drugged up all day' (Inmate, 22 years old) or who are not constantly subject to disciplinary measures (i.e. locked up in isolation cells all the time).

Although the research subjects are critical of the institution and, thus, are interested in the fact that the research serves to highlight the deplorable conditions in which they live, there always exist in every prison a group of prisoners tacitly excluded from research studies, both due to indications of the staff:

No madam..., he can't come [to the interview] because he's in the isolation cell, you should remove him from the list as that bloke *lives* in isolation, he has problems with the whole world, you'll never be able to interview him.

(Prison assistant, assigned to the mobility
of the inmates in the prison)

and also due to indications of other inmates who do not consider them suitable to talk about life in prison:

> It's not worth you interviewing them ... they have no idea where they are, they are *cachivaches*[4]: when they're not in isolation, they're dealing... they can't tell you anything, what do you need to interview them for? Best if you talk to Pedro T., or José C., they've done something with their lives in here.
>
> (Inmate, 31 years old)

Resistance and managing pressure

To help researchers to observe the institution without having to adopt the lens that the different subjects naturally – and often in good faith – offer them and to avoid the preliminary selection that apparently privileged contacts (whether prison staff or inmates themselves) feel they need to make for them, at least two suggestions can be made.

Prison as field

First of all you should consider as object of research the whole field of the prison. 'Thinking in terms of field' as Bourdieu (1992, 66) explains, 'means thinking in a relational manner'. Prison should be considered as a network of relations between positions which are defined by their current and potential status within the structure that distributes different forms of power (i.e. capital) which offers access to the profits which can be won in that field. It is clearly a field which is subject to certain formalities, which seem to be rigidly codified in terms of criteria for defining access. Nonetheless, taking on the field of prison as object of research means first of all going beyond a mere formal description. The huge amount of norms and regulations can easily be deceptive, prison seems to be a world saturated by official norms, but you soon realise that these are de facto used 'a posteriori' to legitimate decisions which are made 'on the field' (cf. Sarzotti 2010). Only in the field is it possible to try to reconstruct and describe the structure which supports the functioning of the institution. As the epigones of prison sociology teach us, total domination does not exist and prison is a field which is dramatically marked by negotiation and by compromises which take place daily between the subjects which inhabit this space in their different roles (Clemmer 1940; Sykes 1958). Even here 'those who dominate ... always have to deal with the resistance and demands, be they political or not, of the dominated' (Bourdieu 1992, 72).

We thus discover – as suggested by Sykes (1958) – that a system of apparently anti-institutional values still exists. Those values encourage prisoners to limit clashes inside the prison and to enact them with the institution only if necessary, and this in reality is a determining factor in keeping order (apparently due to the rigidity of the rules) within the prison: knowing how to 'do one's own time' (not creating conflicts, managing resources and relations adequately) is an affirmation – from both the prisoners and the guards – which brings together the provisions of the 'inmate code' (Sykes 1958) and the institutional imperatives. Worlds which would appear to be in contraposition thus reveal themselves to refer positively to the same codes of behaviour which are essential for the functioning of the institution, in a contiguity which a partial study of the field would not be able to shed light on:

He's a tough one, nobody bothers him and he doesn't give anyone a hard time, you can trust him, and here trust is a rare and bloody precious good: all respect to him, he *knows how to do his own time*.

(Inmate, 28 years old)

He's pretty calm, never made trouble, if only they were all like that, he's someone who *really knows how to do his own time*.

(Penitentiary police inspector, talking to educators during a meeting of the Observation and Treatment Group)

From a relational perspective, the attempts made by individuals – whether they are prison workers or inmates – to influence our choices, to select our sources, to define the spaces of our research can no longer be interpreted simply as obstacles, but on the contrary, they become important elements for an understanding of the dynamics taking place in the field, like the ideologies which are supported. Their attempts to influence our representations cannot but themselves become the object of our research.

Horizontal relationships

The second suggestion regards the researcher's relationship with their research subjects. In order for our potential sources to grant us the respect necessary for us to be adequate interlocutors we must be willing to establish horizontal relations. The researcher has to establish a relationship of mutual recognition and listening, overcoming the structure of socially recognised credibility, without giving in to the temptation of diametrically opposing it. The issues which can arise in relationships with the various figures who populate the prison can be considered separately. Often the first threshold to pass is that of those who govern the institution. Whether you have been invited to carry out research in prison[5] or whether formal authorisation (from the administration) has been obtained through request, the researcher often finds himself or herself walking that fine line between official recognition of their role and the diffidence of those who intend to defend themselves from an unwanted intrusion.

As we have already noted, even those who work within the prison often have an ambivalent rapport with the researcher: on the one hand they see the potential of the research in terms of recognition of their own work; on the other they fear an excessive workload or hindrance to their daily work. In both cases, the strategy is to develop the ability to promote yourself as a resource: organise information, further explore themes which are on the agenda or be a means of granting some recognition for the professional roles which are often disregarded. Even when not directly linked to the research objective, planning for the production of some outputs which would be of use to prison workers can determine the success of the project:

> I'm pleased that you're doing this job for me, look, we didn't even know how many are enrolled at the university... some prisoners leave, others are transferred... and who is it that has time to update the lists... you will leave them for us, won't you?
>
> (Educator)
>
> The administration does similar research, but that remains internal, it's for the efficiency of the service. Nobody ever talks about the social value of our work, ever.
>
> (Chief of state correction officers)

A different issue is that of the relationship with the prisoners. In this case the main obstacle is linked to the social distance between the researcher and the interviewee and the frequent expectation that there will be some form of judgment on the part of the researcher. From this point of view we cannot hide the devastating impact that the meeting with a disenchanted researcher can have on a prisoner, particularly when, in the prisoner's unconscious, the researcher is seen to be, at least initially, contiguous with the institution. Showing that you are critical of the dominant rehabilitation paradigm which is interiorised, or however instrumentally claimed, even by the prisoners themselves, can have a destabilising effect and create confusion and suspicion in the subjects interviewed. Conversely, it can promote empathy and a supposed affinity which can then be difficult to manage.

Sometimes making one's critical perspective explicit can lead to a clear rejection and end the relationship with the interviewee. This is the case in the event of real (desire for) interiorisation of the philosophy of rehabilitation – which in our experience occurs most often in the case of young subjects with long sentences – as well as in the event of apparently real success of rehabilitation (which often occurs despite – and not thanks to – the experience of detention). But if and when these initial difficulties in the relationship are overcome, it finally becomes easier to abandon the game of reciprocal expectations and construct a real space for dialogue. This can be fostered by the ability to clearly transmit certain messages: we are here to reconstruct the story from your point of view, we are not here to judge and access to certain material or symbolic resources does not depend on us. It is worth remembering Pierre Bourdieu's (1993) invitation here to 'put yourself in another's shoes':

The sociologist can make the most socially distant interviewee feel legitimate in being what he/she is, if he can show through the tone and above all content of his questions that, without expecting to annul the social distance which separates them (unlike the populist vision whose blind point is precisely the point of view), he can put himself in his/her shoes through his thoughts (*se mettre à sa place en pensée*).

(Bourdieu 1993, 10)

A profound knowledge of the field one is working in is a determining factor in successfully enacting such relations: '... the interviewer has some chance of really measuring up to his (research) object only if he possesses great knowledge about it which can be acquired, sometimes, through an entire life of research...' (Bourdieu 1993, 10). When the authorisation to carry out the research does not arrive or access to the field is particularly limited the researcher is forced to use his or her own wits:

After having waited about 8 months for an authorisation from the Ministry di Grazia e Giustizia which would allow him to proceed with some interviews with migrant subjects held in the district prisons of northern Italy, the colleague received a list of names, decided by the directors of the institutes on the basis of inscrutable criteria ... You can't enter prisons as a researcher in our country. How do you enter prison? As somebody who has been accused or convicted: clearly the price to pay is too high. As an employee or contract worker of the prison administration: but sociologists are not included among the staff designated to rehabilitation. As a volunteer, this seems pretty feasible: a contained cost, which entails frequenting Catholic ambients. As observer for an association for human rights. As a university professor, when there are prisoners enrolled at the local university. Let us try putting these last three together and see where they take us. As volunteers we can enter prison when we want, with no advance warning, wander around the corridors and through the sections alone, talk to the prisoners. As observers we are not granted interviews, we have to alert the prison of our visits and we will always be accompanied, but we would have the advantage of being able to visit different institutions, ask for cells to be opened and not know places which are off limits, be able to talk to the doctor, the director, the head of penitentiary police. As university professors we can have extended interviews with prisoners, have them meet our students, work with them, involve some of them in our research. It's better than nothing, let's make the most of it.

(Vianello, Ethnographic diary, July 2012)

Observation of daily life in prison carried out while engaged in different activities does not meet the necessary requisites of scientific investigation; further questions could be raised with regard to the ethics of these strategies on the part of the researcher who is not granted access to the field. But the opportunity to get to know and to 'live' the environment in which you hope to subsequently carry out your research (which obviously must be carried out following all due requirements) is an invaluable resource for the researcher. Conversations and interviews can thus represent 'an undoubtedly privileged moment, in a long series of exchanges, and they have nothing in common with the punctual, arbitrary and occasional meetings of the interviews carried out rapidly by interviewers who have no specific competence' (Bourdieu 1993, 11).

Politics of representation

Once our data had been gathered we were faced with another problem, once again common to all analyses of social marginality, but exacerbated by the field of prison, in relation to the 'politics of representation' (Bourgois 2005, 40). It happened because we have passed the threshold of a prison, which gathers 'the poor, the bad and the dirty' who had 'transgressed the laws of society'.

For a long time critical criminology has highlighted the extreme difficulty (if not guilty ambiguity) which you meet when trying to unravel the undeniable relationship between social disadvantage and deviant behaviour (cf. Sbraccia and Vianello 2010, Chapter 3). Once this link is recognised the issue undoubtedly becomes more complex: lack of socialisation, various dysfunctionalities, subcultures and affiliations on one hand, social inequality, cultural marginality, socio-cultural conditions on the other compete for first place in the explanation of deviant and oppositional behaviours. The causes of crime and the criteria which inform processes of criminalisation end up converging in the definition of that 'punished criminality' (Pavarini 1997) which comes into view when we enter prison: poverty and marginality can clearly be claimed by both views and, as for cruelty, it is unclear whether prisoners find themselves in prison because they are bad or if they are bad because they find themselves in prison.

The analytic's desire to reduce the complexity of reality tends to find the answer in some classic representations of prison and its occupants: nuances are rare and researchers, in their work, tend to search for (or reconstruct) coherence and homogeneity in the messages (Bourgois 2005, 44). Some typical depictions of the 'prison community' take on one or more specific representations of prison (and, obviously, its functions). Linked to these are often stereotypical images of the prison staff who, in different roles, govern the institution. Any deviance from the functional representation of the day is presented as an exception, in the form of a remnant from the past or a taste of what is to come. This is the case both for the educators and for the penitential police, for whom the 'generational' variable is, in many studies, overestimated.

A representation of the prison community (or part of it) as composed of 'good, but poor and oppressed' individuals (forgive the extreme simplification) tends to correspond, in a functionalist perspective, to a representation of prison as a resource. This is what we often read in studies of juvenile prisons, with particular reference to young foreign and unaccompanied minors. In a conflict perspective, it corresponds to a recognition of the experience of detention as a further social disadvantage, as is the case for adults, above all when autochthonous, with particular reference to recidivist rates and the true possibility of social re-integration.

A representation of the prison community as formed of individuals who are 'bad, because they are sick or evil' tends to correspond to the ideology of prison as a place for rehabilitation: a place where that 'critical overhaul' which, however ill-defined, dominates the summaries of the treatment staff and the regulations of the surveillance judiciary has to be made. Where rehabilitation turns out to be impossible (or un-demonstrable), as is often the case, prison is represented as a place of mere containment and the final medium/instrument to defend society (oriented to the die-hards, in spite of the constitutional mandate).

But clearly the prison community is not split between the good and bad, or the oppressed and the evil. To be able to understand them on the one hand you need to suspend moral (and legal) judgment which, following its own internal logic, ends up obstructing the search for relative (and alternative) rationalities. On the other hand, you need to combine it with deconstruction which lends us a careful analysis of the social structure in which the subjects reconstruct their own experiences and give them a meaning. Deconstruction, indeed, 'cannot be taken to the extreme, and it should not impede us from defining and evaluating the experiences of injustice and oppression (...) socially and structurally imposed along the coordinates of race, class, gender and sexuality' (Bourgois 2005, 42).

In the stories of prisoners' lives – and also in those of their jailers and probably in each of our lives – we then risk being able to recognise not only different experiences of poverty, marginality, social disadvantage, but also impulsiveness, aggressiveness, desire to oppress, experiences of not only submission but also perpetration of oppression and violence. Ethnography tends to produce empathetic readings of the subjects it studies and willingly lingers over the reconstruction and recognition of alternative rationalities and their relative justifications. Yet suffering, violence and oppression are key elements of the social interaction which takes place within the total institution, both between prison guards and the prisoners, and between inmates (and at times between guards themselves).

It is normal to be concerned about 'the possibility that the life stories and circumstances narrated (...) can be misunderstood as stereotyped representations (...) or negative portraits' of the prison population (Bourgois 2005, 40): indeed there is considerable risk of producing 'inferiorising narratives', often supported by interviewees' attempts to produce strong identities (sometimes reinforced by dialectal inflexions or profanities which mark their language). On the other hand, 'the rejection of moralistic prejudice and middle class hostility towards the poor – (even more, we would add, of delinquents) – does not mean that the suffering and destruction which pervade' both inside and outside the prison should be hidden. Ignoring or minimising social poverty and the violence which mark the lives of those who end up in prison, often making them 'the subordinate executioners' of themselves (Scheper-Hughes 1992, 172), would mean giving up trying to understand the structural dynamics of oppression.

The same could be said, moreover, for those who work in the prison: the hostility of the so-called middle class towards them is no less – sad (and often denied) destiny of jailers (Foucault 1975) – and the simplifications regarding their work (either all good or all bad) end up often being the same. The representations which generalise surveillance personnel as violent and brutal can never be taken for granted: 'Why is sympathy reserved for the offenders and denied to those who (sometimes in good faith) work in criminal justice, with their own lives, stories, pains, motives and understandings?' (Liebling 2001, 476). They may tend to lie since, as Becker (1967) reminds us, they are responsible for 'things which rarely go as they should go', but the truth is that even the 'subordinates' also lie, while the 'superordinates', sometimes, tell their own truth. But more importantly, we must be aware that bringing to light, when necessary, the use of brutality and violence does not mean taking sides with who is subjected to this, but rather promoting a realistic description of the irresolvable tensions (Garland 1993) which pervade the penal justice system since it is a place destined for the downgrading of status (which is the criminal sentence) (see Pavarini 2006).

It seems clear that this kind of approach to the study of prison requires a truly wide, free and extended access to the 'field of prison' (cf. Sarzotti 2010). It addresses the institution as a whole, the controllers and the controlled, and presupposes researcher independence as regards the ideology which governs the prison. The latter is a direct and specific emanation of the ideology of modern criminal law (cf. Baratta 1982) (see also Sbraccia and Vianello 2010, Chapter 2). The researcher must be able to discuss the legitimacy of prison, at least in relation to its declared aims, not take criminal behaviour as necessarily reproachable, irrational or dysfunctional. Above all, she/he must be able to investigate experiences and recesses of the punishment (and of the punishment per excellence, i.e. prison) to make visible what the institution tends to hide.

Conclusion

This chapter has contributed to the discussion of reflexivity in criminological research through the identification and description of the mechanisms used by the actors of the prison to influence the researcher and to draw his work into the net of the ideology dominant in the institution. Reflexivity is presented in this chapter as a useful tool for the construction of a space, first of all a discursive one, in which the classical opposition between dominant and dominated can be diluted, revealing the extent to which the correctional ideology crosses both. Faced with this risk, reflexivity is presented as an important tool for a critical analysis of this essential dimension of the prison field. In this sense, the chapter owes a debt to the work of Becker (1967) and Bourdieu (1992). Following the former, in particular, it emphasises the call to be aware of the hierarchy of credibility that is operating within the field we approach and to make it explicit when we present the research results. From Bourdieu (1992), in particular, it has taken the sociological notion of field and the consequent possibility of thinking the prison as a network of objective relationships. Some 'practices of resistance' were then presented to future researchers, enabling them to reflexively manage the field and not be subjugated by the institutional logics.

Notes

1. It makes sense, in this case, to claim the possibility of a third wider perspective, able to recognise and balance the opposing views within the field in which the researcher is moving, whose emergence constitutes exactly, according to Gouldner (1975), the task that sociology is proposed (see Liebling 2001).
2. While having visited prisons of several countries (France, Greece, Poland, Portugal, United Kingdom), the research experiences to which we refer mainly concern the Argentine and Italian context. Researches have focused on various aspects of detention: the socialisation to the prison context and the changes in the convict code (Vianello 2013b), the overcrowding from the point of view of prisoners (Vianello 2013a), the collateral consequences of incarceration (Ferreccio 2012), the institutional violence on families of prisoners (Ferreccio 2013).
3. Interacting with the two groups of prison staff stops us from considering them indiscriminately under the generic term 'institutional staff'. At least in the Argentinian context, the staff assigned to custody seems to establish a clearer difference between what they consider 'discursive' – that is, the prison's rehabilitation and re-socialisation project – and the 'reality' of the wings that they work with every day. In other words, prison guards assigned to custody seem more inclined to agree with the scepticism towards the dominant paradigm, which expects 'impossible' justification (Pavarini 1992) of the sentence. Paradoxically, with this behaviour, the concept of the prison as a space of pure neutralisation is reinforced.
4. Word, which in prison jargon, is used to refer to prisoners considered conflictual (by their fellow prisoners) or who 'find it difficult to adapt' (by treatment staff).
5. As Liebling highlights (2001, 479) here there is a question of legitimacy: 'a reputation for integrity and independence within the Prison Service can create the risk of being regarded as "in the Prison Service pocket" in other circles'.

References

Baratta, A. (1982) *Criminologia critica e critica del diritto penale*, Bologna: il Mulino.
Becker, H.S. (1967) 'Whose Side Are We on?' *Social Problems* 14: 239–47.

274 Power, Partisanship and Bias

Bourdieu, P. (1992) *Risposte. Per una antropologia riflessiva*, Torino: Bollati e Boringhieri.
Bourdieu, P. (1993) *La misère du monde*, Paris: Editions du Seuil.
Bourgois, P. (2005) *Cercando rispetto. Drug economy e cultura di strada*, Roma: Derive Approdi.
Cicourel, A. (2011) *Método y medida en sociología*, Madrid: Centro de Investigaciones en Sociología, CIS.
Clemmer, D. (1958 [1940]) *The Prison Community*, New York: Holt, Rinehart and Winston.
Ferreccio, V. (2012) 'La larga sombra de la prisión: un estudio de los daños colaterales del encarcelamiento en Argentina', Paper presented at the 54 International Congress of Americanist, Vienna, 15 July 2012.
Ferreccio, V. (2013) 'Familiares de detenidos y violencia institucional en la provincia de Santa Fe', Paper presented at the Workshop 'Delito y Sociedad', Santa Fe, 4 December 2013.
Foucault, M. (1975) *Sorvegliare e punire. Nascita della prigione*, Torino: Einaudi.
Garland, D. (1993) *Punishment and Modern Society: A Study in Social Theory*, University of Chicago Press.
Goffman, E. (2010 [1961]) *Asylums. Le istituzioni totali: i meccanismi dell'esclusione e della violenza*, Torino: Einaudi.
Liebling, A. (2001) 'Whose Side Are We on? Theory, Practice and Allegiances in Prison Research' *British Journal of Criminology* 41: 472–84.
Marquart, J.W. (1986) 'Doing Research in Prison: The Strengths and Weaknesses of Full Participation as a Guard' *Justice Quarterly* III, 1: 15–32.
Pavarini, M. (1992) 'Historia de la pena. La justificación imposible' *Delito y Sociedad. Revista de Ciencias Sociales* I(1): 22–36.
Pavarini, M. (1997) 'La criminalità punita. Processi di carcerizzazione nell'Italia del XX secolo'. In L. Violante (ed.) *La criminalità*, Torino: Einaudi.
Pavarini, M. (2006) 'La 'lotta per i diritti dei detenuti' tra riduzionismo e abolizionismo carcerari' *Antigone. Quadrimestrale di critica del sistema penale e penitenziario* I(1): 82–96.
Rostaing, C. (2006) 'La comprensión sociologique de l'experience carcérale' *Revue européenne des sciences sociales* XLIV(135): 29–43.
Sarzotti, C. (2010) 'Il campo giuridico del penitenziario: appunti per una ricostruzione'. In E. Santoro (ed.) *Diritto come questione sociale*, Torino: Giappichelli, pp.123–79.
Sbraccia, A. and Vianello, F. (2010) *Sociologia della devianza e della criminalità*, Bari and Roma: Laterza.
Scheper-Hughes, N. (1992) *Death Without Weeping: The Violence of Everyday Life in Brazil*, University of California Press.
Sykes, G. (1958) *The Society of Captives: A Study of a Maximum-Security Prison*, Princeton University Press.
Vianello, F. (2013a) 'Daily Life in Overcrowded Prisons: A Convict Perspective on Italian detention' *Prison Service Journal*, May 2013, 207: 27–33.
Vianello, F. (2013b) 'Biographical trajectories, prison careers and effects of detention', Paper presented at the Interlabo on 'Doing research in Prison', Groupe Européen de Recherche sur les Normativités (Gern), Padoue, 11 October 2013.

21
'You Are What You Research': Bias and Partisanship in an Ethnography of Boy Racers

Karen Lumsden

Introduction

Despite social researchers directing a great deal of attention to methodological and theoretical arguments relating to bias and partisanship, and the reflexive turn within the social sciences, explicit reflections of the operation and experience of these in criminological research have been scarce. In a sense, partisanship is frequently presented as if it needed little supporting argument and is discussed in ways that cover over controversial issues. These arguments are not taken seriously by social researchers because they are seen to have been undercut by developments in the philosophy and sociology of science (Hammersley 2000). According to Hammersley (2000, 11): 'Nor do we find, in the literature on researcher partisanship, explicit value arguments about what goals research ought to serve. Instead, '"whose side to be on" is treated as a foregone conclusion, as if the world were made up of "goodies" and "baddies"'. However, when conducting ethnographic research on deviant or criminal cultures the researcher can be required to balance the interests of powerful or elite groups with those of the less powerful or the 'underdogs' (Gouldner 1973). Thus, it is essential that the criminologist is visible in the text in order to ensure that he/she does not exploit his/her authorial position (Brewer 2000). According to Devine and Heath (1999), the best way to proceed is not to pretend to be value neutral, but to be honest about one's own perspectives and beliefs on any given research topic and then seek to represent the data in as objective a way as possible.

This chapter offers a retrospective analysis of the role of bias and partisanship in criminological research with boy racers and social groups

Parts of this chapter were previously published in Lumsden, K. (2013) '"You Are What You Research": Researcher Partisanship and the Sociology of the "Underdog"' *Qualitative Research* 13(1): 3–18.

affected by their behaviour (including local residents, police, council officials, journalists and politicians) in Aberdeen, Scotland from 2005 to 2008
(see Lumsden 2013a). Boy racers (as they are referred to in the United
Kingdom, Australia and New Zealand) are viewed as deviant and problematic
due to their occupation of urban space and the public highways. They contest the normative practices of car culture via their engagement in the ritual
of car modification[1] and supposed participation in illegal and risky driving
behaviours such as speeding and street racing. The boy racer label denotes
a combination of themes including youth, masculinity and deviance which
are intertwined with the car (and car cultures) often resulting in 'moral panics' (Cohen 2002[1972]) over youths' appropriation of this highly valued
consumer good (Lumsden 2013a, 2). My interest in the issue was spurred
by the increased visibility of the subculture in the local and national press
which resulted in a regional 'moral panic' concerning Aberdeen's boy racers
(Lumsden 2009, 2013a).

   In this study, the decision was made not to side with those research participants in powerful or superior positions (such as politicians, journalists or the
authorities). This resulted in an unconscious siding with the 'underdogs' –
members of the boy racer subculture. However, it is argued that certain
social situations require the researcher to engage in advocacy and give voice
to marginal or subordinate groups (Lumsden 2013b). The discussion also
touches upon the prevalence of media culture as well as the dynamics of
making our work public at key stages of the research process.

An ethnography of boy racers

Since the late 1960s, young drivers have collectively gathered at Aberdeen's
Beach Boulevard in order to socialise with like-minded car enthusiasts, display their modified cars and engage in daring driving manoeuvres with
the aim of receiving public acclamation from fellow drivers and spectators.
These boy racers, or as they are locally known, 'Bouley Bashers', are firmly
cemented in the history and lore of Aberdeen. Generations of youths have
participated in the car (sub)culture. At night, the Beach Boulevard comes
alive to the sound of revving engines, roaring car exhausts and the blare
of music from car stereo systems. The subculture has at its centre the prop
or totem of the car: a ritualistic symbol which helps frame the behaviours,
dialogue and practices of its members. Moreover, although it is largely a
male-dominated subculture, a growing number of females participate. In the
eyes of the media, local community, politicians and authorities, the 'Bouley
Bashers' are the villains of this narrative.

   The purpose of the research was to shed light on the unexplored world of
the boy racer in Aberdeen. It was a Friday night in September 2006 when
I first met the gatekeeper Debbie:[2]

I had to drive around the block a few times because I couldn't find a space to park, nor could I see Debbie's car. She had told me to look out for a red modified Seat Ibiza. Eventually I spotted her driving behind me we both parked up on the tramlines.[3] Debbie invited me to sit in the front passenger seat of her car so we could chat. She apologised for being late but said that she was being careful because the police were watching her ... She told me that you have to watch out for the police. They've told the drivers that they are allowed to park on the tramlines but it is illegal to drive on pavements so if they catch them doing so then they'll fine them £30 ... They also aren't allowed to park beyond the pedestrian crossing because it's dangerous. Unfortunately she can't ensure that everyone knows the rules and obeys them just like the neighbourhood police officer can't make sure that all of his officers know the drivers at the Beach Boulevard and whether to fine them, warn them or use discretion. She said: 'It's very much an "us and them" situation'.

(Fieldnotes, September 2006)

It was during my first meeting with Debbie and through hearing her account of various outside groups that I was reminded of the political nature of the research. Upon commencing the fieldwork the topic was already highly contentious in terms of local politics, policing and the public imagination. For instance, local newspaper the *Evening Express* reported:

A major route through Aberdeen could be closed to traffic every night under controversial proposals being drawn up by a city councillor. To prevent boy racers using the Beach Boulevard as a night-time racetrack, Councillor Jim Hunter has hit on a radical plan ... The plans were revealed last night at a highly charged meeting to discuss the impact of the so-called 'Bouley Bashers' on the beach area ... More than 50 locals and business people joined Member of Parliament Frank Doran and representatives from Grampian Police to discuss the boy racer situation. Many claimed the noise from the racers' exhausts and from their car stereos kept them awake until the early hours. They said gangs of youths had been spotted jumping on car bonnets, littering the area and racing along the streets as late as 4am. One hotel manager insisted he was losing business – five guests had walked out over the weekend after protesting about the noise from cars ...

(*This is North East Scotland* 2004)

The boy racers were socially situated as the 'underdogs' in terms of the silencing of their voices and the privileging of the voices of the outside groups in public discourse(s) such as media reports and reality television *exposés*. There were attempts by the police to include the drivers at community meetings and through participation at the Grampian Police Drivers' Group.[4] However, the authorities were mainly representing the interests of local residents and businesses. The implementation of powers under the Antisocial Behaviour (Scotland) Act 2004 (including Seizure of Vehicles, Dispersal Orders and Antisocial Behaviour Orders) also heightened the political and public visibility of the research topic. The use of this legislation in Aberdeen was highlighted at the Prime Minister's Question Time in June 2005 where the Labour Member of Parliament for Aberdeen South stated:

> The people of Beach Boulevard in Aberdeen have been able to sleep at night for the past three months because of the implementation of a dispersal order against the boy racers, or as they are known locally, Bouley Bashers, who have made residents' lives a misery for years.

The then Prime Minister Tony Blair responded:

> I strongly support anti-social behaviour legislation...I urge communities to look at the available powers and make sure that the police, local authorities and local residents are using them properly...The idea that these powers are an affront to civil liberties is patently absurd, because they protect the civil liberties of the decent, law-abiding majority.
>
> (Engagements 2005)

The longitudinal nature of this qualitative study meant that I was witness to the discussion of these issues among social groups, the proposal and implementation of measures, the effect these had on the group and the reactions and views of the young motorists. Each group had a vested interest in the issue and thus an awareness of this on my part was necessary from commencement of the fieldwork.

The study consisted of participant observation with the subculture at Aberdeen's seafront and at various car shows and events across Scotland and semi-structured and ethnographic interviews with the drivers. One hundred and fifty hours were spent in the field and eight semi-structured interviews were conducted with the racers. Access was granted via the Grampian Police Drivers' Group in which police officers regularly met with a group of young drivers from the beach area of the city. Ethnographic research was also conducted online and involved observation of websites[5] hosted by the two gatekeepers, Debbie and Robert.

In terms of the outside groups, semi-structured interviews were conducted with four local residents (and one group interview with four residents present), a Member of Parliament, a Member of the Scottish Parliament, a local councillor, three journalists, two council officials and four officers from Grampian Police. These were conducted at the beginning of the research, before access had been negotiated with the subculture. Participant observation was also conducted at a community meeting involving these groups. The interviews were recorded and fully transcribed. Content analysis was employed to over 200 newspaper articles which focused on boy racers in Aberdeen from daily local newspapers the *Evening Express* and the *Press & Journal*; weekly local newspapers the *Independent* and the *Citizen*; and national media outlets such as *BBC News*, the *Scotsman*, the *Guardian* and the *Times*. The following section provides an analysis of the influence of bias and partisanship in research with the outside groups before considering fieldwork experiences and dissemination of research findings via the media.

Siding with the 'underdogs'

The outside groups: 'What angle are you taking on this issue?'

When researching the outside groups I was aware of attempts by respondents to steer or influence the research, since each had their own interests to protect. When interviewing politicians, each respondent attempted to alter the interview schedule and only answered the questions they were comfortable with. Local journalists answered questions in such a way that it reflected the editorial view of the newspaper in question. In these cases, it was clear that the power relationship between interviewer and interviewee rested with the interviewee, who attempted to control the format and content of the interview. Since the subculture was highly visible in politics, the media and the public imagination, respondents used the interviews to convey particular messages. During interviews respondents often asked me: 'What angle are you taking on the issue?' My answer was that I was researching each of the groups involved in the issue, including the boy racer subculture. Hence I was choosing to adopt a neutral and unbiased stance.

When attending a public road safety event held by Grampian Police at Aberdeen's Beach Boulevard, an intended forum through which young motorists could meet and talk with police officers and members of the local community, a police officer informed me:

'There have been a large number of complaints from residents and businesses in the area and as a result of this something has to be done. Residents have paid large amounts of money for flats with nice scenery not to have it ruined by Bouley Bashers. We – the police – have always let boy racers get away with being at the beach but we won't any longer. The council's idea of planting flowers all the way down the Boulevard won't work because they will just be vandalised. We'll be using ASBOs[6] in the area so anybody causing a nuisance can be sent away from the area until 8am the next day. We're trying to be fair to both the Bouley Bashers and the residents because we understand that people spend a lot of money on their cars for them to look nice'. However it didn't seem this way to me.

(Fieldnotes, February 2005)

From this point, I had developed an understanding of the boy racers as the underdogs through the reaction of social groups, such as the authorities and local residents, to their presence. Related to this were the numerous measures adopted in order to deter them from Aberdeen's seafront. In another conversation with a local police officer I was asked what my opinion was regarding the proposal to close the Beach Boulevard road each evening:

> I was asked by Officer [...] what my opinion is of the road being closed at night. I had to try not to appear to have an opinion on it so tried to give an answer which meant that I agreed with Grampian Police but also thought there are some reasons why it should be open. I answered something along the lines of, 'Closing the road would probably benefit certain groups such as the residents but I'm sure there are also a number of good arguments as to why it should be open. I don't really know enough to fully answer'.

(Fieldnotes, July 2006)

When negotiating access there was also an underlying presumption from members of the outside groups that I would be sympathetic to their cause and 'take their side'. When conducting the research, I believed that my awareness of these attempts made me more conscious of my own values, beliefs and background and how these may influence the research, my relationships with respondents and my accounts of the outside groups and the racers. Although this is the case, it resulted in what Gouldner (1968) terms a 'sociology of the underdog'.

The researcher as spy: Trust in the field

On commencing the fieldwork with the subculture, the research participants seemed suspicious of my intentions and the purposes of my research. This has previously been reflected upon elsewhere (Lumsden 2009) where I note that the group's reluctance to participate in the research may have been linked to the tendency for the media to misrepresent and misquote members of the group. For instance in the *Press & Journal* (2003) it was claimed that: 'Last night drivers were defensive about the scheme and were unwilling to speak to the media, claiming that they did not want their comments to be "twisted"'. Hence, participants, including Robert and Debbie, were critical and suspicious of my research as a result of my 'outsider' status. Robert accused me of being a 'narc' and a 'spy for the authorities'. Trust had to be built up and (re)negotiated with research participants throughout the course of the fieldwork.

Research participants continually highlighted their victimisation and stigmatisation at the hands of the outside groups including most notably, and because they had more contact with them, the police and local residents. On the first occasion I met Debbie she informed me in relation to the subculture and the police that it was: '... very much an "us and them" situation'. Paul also had a negative view of the police:

> While we were sitting watching the cars drive past Paul pointed over to a grey Nova in the distance driving along the seafront. A police car followed closely behind for a while before the officers decided to stop the driver of the car. Paul laughed and remarked: 'There they go again. They'll probably pull him over for whatever reason they can come up with'.
>
> (Fieldnotes, November 2004)

I had to prove to the drivers that I did not belong to one of the outside groups, nor was I spying on behalf of the authorities. The racers also applied the 'us and them' distinction to certain individuals within the subculture who they did not class as legitimate participants. They experienced this exclusion at various car shows. For example, at an Italian car show in St. Andrews, Scotland in 2007, the Fiat Group's presence was challenged by those belonging to other groups such as the Alfa Romeo group. A feeling of camaraderie and belonging was also evident in terms of their public performances on the roads and the reaction from other motorists to the modified car which can be viewed as a symbol of resistance against bourgeois means of consumption (Vaaranen 2004). Hence, as Gouldner (1973) notes in his critique of Becker (1967), the labelling theory of deviance does not account for 'underdogs' as rebellious or resistant to the status quo, which members of the subculture often were.

Giving a voice to the racers

Further evidence of partisanship and the influence of my values can be found in my contact with gatekeepers after leaving the field. Importantly, this concerns the opportunity to involve research participants in media discussions regarding their subculture. The first opportunity occurred in 2007 while I was still in the field. I was contacted by producers at *BBC*[7] *Radio Scotland* who were including a discussion on the implementation of seizure of vehicles powers under the Antisocial Behaviour (Scotland) Act 2004 in their lunch time *Scotland Live* programme. The interview included participation from a politician, a representative from a road safety charity, (minimal participation from) myself and a group of three drivers from Aberdeen, including Debbie. Although the producers had specifically requested that

282 Power, Partisanship and Bias

I ask the drivers if they would participate, I also felt that this would be an ideal opportunity for them to liaise with the media in attempts to explain the reasons for their participation in the scene and their views on Antisocial Behaviour Orders (ASBOs). Hence, I believed this would allow them to voice their thoughts, which had been largely silenced (or misconstrued) in the local and national press. Overall, the interview was positive with the drivers feeling that they had successfully communicated their views in the short segment which was available to them. However, on reflection this event along with the next sheds insight into my views of the media, the drivers and other social groups during the research. My attempts to positively promote the subculture via their involvement with the media raise issues regarding partisanship and also highlight the feelings of guilt which go hand-in-hand with ethnographic fieldwork. In a sense, I felt that this was one means by which I could repay research participants for granting me access to the subculture.

The second incident occurred in 2009 (a year after leaving the field) when I was contacted by a reporter for the Scottish section of the *Times* who wanted to feature an article on 'girl racers' (see McIntosh 2009). She had become aware of my research and the subculture of boy racers through an interview I had taken part in for *BBC Radio 4's Thinking Allowed* programme. Again, I contacted Debbie who I believed would be interested in promoting a positive image of the subculture (and the car modification scene), especially given the gender-related angle the newspaper wished to take. Debbie and other female car modifiers were willing to be interviewed and to have their cars photographed for the report. They explained that this would hopefully allow them further positive exposure in the public eye with regard to a pastime which they took seriously and invested a great deal of time and money in. Yet again, this example highlights my unconscious decision to side with the 'underdogs' with regard to encouraging them to have their own voice through not just myself as a researcher, but also the media. Reflections such as these highlight the need for criminologists to view their own beliefs and decisions with the same critical attitude as they do those held by others (Gouldner 1973).

Discussion: Unintended consequences

The work of Gouldner (1973) and Becker (1967) helps highlight the ambiguities and dilemmas which arise from partisanship. Criminologists should not avoid 'taking sides' in research. Value neutrality is a myth and attempts to mitigate bias are largely unrealistic and thus doomed to fail. Research: '...will inevitably be affected by the values of the researcher – regardless of whether their value position is made explicit. Moreover, a researcher's own values and biases may lead them to prioritise certain accounts over others – even if unwittingly' (Devine and Heath 1999, 39). Perhaps researchers should stop worrying about achieving that mythic objectivity and instead focus on the construction of various kinds of texts – realist tales, confessional tales, impressionist tales, layered accounts, autoethnographies, journals, performance texts and so on (Van Maanen 1988).

Although the racers were socially situated as the 'underdogs', they were not always passive and entered into a dialogue with the police for instance. They were aware of their marginal position within society and their labelling by 'outside' groups. As a result of this, I had to gain their trust in the course of my fieldwork. My interactions with the groups involved clearly influenced my representation of the subculture when writing up and disseminating findings via academia and the media. I went into the field with the assumption (gleaned from popular representations of the boy racer in popular culture and the media) that the subculture was problematic and that in terms of their driving behaviours boy racers were dangerous, reckless and irresponsible. This image of the boy racer was largely taken-for-granted and unchallenged by members of the outside groups. In my interactions with certain research participants, such as journalists and politicians, I did not feel that I was receiving an honest response. Unsurprisingly perhaps, they were 'towing the line' in terms of their position within society. They were representing their own professional interests. They were explicit in their expectations that I would take their side in response to the boy racer 'problem'. However, I was somewhat naive in that while I was aware of partisanship on the part of the outside groups, I did not consider this in relation to the subculture. This is evident in my fieldnotes where I reflect on bias and values in interactions with outside groups, but not with the drivers themselves. This highlights what Gouldner (1973) draws our attention to – the tendency for sociologists to engage in a type of 'underdog identification'. Those involved in the research each had their own expectations about my role in the research and whose story I should privilege. The researcher is thus required to walk a tight rope in that they cannot threaten access or interactions with the researched by directly challenging them, but they must also attempt to remain true to their own values and beliefs.

Attempts were made to give voice to participants via the media in addition to the dissemination of research findings. Some social situations call for advocacy and the inclusion of marginal or subordinate voices as a means by which to dismantle unjust power structures. In this instance, it was necessary to take the side of the 'underdog' – the boy racer. This reflexive approach is beneficial in that it gives us new information concerning social worlds which many members of society know nothing or little about. This was the aim of my research: to gain a detailed sociological understanding of this hitherto unexplored social world, to glimpse the internal dynamics of the subculture, to gain understanding of youths' participation and how social characteristics such as gender, class, regional identity, ethnicity and age played out. Was the public perception and media representation of the sub-culture accurate in terms of the youths' driving practices? Was the response of outside groups accurate in terms of the threat it was claimed the boy racers posed? Was there evidence of a 'moral panic' concerning this youth subculture? Through adopting the standpoint of the 'underdog' it is possible to explore these questions. However, this must still be done from the posi-tion of the 'outsider'. I could not identify myself with the 'underdogs' since I was not a member of their group. I could only present their case. More-over, through adopting an 'outsider' status, it was possible to retain a certain intellectual and emotional distance from the researched and to successfully negotiate the problems of representation and legitimation which ethnographers face.

Conclusion

The above examples demonstrate that I chose to side with the boy racers who were socially situated as the 'underdogs' in contrast to the outside groups. In research involving a plethora of actors – from the racers, to the police, local residents, businesses, journalists, politicians, council officials and general public – it was impossible not to be influenced by my val-ues and beliefs and the expectations of the social actors I was observing or interviewing. As criminologists, we are shaped by our interactions with the researched and we form our own opinions about the group we are study-ing and their treatment by those in positions of power and privilege. The subculture was already politically contentious and thus high on the pub-lic and media agenda(s). Hence, the idea that I could successfully conduct ethnographic research without being influenced by my values and beliefs or those of a particular group was, in this case, unreasonable. Ethnographers will undoubtedly take sides in the course of their research investigations whether they are willing to admit this or not.

A final important point raised concerns the dissemination of research find-ings. The discussion highlights the issues encountered when we liaise with the media in criminological research. Whether I liked it or not, the media were intertwined with this research from the beginning to the end (and beyond in terms of dissemination of research findings). The media interest in the issue of boy racers had fuelled my curiosity into their world. Ironically, in the end, the research findings and the voice(s) of the researched fed back into the apparatus of the mass media. Interactions with the media were an explicit attempt to debunk the myth of the boy racer via research findings and by giving a voice to those research participants who had helped in the course of the fieldwork. Reflecting on these can help us to unravel the role of our values and beliefs in research and how these are further shaped by the researched. In this instance, I pursued these avenues for dissemination as an additional means to give voice to the 'underdogs'. This was tied to notions of research bargaining and in giving something back to those gatekeepers who granted me access to their social world. Thus, criminological research does not occur in a vacuum and more reflection is needed on our experiences with the media and other stakeholders when disseminating research findings. Our engagements in 'public criminology' raise a whole host of methodological, philosophical, political, moral and ethical dilemmas which must be the subject of further debate and scrutiny.

Notes

1. 'Modding' involves taking a standard car and altering its physical appearance (including the interior and exterior) as well as its performance. Typical exterior modifications include tyres and alloys, lowering the suspension, bigger and louder exhausts, tinted windows, smoked-out lights, body kits, bumpers, spoilers, bonnet vents and under-car neon lights. Interior modifications include sports seats and in-car entertainment (ICE) such as stereos, sub-woofers, speakers, amplifiers, DVD/Blue Ray players, games consoles or computers (Lumsden 2013a, 114).
2. Pseudonyms are used in order to protect the identities of research participants.
3. The tramlines ('trammers') are an area at Aberdeen's seafront where the last remnants of the city's old tram lines remain. Drivers use this space to socialise.
4. Consisted of local police officers and representatives from the subculture (including my gatekeepers) who met approximately every three months to discuss issues pertaining to the Beach Boulevard.
5. This included a website dedicated to the hobby of car modification and one dedicated to Fiats.
6. Antisocial Behaviour Orders.
7. British Broadcasting Corporation.

References

Antisocial Behaviour (Scotland) Act (2004) [asp 8].
Becker, H.S. (1967) 'Whose Side Are We On?' *Social Problems* 14: 239–47.
Brewer, J.D. (2000) *Ethnography*, Buckingham: Open University Press.
Cohen, S. (2002[1972]) *Folk Devils and Moral Panics*, 3rd edn, London: Routledge.
Devine, F. and Heath, S. (1999) *Sociological Research Methods in Context*, Basingstoke: Palgrave.
Engagements (2005) *House of Commons Debates* (15 June 2005). URL (accessed 5 July 2005): www.TheyWorkForYou.com
Gouldner, A. (1968) 'The Sociologist as Partisan' *American Sociologist* 3(2): 103–16.
Gouldner, A. (1973) *For Sociology*, London: Allen Lane.
Hammersley, M. (2000) *Taking Sides in Social Research*, London: Routledge.
Lumsden, K. (2009) '"Do We Look Like Boy Racers?" The Role of the Folk Devil in Contemporary Moral Panics' *Sociological Research Online* 14(1): http://www.socresonline.org.uk/14/1/2.html
Lumsden, K. (2013a) *Boy Racer Culture: Youth, Masculinity and Deviance*, London: Routledge.
Lumsden, K. (2013b) '"You Are What You Research": Researcher Partisanship and the Sociology of the "Underdog"' *Qualitative Research* 13(1): 3–18.

McIntosh, L. (2009) 'Women Car Enthusiasts Head for Race Tracks and Streets of Aberdeen' *The Times Online* (22 August 2009). URL (accessed 3 January 2010): http://www.timesonline.co.uk/tol/news/uk/scotland/article6805957.ece

Press & Journal (2003) 'Gathering of City Boy Racers Is Hailed as a Success' (3 June 2003).

This is North East Scotland (2004) 'Plans to Close Beachfront Road in Bid to Stop Disruptive "Bouley Bashers"' (21 September 2004). URL (accessed 10 January 2005): http://www.thisisnorthscotland.co.uk/new/util/content/jsp?id=10989735

Vaaranen, H. (2004) 'The Emotional Experience of Class: Interpreting Working Class Kids' Street Racing in Helsinki' *The ANNALS of the American Academy of Political and Social Science* 595(1): 91–107.

Van Maanen, J. (1988) *Tales of the Field*, Chicago: University of Chicago Press.

Part VI

Reflexivity and Innovation: New Contexts, Challenges and Possibilities

Editors' Introduction

Karen Lumsden and Aaron Winter

In this final part of the book, *reflexivity and innovation*, we turn to discussions of the future of criminological research and examples of innovation in policy, practice and research methods in particular cases and contexts – from the virtual to the international. In Chapter 22, James Banks describes his research on online gambling, examining a context and social sub-culture made possible through technological innovation and presenting new challenges to the ethnographer. He considers the responsibility of criminologists as virtual ethnographers to reflexively interrogate their roles, methods and interpretations when examining online cultures, as well as how the researcher's biography, presuppositions and cultural position impacted upon the study of an online gambling subculture. In Chapter 23, Jarrett Blaustein then describes how a researcher's direct immersion in an active policy node can create unique opportunities to exercise reflexivity and achieve a transnational criminology of harm production. This involves moving beyond ex post facto critiques of ethnocentrism and the struc-tural inequalities associated with transnational criminology and actively mitigating the potential consequences of one's participation in the field. Blaustein reflects on the ethical dilemmas he encountered while completing ethnographic fieldwork with UNDP's Safer Communities project in Bosnia-Herzegovina. Finally, in Chapter 24, Hannah Graham and Rob White discuss the challenges, paradoxes and opportunities encountered in conducting international criminological research about innovative justice initiatives and creative ways of working with offenders. They argue that claims of 'inno-vation' and 'success' are inevitably relative and contextualised, subject to diverse interpretation and frequently contested. Yet, innovation inspires and resonates beyond itself; 'quiet revolutions' are being achieved in unorthodox ways and unlikely places around the world.

22
Online Gambling, Advantage Play, Reflexivity and Virtual Ethnography[1]

James Banks

Introduction

Ethnographic research has a long lineage within criminological inquiry with researchers utilising such approaches to shed light on the lived meanings of a host of groups who operate at the margins of conventional society. More recently, cultural criminologists have adopted immersive ethnographic techniques to research communities as diverse as 'dumpster divers' (Ferrell 2006), terrorists (Hamm 2002) and illegal motorbike racers (Librett 2008). Criminologists (Zaitch and Leeuw 2010; Banks 2013) have also begun to employ ethnographic techniques to examine hard-to-reach cultures that inhabit virtual environments, yet this has not been accompanied by an adequate consideration of the dilemmas that emerge throughout the research process.

This chapter considers the responsibility of criminologists as virtual ethnographers to reflexively interrogate their roles, methods and interpretations when examining online cultures. Numerous dialectic tensions shape researcher's methodologies, behaviours and research outputs. In particular, physical foundations and modernist ontologies operate as principal frames of reference for the virtual ethnographer and inform their premises, processes and interpretations. The chapter will evidence the importance of reflexivity in virtual ethnography through a tripartite analysis of the research process: examining *inquiry*, *analysis* and *representational* stages. First, the chapter will demonstrate how identifying a field of inquiry, negotiating access and collecting data, while typically depicted as merely procedural, act as important indicators of the values and assumptions the researcher assigns to themselves, the researched and the research context. More pertinently, these inquiry processes may be best understood as being intrinsically tied to the construction of identity and this profoundly shapes what is to be studied and what position is adopted by the researcher towards the research subject. Second, decision-making regarding the textual performance of the researched, what is real and what is virtual and the role undertaken by the researcher (is s/he a participant or observer?), will impact significantly on the analysis of data. Reflexive attention to the 'analytical lens' – for instance what is collected and considered as data – is essential if criminologists are to illuminate the lived experience of virtual cultures. Third, writing and presenting research findings should offer an essential reflexive juncture. Representational revision and the reshaping of cultures can occur, as criminologists endeavour to adhere to academic writing conventions, conform to journal style and meet the requirements of target audiences. While neither mutually exclusive nor exhaustive, inquiry, analysis and representational stages of the research process offer critical reflexive junctures at which criminologists must endeavour to interrogate their research roles, methods, understandings and interpretations. Here, reflexivity is employed as 'a sensitizing device to counteract the tendency to present ethnographic reports as portrayals of an objective reality' (Hine 2000, 56). Consideration is given to how my biography, presuppositions and cultural position impacted upon my study of an online gambling subculture that I term 'advantage players'. In turn, it is argued that a rigorous ethnographic inquiry of online cultures may only be achieved if the researcher is reflexive to the complex interrelationships between self, other and context.

The study: Advantage play, gambling, crime, victimisation and virtual ethnography

This paper is derived from the procedural dilemmas that arose during the researcher's virtual ethnography (Hine 2000) of an online advantage play subculture. At its simplest, advantage play refers to the legal use of strategies of mathematical advantage when 'gambling' online in order to substantially reduce or remove the risk inherent in the transaction. Advantage players seek to exploit weaknesses in gambling operator's products and promotions to generate profits. These weaknesses are typically found in sports and horse betting, casino games (such as blackjack and roulette) and slot machines. Advantage players use a number of strategies including, but not limited to, matched betting,[2] bonus hunting[3] and arbitrage.[4]

Remote communications, in the form of the Internet, smart phones and digital television, have been central to the increased availability of gambling. Most notably, the rapid development of the Internet as a public and commercial vehicle provides significant opportunity for gambling online. The online gambling market has been promoted by the leisure and entertainment industry as a site of safe risks where consumers can partake in a panoply of aleatory activities. However, the geographical indeterminacy of the web, coupled with the limitations of state-based law, has given rise to a patchwork global regulatory network from which opportunities for criminal enterprise abound. Beyond the 2,347 licensed online gambling sites, there are an estimated 12,476 sites that are 'wild' or 'savage' in nature (CERT-LEXSI 2006). Wild sites are gambling organisations that operate without a licence, while savage sites actively engage in criminal activity, including theft of payments, theft of means of payment, identity theft and money laundering. With gambling sites actively operating as vehicles for criminal enterprise or as sources of crime, it is unsurprising that advantage players interpret this landscape as one full of danger and deviance. The challenges facing the advantage player (or online gambler) are neatly summarised by one respondent:

> [T]he online gambling market is primarily made up of rogue books. Beyond the high street names – and even some of their practices are questionable – there are hundreds more books that dip in and out of criminal activity. Still, as you well know, there is a lot of tax free money to be made from this game so it is well worth the risk.

An understanding of how advantage players make sense of – and navigate through – an online gambling environment that gives rise to crime and victimisation was achieved through both the researcher's participation in advantage play and the covert participant observation of an online forum frequented by advantage players, over an 18-month period (see Banks 2013). While there is a small body of criminological research that has utilised participant observation to examine virtual subcultures (see Mann and Sutton 1998), to date criminological research rarely provides opportunity for the unravelling of lived meanings through the experiential immersion of the researcher in online communities. The opportunity to undertake a virtual ethnography enabled the researcher to become 'submerged in the situated logic and emotion' (Ferrell and Hamm 1998, 8) of the research subject. This 'methodology of attentiveness' (Ferrell and Hamm 1998, 10) provided the researcher with a unique opportunity to explore the intersections between gambling, crime and victimisation online. The online forum was identified and chosen because of its position as the principal 'meeting place' for advantage players and the hub of information and experience sharing for this subcultural grouping. This provided a suitable venue in which to explore the meanings and practices of advantage players, but also required continual critical reflection of, and reflexivity to, the methodological approach and research sensibilities that shaped inquiry, analysis and representational stages of this process.

Inquiry

There are a number of dilemmas which shape the inquiry stage of any virtual ethnography as researchers seek to identify a field of inquiry, negotiate access and collect data. As co-creators of fields of study, researchers as virtual ethnographers must be reflexive of their roles in the inquiry process. C. Wright Mills (1959, 207) suggests that sociological inquiry begins 'with what interests the individual most deeply, even if it seems altogether trivial and cheap'. The field of inquiry to be examined and, in turn, how it is interpreted is shaped, in part, by the researcher's biography and life history. Being reflexive of my own biography resonated throughout this inquiry into the world of advantage players. Having previously worked for a well-known high street bookmaker for over two years, I held a considerable lay interest in the sociology of gambling, but also certain preconceptions about online gambling and gambling more generally. Initially, distinguishing between gambling and advantage play proved challenging, as I was extremely sceptical of claims that participants could 'account for chance'. However, as investigation progressed a more nuanced understanding of the ways in which individuals engaged with betting establishments emerged. Life history and biography were certainly influential in how I chose gambling as my object of inquiry, but it was my local biographical context which shaped the focus on online gambling. The research was conducted without funding and with limited time available to engage in research activities. Given these two preconditions, the online environment provided a suitable and readily available field of inquiry.

How the researcher defines the field boundaries is a critical reflexive juncture. Unlike traditional ethnographic studies, which are typically determined geographically or physically, in a virtual ethnography the field of study is dictated by connectivity or interaction (Hine 2000, 2005; Markham 2005). With the Internet based on networks and connections, nodes or 'places' where connections meet act as important ethnographic boundaries. Similarly, discourse may be used as a way to identify boundaries and delineate what does or does not fall within the remit of 'the field'. Nevertheless, there is no correct way to determine field boundaries, which are shaped by the decision-making of the individual researcher:

> Boundary markers are underwritten by the researcher's choices about how to find data sites, which search engines to use to sample, whom to interact with, what to say in interaction with participants, what language to use, when to seek and conduct interviews (including both time of day and considering time zones), and so forth.
>
> (Markham 2005, 801)

Thus, the field of study is not already mapped but is sketched and amended as a key feature of the ethnographic process. What is essential, however, is that the virtual ethnographer is conscious of how his/her choices and actions determine the boundaries of his/her field of study.

As this study focused upon an individual gambling subculture, the online forum's interface acted as a clear field site for investigation. This provided a suitable node where 'interactions of interest' (Markham 2005, 801) took place and could be collected, read and analysed through their textual and visual formations. However, as a 'link based phenomenon' (Steinmetz 2012, 29), the Internet is inherently multi-sited, with information often disseminated through hyperlinks which will redirect individuals to different web pages. Whether or not the field site includes hyperlinked material poses a significant dilemma for the researcher. Failure to redirect data collection to material outside of the forum field site may result in the loss of important cultural and contextual information. In this study, many of the links redirected the researcher to unlicensed online gambling sites. As one advantage player notes, unlicensed operators can pose a number of risks:

> There is risk in all my interactions when using online gambling sites. To highlight but a few... there is the risk when it comes to bet settlement, the risk when it comes to bonuses and their winnings, the risk of often vague terms being used to 'rule' against me and the risk of not receiving a payout. Another issue to consider is the risk to personal data. A company may payout and so on, but if you feel the methods they use to deal with sensitive information are poor... then I would have to reassess the risk of playing there.

In responding to such risks, I engaged in high level of preparation and research similar to that exhibited by the advantage play community who fastidiously investigate each new betting establishment that appears on the market. Ownership and betting histories are uncovered, licensees established and records of payment explored, in order to make an assessment of the risk posed to monies that may be deposited and wagered. As one participant observed:

> Research is essential. It may be mundane, but you won't find me depositing until I know who the operators are, more importantly if and where they are licensed. Then it's a case of carefully reading and recording the terms and conditions of the bonus. It's sheer folly to deposit without doing your research.

Ultimately, following each and every single hyperlink proved too onerous a task for the individual researcher constrained by limited research time and resources. Assessing the risk posed by individual operators was central to deciding which online gambling sites to engage with and which to exclude from analysis. In engaging in such decision-making, I actively and consciously contributed to the construction of the field of inquiry which, in turn, pre-structured the data, findings and conclusions of my virtual ethnography.

Given the connectivity of the Internet, face-to-face contact is unlikely in online participant observation. As such, negotiating access and collecting data may differ significantly from a traditional ethnographic study. Gaining access to the field site poses a particular dilemma for the researcher who must balance effective data collection against the ethical concerns which may arise during the investigative process. Gatekeepers have played important roles in traditional criminological ethnographies (see Whyte 1955), providing researchers with access to field sites, orientating and guiding them through such landscapes and acting as a mediator between the researcher and the researched. Virtual ethnographies also pose problems of access, yet unlike traditional ethnographies in which just one gatekeeper is often required, the seamless network of connections may necessitate individual gatekeepers for individual nodes. The researcher will do well to gain access to all nodes through just one gatekeeper and accessing as many gatekeepers as there are relevant nodes is likely to prove challenging. As such, greater time may need to be spent establishing access to multiple field sites, in turn limiting time for data collection and analysis.

Whether to engage in covert or overt participation and participant observation and the implications of such decision-making for both the researcher and the researched are particularly pertinent in virtual ethnographies that examine forum interactions. In overt participant observation, forum profiles and signatures may be developed to meet the ethnographer's needs in the field site. Including information about the researcher's reasons for being on a message board in their user profile is a suitable approach to address forum moderators or users' suspicions or concerns, gain access and collect data. However, affiliations with criminal justice institutions or departments may be omitted from profiles as they can limit site access or impact upon the behaviour of the researched, particularly when studying criminal or deviant activities.

By contrast, in covert research the principle of informed consent is transgressed as participants are unaware that they are the subjects of research inquiry. Covert participant observation or 'lurking' may be employed as an approach in which the researcher 'very self-consciously locates himself at the periphery of a social setting [and] pays strict attention to his degree of obtrusiveness in the situation' (Strickland and Schlesinger 1969, 248). As Hine (2000) has pointed out, lurking limits the researcher's participation in the online community to the detriment of their understanding of that community. However, understanding may be sacrificed in order to prevent the researcher's presence changing the behaviour of the observed group. The advantage play site I examined is an openly accessible virtual public arena, which lessened the requirement for informed consent. Similarly, the site's accessibility ensured that the issue of privacy was also annulled. Participants of the advantage play site are fully aware that the website message boards and instant messaging service's archives are open access with information disseminated freely into the public arena. Moreover, it was made clear throughout the observation period that participants suspected that their discussions and actions were being monitored by certain gambling organisations and businesses.

Engaging in covert participant research was dictated by the fact that advantage players are, by the nature of their activities, furtive individuals. In particular, they demonstrate a deep commitment not to promote themselves, their profits or their actions. Advantage players recognise that generating profits has become more difficult, as bookmakers have become aware of this increasing threat to their revenues. They also acknowledge that limiting the number of individuals engaged in such practices can result in simpler and more profitable products and promotions. Furthermore, with some individuals generating significant sums of money per month, the threat of possible taxation is given serious discussion. Unsurprisingly, this has led to efforts to restrict knowledge of their activities, which indicated that overt research in which informed consent would be secured was likely to be both an inappropriate and unproductive methodological approach to engaging with this subcultural grouping.

I also needed to develop the skills of subterfuge in order to immerse myself in advantage play and collect data from gambling sites while mitigating the risk posed by (potentially rogue) bookmakers. Advantage players seek not to draw attention to themselves through their betting patterns, that is, by betting on out of line odds or obscure markets. If they fail to appear to be 'mug punters',[5] limits may be placed on the amount they can bet, the amount they can bet on certain events or which markets they may wager on. Placing limits on markets, what advantage players call a 'gubbing', can have significant ramifications for the individual. The player may be unable to complete the rollover and withdraw their money successfully. Moreover, advantage players must seek to keep their account 'alive' in order to take part in future promotions and bonuses. An account on which bets are limited to pennies, or worse still account closure, can deprive the advantage player of an important revenue stream. To avoid such outcomes, advantage players often partake in what is known as 'cover play', betting on a range of markets alongside the promotion from which profits may be derived:

> If I have a largish wager requirement to complete, I tend to try to keep to betting on main markets such as the Premier League, Primera, Serie A etc. I also look to mix my bets up, some large, some small. I may also have a bit of a play around on the slots. Obviously, with some books you want to get in and out as quickly as possible, but with others taking your time and also taking a bit of a loss on your profits can lead to future bonuses if they think you are a profitable customer.

Methodical preparation and planning, coupled with meticulous research and a carefully considered approach to engaging with specific bookmakers, was essential if I was to successfully negotiate 'the edge', maintain my accounts, collect data and avoid victimisation.

The ethical dilemmas that shape access and data collection require the researcher to be reflexive throughout the ethnographic process. Moreover, identifying a field, securing access and collecting data are heavily influenced by the identity of the researcher and careful consideration should be given to how biography, life history and the methodological decision-making of the researcher shape and structure the data collected.

Analysis

Traditional criminological research training focuses upon data collection and analysis from physically co-present environments, largely ignoring computer-mediated communication contexts. In computer-mediated communication contexts, the researcher needs to respond to the dilemma of what stimuli are to be categorised as 'data', what is to be excluded and how data can be filtered into appropriate categories for interpretation and analysis. Reflexive attention to the analytical lens, through which researchers examine the visual, verbal and interactive data presented online, is essential if they are to develop appropriate analyses that are able to accurately describe, interpret and explain the phenomena under study. What researchers attend to, collect and consider data will shape the elements that are identified, explored or ignored.

As this research was underpinned by the principles of grounded theory (Glaser and Strauss 1967; Charmaz 2008; Corbin and Strauss 2008), fieldnotes were studied for patterns in attitudes, understandings and experiences of online gambling, gambling organisations, advantage play, crime and victimisation. As such, the thematic codes and categories were developed from within rather than prior to data collection, surfacing as I examined forum discussions and exchanges. However, it should be cautioned that 'while the analysis may indeed emerge from the data, the researcher determines a priori what constitutes data in the first place, making this decision point a crucial reflection point' (Markham 2005, 806). Reflecting on this interpretative path is essential if researchers are to demonstrate consistent and comprehensible decision-making throughout the methodological process.

Interpretative choices regarding meaningful information – utterances and interjections, typographical, grammatical and syntactical 'errors', spelling and typing ability – are all likely to shape analysis. When examining online message boards the analytical lens of the researcher must be attuned to textual messages and the complexities of human expression inherent in such discourse. The multitude of different textual utterances, punctuation and use of emoticons should be given careful attention, as they will provide important insights into a subculture's collective meaning, conventions and stylised representations. Problematically, as the researcher is often interpreting discourse 'from the outside' they may not hold the appropriate knowledge of the subcultural argot, aesthetics and stylised presentation which shape forum interactions. Initially, I struggled to decipher the various abbreviations, cognomens and terminology employed by the advantage play community. This can impede interpretation and analysis of discourse, both its form and content, and, in turn, our understanding of the acts, actions and presentation(s) of participants under study. Moreover, it is essential that the researcher questions the extent to which the identity of participants is shaped by their own discourse, actions and intentions and not the individual inclinations and cultural predispositions of the researcher. This is particularly pertinent, given that the role of the criminological researcher in exploring relatively new online subcultures, such as advantage players, may be to write culture, and not merely reflect it (Clifford and Marcus 1986).

Distinguishing between what is or is not authentic also poses a significant challenge for the virtual ethnographer and warrants careful consideration of the research design. As Markham (2003, 150) importantly recognises: 'cyberculture continues to privilege the researcher's body as the site of experience, the reliant gauge of authenticity, and the residence of knowledge'. Yet, unlike traditional ethnographic environments, the virtual ethnographer does not have recourse to many of the senses – smell, touch, taste and hearing – that would enable them to make sense of the researched, their environment and context. Moreover, the displacement between the virtual ethnographer and their field of study prevents them from understanding the physical context that frames online interactions. External forms of structuration, the physical and aesthetic characteristics of forum users, the smells, sounds, gestures and mimics that characterise interaction are lost in computer-mediated communication contexts. Instead the virtual ethnographer uses textual and visual information as representation of subcultural participants, which replaces these more typical analytical and interpretative filters.

Ultimately, what is considered data, what is considered meaningful information and the limitations of researcher knowledge and sense making filters warrant critical reflection, in order to address methodological flaws and best answer the research question posed.

Representation

In traditional ethnographic studies, embodied research experiences are explored, analysed and represented before being written up in textual forms through research reports, journal articles and monographs. By contrast, in text-based computer-mediated communication contexts, such as this study, the research participants are embodied through text and it is this text which is then subject to representation in a form palatable to an academic audience. In online environments such as the advantage play forums: 'Writing gives appearance to body and thought' (Markham 2003, 152). It is through text that embodiment takes place, self and contexts are constructed and language shifts from an abstraction to a reality.

How text is constructed for presentation or publication has significant ramifications for the members of the advantage play subculture. Textual messages represent the self – either deliberately or not – so how researchers reconstruct or reconfigure participants' sentences impacts upon how cultural members are represented and imagined. As a researcher I held a great deal of power with regard to representing the lived experiences of advantage players, their identities and their actions. As the online subculture I was:

> studying is for all intents and purposes located solely in the pixels on a computer screen, the choices we make to attend to, ignore, or edit these pixels has real consequences for the persons whose manifestations are being altered beyond and outside their control. Hence, if someone types solely in lowercase and uses peculiar spelling, the researcher's correction of grammar may inappropriately ignore and thus misrepresent a participant's deliberate presentation of self. If someone spells atroshiously or uniQueLY, and the researcher corrects it in the research report to make it more readable, a person's creation of identity may be the price of smooth reading.
>
> (Markham 2003, 149–50)

When writing for publication subcultural groups and individual members' identities are presented, framed and embodied by the researcher. However, these identities are also *reconfigured* by the researcher. While this applies to more traditional research approaches, it is particularly pertinent in virtual environments where text is the primary, if not the only, data through which identity is constructed. Journalistic style and editorial processes can significantly reshape utterances and, in turn, research participants' embodied self. Typographical, grammatical and syntactical errors may be corrected in order to enhance readability, while font size, typeface and colour will be standardised to meet a journal's requirements. Fragmented, disjunctive and asynchronous text may be reorganised and produced in a linear, commonsensical and simplified format that makes sense to a specific readership. However, such formatting can lead to the study becoming an abstraction, as conventions in editing and presenting research in written and verbal forms can lead to disingenuous and inaccurate representations of participants' voices. A sensitivity to the fact that: 'Every choice we make about how to represent the self, the participants, and the cultural context under study contributes to how these are understood, framed, and responded to by readers, future students, policy makers, and the like' (Markham 2005, 811) is required from the researcher.

The Internet affords a high degree of anonymity for both the researcher and research participants, but during the course of the study participants often revealed personal details and imparted information which could make them traceable. In response, every effort was made to protect the identities of participants. All names and pseudonyms were removed and all direct quotation shortened or information aggregated, in order to maintain the anonymity of the researched. Ultimately, these representational processes impact upon the identity and autonomy of the research participants under study.

Conclusion

The chapter demonstrates how my construction of the lived meaning of advantage players was shaped, in part, by my own biography, methodological interpretations, decision-making and behaviours. Virtual environments certainly offer new opportunities for criminologists to engage in ethnographic fieldwork, but they also require a considered and reflexive approach to the research process – throughout inquiry, analysis and representational stages. Employing reflexivity as a 'sensitising device' enriched my understanding of how I shaped the research process and its findings. Decision-making with regard to the field of study, what is considered to be meaningful data and how this information was conveyed was not merely procedural, but significantly influenced my representation of the lived experiences of advantage players. Criminologists as virtual ethnographers must seek to grapple with methodological dilemmas, innovate and improvise in order to develop research approaches and sensibilities that are responsive to context in which such studies take place. However, it is also important that we are mindful that how we record, (re)construct, represent and convey (sub)cultural identities and actions has significant ramifications for how such groups and individuals are understood and responded to by a variety of academic and lay audiences.

Notes

1. Banks, J. (2013) 'Edging Your Bets: Advantage Play, Gambling, Crime and Victimisation' *Crime, Media, Culture* 9(2): 171–87.
2. Matched betting is a technique used by individuals to generate profits from free bets and other incentives offered by bookmakers.
3. Bonus hunting involves generating profits from online casino and poker room bonuses.
4. Opportunities for arbitrage or 'arbing' arise on betting markets, due to differences in bookmaker's and betting exchange's odds on the outcome of particular events.

5. 'Mug punter' is a derogatory expression used by the advantage play community to refer to individuals who engage in gambling.

References

Banks, J. (2013) 'Edging Your Bets: Advantage Play, Gambling, Crime and Victimisation' *Crime, Media, Culture* 9(2): 171–87.

CERT-LEXSI (2006) *Cyber-Criminality in Online Gaming.* URL (accessed 5 May 2013): http://www.lexsi.com/telecharger/gambling_cybercrime_2006.pdf

Charmaz, K. (2008) 'Grounded Theory as an Emergent Method'. In S.N. Hess-Biber and P. Leavy (eds) *Handbook of Emergent Methods*, New York: Guildford Press, pp.155–70.

Clifford, J. and Marcus, G. (1986)*Writing Culture*, Berkeley: University of California Press.

Corbin, J.A. and Strauss, A. (2008) *Basics of Qualitative Research*, 3rd ed, London: Sage.

Ferrell, J. (2006) *Empire of Scrounge: Inside the Urban Underground of Dumpster Diving, Trash Picking, and Street Scavenging*, New York: New York University Press.

Ferrell, J. and Hamm, M. (1998) 'True Confessions: Crime, Deviance and Field Research'. In J. Ferrell and M. Hamm (eds) *Ethnography at the Edge: Crime, Deviance and Field Research*, Boston: Northeastern University Press, pp.2–19.

Glaser, B. and Strauss, A. (1967) *The Discovery of Grounded Theory*, Chicago: Aldine.

Hamm, M. (2002) *In Bad Company: America's Terrorist Underground*, Boston: Northeastern University Press.

Hine, C. (2000) *Virtual Ethnography*, London: Sage.

Hine, C. (2005) *Virtual Methods: Issues in Social Research on the Internet*, New York: Berg Publishers.

Librett, M. (2008) 'Wild Pigs and Outlaws: The Kindred Worlds of Policing and Outlaw Bikers' *Crime, Media, Culture* 4(2): 257–69.

Mann, D. and Sutton, M. (1998) 'NetCrime: More Change in the Organisation of Thieving' *British Journal of Criminology* 38(2): 201–29.

Markham, A.N. (2003) 'Representation in Online Ethnographies: A Matter of Context Sensitivity'. In J. Hall, S. Chen and M. Johns (eds) *Online Social Research: Theory, Method, Practice*, New York: Peter Lang, pp.131–45.

Markham, A.N. (2005) 'The Politics, Ethics, and Methods of Representation in Online Ethnography'. In N. Denzin and Y. Lincoln (eds) *Handbook of Qualitative Research*, London: Sage, pp.793–820.

Steinmetz, K.F. (2012) 'Message Received: Virtual Ethnography in Online Message Boards' *International Journal of Qualitative Methods* 11(1): 26–39.

Strickland, D.A. and Schlesinger, L.E. (1969) '"Lurking" as a Research Model' *Human Organisation* 28(3): 248–50.

Whyte, W.F. (1955) *Street Corner Society: The Social Structure of an Italian Slum*, Chicago: University of Chicago Press.

Wright Mills, C. (1959) *The Sociological Imagination*, London: Oxford University Press.

Zaitch, D. and Leeuw, T. de (2010) 'Fighting with Images: The Production and Consumption of Violence Among Online Football Supporters'. In K. Hayward and M. Presdee (eds) *Framing Crime. Cultural Criminology and the Image*, London: Routledge-Cavendish, pp.172–88.

23
Reflexivity and Participatory Policy Ethnography: Situating the Self in a Transnational Criminology of Harm Production

Jarrett Blaustein

Introduction

The concept of reflexivity is central to research that aspires to interpret and reconstruct global, comparative and transnational dimensions of crime and its control. It is crucial for understanding how and why criminal justice policies travel between contexts and for interrogating the motives and the interests of the agents and the institutions which facilitate these 'policy transfers' (Jones and Newburn 2007). Reflexivity in the context of global criminology can be understood as the idea that '[t]here is no one-way street between the researcher and the object of study; rather, the two affect each other mutually and continually in the course of the research process' (Alvesson and Sköldberg 2009, 79). The reflexive praxis described by Alvesson and Sköldberg (2009) holds important methodological implications for criminologists who are interested in studying globalisation 'as an interactive rather than a hegemonic process' (Cain 2000), in other words, a process that is continuously shaped by local and global forces. The concept is therefore crucial for understanding how globalisation facilitates the diffusion of 'Western' mentalities of crime and punishment throughout the Global South (see Chan 2005) and it provides a vehicle for working towards the actualisation of what Bowling (2011, 374 original emphasis) describes as 'a **criminology of harm production** emphasizing the role of the discipline

I would like to thank my colleague Sarah Wydall, participants who attended the ESRC seminar on 'Crime Control and Devolution: Policy-Making and Expert Knowledge in a Multi-tiered Democracy' that took place in Edinburgh on 13 December 2013 and the editors for their feedback on previous drafts of this chapter. I would also like to thank my former colleagues and research subjects at UNDP in BiH for their support.

in documenting the harms produced by global crime control practices and the role of criminologists in speaking truth to power...'.

For researchers afforded the opportunity to utilise ethnographic methods to access the global fields through which transnational criminal justice policy meaning is negotiated and constructed, the 'global' aspect of interactive globalisation can be reconstructed via the researchers' active reflections about how their background, experiences and ethnocentric preconceptions shape their interactions with the field and their interpretations of it. The 'local' aspect can be represented through the researchers' reflections of how their interpretations and interactions may have been altered as a direct result of their progressive immersion in the setting. Continuous reflection during one's field work may allow a researcher to actively situate his/her 'self' within the field of study and recursively mitigate his/her own harm-generating potential. Retrospective analysis further provides the researcher with a method of reconstructing this praxis and representing it in textual form.

This chapter illustrates the alleviatory potential of participatory research on international criminal justice policy transfers in the Global South using retrospective analysis of my ethnographic research with United Nations Development Programme's (UNDP) pilot 'Safer Communities' project in Bosnia-Herzegovina (BiH). The field work took place over a period of three months between January and April 2011 and my access agreement with UNDP in BiH afforded me the unique opportunity to overtly immerse myself in the institutional culture of a multi-lateral international development agency that was actively developing a community safety project for transplant to BiH. Through my roles as a doctoral researcher and a 'Project Intern' with the Safer Communities team, I used overt participant observation, ethnographic interviewing and observational methods to interpret the power asymmetries affecting the police development assistance process and the mediatory capacity of various stakeholders including international development workers and local police officers (see Blaustein 2014).

With this chapter, I reflect specifically on my personal contributions to the development of a UNDP policy brief that outlined the case for introducing community safety partnership reforms to the City of Sarajevo in 2011. The example illustrates that a researcher's awareness of the reflexive praxis described by Cain (2000) can foster the realisation of a particular variant of Bowling's (2011, 374) transnational criminology of harm production that involves limiting the impact of one's presence unless it is clear that it will not exacerbate structural asymmetries or generate what Cohen (1988, 190) describes as 'paradoxical damage', that is, the possibility that even a 'benevolent' criminal justice policy transfer can inadvertently generate harms due to cultural and structural differences between the context of origin and the recipient society (Cohen 1988, 190). To this effect, the chapter highlights how a researcher's direct immersion in an active policy node[1] can create unique opportunities for this individual to move beyond ex post facto critiques of ethnocentrism and the structural inequalities associated with international police development assistance programmes (Ryan 2011; Ellison and Pino 2012) by addressing these issues on a continuous basis as a participant. To be successful in this capacity, the researcher as a cultural and contextual outsider must accept the limits of his/her expertise and exercise modesty in his/her interactions with local stakeholders so as not to undermine their power. Reflexivity as a component of participatory policy research thus provides the researcher with a means of simultaneously achieving a transnational criminology of harm production which allows them to interpret the 'harms produced by global crime control practices' (Bowling 2011, 374) and to achieve modest impact by speaking *truths* to power rather than a singular 'truth'. This distinction is important because it recognises that the reflective praxis of ethnographic research in a transnational setting illuminates a plurality of perspectives and experiences that must not be marginalised by the research process lest key local stakeholders be denied meaningful opportunities to interact with globalisation.

Situating safer communities

Policies associated with the concept of a community safety partnership have proliferated throughout the Global South over the past two decades.[2] They represent an increasingly popular feature of plural policing and crime control models in advanced Western democracies, and their touted success and purported value as locally responsive models governing security at the community level rendered the models an attractive template for entrepreneurial reformers looking to capitalise on an emergent market for police development assistance in developing, transitional and post-conflict societies (Crawford 2009). Community safety partnerships were first introduced to BiH in 2003 by two different international development agencies, the UK's Department for International Development and the Swiss Agency for Development and Cooperation. The logic was that establishing local 'citizen security forums' (CSFs) would complement local community policing initiatives by improving the capacity of the police to initiate holistic solutions to addressing local public safety issues.

By 2009, both of these agencies had either withdrawn their support for community safety reform projects in BiH or were in the final stages of doing so. Members of UNDP's Small Arms Control and Prevention (SACBiH) project learned of this impending policy vacuum and developed a proposal to provide continued support for five CSFs in the municipalities of Bratunac, Prijedor, Sanski Most, Visegrad and Zenica. UNDP approved the project and the SACBiH team proceeded to pilot its 'Safer Communities' project using limited seed funding provided by the SACBiH budget and a small grant from the Danish government. The seed funding covered the salary for an in-house Community Policing Advisor who, along with the SACBiH Project

Manager and a Project Associate, worked with these forums to develop their administrative capacities and develop relevant project activities designed to address local sources of insecurity. Situating my 'self' in the Safer Communities project meant continuously working to gauge the nature and the impact of my involvement with the project by reflecting on how my mentality and actions were being influenced by my progressive immersion in a transnational field as well as the structural politics of liberal state-building in BiH (see Blaustein 2014).

My ethnography of the Safer Communities project highlighted the problems of aid dependency and the ethnocentric proclivities of international development workers tasked with financing community safety partnerships designed to improve the local accountability and responsiveness of security governance in a fledgling, fragmented democracy (Blaustein 2014). Like other critiques of police development assistance (see Ryan 2011; Ellison and Pino 2012), I concluded that the capacity of international development workers to initiate police reforms that prioritised the needs of local policy recipients over the interests of powerful international donors was severely restricted by structural constraints and the limited availability of core funding to support locally defined project activities (Blaustein 2014). Although pessimistic, my conclusion was not entirely fatalistic as my participant observation illuminated the malleability of our collective habitus[3] as well as our agentive capacity as individual members of the Safer Communities project team. Our agency enabled us to participate in a recursive process of 'policy translation' (Lendvai and Stubbs 2009) by assuming the role of transnational policy mediators. This analysis was consistent with Cain's (2000) description of globalisation as an interactive process discussed in the following section.

Policy translation and transnational criminology

'Policy translation' is a conceptual off-shoot of the more widely used term 'policy transfer' which Dolowitz and Marsh (1996, 344) define as the process whereby 'knowledge about policies, administrative arrangements, institutions etc. in one time and/or place is used in the development of policies, administrative arrangements and institutions in another time and/or place'. A growing literature on transnational criminology is critical of policy transfers initiated by Western actors to promote the 'democratisation', 'modernisation' and 'transformation' of criminal justice institutions determined to be underdeveloped or indigenous in the Global South (see Bowling 2011). These concerns draw from Cohen's (1998) discussion of the potential consequences of introducing 'Western Crime Control Models' to the 'Third World' and suggest that these policy transfers are one directional and driven by the interests of powerful donors rather than the needs of recipient societies. The objects of these transfers are said to cause 'paradoxical damage' (Cohen 1998, 189–94; Bowling 2011) to recipient societies and have been described as tainted by ethnocentrism (Cain 2000; Nelken 2009). From a normative perspective, policy transfers associated with police reform in the context of transitional democracies have also been criticised for undermining the political freedoms of recipient societies (Ryan 2011; Ellison and Pino 2012).

Cain's (2000, 86) discussion of ethnocentrism and the interactive character of globalisation provides an important framework for developing a reflexive, 'transnational criminology of harm production' (Bowling 2011). Rather than presenting a deterministic account of globalisation, Cain's analysis recognises that local actors have an important role to play in mitigating the paradoxical damage and structural inequalities of international policy transfers. Cain (2000, 86) writes:

> The trajectory is usually from the more to less powerful, but the recipient groups may, if they choose, if they are strong enough, interact with that idea, re-situate it within their own discourses and practices, modify it, make it their own, and so create an alternative model, which, ideally should then find its own place in a global pool of possibilities.

The remainder of this chapter expands upon the argument that human agency can mediate the forces of globalisation and play a role in mitigating the harms generated by international criminal justice policy transfers. It does so by illuminating the reflexive capacity of researchers and their capacity to alleviate the 'paradoxical damage' (Cohen 1988) that may result from field work in a transnational setting.

Situating my 'self' in safer communities

In assuming the role of a Project Intern with UNDP's Safer Communities team, I contributed to an active police development assistance project in a weak and structurally dependent society. I drafted numerous concept notes that explored the marketability of the project to prospective donors; contributed to the project's sustainability report; conducted a five-week qualitative study of community policing in Sarajevo; and authored a policy brief that outlined UNDP's recommendations for introducing the community safety partnership model to Sarajevo. I openly jotted about my experiences in a small field diary and I spent my evenings reconstructing the days' events as fieldnotes. These fieldnotes established a record of key project activities, documented the institutional culture of UNDP in BiH, reflected on my contributions to the project and described my ongoing interactions with various stakeholders such as my colleagues.

I was assigned the policy brief by the Project Manager in only the second week of the internship. The plan was for me to research and write the report and the Project Manager would provide me with regular feedback. I was also informed that in the next couple of weeks, we would meet with a senior municipal official from Sarajevo Canton to seek his political support for the proposal. Once drafted, the final report would then be reviewed and approved by the Project Manager, translated into Bosnian and submitted to the municipal official and the Minister for Interior Affairs for Sarajevo Canton. I quickly established that the assignment reflected the UNDP's capacity development ethos and its advocacy of generating local ownership of its reforms. In order to align my work with what I interpreted to be the habitus of my colleagues, I made a concerted effort to embrace these principles and use them to structure my work.

The ethics of participation

Despite my admiration for UNDP's 'capacity development' ethos, I had personal reservations about the long-term consequences of my participation in this task. The prospect of taking on the assignment and using it to develop a personal understanding of how development workers at UNDP interpret and contribute to police development assistance was appealing yet the prospect of developing policy recommendations for government officials in a foreign country was intimidating. I lacked local knowledge and feared that if I did somehow manage to produce a competent report my recommendations would inevitably be tainted by my ethnocentric interpretation of the city's problems and my naivety about local politics and governing institutions that would presumably shape the implementation process. What I found perhaps most disconcerting at this early stage of my field work was that my colleagues appeared to be treating me as an expert on the community safety partnership model due to my educational background and long-term residence in the United Kingdom. To accord somebody expert status is to empower that individual and I did not wish to be empowered because I recognised that my knowledge of operational aspects of community safety partnerships was almost entirely academic. At this point in my research I had yet to encounter the formal terminology of 'paradoxical damage' (Cohen 1988) but my hastily jotted fieldnotes indicate that even a novice researcher is capable of reflecting on his/her harm-generating potential as a participant:

> I arrive at the office at 8 am [and] the Project Manager tells me...that I am to write a policy brief extolling the virtues of the Safer Communities model for application in Sarajevo and add some recommendations [for] how it should be implemented in relation to the city's structures/institutions...I am very excited about this prospect but it occurs to me that I have no idea what I am doing or how to even write a policy brief! I hope that I do not ruin the state of policing in Sarajevo...any more than it already is at least.

> (Fieldnotes, 21 January 2011)

In order to ethically justify my participation in this particular task, I decided that I would need to establish that the policy brief was actually warranted on the basis of local needs. The emphasis on local needs reflected both my interpretation of UNDP's capacity development ethos and my commitment to the harm principle. The fact that my ethical obligation as a researcher aligned with UNDP's commitment to capacity development in this particular instance was important because it ensured that my ethical judgment would also influence the team's decision of whether or not to promote the model in Sarajevo Canton.

Working with my colleagues, I established that my participation was ethically justifiable because there was an evident rationale for pursuing the project in relation to local needs. Specifically, we determined that there was a lack of coordination between the police and different municipal agencies and that this might be addressed through the creation of a 'CSF'. The secondary data that we consulted in forming this judgment consisted of a public perceptions survey that was commissioned by UNDP in BiH in the Fall of 2010 and an evaluation report on local community policing practices throughout Bosnia that was written and researched by a UK-based UNDP Evaluation Consultant in 2010.[4] The decision also benefitted from the subjective experiences of my colleagues who were long-term residents of Sarajevo. My colleagues openly reflected on their perceptions of the security situation in Sarajevo and the advantages and limitations of the capacity development approach as a means of promoting local ownership of security sector reforms. These reflections allowed me to critically interpret the empirical evidence; they also represented a valuable source of data for my research.

Safer communities as interactive globalisation

In early February, I met with a senior municipal official in Sarajevo to discuss the policy brief and to generate local support for implementing the proposal. Also in attendance was the Safer Communities team's Project Manager and a graduate student from the University of Sarajevo who had volunteered his time to contribute to the research for the policy brief. The encounter and my colleagues' subsequent reactions to my concerns illustrate the interactive nature of globalisation described by Cain (2000).

At the beginning of the meeting, the official made it clear that he was interested in specific policy recommendations that could be used to improve community safety in Sarajevo. The meeting then took an unexpected turn when the official proceeded to discuss his interest in working with UNDP to develop sentencing reforms having recently read about the benefits of 'alternative sentences' (for instance, community penalties) in Serbia and believed that they might help to reduce overcrowding of prisons in BiH (Fieldnotes, 3 March 2011). From the meeting, I quickly determined that the official's interpretation of 'community safety' was significantly broader than my own or that of UNDP in BiH and I left there fearing that I was in over my head. I returned to the office and discussed my concerns with the project's Community Policing Advisor who assured me that it was not our role as development workers to propose concrete policy recommendations. Rather, the Community Policing Advisor told me, 'UNDP is about giving local stakeholders the tools to do this' and that this was why we advocated a flexible framework for establishing CSFs in local communities. Along these lines, a second member of the Safer Communities team advised me to 'keep it broad' and 'avoid too much detail' because we need to 'let them figure it out for themselves' (personal communications, 3 March 2011).

The municipal official as a local stakeholder and my colleagues in their capacity as representatives of a global institution each recognised that the content of the policy brief would be decided upon within a transnational policy node that was largely inaccessible to the prospective policy recipients. This interaction therefore illustrates the power imbalance between the global and the local with respect to international police development assistance in BiH. My colleagues, however, were aware of structural asymmetries inherent to their work and they worked to facilitate balanced interactions wherever possible. In this instance, my colleagues did so by advising me to 'keep it broad' so that a plurality of local actors would later have a meaningful opportunity to interact with our recommendations and adapt or reject them for application in Sarajevo Canton as they saw fit. As a cultural outsider, I felt reassured by this guidance because it provided me with a suitable justification for extracting myself from a situation in which I feared that I would find myself 'speaking truth to power' (Bowling 2011) that I had yet to fully comprehend.

Final drafts

I submitted a draft of the policy brief to the Project Manager on 31 March 2011. I had actually finished drafting the report weeks earlier but held-off on submitting it in order to afford myself a chance to reflect on the evidence generated from a parallel study that I had been conducting which focused on the actual implementation of community policing in Sarajevo. Based on my observation of two specialist community policing units, I hastily added a final paragraph to the policy brief that included a specific recommendation that:

> Based on the findings of a recent assessment of [community policing] activities in Grad Sarajevo, it is our recommendation that a citizen security forum be established in [a specific municipality] at the earliest possible convenience...It is clear to us that launching this forum would help to reinforce the authority of these CBP officers in the eyes of their partners as well as to enhance their capacity to respond to less conventional community safety issues that they regularly encounter

during the course of their duties. For example, such a forum would provide the officers with a functional venue for addressing issues such as stray dogs or poor street lighting as it would serve to enhance the transparency of this problem-solving process and create additional pressures on key service providers to respond to the community's needs in a timely manner.

(Draft of Policy Brief, 31 March 2011)

The Project Manager cut the entire paragraph from the final version of the policy brief because it was too specific and thus, incompatible with the capacity development ethos.

The final version of the policy brief which was ultimately submitted to the Deputy Mayor and the Ministry of Interior Affairs in July 2011 contained no specific recommendations. Rather, the Executive Summary (translated) proposed that:

A Community Steering Board (CSB) should be formally established through cooperation between the Mayor's office and the Ministry of Interior Affairs by [date withheld] to oversee the implementation and institutionalization of this plan by the end of the year;

CSB should create an Operational Security Plan (OSP) based on SARA methodology that defines the city's community safety and security priorities annually and a rulebook that will serve to guide the activities of Citizen Security Forums (CSF) at the municipal level;

Establishment of discretionary budget (renewable) that will enable CSB to coordinate and financially support CSF activities that aligns with CSB Operational Safety Plan;

CSFs should be formally established within each municipality. CSFs should be officially recognized by the municipal councils (similar to 'Commissions');

Establishment of discretionary budget through the municipal councils (renewable) that will enable CSFs to implement community safety projects in cooperation with key service providers;

Formal requirement that municipal-level Mayors serve as permanent members in CSFs;

CSFs designate procedure for utilizing SARA methodology to identify and address [community-level] security and public safety issues.

(UNDP 2011, 4)

Exiting the field has since made it difficult for me to gauge the impact of this document and of my participation with the project but I have learned from the graduate student who attended the meeting with the Deputy Mayor that the policy brief prompted the formation of a working group comprised of local government officials, criminal justice practitioners and local academics from the University of Sarajevo who met to discuss the proposals in September 2011. Insofar as my participation appears to have fostered a public dialogue that was relevant and accessible to a diverse group of local stakeholders, I am content that my modest contribution to the field did not serve to marginalise the preferences of local citizens. Nor did my participation 'speak truth to power' (Bowling 2011) by constructing or validating a 'solution' to an externally defined problem. I am therefore grateful to my colleagues for welcoming me into their world and continuously helping me to conduct myself in a manner consistent with the harm principle.

Conclusion

This chapter demonstrated the need for modest engagement with a transnational field by reflecting on my ethnography of the Safer Communities project in BiH and through my discussion about why justifying a modest policy intervention on the basis of an outsider's interpretation of local needs is challenging for both methodological and ethical reasons. Methodologically, the researcher is limited by his/her ethnocentrism and his/her status as a cultural outsider. These limitations, combined with the fact that the researcher may not be a permanent member of the field, highlight the ethical imperative for researchers to minimise impact if it may generate harm. Reflexive awareness supports one's ability to achieve this 'transnational criminology of harm production' (Bowling 2011) and to facilitate deliberations that create opportunities for local stakeholders to meaningfully participate in globalisation as an interactive process. A 'transnational criminology of harm production' (Bowling 2011) in this sense is concerned with both the harms generated by others and the harms or the potential harms generated by one's 'self'.

The reflexive praxis which makes this transnational criminology of harm production achievable through one's field work is grounded in Cain's (2000) discussion of interactive globalisation, Cohen's (1998) reflections on 'paradoxical damage' in the Third World and most recently in Bowling's (2011) work on 'transnational criminology'. The ethos does not reject the possibility that international research on policing and police development assistance in the Global South may generate positive impact but rather it recognises that often, less is more. On a methodological level, it further suggests that an ethnographic approach readily lends itself to a transnational criminology of harm production because its epistemological orientation assumes that the researcher is inseparable from their field of study. Reflexive awareness provides ethnographers with a means of interpreting the subjectivities generated through their participant observation and it also provides them with a means of regulating their own ethnocentric interactions with the field.

However, it should also be considered that mixed-method approaches may also be reconciled with a transnational criminology of harm production and benefit from its call for modesty. For example, Northern criminologists training Southern practitioners and researchers to utilise experimental and quasi-experimental methods as a means of supporting criminal justice transformation must exercise reflexive awareness lest their instructions and the resultant experimental designs reflect their own ethnocentric definitions of the field instead of those of key local stakeholders. For this reason, leading proponents of experimental criminology including Peter Neyroud have discussed the importance of grounding experiments in a solid foundation of ethnographic research (see Hills et al. 2013). The implication is that a transnational criminology of harm production can accommodate various methods but that it requires researchers to acknowledge their limitations and the potential implications of their involvement in an active policy process. They must reflect on the ways in which structural power asymmetries may enhance their perceived expertise and disassociate themselves with the expert label when necessary. They must do these things before they 'speak truth to power' (Bowling 2011) or better yet, work to ensure that their research speaks truths to power. Finally, they must resist the temptation to construct a problem to solve simply because the occasion or an attractive template presents itself.

Notes

1. A policy node describes a social space at which different actors, institutions and structures converge for the purpose of shaping an active policy-making process. The nodal space may correspond to an institutional setting or emerge through the interactions between different institutional stakeholders. The Safer Communities project represented an ideal policy node for using participatory policy ethnography to interpret the transnational power dynamics of police development assistance because it was temporally stable (i.e. it was located within an established institutional setting) yet the prospect of future instability that arose from UNDP's constant need to justify the existence of the node to current and prospective donors facilitated a reflective dialogue regarding the aims and impact of the project (see Blaustein 2014).
2. Some of the background and conceptual material from this section is based on Blaustein (2014).
3. Habitus refers to structured mentalities and dispositions that shape the practices and perceptions of the individuals who collectively populate a field. This simplified definition of habitus draws from definitions by Elias (2000) and Bourdieu (1977) and is intended to emphasise the idea that habitus is shaped by the continuous interplay between structure and agency and between objective and subjective forces.

4. The public perceptions survey and the evaluation report are internal UNDP documents. My access agreement with UNDP established my permission to reference these documents. The data should not be treated as 'scientific', it is for illustrative purposes only.

References

Alvesson, M. and Sköldberg, K. (2009) *Reflexive Methodology*, London: Sage.

Blaustein, J. (2014) 'The Space Between: Negotiating the Contours of Nodal Security Governance through "Safer Communities" in Bosnia-Herzegovina' *Policing and Society* 24(1): 44–62.

Bourdieu, P. (1977) *Outline of a Theory of Practice*, Cambridge: Cambridge University Press.

Bowling, B. (2011) 'Transnational Criminology and the Globalization of Harm Production'. In C. Hoyle and M. Bosworth (eds) *What Is Criminology?* Oxford: Oxford University Press, pp.361–80.

Cain, M. (2000) 'Orientalism, Occidentalism and the Sociology of Crime' *British Journal of Criminology* 40(2): 239–60.

Chan, J. (2005) 'Globalisation, Reflexivity and the Practice of Criminology'. In J. Sheptycki and A. Wardak (eds) *Transnational & Comparative Criminology*, Abingdon: Glasshouse Press, pp.337–57.

Cohen, S. (1988) 'Western Crime-Control Models'. In S. Cohen (ed.) *Against Criminology*, New Brunswick: Transaction Books, pp.172–202.

Crawford, A. (2009) *Crime Prevention Policies in Comparative Perspective*, Cullompton: Willan.

Dolowitz, D. and Marsh, D. (1996) 'Who Learns What from Whom: A Review of the Policy Transfer Literature' *Political Studies* XLIV: 343–57.

Elias, N. (2000) *The Civilizing Process*, London: Blackwell.

Ellison, G. and Pino, N. (2012) *Globalization, Police Reform and Development*, Basingstoke: Palgrave MacMillan.

Hills, A., Neyroud, P., and Sheptycki, J. (2013) 'Experimental Criminology and Evidence-based Policing: The Future of Democratically Responsive Policing in the Global South?' At the *European Society of Criminology Conference*, September 2013, Budapest, Hungary.

Jones, T. and Newburn, T. (2007) *Policy Transfer and Criminal Justice*, Maidenhead: Open University Press.

Lendvai, N. and Stubbs, P. (2009) 'Assemblages, Translation and Intermediaries in South East Europe' *European Societies* 11(5): 673–95.

Nelken, D. (2009) 'Comparative Criminal Justice: Beyond Ethnocentrism and Relativism' *European Journal of Criminology* 6(4): 291–311.

Ryan, B. (2011) *Statebuilding and Police Reform: The Freedom of Security*, Abingdon: Routledge.

UNDP (2011) Kratki Pregled Politika: Partnerstvo za Signurnije Zajednice Grada Sarajevo. Sarajevo.

24
Innovative Justice: According to Whom?

Hannah Graham and Rob White

Introduction

This chapter offers critical reflections about the challenges, paradoxes and opportunities involved in conducting international criminological research about innovative justice initiatives and creative ways of working with offenders. Engaging with people and pioneering projects at the frontiers of justice become even more intriguing and complex when these are to be done across cultures and national borders. Claims of 'innovation' and 'success' are inevitably relative and contextualised, subject to diverse interpretation and frequently contested. In this chapter, we briefly describe an international research initiative we are conducting, offering an analytical critique of its core components and some of the key questions that have emerged in the process.

Pursuing innovative justice

'Innovative Justice' is an international research initiative that consolidates and disseminates information about creative, collaborative and pioneering approaches to justice. Established in early 2013 in Tasmania, Australia, the study involves local, regional and international data collection and interdisciplinary collaboration. The study and its findings are to be disseminated in a number of forms and forums, including a book (Graham and White 2014) and a website. A few research questions capture our interest: What constitutes innovative justice? How are ex/offenders, practitioners and communities creatively engaged in innovative justice? What social and other consequences flow from adoption of innovations in criminal justice, and for whom?

We are seeking to shift away from punitive and highly politicised representations of criminality and criminal justice, the normal grist for the media mill in many jurisdictions. Instead, this research centres on the lived experiences and stories of ex/offenders, practitioners and other stakeholders which can serve as refreshing counter-frames to normative media representations that distort the human condition, entrench patterns of othering and justify coercion. As Brayford et al. (2010) put it, we are passionate about discovering 'what else works?'

Our concerns in this regard should not be seen as somehow naïvely ignoring or glossing over systemic or individual failures and the volatile scenarios that regularly occur in criminal justice systems and prisons around the world. Public anxieties, stereotypes and sensationalistic media coverage of these things will not cease. For our part, we refuse to build research agendas and academic careers upon fuelling the expansion of retributive justice and the endemic preoccupation with risk exemplified in such trends. Rather, this study seeks to add to, counterbalance and, to a certain extent, challenge the normative and traditional using new insights, intelligent ideas and hopeful results.

In the 'Innovative Justice' research, mixed methods are used to gather personal stories, practice wisdom and experience from interviews and ethnographic observation, secondary data analysis (e.g. media articles, annual reports, social media content) and photographic snapshots to offer evocative glimpses into excellent projects that largely happen 'behind closed doors'. The following serve as examples of the range and types of initiatives that are of interest:

- *Gardening, horticulture and 'green justice':* including community gardens in prisons and communities where offenders, practitioners and volunteers cultivate healthy produce, which is distributed to people in disadvantaged communities in partnership with charities and community groups. Also of interest are 'green collar jobs' training initiatives, sustainability in prisons initiatives and community-based environmental conservation initiatives involving ex/offenders;
- *Animal welfare and animal therapy:* including offenders volunteering as animal foster carers in collaboration with animal welfare organisations or training assistance dogs to be given as companions for people with disabilities, and the therapeutic benefits of using assistance dogs with witnesses, victims of crime and defendants in the courtroom and forensic interviews;
- *The arts:* including performing arts and prison theatre productions, offender art exhibitions in collaboration with museums and galleries, offenders being trained and paid to produce high-quality needlework and embroidery and fashion design and runway shows in prison and the community;
- *Creative prison industries and entrepreneurship initiatives:* including meaningful paid work that aids offenders to develop their skills and entrepreneurship abilities in preparation to gain and maintain employment in the community;

- *Natural disaster aid and recovery efforts:* including offenders volunteering in preventative efforts as well as recovery efforts with at-risk communities and residents before and after natural disasters and extreme weather events;
- *Environmental conservation:* including collaborative initiatives between environmental organisations, scientists and researchers and corrective services to restore places and environments that have been damaged, raise endangered species of animals, propagate plants;
- *Education initiatives:* including initiatives where new and inspiring approaches encourage ex/offender participation in learning and training or take on the role of trainer, researcher or educator;
- *Sports and health initiatives:* including prisoners on day release volunteering as accredited umpires for football and cricket events in the community, large-scale sporting events and competitions and other health projects;
- *Tailor-made initiatives with unique groups of people:* including court innovation and therapeutic justice initiatives, restorative peace-making initiatives to resolving conflicts, specialist policing initiatives and creative initiatives with different types and groups of offenders (e.g. indigenous offenders, offenders with cognitive disabilities, violent offenders, terminally ill prisoners and terrorist or politically or religiously motivated hate crime offenders);
- *Social inclusion and systems innovations:* including whole-of-government approaches to offender reintegration and desistance, community-wide awareness raising campaigns that promote social inclusion and human rights, and reduce stigma and inequality.

The science and evidence base that underpin these initiatives may be well established and patently obvious, intentionally inconspicuous or, in some cases, still emerging. Our role, as researchers, is to foster knowledge exchange about evidence *and* experience-based practices, linking the applied with the analytical to understand what works for whom, why and in what contexts and conditions.

The research aims to promote innovation and improvement in services and systems that work with ex/offenders

- In the hope of supporting individual *ex/offenders* towards desistance, reintegration and opportunities to live meaningful lives in the community, independent of the criminal justice system;
- To promote greater professional capacity, collaboration and creativity among *practitioners* and their agencies;
- To recognise and celebrate *community* engagement in justice in ways that increase community safety and advance social inclusion and citizenship.

The research will be used to produce a conceptual framework and other resources for understanding and theorising what constitutes 'innovative justice'. In this, we draw on criminological scholarship, as well as considering new applications of theory and practice relating to social innovation, entrepreneurship and intrapreneurship, and the broader social sciences. Researching and conceptualising innovative justice is not an easy mission, but it is proving to be one of the more inspiring and fruitful pursuits of our professional careers.

The intellectual origins of this study and our conceptualisation of innovative justice are inspired and informed by critical criminology, restorative justice and desistance scholarship. Critical criminologists advocate pressing reasons for why criminal justice institutions and processes need to change and innovate, emphasising inequalities in who is subject to punishment and social control and exposing the failings and harms of traditional approaches (see Garland 2001; Scraton 2007; Scraton and McCulloch 2009; Wacquant 2009; Reiman and Leighton 2012). Restorative justice highlights the importance of working together to repair harm and support reintegration, ensuring that offenders, victims, families and communities are active in the design and practice of criminal justice interventions (Braithwaite 1989; Zehr 1990; Walgrave 2008; Van Wormer and Walker 2013). Desistance scholars seek to explain how and why people stop offending and change, offering empirical and practical insights into how services, structures and social relations within and beyond the criminal justice system can be reconfigured to successfully support change (see Maruna 2001; Farrall and Calverley 2006; McNeill 2006, 2012a; Porporino 2010, Graham 2012; McNeill et al. 2012a, 2012b). The common strength of these areas is the pragmatism with which the analytical is linked to the applied and the capacity to acknowledge the influence of agency, context *and* structure – which is highly relevant to an international study considering what constitutes innovative justice and why. In keeping with such intellectual origins, a necessary part of our own reflexive practice is to question and critique the core concepts that we employ.

What do we mean by innovative?

Innovation is imbued with connotations of excellence, entrepreneurial ingenuity and creativity. A basic premise of the term 'innovative' is that something is being created, trialled or experienced that presents a new better way in which to provide a product, service or solution to an existing problem or mode of service delivery. The emphasis is on novelty, although as a process innovation may refer to the bringing together of various ideas and practices in a new reconfiguration or to specific ideas and methods that lead to a better end result. Innovation is thus tied to performance. In an institutional context, it is about improving service efficiencies as part of producing something else (e.g. more effective staff interactions and collaborative partnerships) and/or improving the outputs and impact associated with the service (e.g. reducing reoffending rates). Again, the question of performance and quality according to whom remains pertinent.

Within the context of criminal justice, innovation has a number of dimensions. Consider, for example, the sources of innovation. New ways of doing things, new programmes, new projects and new policies can emerge for a variety of different reasons: from client or staff suggestions for improvement (based upon experience at the coalface) through to the necessity to respond to major system failures (such as cost blow-outs due to soaring prison populations). New ways of doing things may start via informal processes, before becoming institutionalised. For example, family group conferencing in New Zealand not only had its conceptual and cultural origins in Mâori social life, but it was instigated, informally, by Mâori practitioners who, tired of the failures of the pre-existing system, put their own ways of working in its place 'without permission'. Legitimacy came later, after initial successes became apparent. Trial by doing is a true test of innovation. Yet, when institutionalisation does come, big questions can be asked as to whose interests (Mâori and/or Pâkehâ/white people, the community and/or the criminal justice system) shape the final organisational form and content of the innovation (Tauri 1999).

Reflections on bicultural interventions are also relevant for those in other cultures and countries wanting to learn from and replicate the successes of a given initiative. Understanding diversity within and between cultures and jurisdictions becomes paramount and, in our study, comparative criminological theories and methodologies are essential in guiding cross-cultural analyses (see Nelken 2010, 2011). Innovation and originality are partly in the eye of the beholder. What key stakeholders are doing in Norway or Scotland may be 'old hat' to them, but may present new knowledge to those working in Australia or the United States. Importantly, it is stories told about specific practices from 'somewhere else' that frequently lead to local adaptations and applications. Innovation is not about 'one size fits all'; rather, it is about how people in many different social, cultural, economic and political contexts manipulate, thresh out, realign and try out new concepts, new methods and new practices. Innovation occurs in context and amid complexity. Yet, borrowing and re-purposing ideas is part and parcel of what innovation is about. Innovation resonates beyond itself. This is why the use of case studies in comparative analytical exercises can be so worthwhile, as it can be a catalyst for learning, motivation and change (Heckenberg 2011). To be innovative means to be flexible and to take chances. It does not mean to simply take someone else's ideas and models 'off the shelf' and/or to 'follow the manual'. In criminal justice settings, we are increasingly finding that 'quiet revolutions' (as one practitioner aptly described it) are being driven by 'intrapreneurs', trusted employees or volunteers who work in or have good connections with the system but is granted the freedom to innovate and change things in ways that differ or go beyond the status quo and routine procedures.

Sometimes things seem to happen by chance, as when extenuating circumstances demand something different from offenders than they are otherwise afforded the freedom to do. At such times, inspiration can be drawn from seeing through the veneer of 'master statuses', labels and system imperatives (White and Graham 2010). The expressions on the faces of prisoners when undertaking strenuous physical labour that will benefit someone else in their community (as with natural disaster emergency relief work) may spark ideas about thinking and working differently with some classifications or groups of offenders. A simple 'thank you' from the farmer whose property is being re-built after a cyclone or a community thanksgiving ceremony in recognition of sacrificial and heroic endeavours in bushfire-affected towns can have powerful effects on those upon whom these things are conferred. What is observed, felt and said can aid an offender in the process of becoming something other than a stigmatised labelled 'Other'. In affording them the freedom to take responsibility and help their community when they need it most, we are affording them second chances, opportunities for restored social standing and a strengthened sense of agency and citizenship. Justice done differently has the capacity to make a real difference, especially when pro-social roles and generative activities are formally recognised by authorities, such as parole boards. What counts in this is seeing and speaking of 'offenders' in other than 'offensive' terms (Graham and White 2014). In this research, when we visit prisons, prisoners regularly ask us what we do, even if they have been told in advance. Where appropriate, we enjoy asking them the same question in return, as this is often met with positive responses that have nothing to do with being in prison, for example, 'I'm a gardener, let me show you our community garden', 'I'm an artist' or 'I'm a carpenter, let me show you our workshop'. The time spent meeting people on their terms, doing what they are good at and becoming someone different who is making a difference, positions them as educator and expert in telling their 'good news story' and introduces us to their 'colleagues' and 'friends' (professional or otherwise) who are helping them in the process of change. It is perhaps unsurprising that the language and labels in conversations about innovation and change are rarely negative or pathologising, but processes of self-discovery and positive labelling.

Discovering and trying new and original ideas is one thing, sustaining them is another. When does the innovative cease being innovative? Is it when the latest concept, model or programme becomes institutionalised or mainstream or stops being evaluated? At what point does the 'new' become the 'old', and is this a bad thing? How can sustainability and longevity be fostered in institutionalising innovation into the fabric of the criminal justice system? These are the sorts of questions that remain after the excitement dies down, the novelty wanes and the bureaucrats and bean counters take aim. The vitality of innovation needs sustenance in the same way that liberty requires vigilance. Innovation needs to outlive 'the pilot project' stage and continue irrespective of personalities and electoral cycles. If it is owned by one key driver, it is likely to flounder or fail when that person moves on. The common variables are active participation and collaboration across stakeholders arising from commitment to a common cause. Again, it is here that values have the most to say – and the last word. Innovation does not take place in a social and ethical vacuum. It is inherently about purpose and prospects. This is what gives it its existential weight and its moral authority and quality. We innovate to do 'good', to restore and reciprocate and 'make good' (Maruna 2001) – and if this is not the result or the consequence, then progressive it is not.

The paradoxes of justice

The reflexive pursuit of what constitutes innovative justice, by its nature, entails consideration of positive, negative and ambiguous factors. Rights cannot be considered without due regard for risks and responsibilities. Success and hard-won changes and improvements make little sense without appreciation for how far a person or programme has come over time. Some tensions represent irreconcilable differences, and this is where the paradoxes of justice emerge.

One of the most pressing tensions in this study is thinking about when good things happen in bad places, when outstanding and original practices co-exist and are even co-located in places where average (in the sense of relatively 'neutral' and routine, such as psychosocial 'talking therapies') and even harmful practices also occur. For example, should we draw attention to socially inclusive and progressive initiatives in jurisdictions that also have capital punishment? Are we complicit in upholding what are, in general, brutal and brutalising systems of social control by selecting out the few 'good news stories' that such regimes simultaneously produce? Do such stories belie the reality of the mixed messages that some offenders can change and yet some offenders deserve to be killed for what they have done? Innovative justice in practice, for example, may sit in tension with ongoing inhumane conditions for the many, and their ineligibility to take part in what are still wonderful innovative initiatives.

The death penalty notwithstanding, security classifications and divergence in penal practices mean that there can be ongoing tensions occurring in the same jurisdiction and, indeed, the same prison. Again, some are offered innovative options and chances of a fresh start, meanwhile others are further excluded on the grounds of risk and their past and subject to coercive practices in 'criminogenic' institutions that fail to achieve their corrective mission and may do more harm than good. Paradoxically, both approaches are done in the name of justice. Yet, there is the potential to 'throw out the baby with the bathwater', if we refuse to accept that contradiction and paradox will inevitably arise out of criminal justice systems. It is not necessarily hypocritical to extol the benefits of the progressive intervention that seemingly lies embedded within a larger repressive whole. Systemic change has to start somewhere; hopeful new beginnings may start small and the novel may presage wider transformations to come.

Innovative justice is not a passing fad, nor should novelty connote the trivial and be used to endorse surface-level changes that lack impact and substance. Being clear about the *purpose* of innovation is particularly important in this regard. Innovation can and does have unintended consequences, both good and bad. Accordingly, it is vital that new ideas and methods be evaluated on a continual basis, in specific settings and contexts, and in regard to specific service providers and clientele. Sometimes what is presented as 'innovation' is reflective of 'paradoxical harm'. This refers to instances when governments or agencies accept or implement apparently novel solutions to existing problems, in full knowledge that, in fact, little will change – for workers or for offenders or for families and communities. Changing the labels of 'same practice' does not change the practice. Rehabilitation foisted upon offenders, irrespective of the terms it is clothed in, is still rehab without choice. The paradox of paradoxical harm lies in the promise of progressive change but being left with nothing more than the said reality of the status quo.

Generativity and reciprocity – opportunities for meaningful giving in the context of community – emerge as important factors in innovative justice initiatives and processes, not only for the good work that might be done, but to safeguard against some of the paradoxical harms and pitfalls of justice as it is currently done. Criminal justice, especially in the form of punishment, is not a passive process, nor is it value neutral. Justice and supporting desistance from crime are as much social projects (i.e. we are all responsible) as they are personal ones (i.e. each individual is responsible) (White and Graham 2010; McNeill et al. 2012b). Unfortunately, the former can be misconstrued and misappropriated in ways that impact on the latter and, paradoxically, effectively impede it. Ironically, this is often done with good intentions. The potential contradictions and tensions start to emerge when justice is done to, rather than done *with* offenders. Individual pathologising and paternalism can be subtle or blatantly obvious, depending on the individual as well as the crime. Either way it undermines the very agency that the individual needs to embark on sustained change and redemption and underemphasises, or worse still, ignores the social determinants and conditions that gave rise to their offending behaviour in the first place.

The paradox of justice revolves around how questions of responsibility and redemption are construed within the criminal justice context.

Responding to these issues requires acknowledgement of 'failed citizenship' in two senses: of offenders failing in their citizenship responsibilities as well as having been failed as citizens by the State and others (McNeil 2012b). Responsible citizenship is built upon a foundation of reciprocal and restorative practices that implicate all (Walgrave 2008). In order to effectively safeguard against some of the aforementioned issues, the notion of the 'duality of responsibility' is relevant (White 2008; White and Graham 2010). This refers to, on the one hand, the responsibility of society to address the social determinants of offending (such as poverty, unemployment and racism). On the other hand, a vital part of responsibility is to acknowledge the doing of harm, and that you have actually hurt somebody or damaged something. Taking responsibility means that the offender, too, should have an interest in making things right, in repairing the harm and in addressing the wrongs. Several of the innovative initiatives in our research provide opportunities for doing this, in non-stigmatising ways. This reinforces the essential point that innovative justice is by its very nature a communal and collective process, with implications for everyone associated with it. The other side of the duality of responsibility is the benefits of reciprocity: collectively and individually owning failure and taking responsibility may afford opportunities for owning and sharing success. In this, social, human and economic capital may need to be invested as capital cannot be expended and given by those upon whom it has not been conferred.

If social justice is to underpin criminal justice reforms, then questions of 'success' and 'what works' and 'what helps' demand answers from outside the logic of social control and the realm of conventional offender management. From this perspective, creative interventions that enable rehabilitation and support desistance are innovative only insofar as they push the boundaries and transcend the corrective mission and the urge to punish. Those involved need to be willing to give up adversarial zero sum games (i.e. pitting offenders vs. victims and the community). Innovative justice has an a priori commitment to human rights, desistance and safety for the benefit of all stakeholders – otherwise it is not innovative and it is not just.

Engaging diversity and vulnerability

The overrepresentation of vulnerabilities and inequalities in criminal justice is relevant to a study that seeks to conduct research with vulnerable people as well as contribute to efforts to change the systems in which they find themselves. Engaging with vulnerabilities and diversity necessitates respect, sensitivity to culture and legitimacy. This refers to the perceptions by those involved that processes are fair and appropriate to the task at hand and that they are being treated with respect. If an intervention or service does not have these things, then it is more unlikely to succeed in its purposes (Crawford and Hucklesby 2013). If our research lacks these things, it is less likely to discover the antecedents of social innovation and the cultures and contexts which foster it.

In being mindful of vulnerabilities and inequalities, the concept of responsivity is important, as one innovative initiative for a specific group will not necessarily be helpful for all members of that group. When it comes to innovation, not everyone responds in the same way. This is where the notion of 'co-production' as a driver of innovative justice again comes to the fore (Weaver 2011; Maruna et al. 2012; Barry 2013). For how are interventions and services to be fit for purpose without active and meaningful offender participation, negotiation and decision-making in their design and evaluation? But respect is a two-way street – responsibility is dual. So too, experience and expertise is not the preserve of the offender or client alone. The evidence and contributions of practitioners, sectoral leaders, criminologists and other academics need to be valued and respected as well. Reflexivity and legitimacy entail a certain amount of 'give and take', but do not necessarily mean compromise on fundamentally important values.

In light of these factors and dynamics, the choice of methodology in our research emerges as central for how it shapes the research process and participants' voices. We have chosen to use Appreciative Inquiry in tandem with mixed methods of data collection. Fittingly for our purposes, Appreciative Inquiry originated from business innovation and organisational change research. It is an emerging methodology in criminal justice, one that is gaining increasing credence for its capacity to accommodate diversity and vulnerability with sensitivity. Appreciative Inquiry has proven effective in engaging offenders in prisons, in drug courts and on probation, as well as prison officers, probation officers and other practitioners in research with a view to improving practice and realising organisational change (Liebling et al. 1999; Liebling 2011; Fischer et al. 2007; Robinson et al. 2012, 2013).

An appreciative approach seeks to know what is and considers what could be, re-framing 'the now' in anticipation and imagination of the 'not yet', from the perspective of those involved (Graham 2013). At the heart of Appreciate Inquiry is the recognition of power relations and the synthesis of critical thinking with pragmatic listening. It seeks to avoid making value judgments, in order that the voices of many may be heard. Our research involves hearing diverse perspectives including the judiciary, executive directors and national directors, along with offenders, psychologists, prison officers, scientists, lawyers, ministers of religion, academics, marketing and communications specialists, students, community volunteers and various others. The purpose of this type of listening, however, is action oriented. Appreciative Inquiry re-frames practices and problems away from a deficit focus and preoccupation with risk, instead tapping into opportunities, strengths and hopes for a better, different future (Graham 2013). This choice of methodology fits and flows from the nature of our inquiry: Appreciative

Inquiry necessitates pragmatic reflexivity while encouraging creativity and building capacity for change.

Conclusion

Innovative justice, as we approach it, is a complicated and controversial subject. Innovation rests upon an amalgam of forces and factors, and success is always registered in the integration of theory and practice, the fusion of producer and programme and the interchange between practitioner and those with whom the service is provided. Innovative justice is not just a matter of nice stories and isolated successes for the select few. We are not in the business of 'feel good criminology' that is blind to other issues at hand. Navigating the complexities and tensions that we observe in the field, and that we feel keenly within our own work, is nonetheless worth the effort. This is because innovative justice offers the promise of something better than much of what passes for 'justice' within existing systems of social control today. It has the potential to change lives, in some cases to save lives, and more broadly to transform systems in ways that affect not just individuals but groups, communities and possibly generations.

We do not presume to embark on this exercise as 'experts', but with a healthy degree of humility. While we have developed a certain level of expertise in the field of criminology over time, the point of gathering these fresh stories and case studies, and critically evaluating them, is to broaden our personal, professional and system horizons in ways that will enrich other people's lives and horizons within what are undoubtedly difficult institutional circumstances. Our job therefore is to listen, to collaborate, to interpret and analyse and to disseminate that which holds the promise of progressive change and improvement.

Innovative justice is constructed through practice and experience, involving real people, struggling to make a difference within highly constrictive parameters. Evidence of 'innovation' is not only about emotional connections and empathetic appreciation of goodwill and concerted efforts. It demands critical, albeit appreciative, appraisal of whether there is evidence, as well, of good deeds. Our task hinges upon the interplay of the objective and the subjective, the affective and the effective. This is how we, in the end, are enabled to investigate and describe 'innovative justice'.

References

Barry, M. (2013) 'Desistance by Design: Offenders' Reflections on Criminal Justice Theory, Policy and Practice' *European Journal of Probation* 5(2): 47–65.
Braithwaite, J. (1989) *Crime, Shame and Reintegration,* Cambridge: Cambridge University Press.
Brayford, J., Cowe, F. and Deering, J. (eds) (2010) *What Else Works? Creative Work with Offenders,* Cullompton: Willan Publishing.

Crawford, A. and Hucklesby, A. (eds) (2013) *Legitimacy and Compliance in Criminal Justice*, Abingdon: Routledge.

Farrall, S. and Calverley, A. (2006) *Understanding Desistance From Crime: Theoretical Directions in Resettlement and Rehabilitation*, Berkshire: Open University Press.

Fischer, M., Geiger, B. and Hughes, M. (2007) 'Female Recidivists Speak About Their Experience in Drug Court While Engaging in Appreciative Inquiry' *International Journal of Offender Therapy and Comparative Criminology* 51(6): 703–22.

Garland, D. (2001) *The Culture of Control: Crime and Social Order in Contemporary Society*, Oxford: Oxford University Press.

Graham, H. (2012) 'The Path Forward: Policing, Diversion and Desistance'. In I. Bartkowiak-Théron, and N. Asquith (eds) *Policing Vulnerability*, Annandale: The Federation Press, pp.262–77.

Graham, H. (2013) 'Appreciative Inquiry'. In M. Walter (ed.) *Social Research Methods*, 3rd edn, South Melbourne: Oxford University Press. Available at: http://ecite.utas.edu.au/89192 (accessed 23 May 2014).

Graham, H. and White, R. (2014) *Innovative Justice*, Abingdon: Routledge.

Heckenberg, D. (2011) 'What Makes a Good Case Study and What Is It Good For?' In L. Bartels and K. Richards (eds) *Qualitative Criminology: Stories from the Field*, Annandale: Hawkins Press, pp.190–202.

Liebling, A. (2011) 'Being a Criminologist: Investigation as a Lifestyle and Living'. In M. Bosworth, and C. Hoyle (eds) *What is Criminology?*, Oxford: Oxford University Press, pp.518–29.

Liebling, A., Price, D. and Elliot, C. (1999) 'Appreciative Inquiry and Relationships in Prison' *Punishment and Society* 1(1): 71–98.

Maruna, S. (2001) *Making Good: How Ex-Convicts Reform and Rebuild Their Lives*, Washington, DC: The American Psychological Association.

Maruna, S., McNeill, F., Farrall, S. and Lightowler, C. (2012) 'Desistance Research and Probation Practice: Knowledge Exchange and Co-Producing Evidence Based Practice Models' *Irish Probation Journal* 9: 42–55.

McNeill, F. (2006) 'A Desistance Paradigm for Offender Management' *Criminology and Criminal Justice* 6(1): 39–62.

McNeill, F. (2012a) 'Four Forms of "Offender" Rehabilitation: Towards an Interdisciplinary Perspective' *Legal and Criminological Psychology* 17(1): 18–36.

McNeill, F. (2012b) 'Ex-Offenders' or "Re-Citz"?' Discovering Desistance Blog and Knowledge Exchange. URL (accessed 30 June 2012): http://blogs.iriss.org.uk/discoveringdesistance/2012/06/29/ex-offenders-or-re-citz/

McNeill F., Farrall, S., Lightowler, C. and Maruna, S. (2012a) 'Re-Examining Evidence-Based Practice in Community Corrections: Beyond "A Confined View" of What Works' *Justice Research and Policy* 14(1): 35–60.

McNeill, F., Farrall, S., Lightowler, C. and Maruna, S. (2012b) *How and Why People Stop Offending: Discovering Desistance [IRISS Insight #15]*, Glasgow: Institute for Research and Innovation in Social Services.

Nelken, D. (2010) *Comparative Criminal Justice*, London: Sage.

Nelken, D. (2011) 'Why Compare Criminal Justice?' In M. Bosworth and C. Hoyle (eds) *What is Criminology?* Oxford: Oxford University Press, pp.393–405.

Porporino, F. (2010) 'Bringing Sense and Sensitivity to Corrections: From Programmes to "Fix" Offenders to Services to Support Desistance'. In J. Brayford, F. Cowe and J. Deering (eds) *What Else Works? Creative Work with Offenders*, Cullompton: Willan Publishing, pp.61–85.

Reiman, J. and Leighton, J. (2012) *The Rich Get Richer and the Poor Get Prison: Ideology, Class and Criminal Justice*, 10th edn, Boston: Pearson Education.

Robinson, G., Priede, C., Farrall, S., Shapland, J. and McNeill, F. (2012) 'Doing "Strengths-Based" Research: Appreciative Inquiry in a Probation Setting' *Criminology & Criminal Justice* 13(1): 3–20.

Robinson, G., Priede, C., Farrall, S., Shapland, J. and McNeill, F. (2013) 'Understanding "Quality" in Probation Practice: Frontline Perspectives in England and Wales' *Criminology & Criminal Justice* iFirst doi: 10.1177/1748895813483763.

Scraton, P. (2007) *Power, Conflict and Criminalisation*, Abingdon: Routledge.

Scraton, P. and McCulloch, J. (eds) (2009) *The Violence of Incarceration*, New York: Routledge.

Tauri, J. (1999) 'Explaining Recent Innovations in New Zealand's Criminal Justice System: Empowering Maori or Biculturalising the State?' *Australian & New Zealand Journal of Criminology*, 32(2): 153–67.

Van Wormer, K. and Walker, L. (eds) (2013) *Restorative Justice Today: Practical Applications*, Thousand Oaks: Sage.

Wacquant, L. (2009) *Punishing the Poor: The Neoliberal Government of Social Insecurity*, Durham: Duke University Press.

Walgrave, L. (2008) *Restorative Justice, Self Interest and Responsible Citizenship*, Cullompton: Willan Publishing.

Weaver, B. (2011) 'Co-Producing Community Justice: The Transformative Potential of Personalisation for Penal Sanctions' *British Journal of Social Work* 41(6): 1038–57.

White, R. (2008) 'Prisoners, Victims and the Act of Giving' *Parity* 21(9): 18–19.

White, R. and Graham, H. (2010) *Working with Offenders: A Guide to Concepts and Practices*, Abingdon: Routledge.

Zehr, H. (1990) *Changing Lenses*, Scotsdale: Herald Press.

Index

harm, 1, 23, 29, 38, 40, 127–36, 168,
    301–11, 316, 319–21
  harmless, 51
  harm production, 15, 287, 301–11
hate, 127–37, 241
  hate crime, 12, 125, 127–37, 315
  see also assault; crime; violence
heterosexual, 151–2
  heterosexism, 127
  heterosexist, 151
  see also gender; sexuality
hierarchy, 10–11, 21, 55, 123,
    226, 240
  of credibility, 260, 273
Hispanic, 140–1, 153
  see also ethnicity; race
homicide, 250, 253–6
  rates, 225
  see also murder
Hudson, Barbara, 1, 7, 9

identity, 7–9, 12–13, 32, 75, 78–9, 90, 94,
    99, 125–6, 130, 132, 134–5, 147,
    172, 174, 188, 193, 199, 205, 228,
    262, 283, 289, 291, 297–9
  collective identity, 25
  ethnic identity, 170
  feminist identity, 12, 75, 91–4, 99
  identity politics, 7
  identity work, 115–16
  masculine identity, 122
  place identity, 116
  researcher identity, 10, 30, 91–4, 99,
    115–16, 234, 296
immigrant, 11, 13, 126, 130, 162–76,
    178–89
  crimmigrant, 162–3
  immigration, 13, 126, 130, 162–76,
    178–89
  see also migrant
incarceration, *see* prison
India, 10–11, 22, 47–8, 51–2
inequality, 7, 125, 270, 315
  see also poverty
insider, 82, 162–3, 172, 174, 182–4, 228,
    234, 247–8, 251–3, 256
  see also native; outsider
international, 10–11, 15, 221, 287,
    302–5, 308, 310, 313, 316
  internationalised, 200

internationally, 248
  see also global; national
internet, 221, 290, 292–4, 299
  see also virtual
intersection, 55, 159, 194, 291
  intersectional, 83
  intersectionalities, 12–13, 75–6, 125–6
interview, 11–12, 14, 23–4, 27, 29, 36,
    41–3, 48, 51–5, 58, 62, 64, 71, 75–6,
    82, 90, 95–8, 102–13, 127–8, 130,
    132, 145–6, 164, 167–8, 173–4, 180,
    224, 226, 231, 233–43, 247–56,
    259–73, 278–9, 281–2, 292, 314
  ethnographic, 278, 302
  forensic, 314
  group, 278
  interviewee, 95, 103, 106–13, 131–2,
    166, 239–41, 269, 272, 279:
    interviewing, 14, 95, 107, 111–12,
    168, 194, 198, 231, 233, 235,
    238–9, 242–3, 247–56, 259–73,
    279, 284
  interviewer, 95–6, 113, 237, 279
  semi-structured, 12, 23–4, 36, 75, 278
Italy, 15, 231, 269

journalist, 80, 147, 234, 276, 278–9,
    283–4
judge, 139, 234, 247, 249, 252–3
justice, 1, 2, 138, 162, 164, 194, 198,
    217, 222, 247, 250–1, 260, 313–23
  criminal justice, 9–11, 14, 16, 22, 35,
    37, 90, 112, 214, 231, 233–4, 242,
    272, 294, 301–2, 304–5, 310–11,
    313, 317–23
  criminal justice system, 4, 9, 36, 48,
    126, 164, 197, 209, 216, 247–56,
    314–16, 318–23
  injustice, 8, 13, 96, 126, 163, 167,
    250, 271
  innovative, 11, 15, 287, 313–23
  restorative, 316
  youth, 9, 62–3, 66–72

knife, 14, 206, 224, 227–8
  see also weapon
knowledge, 2–3, 5–7, 10–14, 21–2, 24–5,
    31, 39, 44, 58, 60–1, 76, 81, 90–2,
    96–7, 104–6, 108–10, 112–13,
    115–16, 121, 125–6, 129, 132–4,

231–2, 233–43, 277–8, 284–5, 305–6, 317

politician, 14–15, 141, 162, 231, 234, 276, 279, 281, 283–4

of representation, 270–2

see also government

population, 11, 13, 22, 25, 36–7, 94, 116, 131, 140, 150, 153–4, 178–89, 193, 196–9, 248

hidden, 13, 126, 178–89

prison, 140, 260, 264, 271, 317

vulnerable, 207–10, 239, 250

positivism, 9, 58, 72, 91, 194

anti-positivist, 91

positivist, 1–2, 5, 12, 14, 22, 49, 58–61, 72, 115, 147, 175, 178

postmodern, 6, 104, 194, 199

poverty, 36, 44, 106, 140, 153, 162, 193, 221, 227, 270–2, 321

see also inequality

power, 1–7, 9, 11–12, 14–16, 21, 32, 35, 37, 39–43, 48, 50, 55, 70, 77, 81, 85, 90–2, 94–9, 102, 106, 108–9, 113, 121, 123, 133–6, 144, 148, 193–6, 198–200, 210–11, 213, 224, 226, 228, 231–3, 235–7, 240, 242, 261, 266, 279, 283–4, 298, 302–3, 308, 310–11

dynamic, 37, 41, 90–1, 94–6, 99, 127, 233, 236–7, 242

empower, 44, 86, 94, 99, 172, 306

imbalance, 64, 94–6, 308

powerful, 1–7, 9–10, 13–16, 21, 40, 90, 99, 105, 121, 127, 148, 187, 192–3, 196, 207–8, 217, 231, 233, 235–6, 239, 241, 247–8, 253–6, 275–6, 304–5, 318

powerless, 1–7, 9–10, 12–13, 15–16, 23, 30, 32, 35, 55, 59, 75–8, 85, 90, 96–7, 99, 113, 121, 123, 125–6, 142, 144, 148, 168, 192–3, 197–8, 208, 224, 228, 231, 236, 239, 247, 252

relations, 11–12, 21, 47, 49, 75, 78, 86, 97, 99, 125, 172, 239–40, 322

struggle, 84

tactic, 81

pregnant, 103, 107–8, 110–13, 209

pregnancy, 12, 75, 102–13

see also body; child; family; father; parent; mother

Presdee, Mike, 4, 9, 221

prison, 9–12, 14–15, 21–2, 35–44, 47–55, 102–13, 138–49, 168, 170, 201, 205, 208–17, 226, 231, 234, 259–73, 307, 314–15, 317–19, 322

see also punish

privilege, 3, 93, 97–8, 102, 105–7, 125, 148, 243, 265, 283–4, 297

psychology, 134

punish, 145, 225, 228, 321

capital punishment, 225, 319

punished criminality, 270

punishment, 167, 196, 272, 301, 316, 320

qualitative, 9, 11–14, 23–5, 28, 30, 32, 54, 64, 71, 75, 78, 86–7, 90, 93, 95, 102, 104, 107, 109, 112, 126, 148, 163–5, 169, 178–80, 182, 192–201, 214–15, 233–4, 241, 248, 253–5, 278, 305

see also ethnography; interview; method; reflexivity; research

quantitative, 11, 13, 178–89

see also interview; method; questionnaire; reflexivity; research; survey

queer, 127, 132

see also bisexual; gay; gender; lesbian; LGBTQ; sexual; TLGBQ

questionnaire, 58, 141–2, 144, 146, 181–8, 210

see also method; qualitative; quantitative

race, 3–5, 7–10, 12–13, 50, 75, 103, 125–201, 271

institutional racism, 152

racial, 7–9, 11, 130–1, 138, 140, 154, 159, 221, 227

racism, 127, 140, 152, 162

see also ethnicity

realism, 198, 200

realist, 198, 282

reality, 3, 58, 60, 98, 105, 178, 200, 236, 238, 260, 270, 290, 298

Printed and bound by CPI Group (UK) Ltd, Croydon, CR0 4YY